# Warman's®

# Depression
# Glass

## 3rd Edition

## A VALUE & IDENTIFICATION GUIDE

Ellen T. Schroy

Published by

**krause publications**
An F&W Publications Company

**700 East State Street • Iola, WI 54990-0001**
**715-445-2214 • 888-457-2873**
**www.krause.com**

Please call or write for our free catalog.

Library of Congress Catalog Number: 00-104096
ISBN: 0-87349-618-3
Printed in the United States of America

Note: All listings and prices have been carefully checked for accuracy, but the publisher and editor cannot be responsible for any errors.

# Contents

## Patterns, Items and Values

# Introduction

## Welcome

Welcome to *Warman's® Depression Glass, 3rd Edition*, the latest edition in the Warman's price guides series. This edition is designed to assist collectors, appraisers, auctioneers, and those trying to identify that special piece of heirloom Depression-era glassware. A selection of 170 of the most popular patterns of American glass dinnerware manufactured between the 1920s and 1970s is featured. The third edition includes the standard Adam to Windsor patterns, plus other patterns most eagerly sought after by the collectors of the new millennium.

Each pattern is represented by a color photograph and line drawing to help with the identification process. A listing of known manufactured items and current prices assist in helping to establish the value. The pattern name listed is the one given by the manufacturer, except in the case of numbered patterns, which have now developed more easily recognizable names. A Shape Library has been included to give you an idea of the myriad of shapes plates were manufactured in during this exciting period of American glassware production. A quick identification guide has also been developed which sorts Depression-era glassware by motif, such as circles, fruits, florals, etc. By using this new quick identification guide, you may be able to discern the pattern you are trying to identify.

## History

The history of Depression-era glassware is fascinating in that one must thoroughly investigate the histories of many American glass houses to more fully understand why this glassware is so fascinating to many collectors. By exploring how these companies developed new patterns and new technologies, merged with other companies, and sold their wares, the story becomes clearer.

The name "Depression glass" comes from the fact collectors generally associate mass-produced glassware found in pink, yellow, crystal, or green with the years surrounding the Great Depression in America. Actually, the major manufacturers involved in making Depression-era glass, such as Federal, Hazel Atlas, and U.S. Glass, had established their businesses before the Depression set in. In the case of U.S. Glass, it formed a consortium of many smaller glasshouses in the late 1890s and combined factories, companies, and technologies for producing early American pattern glass.

Some of these factories later went on to produce the glass patterns associated with the Depression era. The Tiffin Glass factory may owe its longevity to the fact that it was part of the U.S. Glass consortium during some difficult times and later survived after the consortium was dismantled. Federal Glass company opened its Columbus, Ohio, plant in 1900. After switching to automation, it soon began production of tumblers and many Depression-era patterns, as well as restaurant wares, allowing its diversification to get the company through some difficult financial times. Collectors cannot easily pick a date and say this is when Depression-era glass started; rather, it was a gradual easing of the American glassware industry into modern mechanical advancements, allowing for the creation of inexpensive, quickly made colorful glassware.

Housewives of the Depression era were able to often enjoy the wonderful colors offered in this new, inexpensive glass dinnerware because they received pieces of their favorite patterns packed in boxes of soap, or as premiums given at "dish night" at the local movie theater. Merchandisers such as Sears & Roebuck and F. W. Woolworth enticed young brides with the colorful wares that they could afford even when economic times were harsh. Because of advancements in glassware technology, Depression-era patterns were mass-produced and could be had for a fraction of what cut glass or lead crystal cost. It was a time when the scoop of a front-end loader, not a handful of this or that, measured chemicals and raw materials. As one manufacturer found a pattern that was pleasing to the buying public, other companies soon followed with their adaptation of a similar design. Patterns included several design motifs, such as florals, geometrics, and even patterns that looked back to Early American patterns like Sandwich glass.

As America emerged from the Great

Depression and life became more leisure-oriented again, new glassware patterns were created to reflect the new tastes of this generation. More elegant shapes and forms were designed, leading to what is sometimes called "elegant glass." Often made by "finer" companies such as Heisey or Fostoria, these glassware patterns were made with formulas that created clearer glass and the patterns no longer had to be designed to hide inconsistencies found so often in inexpensively mass-produced glass. Many companies went back to finishing pieces by hand, raising the quality and the price. Today's collectors often include these more elegant patterns when they talk about Depression-era glassware.

A Timeline that highlights the beginnings, major events, and endings of American glassware manufacturers is included in this edition to show the scope of the companies which helped produce glassware in this era. Also included in this edition is a Color Timeline designed to help identify colors and when they were manufactured. Combining all these clues, along with the pattern identification sketches, will help determine when a pattern was made, by who, when, and in what colors.

## Prices

The prices in *Warman's® Depression Glass* have been established by careful research and compiling data for months from various sources. These sources include advertisements of glassware listed for sale in such sources as *Antique Trader Weekly*, and other trade publications. Visits to auctions, antiques shops, malls, and flea markets yielded still another source of pricing data. Many specialized Depression-era glassware shows and general antiques shows were visited. The newest, and probably most up-to-date, pricing venue is the Internet. Several sites were visited daily to observe what was being offered for sale. A careful eye was used to determine which patterns were being offered, as well as which colors seemed most popular and which forms were being sold.

A huge database was created in the computer to track what was being offered for sale, as well as what was not, at this time. Regional differences were noted and it seemed apparent that advertised prices were fairly constant. Of course, some patterns are more popular in certain areas, but there is no clear definition of what patterns were being collected by any particular geographic area.

Collectors remain individual in their tastes and preferences for certain patterns and colors. Some colors in some patterns are just not being offered for sale in large enough quantities to get a true reading for the price structure. In those cases, a note as to availability has been included to guide the collector in establishing a value. The antiques and collectibles business is based on comparables, and great amounts of data must be analyzed to accurately attribute pricing. Regional differences, condition, and collector desirability are all factors that have affected the pricing included in *Warman's® Depression Glass*.

## Research

Depression-era glassware is one of the best researched collecting areas available to the American marketplace. This is due in large part to the careful research of several people, including Hazel Marie Weatherman, Gene Florence, Carl F. Luckey and Kent Washburn. Their volumes are held in high regard by researchers and collectors today. Many Depression-era glass collectors find their libraries grow as fast as their collections as they search to find what was manufactured in a particular pattern. By carefully researching company records and archives, these authors have allowed us to view what forms were popular, what colors delighted housewives of the era, and what sizes and shapes the patterns include. *Warman's® Depression Glass* has responded to these authors by incorporating the best information they offer into a new source for collectors.

## Reproductions

Reproductions of Depression-era glassware have greatly impacted the market. Whole patterns have fallen in value because collectors are wary of continuing to invest in patterns beset by reproductions. Some patterns, like Miss America, are now experiencing reproductions of reproductions. The well-known clues to identifying the Miss America butter dish are now being compounded by having to recognize the second generation reproduction and its identification clues. Known reproductions, as of January 2003, are identified in the introduction of each pattern as well as being marked in the listing as †. Fantasy pieces, items not originally produced or produced in another color, are also listed as reproductions. Collectors are encouraged to subscribe to the *Antique and Collectors Reproduction News*, P.O. Box 71174, Des Moines, IA 50325. This excellent publication covers all areas of the antiques and collectibles marketplace, and provides information about Depression-era glassware.

## What's Included

Depression-era glassware, as defined by this edition, designates "patterns" produced between 1920 and the late 1970s. Such an expansive time span allows patterns to be included from many manufacturers. The patterns selected reflect dinnerware patterns as opposed to elegant patterns or stemware only patterns. To be included in this edition, a pattern had to meet several criteria:

- Be readily available on the marketplace.
- Include a basic place setting, such as a cup and saucer, plates.
- Be manufactured during the time frame established.
- Be manufactured in America.
- Be eagerly sought by collectors.

Several patterns were included that are considered "handmade" such as Fostoria's American and Tiffin's Flower Garden with Butterflies. These patterns actually cross over into the elegant glassware associated with Depression glass. Because these patterns are currently very popular with collectors, they were chosen to be included along with the machine-made patterns.

Adding new patterns to this third edition was an interesting challenge. A concentrated effort was made to focus beyond the typical Adams to Windsor patterns to see what collectors were searching for, and what types of patterns dealers were carrying in their inventories. As many of the older traditional patterns disappear from the marketplace, they are being replaced by patterns such as Indiana Glass' Constellation pattern, Imperial's Monticello, and Westmoreland's paneled Grape. There are many more patterns to entice collectors. Just as our tastes in fashion change from year to year, so do the styles of glassware. These style changes have spanned many years and helped to create the lovely patterns we consider as Depression-era glassware.

Very expensive items have been included in some patterns to give collectors a comparable value. Depression-era collectors are referred to other volumes that list rare and expensive Depression glass, to firmly establish prices on those very rare items. As in some other areas of the antiques and collectibles marketplace, rare does not always equate to a high dollar amount. And, some more readily found items command lofty prices because of high demand or other factors, not because they are necessarily rare. As collectors' tastes range from the simple patterns to the more elaborate patterns, so does the ability of their budget to invest in inexpensive patterns to ones that cost hundreds of dollars per form.

To maintain the fine tradition of extensive descriptions typically found in Warman's® price guides, as much information as possible has been included as far as sizes, shapes, colors, etc. Whenever possible, the original manufacturer's language was maintained. A glossary is included to help you identify some of those puzzling names. As the patterns evolved, sometimes other usage names were assigned to pieces. Collectors and dealers today face the constant challenge of identifying not only the pattern, but also understanding the original usage. It takes careful attention to detail to be able to discern the differences between berry, dessert, fruit, sauce, and cereal bowls. Color names are also given as the manufacturers originally named them. The Depression-era glassware researchers have many accurate sources, including company records, catalogs, magazine advertisements, oral and written histories from sales staff, factory workers. etc. The dates included in the introductions are approximate, as are some of the factory locations. When companies had more than one factory, usually only the main office or factory is listed. With fine reference books available to collectors, Warman's® Depression Glass concentrates on the pricing aspects of this segment of the antiques and collectibles market, rather than repeat the known company histories.

## Today's Collectors

It became quite evident, through the compilation and analyzing of the databases, that collectors of Depression-era glassware tend to use their treasures. Whether it's for everyday use, or for just special occasions, most reported on enjoying their collections and using them. Some noted that they mix and match patterns, although most seem devoted to one color in a particular pattern. Sometimes colors will be mixed and matched as a collection is created for use purposes. Often the collectors later sell off those pieces that no longer match or go with their patterns. Many Depression-era glass collectors become dealers to support their habit and to lessen their groaning cupboards!

Depression glass has been identified as being one of the hottest areas of interest on the Internet. The ever-growing number of sites available to the serious collector and first-time buyer verifies this statement. Information about company histories, interesting articles, listings of shows, and shops is becoming more easily accessible as this world-wide web gathers collectors together. Purchasing Depression-era glassware via the Internet is a fun way to expand a collection, locate objects not normally found in a region, etc. However, care must be exercised when bidding or purchasing glassware on-line. Buyers should ask the seller the same questions on-line as they would when making a live purchase, i.e. what is the history of the piece, more details about the description, are there any areas of damage, and what is the return policy. Because there are hundreds of Depression-era patterns, sometimes items are misidentified, so a savvy collector must learn to recognize the intricacies of the pattern they are seeking.

Many Depression-era collectors consistently look to each other for support, sharing of knowledge, and searching. This is one area where the Internet has answered a need in that some collectors correspond or "chat" daily about their collections, sharing experiences and dreams. During Depression glass antiques shows, it is not uncommon to see a dealer or collector offering their opinion about the source of a particular piece, what colors are available, etc. This is certainly one area of the antiques and collectibles marketplace where knowledge is freely shared. Perhaps this helps explain why so many young collectors are drawn to this colorful glassware. Information is readily available, standard price guides are used to establish prices, and knowledge is freely shared. Add to that excellent reference books, and you have an ever-increasing pool of collectors. Many exciting treasures await those who actively search for the rainbow of sparkling colors known today as Depression-era glass.

## Thanks

Working on *Warman's® Depression Glass* has been a wonderful experience. Hopefully, it will continue to be a work in progress as readers share their discoveries, stories of special pieces, etc. with me. No book of this nature can ever be 100% complete; there will always be some unknown pieces, unreported colors, or unusual pieces. Company records and catalogs are still to be discovered and shared with collectors. Krause Publications and I are proud to bring you this edition and hope it will meet your expectations.

To facilitate photographing all these beautiful patterns, several Depression-era dealers and private collectors generously loaned us pieces. Each piece was hand selected for the book, carefully washed, and wrapped for transport to the photographer. Photographer Donna Chiarelli carefully positioned each and every piece, adjusting lights and cameras to present each one's best side!

Another type of artist was employed to develop the line drawings. Jerry O'Brien's patience and attention to detail have resulted in these superb drawings. Whenever possible, he worked from an actual example, measuring details, analyzing the pattern from an artist's point of view. Sometimes an actual plate, saucer, or other piece was photocopied and then the lines meticulously traced and enhanced to show the details. After Jerry completed a pencil sketch, the drawings were again evaluated for attention to detail. Finally, the drawings were inked in preparation for use in *Warman's®*. Other patterns, those with a design in a more geometric arrangement, were drawn using more technical drawing skills. Where the pattern repeats evenly around the piece, only a portion is shown, allowing more room for pertinent information. In other patterns, such as Parrot (Sylvan), the whole pattern is shown so that collectors can get a proper prospective as to the location of the parrots, foliage, etc. It's our hope that these detailed drawings will help give you a clearer view of the details associated with these beautiful patterns.

After Jerry completed the task of drawing the pattern, he then provided us with a drawing of a typical plate to be included in our Shape Library. As the book progressed, we were all delighted to see the variations of the Depression-era glassware.

Support and guidance for *Warman's® Depression Glass* has been terrific and freely given by many. Through daily chats on Depression Glass Online Shopper, e-mails, conversations, and letters, I have received encouragement and guidance. Add to that an understanding family willing to pitch in. To all those, I say thanks!

And, most important, thanks to you, the collectors, dealers, and those who read books such as *Warman's® Depression Glass*. For it is you who keep the Depression glass market glittering.

# Glossary

**AOP:** All-over pattern, often found in descriptions to indicate a design that covers the entire piece rather than in just one location.

**Berry bowl:** Used to describe both individual serving dishes and master bowl used as a set to serve berries (strawberries, etc.). Often accompanied by creamer or milk pitcher and sugar bowl.

**Bouillon:** Generally, cup-shaped bowl for serving broth or clear soups, usually has handles.

**Cheese and cracker set:** Serving piece often consists of a comport to hold cheese and large plate for crackers; forms differ. Sometimes, a sherbet is used as comport.

**Cheese dish:** Serving dish, often with domed top, to cover cheese wedge.

**Children's wares:** Dish and tea sets designed to be used by children for play.

**Chop plate:** Large round plate used to serve individual portions of meat and fowl.

**Cider set:** Consists of covered cookie jar (used to hold cider), tray and roly-poly cups and ladle.

**Closed handle:** Solid glass handle.

**Comport:** Container used as serving dish, open with handles, sometimes covered.

**Compote:** Another name for comport.

**Console set:** Decorative large bowl with matching candlesticks.

**Cream soup:** Bowl used to serve cream-type or chilled soups, usually has handles.

**Cup and saucer:** Used to refer to place-setting cup and saucer; some patterns include larger coffee cup or more diminutive tea cup.

**Demitasse cup and saucer:** Term used to describe smaller cup and saucer used for after-dinner beverage.

**Domino tray:** Tray used to hold sugar blocks shaped like dominoes.

**Egg cup:** Stemware with short stem used to hold an egg, usually used with underplate.

**Goblet:** Stemware used to hold water.

**Grill plate:** Dinner-sized plate with lines that divide plate into compartments.

**Ice lip:** Small piece of glass inside of top of pitcher to hold ice in pitcher. May also mean a pinched lip that prevents ice from falling from pitcher.

**Icer:** Vessel with compartment to hold crushed ice to keep main vessel cold, i.e., mayonnaise, cream soup, shrimp, etc.

**Individual-sized pieces:** Smaller sized pieces, often designed for bed tray use. Not to be confused with children's wares.

**Liner:** Underplate or under bowl used to accompany another piece, i.e., finger bowl or sherbet.

**Light (Lite):** Branch found on candlestick used to hold additional candles, i.e., 2 light, 3 light.

**Nappy:** Shallow bowl used as serving dish or in place-setting; often has small handle.

**Oil/vinegar:** Term used to describe cruet or bottle with stopper to hold oil and/or vinegar for salads.

**Platter:** Small, medium or large oval plate used to serve roasts and fowl.

**Ring handle:** Figural round handle, ring-shaped.

**Salver:** Large round plate used as serving piece.

**Sandwich server:** Round plate, often with center handle (made of glass or metal) used to serve tea-type sandwiches.

**Sherbet:** Part of a place-setting used to hold sherbet, often served with matching underplate about the same size as a saucer.

**Snack set:** Plate or small tray with indent to hold punch or coffee-type cup.

**Spooner:** Small, often squatty, open vase-type vessel used to hold spoons upright. Typically, part of table set.

**Spoon tray:** Small bowl-shaped vessel used to hold spoons horizontally, often oval. Often used on buffets, etc., to hold extra place-setting spoons.

**Stand:** Base or additional piece used to hold punch bowl, etc.

**Table set:** Name given to set of matching covered butter dish, creamer, covered (or open) sugar and spooner. An extended table service may include syrup, toothpick holder and salt and pepper shakers.

**Tab handle:** Small solid glass handle useful to grab bowl, etc.

**Toddy set:** Set consists of covered cookie jar (used to hold toddy), tray and roly-poly cups and ladle.

**Tumbler:** Any footed or flat vessel used to hold water or other liquids. Specialized tumblers include ginger ale, juice, iced tea, lemonade, old fashioned and whiskey.

**Wine:** Term used to describe stemware used to hold wine. Depression-era wines have a small capacity, by today's standards.

# Company Timeline

**19th C**  Ohio Flint Glass founded, later becomes part of National Glass Company conglomerate. Indiana Glass Company established in 1907.
Bottle plant at Jeannette, Pennsylvania, which becomes Jeannette Glass Company.

**1853**  McKee and Brothers founded in Pittsburgh, Pennsylvania.

**1887**  Fostoria Glass Company, founded in Fostoria, Ohio, but moves to Moundsville, West Virginia, when fuel supply is depleted.

**1888**  McKee moves to Jeannette, Pennsylvania.

**1890**  Westmoreland Specialty Company established in Grapeville, Pennsylvania. Early manufacture includes bottles and food containers. During World War I, glass candy containers are made. The plant continues on to make colored and opaque glassware in both Depression patterns and later a giftware line.

**1891**  U.S. Glass Company organizes by combining 18 different glass houses located in Pennsylvania, Ohio, and West Virginia. The main offices are in Pittsburgh, as well as some manufacturing.

**1899**  Macbeth merges with Evans, creating Macbeth-Evans. Main factory located in Charleroi, Pennsylvania, with others located in Marion, Bethevan, and Elwood, Indiana, as well as Toledo, Ohio.

**1900**  Federal Glass Company opens Columbus, Ohio, plant. First wares are crystal with needle etching, various decorations, and crackle finish. After switching to automation, they soon begin production of tumblers and many Depression-era patterns, as well as restaurant wares, all at an economical price.

**1901**  Imperial Glass Company organizes. Produces first glass at Bellaire, Ohio, plant in 1904.
Morgantown Glass Works begins production in Morgantown, West Virginia.
New Martinsville Glass Manufacturing Company is established at New Martinsville, West Virginia.

**1902**  Hazel Atlas Glass Company established in Washington, Pennsylvania, a result of the merger of the Hazel Glass Company and its neighboring factory, Atlas Glass and Metal Company. Corporate offices are later established at Wheeling, West Virginia.

**1903**  Morgantown Glass Works reorganizes as Economy Tumbler Company and operates using that name.
Liberty Cut Glass Works established in Egg Harbor, New Jersey. Primarily a cutting house for years, pressed glass is also made.
McKee Brothers reorganizes into McKee Glass Company and continues until 1951.

**1905**  Anchor Hocking Glass Company established in Lancaster, Ohio. Well known by the mid-1920s for their tumbler and tableware production.

**1906**  Fenton Art Glass Company builds new factory, Williamstown, West Virginia. While their giftware lines are well known, some Depression-era glassware is produced.

**1907**  Indiana Glass Company established at Dunkirk, Indiana. Early production is hand pressed. Assembly line patterns evolve during the 1920s, although some still require hand work. Later produce automobile glassware items, become a subsidiary of Lancaster Colony.

**1908**  Lancaster Glass Company, Lancaster, Ohio, built by first president of Fostoria.

**1911**  L.E. Smith begins in the glass trade. A lot of the production of this company remains utilitarian in nature as well as making lenses for automobiles.

10

| 1916 | Paden City Glass Manufacturing Company established at Paden City, West Virginia. Production includes some Depression-era patterns, but is more well known for their elegant lines, vases, lamps and restaurant wares. |
|---|---|
| 1923 | Economy Tumbler Company changes name to Economy Glass Company. |
| 1924 | Fostoria introduces color and starts national magazine advertising campaign. Jeannette touted by trade as "one of the most complete automatic factories in the country." Lancaster becomes subsidiary of Hocking Glass Company. Continues to make kitchen ware, cut and dec tableware under the Lancaster name until 1937. Also makes colored blanks for Standard Glass Company, another Hocking subsidiary, where the glass is etched and cut. Known as Plant #2 to Anchor Hocking. |
| 1927 | Jeannette management ceases all hand operations. |
| 1928 | Jeannette makes green and pink glass automatically in a continuous tank, a first! Trade journals proclaim Clarksburg, West Virginia, Hazel-Atlas factory the "World's Largest Tumbler Factory," which accurately describes the fully automated factory. |
| 1929 | Economy Glass Company changes name back to Morgantown Glass Works, Inc. |
| 1932 | Liberty Cut Glass Works destroyed by fire, never to rebuild. |
| 1937 | Corning Glass Works purchases Macbeth-Evans. Hocking Glass Company merges with Anchor Cap and Closure Corporation, Long Island City, New York, creating the huge Anchor-Hocking Glass Company, which has continued to have a major impact on the glassware industry. Morgantown Glass Works, Inc., closes. |
| 1938 | U.S. Glass moves main offices to Tiffin, Ohio, and production decreases. |
| 1939 | Morgantown Glassware Guild organizes and reopens factory. |
| 1944 | New Martinsville sold and reorganizes as Viking Glass Company. |
| 1949 | Westmoreland Glass Company begins to use impressed intertwined "W" and "G" mark. |
| 1951 | The only operating company of the former U.S. Glass is Tiffin. The rest have all closed. McKee sold to Thatcher Manufacturing Co. |
| 1952 | Fire destroys Belmont plant, Bellaire, Ohio, and with the fire go company records. |
| 1955 | Duncan and Miller molds acquired by Tiffin, who begins to produce colors and crystal wares with these molds. |
| 1956 | Continental Can purchases Hazel-Atlas and continues to sell tableware under name "Hazelware." |
| 1958 | Federal Glass becomes a division of Federal Paper Board Company, and continues glass ware production. |
| 1961 | Jeannette buys old McKee factory in Jeannette and moves there to continue production. |
| 1964 | Brockway Glass Company buys out Continental Can's interest in Hazel-Atlas and begins operation. |
| 1965 | Fostoria Glass Company purchases Morgantown Glassware Guild. |
| 1966 | Continental Can takes over operation of Tiffin until 1969, with glass production continuing. |
| 1971 | Glass production terminated at Fostoria's Morgantown facility, ending the Morgantown Glassware Guild. |
| 1973 | Imperial Glass Company sold to Lenox, Inc. |
| 1980 | Tiffin Glass discontinues operation. |
| 1982 | Westmoreland Glass Company closes factory in May. Reorganizes in July. |
| 1983 | Lancaster Glass purchases Fostoria. Westmoreland begins to use full name as imprinted mark. |
| 1984 | Westmoreland Glass Company again closes Grapeville plant. |
| 1999 | L.G. Wright discontinues operation. Molds, factory equipment liquidated at public auction in May. |
| 2000 | Indiana Glass goes out of business in November. |

# Color Timeline

## Amber
1923: McKee
1923: New Martinsville
1924: Paden City
1924: Westmoreland's Transparent Amber
1924-1941: Fostoria
1925: Indiana
Mid 1920s: Hocking, Imperial and L.E. Smith
1926: Jeannette
Late 1920s: Liberty
1931-1942: Federal's Golden Glow
1960: Westmoreland's Golden Sunset

## Amethyst
1923: McKee
1924: New Martinsville
Mid-1920s: L.E. Smith
1926: Morgantown's Old Amethyst
1933: Paden City
1939: Morgantown's Light Amethyst

## Apple Green
1925: Jeannette

## Black
1920s-1930s: L.E. Smith
1922: Morgantown's India Black
1923 and 1930s: Paden City
1923: New Martinsville
1924: Fostoria
1930: McKee
1931: Hazel-Atlas, Imperial, Lancaster

## Blue
1920s: Lancaster
1923: McKee's Jap Blue and Transparent Blue
1923: New Martinsville
1924: Paden City
1924-1928: Fostoria
1925: McKee's Sky Blue and Westmoreland's
Mid-1920s: Hocking
1926: Imperial, Morgantown's Azure and transparent blue
1927: Imperial's Blue-Green, Morgantown's Ritz
1928: New Martinsville's Alice Blue (medium shade)
1928-1943: Fostoria's Azure Blue (lighter shade)
Late 1920s: Liberty's pale shade
1930: Hocking's Mayfair Blue (medium shade), McKee's Ritz Blue and Chalaine Blue
1931: Imperial's Ritz Blue, Lancaster's pale blue, Westmoreland's Belgian Blue
1933: Fostoria's Regal Blue
1933-1934: Federal's Madonna Blue (medium shade)
1933-1942: New Martinsville's Ritz Blue
Mid 1930s: MacBeth-Evans' Ritz Blue
1936: Hazel-Atlas's Ritz Blue, McKee's opaque Poudre Blue, Paden City's Ceylon Blue

1939: Morgantown's Copen Blue and Gloria Blue
1940: Anchor-Hocking's Fire King
1950s: Indiana's Blue-Green

## Burgundy
1933: Fostoria
1936: Hazel-Atlas (deep shade)

## Canary Yellow
1923: McKee
Mid-1920s: Hocking, L.E. Smith
1924: New Martinsville
1924-1927: Fostoria
1925: Lancaster

## Cobalt Blue
1930: Liberty
1936: Paden City
1939: Morgantown

## Cremax
1939: MacBeth-Evans

## Crystal
1923: Paden City
1930s: Imperial
1935: New Martinsville and Westmoreland—most companies produced crystal throughout their years of production

## Delphite, Delfite
1936: Jeannette

## Fired-On Colors
1920s: Federal and Lancaster
1923: Westmoreland
1926: New Martinsville
Mid 1930s: MacBeth-Evans

## French Ivory (opaque)
1933: McKee

## Green
1920s: Lancaster
1921: Morgantown's Venetian Green
1922: Morgantown's Meadow Green
1923: McKee
1924: Paden City
1924-1941: Fostoria
Mid 1920s: Hocking, Imperial and L.E. Smith
1925: Indiana, McKee's Grass Green and New Martinsville
1926: New Martinsville's Emerald Green
1926-1936: Federal's Springtime Green
1928: MacBeth-Evans' Emerald
Late 1920s: Liberty
1929: Hazel-Atlas, Imperial
1931: Morgantown's Stiegel Green

1931-1933: New Martinsville's Stiegel Green
1933: Fostoria's Empire Green, Hazel-Atlas's Killarney Green, New Martinsville's Evergreen (dark shade)
1936: Paden City's Forest Green
1939: Morgantown's Shamrock Green
1950s: Anchor-Hocking's Forest Green

### Iridescent
1920s: Federal
1920s to present: Jeannette
1934-1935: Federal's Iridescent Amber

### Ivory
1929: Imperial
1933: Indiana (opaque)
1940: Anchor-Hocking

### Ivrene
1930s: MacBeth-Evans

### Jade
1930: McKee
1931: New Martinsville

### Jade Yellow
1923: McKee

### Jadite
1932: Jeannette

### Monax
1920s: MacBeth-Evans

### Mulberry
1924: Paden City

### Opalescent
1923: Morgantown's Alabaster
1931: Westmoreland's Moonstone (blue)
1942: Anchor-Hocking's Moonstone

### Orchid
1927: McKee
1927-1929: Fostoria
1929: Imperial

### Pink
Mid-1920s: Imperial's Rose Marie, Rose
1925: Paden City's Cheriglo
1926: McKee's Rose Pink, Morgantown's Anna

### Red-Amber
1930: Liberty

### Rose
1926: Indiana and Westmoreland
1926-1942: Hocking's Rose (later called Flamingo or Cerise), New Martinsville's Peach Melba (later known as Rose)
1927: Jeannette's Wild Rose, L.E. Smith
1928: MacBeth-Evans
1928-1941: Fostoria's Rose or Dawn
Late 1920s: Liberty

1930: Hazel-Atlas, Lancaster's deep pink
1931-1942: Federal's Rose Glow
1933: Hazel-Atlas's Sunset Pink
1939: Morgantown's Pink Champagne
1947-1949: Jeannette

### Royal Blue
1932: Paden City

### Ruby
1925: Morgantown
1927: McKee
1931: Imperial
1932: Paden City
1933-1942: New Martinsville
Mid-1930s: MacBeth-Evans
1935: Fostoria's Ruby
1939: Anchor-Hocking's Royal Ruby

### Sea Foam
1931: Imperial, Harding Blue, Moss Green or Burnt Almond with opal edge

### Seville Yellow
1931: McKee

### Shell Pink
1958: Jeannette

### Skokie Green
1931: McKee

### Tan
1931: McKee's Old Rose

### Topaz
1921: Morgantown's 14K Topaz
1925: Jeannette
1928: Hocking
1929: Fostoria
1930: Lancaster, Westmoreland (sometimes combined with crystal or black)
1930-mid 1930s: Indiana
1931: Imperial, Liberty, MacBeth-Evans, McKee, Paden City's Golden Glow
1933: Hazel-Atlas
1938-1940s: Fostoria's Golden Tint
1939: Morgantown's Topaz Mist

### Ultramarine
1937-1938: Jeannette

### Vaseline
Mid-1920s: Imperial

### White
1930s: Hazel-Atlas's Platonite (opaque)
1932: Hocking (Vitrock)
1937-1942: McKee (opal) and after World War II

### Wine
1923: New Martinsville

### Wisteria
1931-1938: Fostoria

# Resources

## Collectors' Clubs

### International Associations

**Canadian Depression Glass Association**
119 Wexford Road
Brampton, Ontario L6Z 2T5  Canada
Web site:  http://www.CDGA.com

**Fenton Art Glass Collectors of America, Inc.**
P.O. Box 384
Williamstown, WV 26187

**Fire-King Collectors Club**
1167 Teal Road, SW
Dellroy, OH 44620

**Fostoria Glass Collectors, Inc.**
P.O. Box 1625
Orange, CA 92856

**Fostoria Glass Society of America, Inc.**
P.O. Box 826
Moundsville, WV 26041
Web site: http://home/gte.net/bartholf.fostoria.html

**H. C. Fry Glass Society**
P.O. Box 41
Beaver, PA 15009

**Heisey Collectors of America, Inc.**
169 N. Church St.
Newark, OH 43055

**National Cambridge Collectors Inc.**
P.O. Box 416
Cambridge, OH 43725

**National Candlewick Collectors Club**
275 Milledge Terrace
Athens, GA 30606

**National Depression Glass Association**
P.O. Box 8264
Wichita, KS 67208-0264

**National Duncan Glass Society**
P.O. Box 965
Washington, PA 15301

**National Fenton Glass Society**
P.O. Box 4008
Marietta, OH 45750

**National Imperial Glass Collectors Society**
P.O. Box 534
Bellaire, OH 43906

**National Westmoreland Glass Collectors Club**
P.O. Box 372
Westmoreland City, PA 15692

**Old Morgantown Glass Collectors Guild Inc.**
P.O. Box 894
Morgantown, WV 26507-0894

**Three Rivers Depression Era Glass Society**
Donna Hennen
3275 Sylvan Road
Bethel Park, PA  15102
412-835-1903

**Tiffin Glass Collectors' Club**
P.O. Box 554
Tiffin, OH 44883

**Westmoreland Glass Society, Inc.**
2712 Glenwood
Independence, MO 64052.

### Regional

There are many regional clubs where people gather to discuss Depression-era glassware. Check with the National Depression Glass Association for a club in your region if none are listed below:

**Big "D" Pression Glass Club**
10 Windling Creek Trail
Garland, TX  75043

**Black Hills Depression Glass Club**
1310 Milwaukee
Rapid City, SD 57701

**Buckeye Dee Geer's**
2501 Campbell St.
Sandusky, OH  44870

**Carolina Depression Glass Club**
P.O. Box 128
Easley, SC 29640

**Central Florida Depression Era Glass Club**
P.O. Box 948042
Maitland, FL 32794-8042

**Central Jersey Depression Glass Club**
181 Riviera Drive
Brick Town, NJ 08723

**Charter Oak Depression Glass Club**
P.O. Box 604
Chester, CT 06412

**Cigar City Depression Glass Club**
P.O. Box 17322
Tampa, FL 33612

**Clearwater Depression Glass Club**
10038 62nd Terrace North
St. Petersburg, FL  33708

**CSRA D. G. Club**
1129 Magnolia Ave.
Augusta, GA 30904

**Crescent City Depression Glass Club**
P.O. Box 55981
Metairie, LA 70055

**Depression Era Glass Society of Wisconsin**
1534 S. Wisconsin Ave.
Racine, WI 53403

**Depression Glass Club of Greater Rochester**
P.O. Box 10362
Rochester, NY  14610

**Depression Glass Club of North East Florida**
2604 Jolly Road
Jacksonville, FL   33207

**Evergreen Depression Era Collectors**
312 Golden Gate
Fircrest, WA 98466

**Garden State Depression Glass Club**
93 Idlewild Lane
Matawan, NJ 07747

**Greater San Diego Depression Glass Club**
P.O. Box 3573
San Diego, CA 92103-3573

**Greater Tulsa Depression Era Glass Club**
P.O. Box 470763
Tulsa, OK  74147-0763

**Hazelnut Depression Glass Club**
129 Southcliff Drive
Findlay, OH 45840

**Heart of America Glass Collectors**
14404 E. 36th Terrace
Independence, MO, 64055

**Houston Glass Club**
P.O. Box 1254
Rosenberg, TX 77471-1254

**Hudson Valley Depression Club**
129 Southcliff Drive
Findlay, OH 45840

**Kansas City Depression Glass Club**
12950 East 51st Terrace
Independence, MO 64055

**Illinois Valley Depression Glass Club**
RR 1, Box 52
Rushville, IL 62681

**Iowa Depression Glass Association**
5871 Vista Drive, Apt. 725
West Des Moines, IA 50266

**Land of Sunshine Depression
Glass Club**
P.O. Box 560275
Orlando, FL 32856-0275

**Lincoln Land Depression Glass Club**
1625 Dial Court
Springfield, IL 62704

**Long Island Depression Glass Society**
P.O. Box 147
West Sayville NY 11796

**Low Country Depression Glass Club**
209 Trestle Wood Drive
Summersville, SC 29483

**Montclair Depression Glass Club**
1254 Karesh Ave.
Pomona, CA 91767

**Mountain Laurel Depression
Glass Club**
942 Main St.
Hartford, CT 06103

**North Jersey Dee Geer's**
82 High St.
Butler, NJ 07405

**Northeast Florida Depression
Glass Club**
P.O. Box 338
Whitehouse, FL 32220

**Nutmeg Depression Glass Club**
230 Hillside Ave.
Naugatuck, CT 06770

**Old Dominion Depression
Glass Club**
8415 W. Rugby Road
Manassas, VA 22111

**Peach State Depression Glass Club**
4174 Reef Road
Marietta, GA 30066

**Permian Basin Depression Glass Club**
708 N. Adams St.
Odessa, TX 79762

**Pikes Peak Depression Glass Club**
2029 Devon
Colorado Springs, CO 80909

**Pocono Mountains Depression
Glass Club**
c/o Gwen Hawn
Pocono Lake, PA 18610

**Portland's Rain of Glass, Inc.**
P.O. Box 819
Portland, OR 97207-0819

**Sandlapper Depression Glass Club**
503 Leyswood Drive
Greenville, SC 29615

**South Bay Depression Glass Society**
P.O. Box 7400
Torrance, CA 90504-7400

**South Florida Depression Glass Club**
P.O. Box 845
Boca Raton, FL 33429

**Southern Illinois Diamond H Seekers**
1203 N. Yale
O'Fallon, IL 62269

**Spokane Falls Depression Glass Etc.**
P.O. Box 113
Veradale, WA 99037

**Three Rivers Depression Era
Glass Society**
3275 Sylvan Road
Bethel Park, PA 15102

**Top of Texas Depression Era
Glass Club**
42149 1st St.
Lubbock, TX 79424

**Tri-State Depression Era Glass Club**
RD #6, Box 560D
Washington, PA 15301

**20-30-40 Society, Inc.**
P.O. Box 856
LaGrange, IL 60525

**Western North Carolina**
P.O. Box 116
Mars Hill, NC 28743

**Western Reserve Depression Glass Club**
8669 Courtland Drive
Strongsville, OH 44136.

## Internet Sites

The following Internet Web sites offer information about Depression-era glassware in the form of online articles, references, chats, etc. There are hundreds of Web sites to purchase Depression-era glassware as well as numerous e-auctions.

**DG Shopper Online**
The Depression Glass Super Site
http://www.dgshopper.com
P.O. Box 3411
Albany, OR 97321-0716

**Dictionary of Glass Marks**
http://www.heartland-discoveries.com

**Facets Antiques & Collectibles Mall**
http://www.Facets.net

**Just Glass**
http://www.justglass.com
P.O. Box 20146
Cincinnati, OH 45220.

**Mega Show**
http://www.glassshow.com

## Publications

**Antique & Collector's
Reproduction News**
P.O. Box 12130
Des Moines, IA 50312

**Kitchen Antiques & Collectible News**
4645 Laurel Ridge Drive
Harrisburg, PA 17110

**The Fire-King News**
K & W Collectibles, Inc.
P.O. Box 473
Addison, AL 35540

# References

## General Depression Glass References

Tom and Neila Bredehoft, *Fifty Years of Collectible Glass, 1920-1970*, Antique Trader Books, Volume 1, 1997, Volume 2, 2000.

Monica Lynn Clements and Patricia Rosser Clements, *Cobalt Blue Glass*, Schiffer Publishing, 1998.

—*Price Guide to Pink Glass*, Schiffer Publishing, 1999.

Debbie and Randy Coe, *Elegant Glass: Early, Depression & Beyond*, Shiffer, 2001.

Gene Florence, *Collectible Glassware from the 40s, 50s, & 60s, 6th Edition*, Collector Books, 2002.

—*Collector's Encyclopedia of Depression Glass, 15th Edition*, Collector Books, 2002.

—*Elegant Glassware of the Depression Era, 10th Edition*, Collector Books, 2003.

—*Kitchen Glassware of the Depression Era, 5th Edition*, Collector Books, 1995, revised 1999.

—*Stemware Identification*, Collector Books, 1996.

—*Very Rare Glassware of the Depression Years*, 1st Series (1988, 1990 value update), 2nd Series (1990), 3rd Series (1993, 1995 value update), 4th Series (1995), 5th Series (1996), 6th Series (1999), Collector Books.

Jay L. Glickman, *Yellow-Green Vaseline! A Guide to the Magic Glass*, Antique Publications, 1991.

Phillip Hopper, *Forest Green Glass with Price Guide*, Schiffer Publishing, 2000.

—*Royal Ruby*, Schiffer Publishing, 1998.

—*More Royal Ruby*, Schiffer Publishing, 1999.

Ralph and Terry Kovel, *Kovel's Depression Glass & Americana Dinnerware Price List, 6th Edition*, Three Rivers Press, 1998.

Carl F. Luckey and Debbie Coe, *Identification and Value Guide to Depression Era Glassware, 4th Edition*, Krause Publications, 2002.

Barbara and Jim Mauzy, *Mauzy's Comprehensive Handbook of Depression Glass Prices*, Schiffer Publishing, 1999.

—*Mauzy's Depression Glass, A Photographic Reference with Prices*, Schiffer Publishing, 1999.

James Measell and Barry Wiggins, *Great American Glass of the Roaring 20s and Depression Era*, Antique Publications, 1998.

Naomi L. Over, *Ruby Glass of the 20th Century*, Antique Publications, 1990, 1993-94 value update.

—*Ruby Glass of the 20th Century, Book 2*, Antique Publications, 1999.

Marlene Toohey, *A Collector's Guide to Black Glass*, Antique Publications, 1988.

—*A Collector's Guide to Black Glass, Book 2*, Antique Publications, 1999.

Kent G. Washburn, *Price Survey, 4th Edition*, published by author, 1994.

Hazel Marie Weatherman, *Colored Glassware of the Depression Era, Book 2*, published by author, 1974, available in reprint.

—*1984 Supplement & Price Trends for Colored Glassware of the Depression Era, Book 1*, published by author, 1984.

## Specific Company References

Duncan: Gail Krause, *The Encyclopedia of Duncan Glass*, published by author, 1984; *A Pictorial History of Duncan & Miller Glass*, published by author, 1986; *The Years of Duncan*, published by author, 1980; Leslie Piña, *Depression Era Glass By Duncan*, Schiffer Publishing, 1992.

Fenton: Robert E. Eaton, Jr., *Fenton Glass: The First 25 Years Comprehensive Price Guide*, The Glass Press, 1995, 1997 value update, distributed by Antique Publications; *Fenton Glass: The 1980s Decade Comprehensive Price Guide*, The Glass Press, 1996, 1997 value update, distributed by Antique Publications; William Heacock, *Fenton Glass: The First Twenty-Five Years* (1978), *The Second Twenty-Five Years* (1980),

*The Third Twenty-Five Years* (1989), available from Antique Publications; Alan Linn, *Fenton Story of Glass Making*, Antique Publications, 1996; James Measell, *Fenton Glass, The 80s Decade*, Antique Publications, 1966, Members of the Fenton Art Glass Collectors of America, *Fenton Glass: The Third 25 Years Comprehensive Price Guide to Fenton Glass*, Antique Publications, 1995, distributed by Antique Publications; Ferill J. Rice (ed.), *Caught in the Butterfly Net*, Fenton Art Glass Collectors of America, The Glass Press, 1995; Margaret and Kenn Whitmyer, *Fenton Art Glass 1907-1939*, Collector Books, 1996.

**Fire King:** Monica Clements and Patricia Rosser Clements, *Guide to Fire King Glassware*, Schiffer Publishing, 1999; Gene Florence, *Anchor Hocking's Fire-King & More*, Collector Books, 1997; Joe Keller and David Ross, *Jadite - An Identification and Price Guide*, Schiffer Publishing, 1999; Garry and Dale Kilgo, Jerry and Gail Wilkins, *Collectors Guide to Anchor Hocking's Fire-King Glassware*, K & W Collectibles Publisher, 1991; *Fire King Glassware, A Collector's Guide to Anchor Hocking, 2nd Edition*, K & W Collectibles Publisher, 1998.

**Fostoria:** Frances Bones, *Fostoria Glassware 1887-1982*, Collector Books, 1999; Ann Kerr, *Fostoria: An Identification and Value Guide, Volume I, Pressed, Blown & Hand Molded Shapes*, Collector Books, 1994, 1997 values; *Fostoria: An Identification and Value Guide, Volume II, Etched and Carved & Cut Designs*, Collector Books, 1996; Milbra Long and Emily Seate, *Fostoria Stemware, The Crystal for America*, Collector Books, 1997; *Fostoria Tableware, 1924-1943*, Collector Books, 1999; *Fostoria Tableware, 1944-1986*, Collector Books, 1999; Leslie Piña, *Fostoria American Line 2056*, Schiffer Publishing, 1999; *Fostoria Designer George Sakier*, Schiffer Publishing, 1996; *Fostoria*, Schiffer Publishing, 1995; Joann Schleismann, *Price Guide to Fostoria, 3rd Edition*, Park Avenue Publications; Sidney P. Seligson, *Fostoria American, A Complete Guide, 2nd Edition*, published by author.

**Imperial:** Margaret and Douglas Archer, *Imperial Glass*, Collector Books, 1978, 1993 value update; Myrna and Bob Garrison, *Imperial Cape Cod Tradition to Treasure, 2nd Edition*, published by authors, 1991; National Imperial Glass Collectors Society, *Imperial Glass Encyclopedia, Volume I: A-Cane*, Antique Publications, 1995; *Imperial Glass Encyclopedia, Volume II: Cape Cod to L*, Antique Publications, 1998; *Imperial Glass Encyclopedia, Volume III, M-Z*, Antique Publications, 1999; National Imperial Glass Collectors Society, *Imperial Glass 1966 Catalog*, reprint, 1991 price guide, Antique Publications.

**Morgantown:** Jerry Gallagher, *A Handbook of Old Morgantown Glass, Volume I: A Guide to Identification and Shape*, published by author, 1995; Jeffrey B. Snyder, *Morgantown Glass: Depression through 1960s*, Schiffer Publishing, 1998.

**New Martinsville:** James Measell, *New Martinsville Glass*, Antique Publications, 1994.

**Tiffin:** Fred Bickenhauser, *Tiffin Glassmasters, Book I (1979), Book II (1981), Book III (1985)*, Glassmasters Publications; Ed Goshe, Ruth Hemminger and Leslie Piña, *Tiffin Depression-Era Stems and Tablewares*, Schiffer Publishing, 1998; *40s, 50s, & 60s Stemware by Tiffin*, Schiffer Publishing, 1999; Kelly O'Kane, *Tiffin Glassmasters, The Modern Years*, published by author, 1998; Bob Page and Dale Fredericksen, *Tiffin Is Forever*, Page-Fredericksen, 1994; Leslie Piña and Jerry Gallagher, *Tiffin Glass*, Schiffer Publishing, 1996.

**Westmoreland:** Lorraine Kovar, *Westmoreland Glass, Volumes I and II (1991), Volume III (1998)*, Antique Publications, 1991; *Westmoreland Glass 1950-1984 Volume I Comprehensive Price Guide*, published by author, 1998; *Price Guide to Westmoreland's Paneled Grape Pattern*, published by author, 1997; Charles West Wilson, *Westmoreland Glass*, Collector Books, 1996.

# Color Identification Guide

Blue, back row, from left: Lace Edge, Radiance, and Bubble; front row from left: Mayfair and Ships.

Green #1, from left: Floral and Diamond, Colonial, U.S. Swirl, Thistle, Pyramid, Daisy, and Fire-King Restaurantware.

Green #2, from left: Laurel, Rosemary, Westmoreland Vaseline basket, Parrot, and Thumbprint.

*Pink #1, back row, from left: Nora Bird, Fire-King Swirl, Petalware, and Diana; front row from left: Fortune and Hobnail.*

*Pink #2, back row, from left: Lincoln Inn, Open Lace, and Ovide; front row from left: Moondrops (cup and saucer), Sharon, Diana (coaster), and Peacock & Wild Rose.*

*Yellow #1, from left: Madrid, Patrick, Jubilee, Mayfair, Orchid, Madrid, and Roxana.*

*Yellow #2, from left: Crow's Foot, Princess (apricot grill plate), Daisy, Rock Crystal (front).*

# Shape Guide

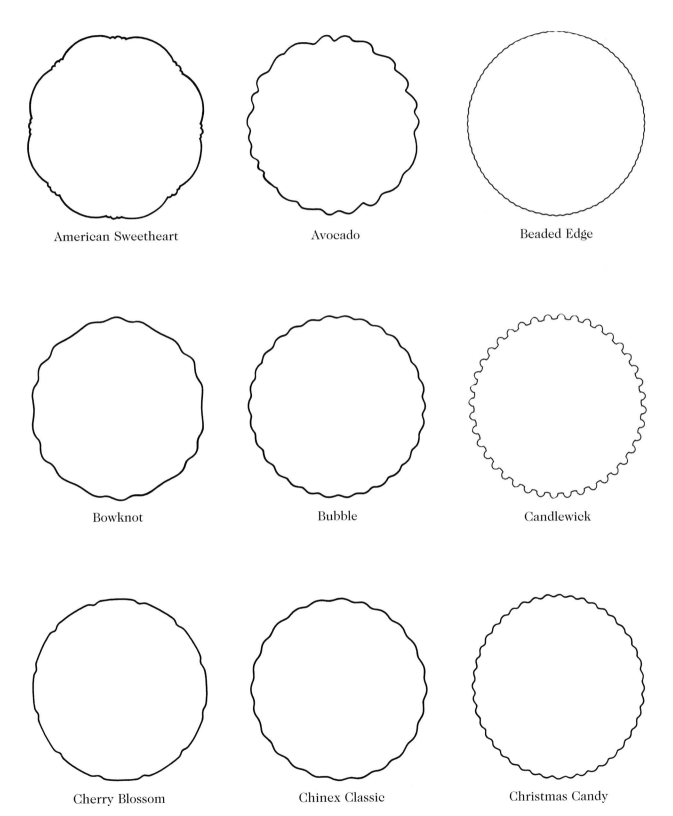

American Sweetheart

Avocado

Beaded Edge

Bowknot

Bubble

Candlewick

Cherry Blossom

Chinex Classic

Christmas Candy

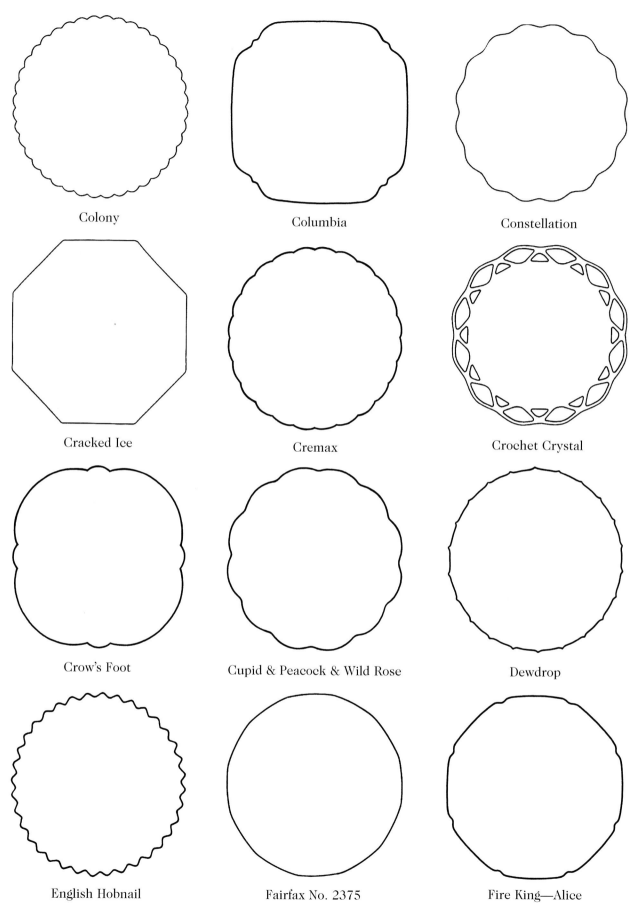

Colony

Columbia

Constellation

Cracked Ice

Cremax

Crochet Crystal

Crow's Foot

Cupid & Peacock & Wild Rose

Dewdrop

English Hobnail

Fairfax No. 2375

Fire King—Alice

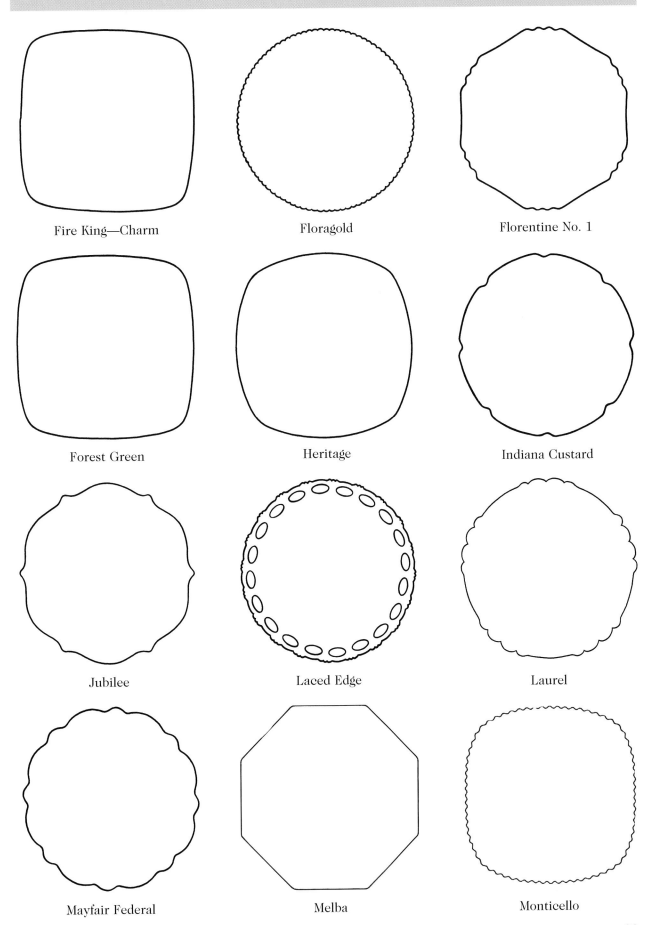

Fire King—Charm

Floragold

Florentine No. 1

Forest Green

Heritage

Indiana Custard

Jubilee

Laced Edge

Laurel

Mayfair Federal

Melba

Monticello

Moonstone

Mt. Pleasant

Nora Bird

Old Café

Orchid

Oyster & Pearls

Paneled Grape

Parrot

Patrick

Pineapple & Floral

Pioneer

Pretzel

Radiance

Ripple

Rock Crystal

Romanesque

Roxana

Royal Lace

Royal Ruby

Sandwich

Sierra Pinwheel

Starlight

Sunburst

Swirl

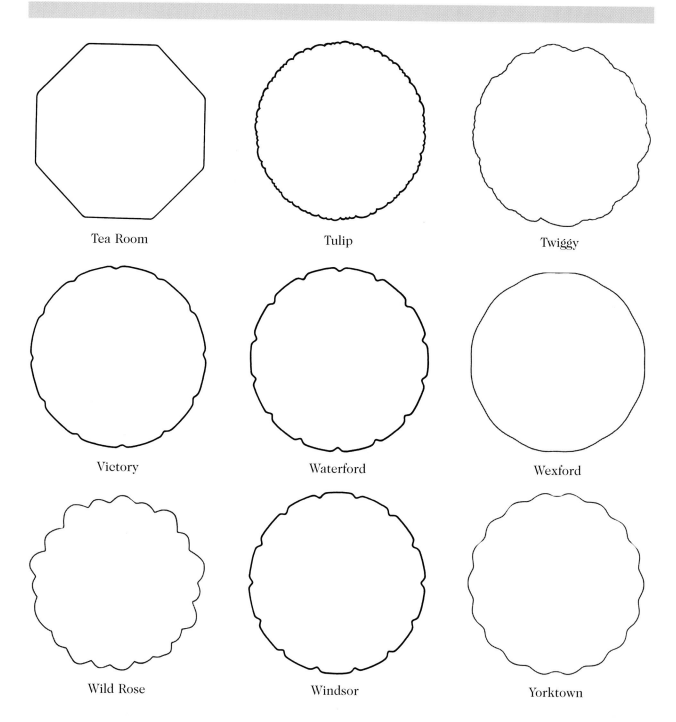

Tea Room

Tulip

Twiggy

Victory

Waterford

Wexford

Wild Rose

Windsor

Yorktown

# Thumbnail Guide

Depression-era glassware can be confusing. Many times one manufacturer came up with a neat new design and as soon as it was successful, other companies started to make patterns that were similar. To help you figure out what pattern you might be trying to research, here's a quick identification guide. The patterns are broken down into several different classifications by design elements. Try comparing your piece to these and then consult the detailed pattern listing and larger drawing for more information.

**Art Deco**
Ovide

**Baskets**
Lorain

**Beaded Edges**
Beaded Edge
Candlewick

**Birds**
Parrot

**Birds**
Delilah Bird
Nora Bird
Peacock & Wild Rose
Georgian

**Blocks**
Beaded Block

**Blocks**
Colonial Block

**Bows**
Bowknot

**Coins**
Coin

**Cubes**
Cube
American

**Diamonds**
English Hobnail
Golf Ball
Miss America
Holiday
Laced Edge

**Diamonds**
Diamond Quilted
Windsor
Waterford
Peanut Butter
Cape Cod

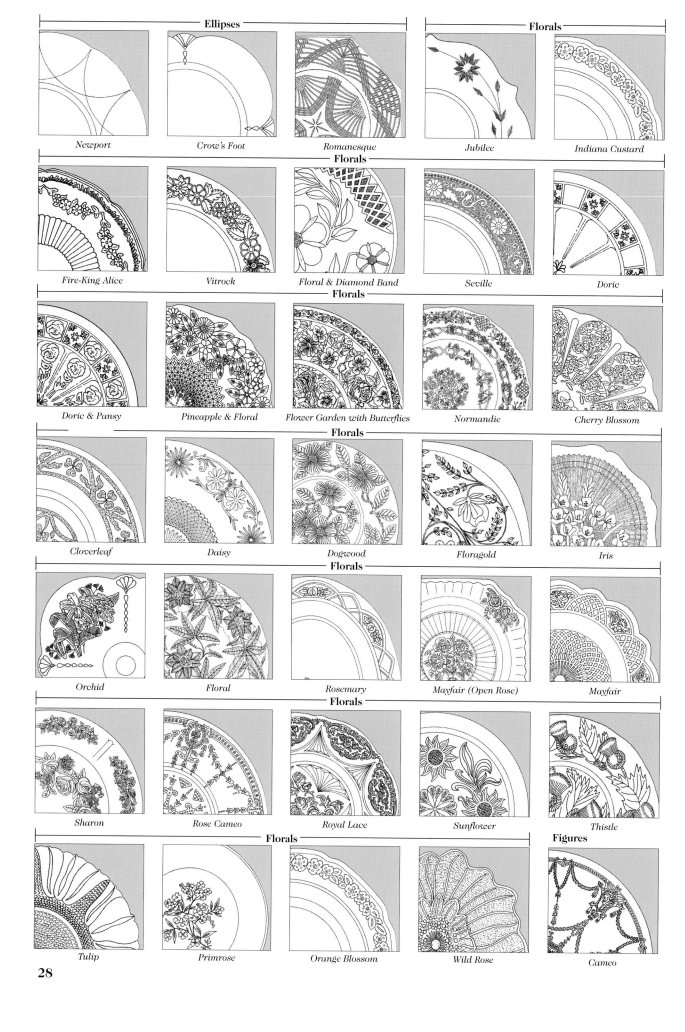

## Ellipses

Newport

Crow's Foot

Romanesque

## Florals

Jubilee

Indiana Custard

## Florals

Fire-King Alice

Vitrock

Floral & Diamond Band

Seville

Doric

## Florals

Doric & Pansy

Pineapple & Floral

Flower Garden with Butterflies

Normandie

Cherry Blossom

## Florals

Cloverleaf

Daisy

Dogwood

Floragold

Iris

## Florals

Orchid

Floral

Rosemary

Mayfair (Open Rose)

Mayfair

## Florals

Sharon

Rose Cameo

Royal Lace

Sunflower

Thistle

## Florals

Tulip

Primrose

Orange Blossom

Wild Rose

## Figures

Cameo

**28**

**Figures**

*Cupid*

**Fruits**

*Avocado*

*Cherryberry*

*Della Robbia*

*Strawberry*

**Fruits**

*Fruits*

*Paneled Grape*

**Geometric & Line Designs**

*Starlight*

*Star*

*Early American Prescut*

**Geometric & Line Designs**

*Park Avenue*

*Pioneer*

*Cracked Ice*

*Sierra Pinwheel*

*Cremax*

**Geometric & Line Designs**

*Tea Room*

**Honeycomb**

*Hex Optic*

*Aunt Polly*

**Horseshoe**

*Horseshoe*

**Lacy Designs**

*Heritage*

**Lacy Designs**

*Harp*

*Sandwich (Duncan Miller)*

*Sandwich (Hocking)*

*Sandwich (Indiana)*

*S-Pattern*

**Leaves**

*Sunburst*

*Fire-King Peach Luster*

*Laurel*

*Christmas Candy*

**Loops**

*Pretzel*

**Loops**

*Crocheted Crystal*

**Petals**

*Victory*

*Block Optic*

*Circle*

*Colonial*

29

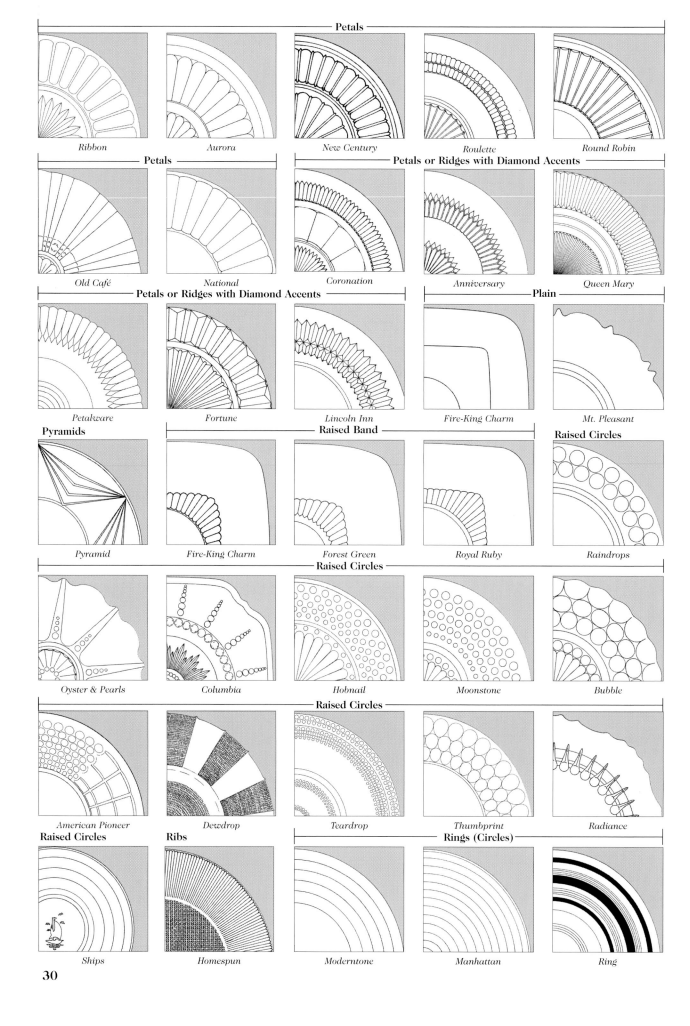

Petals

*Ribbon*  *Aurora*  *New Century*  *Roulette*  *Round Robin*

Petals — Petals or Ridges with Diamond Accents

*Old Café*  *National*  *Coronation*  *Anniversary*  *Queen Mary*

Petals or Ridges with Diamond Accents — Plain

*Petalware*  *Fortune*  *Lincoln Inn*  *Fire-King Charm*  *Mt. Pleasant*

Pyramids — Raised Band — Raised Circles

*Pyramid*  *Fire-King Charm*  *Forest Green*  *Royal Ruby*  *Raindrops*

Raised Circles

*Oyster & Pearls*  *Columbia*  *Hobnail*  *Moonstone*  *Bubble*

Raised Circles

*American Pioneer*  *Dewdrop*  *Teardrop*  *Thumbprint*  *Radiance*

Raised Circles — Ribs — Rings (Circles)

*Ships*  *Homespun*  *Moderntone*  *Manhattan*  *Ring*

30

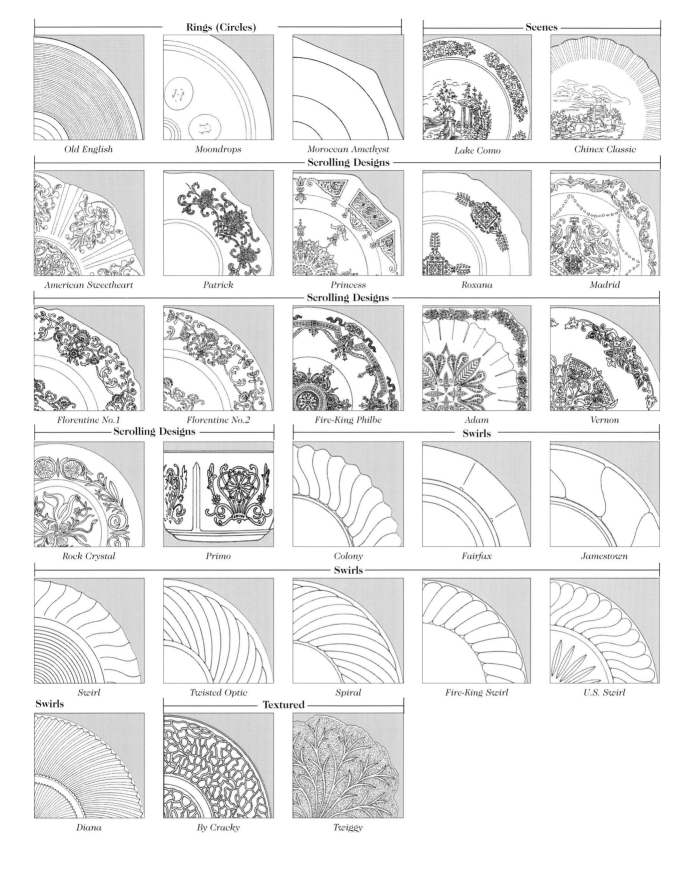

**Rings (Circles)**

*Old English*

*Moondrops*

*Moroccan Amethyst*

**Scenes**

*Lake Como*

*Chinex Classic*

**Scrolling Designs**

*American Sweetheart*

*Patrick*

*Princess*

*Roxana*

*Madrid*

**Scrolling Designs**

*Florentine No.1*

*Florentine No.2*

*Fire-King Philbe*

*Adam*

*Vernon*

**Scrolling Designs**

*Rock Crystal*

*Primo*

**Swirls**

*Colony*

*Fairfax*

*Jamestown*

**Swirls**

*Swirl*

*Twisted Optic*

*Spiral*

*Fire-King Swirl*

*U.S. Swirl*

**Swirls**

**Textured**

*Diana*

*By Cracky*

*Twiggy*

31

# Adam

Manufactured by Jeannette Glass Company, Jeannette, Pa., from 1932 to 1934.

Made in crystal, Delphite blue, green, pink, some topaz and yellow. Delphite 4" h candlesticks are valued at $250 a pair. A yellow cup and saucer are valued at $200, and a 7-3/4" d yellow plate is valued at $115. Production in topaz and yellow was very limited. Crystal prices would be approximately 50 percent of the prices listed for green.

**Reproductions:** † Butter dish in pink and green.

| Item | Green | Pink |
|---|---|---|
| Ashtray, 4-1/2" d | 28.00 | 32.00 |
| Berry Bowl, small | 20.00 | 18.50 |
| Bowl, 9" d, cov | 95.00 | 80.00 |
| Bowl, 9" d, open | 45.00 | 30.00 |
| Bowl, 10" l, oval | 40.00 | 40.00 |
| Butter Dish, cov † | 400.00 | 145.00 |
| Cake Plate, 10" d, ftd | 38.00 | 35.00 |
| Candlesticks, pr, 4" h | 125.00 | 100.00 |
| Candy Jar, cov, 2-1/2" h | 120.00 | 115.00 |
| Casserole, cov | 95.00 | 80.00 |
| Cereal Bowl, 5-3/4" d | 50.00 | 48.00 |
| Coaster, 3-1/4" d | 25.00 | 35.00 |
| Creamer | 30.00 | 28.00 |
| Cup | 28.00 | 30.00 |
| Dessert Bowl, 4-3/4" d | 25.00 | 25.00 |
| Iced Tea Tumbler, 5-1/2" h | 70.00 | 75.00 |
| Lamp | 500.00 | 500.00 |
| Pitcher, 32 oz, round base | - | 125.00 |
| Pitcher, 32 oz, 8" h | 48.00 | 45.00 |
| Plate, 6" d, sherbet | 15.00 | 18.00 |
| Plate, 7-3/4" d, salad, sq | 20.00 | 24.00 |
| Plate, 9" d, dinner, sq | 35.00 | 40.00 |
| Plate, 9" d, grill | 35.00 | 35.00 |
| Platter, 11-3/4" l, rect | 38.00 | 35.00 |
| Relish Dish, 8" l, divided | 27.00 | 20.00 |
| Salt and Pepper Shakers, pr, 4" h | 130.00 | 95.00 |
| Saucer, 6" sq | 12.00 | 10.00 |
| Sherbet, 3" | 40.00 | 35.00 |
| Sugar, cov | 48.00 | 42.00 |
| Tumbler, 4-1/2" h | 35.00 | 38.00 |
| Vase, 7-1/2" h | 60.00 | 250.00 |
| Vegetable Bowl, 7-3/4" d | 30.00 | 30.00 |

Adam, green plate.

Adam, pink pitcher and green ashtray.

# American

Manufactured by Fostoria Glass Company, Moundsville, Va., from 1915 to 1986.

Made in crystal, some amber, blue, green, yellow, pink, pink tinting to purple in the late 1920s, white, red in 1980s, and currently in red and crystal for Lancaster Colony by Dalzell Viking. Prices for colors fluctuate greatly.

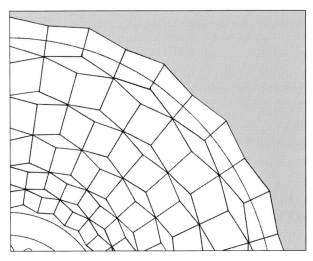

| Item | Crystal |
|---|---|
| Almond Bowl, 3-3/4" l, oval | 18.00 |
| Appetizer Insert, 3-1/4" | 30.00 |
| Appetizer Tray, 10-1/2" l, 6 inserts | 250.00 |
| Ashtray, 2-7/8" w, sq | 10.00 |
| Ashtray, 3-7/8" l, oval | 25.00 |
| Ashtray, 5" w, sq | 35.00 |
| Ashtray, 5-1/2" l, oval | 20.00 |
| Banana Split, 9" x 3-1/2" | 995.00 |
| Basket, open handle | 125.00 |
| Basket, 10", c1988 | 40.00 |
| Basket, 7" x 9", reeded handle | 95.00 |
| Beer Mug, 4-1/2" h, 12 oz | 70.00 |
| Bell | 650.00 |
| Biscuit Jar, cov | 800.00 |
| Bitter Bottles, 5-3/4" h, 4-1/2 oz, 2-pc set | 310.00 |
| Boat, 8-1/2" d | 15.00 |
| Boat, 9" d, 2 parts | 12.00 |
| Boat, 12" l | 17.50 |
| Bonbon, 6" d, 3 ftd | 15.00 |
| Bonbon, 7" h, 3 ftd | 15.00 |
| Bonbon, 8" d, 3 ftd | 17.50 |
| Bowl, 4-1/2" d, 1 handle, round or square | 12.00 |
| Bowl, 4-1/2" d, oval | 15.00 |
| Bowl, 5" d, handle, tricorner | 15.00 |
| Bowl, 7" d, 4-1/2" h, cupped | 50.00 |
| Bowl, 8" d, deep | 50.00 |
| Bowl, 8" d, ftd | 55.00 |
| Bowl, 8-1/2" d, 2 handles | 65.00 |
| Bowl, 9" l, oval #4836 | 25.00 |
| Bowl, 9-1/2" d, 6" w, 3 parts | 60.00 |

| Item | Crystal |
|---|---|
| Bowl, 10" d, deep | 48.00 |
| Bowl, 10" d, 14" d liner | 50.00 |
| Bowl, 11-1/2" d rolled edge | 75.00 |
| Bowl, 11-3/4" l, oval, deep | 40.00 |
| Box, cov, 4-1/2" x 4-1/2" | 200.00 |
| Brush Tray | 50.00 |
| Bud Vase, 6" h, flared | 45.00 |
| Bud Vase, 6" h, ftd | 40.00 |
| Bud Vase, 8-1/2" h, cupped | 40.00 |
| Bud Vase, 8-1/2" h, flared | 45.00 |
| Butter Dish, cov, 1/4 lb | 45.00 |
| Butter Dish, cov, 7-1/4" d, round plate | 135.00 |
| Cake Plate, 10" d, 2 handles | 24.00 |
| Cake Plate, 12" d, 3 ftd | 20.00 |
| Cake Stand, 10" round, pedestal foot | 125.00 |
| Cake Stand, 10" sq, pedestal foot | 310.00 |
| Cake Stand, 11" d, round, pedestal foot | 195.00 |
| Cake Tray, 10-1/2" d, crook-shaped handle | 45.00 |
| Candelabrum, 6-1/2", 2 light, bell base, bobeche, pr | 125.00 |
| Candle Lamp, 8-1/2" h, chimney, candle part, 3-1/2" | 170.00 |
| Candlestick, 2", chamber, fingerhold | 60.00 |
| Candlesticks, pr, 3", round, ftd | 24.00 |
| Candlesticks, pr, 4-3/8", 2-light, round foot | 95.00 |
| Candlesticks, pr, 6", octagon foot | 65.00 |
| Candlesticks, pr, 6-1/2", 2-light, bell base | 265.00 |
| Candlesticks, pr, 6-1/4", round foot | 360.00 |
| Candlesticks, pr, 7", sq, column | 225.00 |
| Candlesticks, pr, 7-1/4", Eiffel Tower | 375.00 |

| Item | Crystal | Item | Crystal |
|---|---|---|---|
| Candy Box, cov, 3 parts, triangular | 95.00 | Cordial Bottle, 7-1/4" h, 9 oz | 95.00 |
| Candy Box, cov, 7" x 5" | 500.00 | Cordial Set, four decanters, chrome holder | 2,285.00 |
| Catsup Bottle | 145.00 | Cosmetic Box | 850.00 |
| Celery Tray, 10" l, oblong | 35.00 | Cream Soup Bowl, 5" d, two handles | 95.00 |
| Centerpiece Bowl, 9-1/2" d | 45.00 | Cream Soup Liner | 20.00 |
| Centerpiece Bowl, 11" d | 45.00 | Creamer and Sugar Tray, 6-3/4" l, handle | 15.00 |
| Centerpiece Bowl, 11" d, tricorner | 45.00 | Creamer, 3 oz, 2-3/8" h, tea size | 10.00 |
| Centerpiece Bowl, 15" d, hat-shape | 165.00 | Creamer, 4-3/4 oz, individual size | 11.50 |
| Cheese and Cracker, 5-3/4" comport, 11-1/2" d plate | 125.00 | Creamer, 9-1/2 oz | 14.00 |
| Chocolate Tray, 7" x 5" x 1-7/8" deep | 695.00 | Cruet, orig stopper, 5 oz | 32.00 |
| Cigarette Box, cov, 4-3/4" | 60.00 | Cruet, orig stopper, 7 oz | 35.00 |
| Claret, 4-5/8" h, 3-1/2 oz, plain bowl, #5056 | 65.00 | Crushed Fruit, cov, spoon, 9-1/2" h | 2,125.00 |
| Claret, 4-7/8" h, 7 oz, #2056 | 75.00 | Crushed Fruit, cov, spoon, 10" h | 1,425.00 |
| Coaster, 3-3/4" d | 20.00 | Cup, flat | 8.50 |
| Cocktail, 2-7/8" h, cone, ftd, 3 oz, #2506 | 20.00 | Cup, ftd, 7 oz | 7.50 |
| Cocktail, 4" h, 3-1/2 oz, plain bowl, #5056 | 18.00 | Decanter, stopper, 24 oz, 9-1/4" h | 150.00 |
| Cologne Bottle, orig stopper, 5-3/4" h, 6 oz | 95.00 | Dresser Set, pr cov powder boxes, tray | 500.00 |
| Cologne Bottle, orig stopper, 7-1/4" h, 9 oz | 90.00 | Dresser Tray, 11" | 450.00 |
| Comport, 5" d, covered | 25.00 | Finger Bowl, 4-1/2" d, underplate | 110.00 |
| Comport, 8-1/2" d, 4" h | 45.00 | Float Bowl, 10" d | 45.00 |
| Comport, 9-1/2" d, #3237 | 75.00 | Float Bowl, 10" l, oval | 35.00 |
| Condiment Bottle | 115.00 | Float Bowl, 11-1/2" d | 55.00 |
| Condiment Set, 2 oils, 2 shakers, mustard, tray | 325.00 | Float Bowl, 11-1/2" l, oval | 45.00 |
| Condiment Tray, clover leaf | 375.00 | Flower Pot, orig flower frog center, 5-1/2" h, 9-1/2" w | 2,700.00 |
| Cookie Jar, cov, 8-3/4" h | 800.00 | Fruit Bowl, 10-1/2" d, 3 ftd | 40.00 |
| Cordial, 3-1/8" h, 1 oz, plain bowl, #5056 | 25.00 | Fruit Bowl, 11-1/2" d, 2-3/4" h, rolled edge | 45.00 |

*American, relish, plate and tumbler.*

| Item | Crystal |
|---|---|
| Fruit Bowl, 13" d, shallow | 65.00 |
| Fruit Bowl, 4-3/4" d, flared | 18.00 |
| Fruit Bowl, 16" d, pedestal foot | 250.00 |
| Fruit Cocktail, 4-3/4" h, 4-1/2 oz, hex foot, #2506 | 40.00 |
| Glove Box, cov, 9-1/2" x 3-1/2" | 325.00 |
| Goblet, 9 oz, 4-3/8" h, low foot, #2056 | 12.00 |
| Goblet, 10 oz, 6-1/8" h, plain bowl, #5056 | 12.50 |
| Goblet, 10 oz, 6-7/8" h, hex foot, #2056 | 16.00 |
| Hair Receiver, 3" x 3" | 1,000.00 |
| Hairpin Box, cov, 3-1/2" x 1-3/4" | 1,700.00 |
| Handkerchief Box, cov, 5-5/8" x 4-5/8"** | 700.00 |
| Hat, 2-1/8" | 30.00 |
| Hat, 3" h | 35.00 |
| Hat, 4" h | 45.00 |
| Hat, western style | 200.00 |
| Hurricane Lamp, 12" h, complete | 425.00 |
| Ice Bucket, tongs | 90.00 |
| Ice Cream Saucer, 2 styles | 55.00 |
| Ice Cream Tray, 13-1/2" l, oval | 300.00 |
| Ice Dish for 4 oz crab or 5 oz tomato liner | 65.00 |
| Ice Dish Insert | 18.00 |
| Ice Tub, with liner, 5-3/8" | 95.00 |
| Ice Tub, with liner, 6-1/2" | 100.00 |
| Iced Tea Tumbler, handle | 215.00 |
| Iced Tea Tumbler, 12 oz, 5-3/4" h, 12 oz, low foot, #2056 | 22.00 |
| Jam Pot, cov | 125.00 |
| Jelly Bowl, 4-1/4" d, 4-1/4" h | 20.00 |
| Jelly Bowl, cov, 4-1/2" d, 6-3/4" h | 28.00 |
| Jelly Comport, 4-1/2" d | 25.00 |
| Jelly Comport, 5" d, flared | 70.00 |
| Jelly Comport, cov, 6-3/4" d | 35.00 |
| Jewel Box, cov, 3-1/2" x 6" | 1,600.00 |
| Jewel Box, cov, 4-1/4" x 3-1/4", 2 drawers | 1,800.00 |
| Jewel Box, cov, 5-1/4" x 2-1/4" | 325.00 |
| Juice Tumbler, 5 oz, straight sides, flat | 15.00 |
| Juice Tumbler, 4-1/8" h, 5 oz, ftd, plain bowl | 15.00 |
| Juice Tumbler, 4-3/4" h, 5 oz, ftd, #2056 | 15.00 |
| Ketsup Bottle, orig stopper | 160.00 |
| Lemon Bowl, cov, 5-1/2" d | 45.00 |
| Lemonade Tumbler, 11 oz, 5-3/4" h, ftd | 500.00 |
| Lily Pond Bowl, 12" d | 65.00 |
| Marmalade, cov, chrome spoon | 125.00 |
| Mayonnaise, div | 25.00 |
| Mayonnaise, ladle, pedestal foot | 45.00 |
| Mayonnaise, liner, ladle | 35.00 |
| Molasses Can, 11 oz, 6-3/4" h, 1 handle | 450.00 |
| Muffin Tray, 10" l, 2 upturned sides | 35.00 |
| Mustard, cov | 45.00 |
| Napkin Ring | 45.00 |
| Nappy, 4-1/2" | 15.00 |
| Nappy, 4-3/4" x 8" | 150.00 |
| Nappy, 5" d | 18.00 |
| Nappy, 5" d, cov | 30.00 |

| Item | Crystal |
|---|---|
| Nappy, 6" d | 15.00 |
| Nappy, 7" d | 17.50 |
| Nappy, 8" d | 20.00 |
| Old Fashioned Tumbler, 3-3/8" h, 6 oz, flat | 10.00 |
| Olive, 6" l, oblong | 22.00 |
| Oyster Cocktail, 3-1/2" h, 4-1/2 oz, #2056 | 18.00 |
| Oyster Cocktail, 3-1/2" h, 4 oz, plain bowl | 16.50 |
| Pastry Server, orig spoon, orig box | 45.00 |
| Pastry Stand, ftd, 8-1/2" or 9-3/4" d | 500.00 |
| Perfume Bottle, orig stopper **** | 100.00 |
| Pickle Jar, pointed cov, 6" h | 650.00 |
| Pickle, 8" l, oblong | 25.00 |
| Picture Frame | 18.00 |
| Pin Tray, oval, 5-1/2" x 4-1/2" | 120.00 |
| Pitcher, 1 pt, 5-3/8" h, flat | 35.00 |
| Pitcher, 1 qt, flat | 40.00 |
| Pitcher, 1/2 gal, 8", ftd | 90.00 |
| Pitcher, 1/2 gal, ice lip, 8-1/4", flat bottom | 165.00 |
| Pitcher, 1/2 gal, without ice lip | 265.00 |
| Pitcher, 2 pt, 7-1/4" h, ftd | 70.00 |
| Pitcher, 3 pt, 8", ftd | 75.00 |
| Pitcher, 3 pt, ice lip, 6-1/2", ftd, fat | 65.00 |
| Plate, 6" d, bread and butter | 12.00 |
| Plate, 7" d, salad | 15.00 |
| Plate, 7-1/2" x 4-3/8", crescent salad | 45.00 |
| Plate, 8" d, sauce liner, oval | 28.00 |
| Plate, 8-1/2" d, lunch | 18.00 |
| Plate, 9-1/2" d, dinner | 24.00 |
| Platter, 10-1/2" l, oval | 40.00 |
| Platter, 12" l, oval | 55.00 |
| Platter, 13-1/2" l | 850.00 |
| Pomade Box, 2" sq | 365.00 |
| Preserve Bowl, cov, 5-1/2" d, two handles | 85.00 |
| Puff Box, cov, round | 950.00 |
| Puff Box, cov, square | 2,700.00 |
| Punch Bowl, 14" d, high foot, base, 2 gallon | 250.00 |
| Punch Bowl, 14" d, low foot, base | 275.00 |
| Punch Bowl, 18" d, low, 3-3/4 gallon | 325.00 |
| Punch Cup, flared rim | 12.00 |
| Punch Cup, straight edge | 10.00 |
| Relish Boat, 12" l, 2 part | 16.50 |
| Relish Tray, 6-1/2" x 9", 4 part | 42.00 |
| Relish/Celery, 11" l, 3 part | 30.00 |
| Ring Holder | 850.00 |
| Rose Bowl, 3-1/2" d | 50.00 |
| Rose Bowl, 5" d | 40.00 |
| Salt and Pepper Shakers, pr, tray, 2" h | 24.00 |
| Salt Shaker, 3" h | 20.00 |
| Salt Shaker, 3-1/2" h | 7.50 |
| Salt Shaker, 3-1/4" h | 9.50 |
| Salt, individual | 15.00 |
| Sandwich Plate, 9" d, small center | 20.00 |
| Sandwich Plate, 10-1/2" d, small center | 22.00 |
| Sandwich Plate, 11-1/2" d, small center | 22.00 |
| Sandwich Tray, 12" d, center handle | 35.00 |

| Item | Crystal |
|---|---|
| Sauce Boat | 50.00 |
| Saucer | 3.25 |
| Service Tray, 9-1/2", 2 handles | 32.00 |
| Sherbet, 4-1/2 oz, 3-1/2" h, handle | 95.00 |
| Sherbet, 4-1/2 oz, 4-3/8" h, flared, #2056 | 9.00 |
| Sherbet, 4-1/2 oz, 4-1/2" h, #2056-1/2 | 9.00 |
| Sherbet, 5 oz, 3-1/2" h, low, #2056-1/2 | 12.00 |
| Sherbet, 5-1/2 oz, 4-1/8" h, plain bowl, #5056 | 8.50 |
| Shrimp Bowl, 12-1/4" d | 395.00 |
| Spooner, 3-3/4" h | 60.00 |
| Strawholder, 10" h, cov | 265.00 |
| Sugar Shaker | 50.00 |
| Sugar, cov, 2 handles | 22.00 |
| Sugar, cov, 6-1/4" h | 65.00 |
| Sugar Cube Holder | 450.00 |
| Sugar, handle, 3-1/4" h | 55.00 |
| Sugar, tea, 2-1/4" h | 15.00 |
| Sundae, 3-1/8" h, 6 oz, low foot, #2056 | 8.50 |
| Sweet Pea Vase, 4-1/2" h | 75.00 |
| Syrup, drip-proof top | 95.00 |
| Syrup, 6 oz, non-pour screw top, 5-1/2" h | 200.00 |
| Syrup, 6-1/2 oz, Sani-cut server, #2056-1/2 | 175.00 |
| Syrup, 10 oz, glass cov, 6" liner plate | 145.00 |
| Tea Tumbler, 5" h, 12 oz, #2056-1/2 | 17.50 |
| Tea Tumbler, 5-1/2" h, plain bowl, #5056 | 15.00 |
| Tea Tumbler, 5-1/4" h, 12 oz, flat, flared | 17.50 |
| Tidbit Tray, metal crook-shaped handle | 30.00 |
| Toddler set, baby tumbler, bowl | 85.00 |
| Tom and Jerry Mug, 3-1/4" h, 5-1/2 oz | 42.00 |
| Tom and Jerry, 12" d, small punch bowl, pedestal foot** | 240.00 |
| Toothpick Holder | 25.00 |
| Torte Plate, 13-1/2" d, oval | 65.00 |
| Torte Plate, 14" d | 90.00 |
| Torte Plate, 18" d | 150.00 |
| Torte Plate, 20" d | 250.00 |
| Torte Plate, 24" d | 275.00 |
| Tray, cloverleaf | 250.00 |
| Tray, 5" x 2-1/2", rect | 80.00 |
| Tray, 6", oval, handle | 45.00 |
| Tray, 10" w, sq | 115.00 |
| Tray, 10" w, sq, 4 parts | 85.00 |
| Tray, 10-1/2" x 5", oval, handle | 48.00 |
| Tray, 10-1/2" x 7-1/2", rect | 75.00 |
| Tray, 10-3/4" sq, 4 parts | 175.00 |
| Tray, 12" d, round | 185.00 |
| Tray, 14-1/8", 5 parts*** | 160.00 |
| Trifle Bowl, 8" d, 4" h | 300.00 |
| Trophy Cup, 8" d, ftd, 2 handles | 145.00 |
| Tumbler, 3-7/8" h, straight sides, #2056-1/2 | 17.50 |
| Tumbler, 4-1/8" h, 8 oz, flat, flared | 10.00 |
| Tumbler, 4-7/8" h, 9 oz, ftd | 12.00 |
| Urn, 6" h, sq, pedestal foot | 32.00 |
| Urn, 7-1/2" sq, pedestal foot | 60.00 |
| Vase, 6" h, straight side | 38.00 |

| Item | Crystal |
|---|---|
| Vase, 6-1/2" h, flared rim | 18.00 |
| Vase, 7" h, flared | 75.00 |
| Vase, 8" h, flared | 85.00 |
| Vase, 8" h, porch, 5" d | 315.00 |
| Vase, 8" h, straight side | 45.00 |
| Vase, 9" h, sq pedestal foot | 60.00 |
| Vase, 9-1/2" h, flared | 300.00 |
| Vase, 10" h, cupped in top | 250.00 |
| Vase, 10" h, flared | 95.00 |
| Vase, 10" h, porch, 8" d | 3,600.00 |
| Vase, 10" h, straight side | 95.00 |
| Vase, 10" h, swung | 295.00 |
| Vase, 12" h, straight side | 125.00 |
| Vase, 12" h, swung | 295.00 |
| Vase, 14" h, swung | 310.00 |
| Vase, 20" h, swung | 395.00 |
| Vase, 22-1/2" h, swung | 1,000.00 |
| Vegetable Bowl, 9" l, oval | 32.00 |
| Vegetable Bowl, 10" l, oval, 2 parts | 35.00 |
| Wash Bowl and Pitcher | 2,650.00 |
| Water Bottle, 9-1/4" h, 44 oz | 750.00 |
| Wedding Bowl, cov, 6-1/2" w, 5-1/4" h, sq, pedestal | 160.00 |
| Whiskey, 2 oz | 12.00 |
| Whiskey Tumbler, 2-1/4" h, 6 oz, #2056 | 16.00 |
| Wine, 4-3/8" h, 2-1/2 oz, hex foot, #2056 | 22.00 |

* Handkerchief Box, cov, 5-5/8" x 4-5/8" in blue is valued at $800.
** Tom and Jerry, 12" d, small punch bowl, pedestal foot in blue sold in 1999 for $12,000.
*** Tray, 14-1/8" d, 5 part, in blue, is valued at $425.
**** Perfume Bottle, orig stopper, 5-1/2" h, in amber, $425.

*American, bowl.*

# American Pioneer

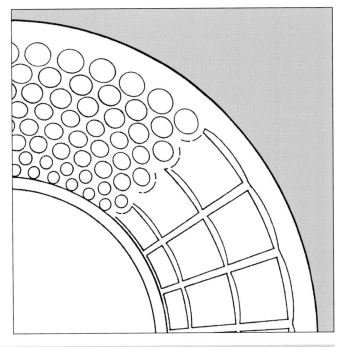

Manufactured by Liberty Works, Egg Harbor, N.J., from 1931 to 1934.

Made in amber, crystal, green, and pink.

| Item | Amber | Crystal | Green | Pink |
|------|-------|---------|-------|------|
| Bowl, 5" d, handle | 45.00 | 24.00 | 27.50 | 24.00 |
| Bowl, 8-3/4" d, cov | - | 115.00 | 125.00 | 115.00 |
| Bowl, 9" d, handle | - | 24.00 | 30.00 | 24.00 |
| Bowl, 9-1/4" d, cov | - | 120.00 | 150.00 | 120.00 |
| Bowl, 10" d | - | 50.00 | 70.00 | 60.00 |
| Candlesticks, pr, 6-1/2" h | - | 75.00 | 95.00 | 75.00 |
| Candy Jar, cov, 1 pound | - | 100.00 | 115.00 | 110.00 |
| Candy Jar, cov, 1-1/2 pound | - | 70.00 | 125.00 | 95.00 |
| Cheese and Cracker Set, indented plate and compote | - | 50.00 | 65.00 | 55.00 |
| Coaster, 3-1/2" d | - | 30.00 | 35.00 | 32.00 |
| Cocktail, 3 oz, 3-13/16" h | 45.00 | - | - | - |
| Cocktail, 3-1/2 oz, 3 -15/16" h | 45.00 | - | - | - |
| Console Bowl, 10-3/4" d | - | 50.00 | 75.00 | 60.00 |
| Creamer, 2-3/4" h | - | 20.00 | 22.00 | 25.00 |
| Creamer, 3-1/2" h | 60.00 | 30.00 | 32.00 | 30.00 |
| Cup | 24.00 | 12.00 | 15.00 | 12.00 |
| Dresser Set, 2 cologne bottles, powder jar, 7-1/2" tray | - | 300.00 | 345.00 | 365.00 |
| Goblet, 8 oz, 6" h, water | - | 40.00 | 45.00 | 40.00 |
| Ice Bucket, 6" h | - | 50.00 | 80.00 | 65.00 |
| Juice Tumbler, 5 oz | - | 40.00 | 45.00 | 40.00 |
| Lamp, 1-3/4", metal pole, 9-1/2" | - | - | 85.00 | - |

| Item | Amber | Crystal | Green | Pink |
|---|---|---|---|---|
| Lamp, 5-1/2" round, ball shape | 175.00 | - | - | 70.00 |
| Lamp, 8-1/2" h | - | 90.00 | 115.00 | 110.00 |
| Mayonnaise, 4-1/4" | - | 60.00 | 90.00 | 60.00 |
| Pilsner, 5-3/4" h, 11 oz | - | 100.00 | 110.00 | 100.00 |
| Pitcher, cov, 5" h | 295.00 | 150.00 | 225.00 | 165.00 |
| Pitcher, cov, 7" h | 325.00 | 175.00 | 250.00 | 195.00 |
| Plate, 6" d | - | 12.50 | 17.50 | 12.50 |
| Plate, 6" d, handle | 25.00 | 12.50 | 17.50 | 12.50 |
| Plate, 8" d | 28.00 | 10.00 | 13.00 | 14.00 |
| Plate, 11-1/2" d, handle | 40.00 | 20.00 | 24.00 | 20.00 |
| Rose Bowl, 4-1/4" d, ftd | - | 40.00 | 50.00 | 45.00 |
| Saucer, 6" sq | 10.00 | 4.00 | 5.00 | 5.50 |
| Sherbet, 3-1/2" h | - | 18.00 | 22.00 | 20.00 |
| Sherbet, 4-3/4" h | - | 32.50 | 40.00 | 30.00 |
| Sugar, 2-3/4" h | - | 20.00 | 27.50 | 25.00 |
| Sugar, 3-1/2" h | 50.00 | 20.00 | 27.50 | 25.00 |
| Tumbler, 8 oz, 4" h | - | 32.00 | 55.00 | 35.00 |
| Tumbler, 12 oz, 5" h | - | 40.00 | 55.00 | 40.00 |
| Vase, 7" h, 4 styles | - | 115.00 | 145.00 | 115.00 |
| Vase, 9" h, round | - | - | 245.00 | - |
| Whiskey, 2 oz., 2-1/4" h | - | 50.00 | 100.00 | 50.00 |

*American Pioneer, green plate, cup, and saucer.*

# American Sweetheart

Manufactured by Macbeth-Evans Glass Company, Charleroi, Pa., from 1930 to 1936.

Made in blue, Monax, pink, and red. Limited production in Cremax and color-trimmed Monax. Prices for Monax with color-trim, pink, and red are listed on page 41.

| Item | Blue | Cremax | Monax |
|---|---|---|---|
| Berry Bowl, 3-1/4"d, flat | - | - | - |
| Berry Bowl, 9" d | - | 50.00 | 75.00 |
| Cereal Bowl, 6" d | - | 19.50 | 20.00 |
| Chop Plate, 11" d | - | - | 24.00 |
| Console Bowl, 18" d | 1,400.00 | - | 475.00 |
| Cream Soup, 4-1/2" d | - | - | 135.00 |
| Creamer, ftd | 195.00 | - | 11.50 |
| Cup | 160.00 | - | 15.00 |
| Lamp Shade | - | 450.00 | 500.00 |
| Pitcher, 60 oz, 7-1/2" h | - | - | - |
| Pitcher, 80 oz, 8" h | - | - | - |
| Plate, 6" d, bread and butter | - | - | 7.50 |
| Plate, 8" d, salad | 125.00 | - | 10.00 |
| Plate, 9" d, luncheon | - | - | 14.00 |
| Plate, 9-3/4" d, dinner | - | - | 25.00 |
| Plate, 10-1/4" d, dinner | - | - | 30.00 |
| Platter, 13" l, oval | - | - | 85.00 |
| Salt and Pepper Shakers, pr, ftd | - | - | 395.00 |

| Item | Blue | Cremax | Monax |
|------|------|--------|-------|
| Salver Plate, 12" d | 275.00 | - | 30.00 |
| Saucer | 25.00 | - | 7.00 |
| Serving Plate, 15-1/2" d | 425.00 | - | 250.00 |
| Sherbet, 3-3/4" h, ftd | - | - | 15.00 |
| Sherbet, 4-1/4" h, ftd | - | - | 25.00 |
| Soup Bowl, flat, 9-1/2" d | - | - | 95.00 |
| Sugar Lid | - | - | 300.00 |
| Sugar, open, ftd | 195.00 | - | 15.00 |
| Tidbit, 2 tiers | 350.00 | - | 95.00 |
| Tidbit, 3 tiers | 750.00 | - | 275.00 |
| Tumbler, 5 oz, 3-1/2" h | - | - | - |
| Tumbler, 9 oz, 4-1/4" h | - | - | - |
| Tumbler, 10 oz, 4-3/4" h | - | - | - |
| Vegetable Bowl, 11" | - | - | 90.00 |

*American Sweetheart, Monax large plate.*

*American Sweetheart, Monax sugar and creamer.*

| Item | Monax with color-trim | Pink | Red |
|---|---|---|---|
| Berry Bowl, 3-1/4"d, flat | - | 80.00 | - |
| Berry Bowl, 9" d | 200.00 | 65.00 | - |
| Cereal Bowl, 6" d | 50.00 | 24.00 | - |
| Console Bowl, 18" d | - | - | 1,100.00 |
| Cream Soup, 4-1/2" d | - | 85.00 | - |
| Creamer, ftd | 110.00 | 18.00 | 175.00 |
| Cup | 100.00 | 20.00 | 95.00 |
| Pitcher, 60 oz, 7-1/2" h | - | 995.00 | - |
| Pitcher, 80 oz, 8" h | - | 795.00 | - |
| Plate, 6" d, bread and butter | 24.00 | 8.00 | - |
| Plate, 8" d, salad | 30.00 | 12.00 | 125.00 |
| Plate, 9" d, luncheon | 45.00 | - | - |
| Plate, 9-3/4" d, dinner | 90.00 | 42.00 | - |
| Plate, 10-1/4" d, dinner | - | 45.00 | - |
| Platter, 13" l, oval | 225.00 | 70.00 | - |
| Salt and Pepper Shakers, pr, ftd | - | 500.00 | - |
| Salver Plate, 12" d | - | 30.00 | 200.00 |
| Saucer | 18.00 | 5.75 | 45.00 |
| Serving Plate, 15-1/2" d | - | - | 350.00 |
| Sherbet, 3-3/4" h, ftd | - | 25.00 | - |
| Sherbet, 4-1/4" h, ftd | 110.00 | 25.00 | - |
| Soup Bowl, flat, 9-1/2" d | 170.00 | 85.00 | - |
| Sugar, open, ftd | 110.00 | 15.00 | 175.00 |
| Tidbit, 2 tiers | - | - | 250.00 |
| Tidbit, 3 tiers | - | - | 600.00 |
| Tumbler, 5 oz, 3-1/2" h | - | 110.00 | - |
| Tumbler, 9 oz, 4-1/4" h | - | 85.00 | - |
| Tumbler, 10 oz, 4-3/4" h | - | 185.00 | - |
| Vegetable Bowl, 11" | - | 80.00 | - |

# Anniversary

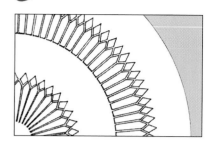

Manufactured by Jeannette Glass Company, Jeannette, Pa., from 1947 to 1949, and late 1960s to mid-1970s. Made in crystal, iridescent, and pink.

| Item | Crystal | Iridescent | Pink |
|---|---|---|---|
| Berry Bowl, 4-7/8" d | 3.50 | 4.50 | 11.00 |
| Butter Dish, cov | 25.00 | - | 50.00 |
| Cake Plate, 12-3/8" w, square | 7.00 | - | 16.50 |
| Cake Plate, 12-1/2" d, round | 8.00 | - | 18.50 |
| Cake Plate, metal cover | 15.00 | - | - |
| Candlesticks, pr, 4-7/8" h | 20.00 | 25.00 | - |
| Candy Jar, cov | 24.00 | - | 45.00 |
| Comport, open, 3 legs | 5.00 | 5.00 | 16.00 |
| Comport, ruffled, 3 legs | 6.50 | - | - |
| Creamer, ftd | 6.00 | 6.50 | 14.00 |
| Cup | 5.00 | 4.00 | 9.00 |
| Fruit Bowl, 9" d | 10.00 | 14.00 | 24.00 |
| Pickle Dish 9" d | 5.50 | 7.50 | 12.00 |
| Plate, 6-1/4" d, sherbet | 2.00 | 3.50 | 4.00 |
| Plate, 9" d, dinner | 5.00 | 8.00 | 17.00 |
| Relish Dish, 8" d | 5.60 | 7.50 | 14.00 |
| Sandwich Server, 12-1/2" d | 6.50 | 10.00 | 20.00 |
| Saucer | 1.00 | 1.50 | 6.00 |
| Sherbet, ftd | 7.00 | - | 10.00 |
| Soup Bowl, 7-3/8" d | 8.00 | 7.50 | 18.00 |
| Sugar, cov | 12.00 | 10.00 | 20.00 |
| Sugar, open, gold trim | 4.50 | - | - |
| Tidbit, metal handle | 14.00 | - | - |
| Vase, 6-1/2" h | 16.00 | - | 30.00 |
| Wall Pocket | 65.00 | - | 90.00 |
| Wine, 2-1/2 oz | 10.00 | - | 20.00 |

*Anniversary, iridescent plate.*

# Aunt Polly

Manufactured by U.S. Glass Company, Pittsburgh, Pa., in the late 1920s.

Made in blue, green, and iridescent.

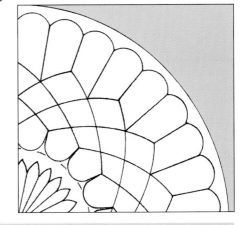

| Item | Blue | Green | Iridescent |
|---|---|---|---|
| Berry Bowl, 4-3/4" d, individual | 18.00 | 10.00 | 10.00 |
| Berry Bowl, 7-1/8" d, master | 45.00 | 22.00 | 22.00 |
| Bowl, 4-3/4" d, 2" h | - | 15.00 | 15.00 |
| Bowl, 5-1/2" d, one handle | 25.00 | 15.00 | 15.00 |
| Bowl, 8-3/8" l, oval | 100.00 | 42.00 | 42.00 |
| Butter Dish, cov | 245.00 | 200.00 | 200.00 |
| Candy Jar, cov, 2 handles | 50.00 | 30.00 | 30.00 |
| Candy Jar, ftd, 2 handles | - | 27.50 | 27.50 |
| Creamer | 60.00 | 32.00 | 32.00 |
| Pickle, 7-1/4" l, oval, handle | 42.00 | 17.50 | 17.50 |
| Pitcher, 48 oz, 8" h | 200.00 | - | - |
| Plate, 6" d, sherbet | 12.00 | 6.00 | 6.00 |
| Plate, 8" d, luncheon | 20.00 | - | - |
| Salt and Pepper Shakers, pr | 245.00 | - | - |
| Sherbet | 15.00 | 12.00 | 12.00 |
| Sugar | 195.00 | 95.00 | 95.00 |
| Tumbler, 8 oz, 3-5/8" h | 30.00 | - | - |
| Vase, 6-1/2" h, ftd | 48.00 | 30.00 | 30.00 |

*Aunt Polly, blue sherbet.*

# Aurora

Manufactured by Hazel Atlas Glass Company, Clarksburg, W.V., and Zanesville, Ohio, in the late 1930s.

Made in cobalt (Ritz) blue, crystal, green, and pink.

| Item | Cobalt Blue | Crystal | Green | Pink |
|---|---|---|---|---|
| Bowl, 4-1/2" d | 60.00 | - | - | 60.00 |
| Breakfast Set, 24 pcs, service for 4 | 500.00 | - | - | - |
| Cereal Bowl, 5-3/8" d | 20.00 | 12.00 | 10.00 | 15.00 |
| Cup | 20.00 | 6.00 | 10.00 | 15.00 |
| Milk Pitcher | 27.50 | - | - | 25.00 |
| Plate, 6-1/2" d | 12.50 | - | - | 12.50 |
| Saucer | 6.00 | 2.00 | 3.00 | 6.00 |
| Tumbler, 10 oz, 4-3/4" h | 27.50 | - | - | 27.50 |

*Aurora, blue cereal bowl, berry bowl, and milk pitcher.*

# Avocado

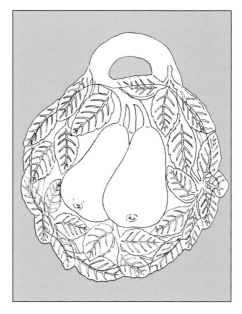

Manufactured by Indiana Glass Company, Dunkirk, Ind., from 1923 to 1933.

Made in crystal, green, pink, and white.

**Reproductions:** † Creamer, 8" pickle, 64 oz. pitcher, plates, sherbet, sugar, and tumblers. Reproductions can be found in amethyst, blue, dark green, frosted green, frosted pink, pink, red, and yellow, representing several colors not made originally.

| Item | Crystal | Green | Pink | White |
|---|---|---|---|---|
| Bowl, 5-1/4" d, 2 handles | 12.00 | 38.00 | 27.50 | - |
| Bowl, 8" d, 2 handles, oval | 17.50 | 30.00 | 25.00 | - |
| Bowl, 8-1/2" d | 20.00 | 60.00 | 50.00 | - |
| Bowl, 9-1/2" d, 3-1/4" deep | 35.00 | 175.00 | 150.00 | - |
| Cake Plate, 10-1/4" d, 2 handles | 17.50 | 60.00 | 40.00 | - |
| Creamer, ftd † | 17.50 | 40.00 | 35.00 | - |
| Cup, ftd | - | 36.00 | 30.00 | - |
| Pickle Bowl, 8" d, 2 handles, oval † | 17.50 | 30.00 | 25.00 | - |
| Pitcher, 64 oz † | 385.00 | 1,100.00 | 900.00 | 425.00 |
| Plate, 6-3/8" d, sherbet † | 6.00 | 22.00 | 15.00 | - |
| Plate, 8-1/4" d, luncheon † | 7.50 | 25.00 | 20.00 | - |
| Preserve Bowl, 7" l, handle | 10.00 | 32.00 | 28.00 | - |
| Relish, 6" d, ftd | 10.00 | 35.00 | 28.00 | - |
| Salad Bowl, 7-1/2" d | 9.00 | 55.00 | 37.50 | - |
| Saucer | 6.00 | 24.00 | 15.00 | - |
| Sherbet, ftd † | - | 75.00 | 55.00 | - |
| Sugar, ftd † | 17.50 | 40.00 | 35.00 | - |
| Tumbler † | 25.00 | 250.00 | 150.00 | 35.00 |

*Avocado, green sugar and creamer.*

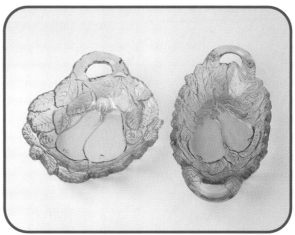

*Avocado, green bowl and relish dish.*

# Beaded Block

Manufactured by Imperial Glass Company, Bellaire, Ohio, from 1927 to the 1930s.

Made in amber, crystal, green, ice blue, iridescent, milk white (1950s), opalescent, pink, red, and Vaseline. Some pieces are still being made in pink and are embossed with the "IG" trademark. The only form known in red is the 4-1/2" lily bowl, valued at $300. The secondary market for milk white is still being established.

| Item | Amber | Crystal | Green | Ice Blue |
|---|---|---|---|---|
| Bowl, 4-1/2" d, lily | 20.00 | 15.00 | 22.00 | 24.00 |
| Bowl, 4-1/2" d, 2 handles | 18.00 | 10.00 | 22.00 | 28.00 |
| Bowl, 5-1/2" sq | 18.00 | 8.00 | 20.00 | 12.00 |
| Bowl, 5-1/2" d, 1 handle | 18.00 | 8.00 | 20.00 | 12.00 |
| Bowl, 6" deep | 24.00 | 12.00 | 24.00 | 15.00 |
| Bowl, 6-1/4" d | 24.00 | 8.50 | 20.00 | 12.00 |
| Bowl, 6-1/2" d, 2 handles | 24.00 | 8.50 | 20.00 | 12.00 |
| Bowl, 6-3/4" d | 28.00 | 12.00 | 28.00 | 14.00 |
| Bowl, 7-1/4" d, flared | 30.00 | 12.00 | 28.00 | 14.00 |
| Bowl, 7-1/2" d, fluted | 30.00 | 22.00 | 30.00 | 24.00 |
| Bowl, 7-1/2" plain | 30.00 | 20.00 | 30.00 | 22.00 |
| Candy Dish, cov, pear shaped | - | - | 395.00 | - |
| Celery, 8-1/4" d | 35.00 | 18.00 | 35.00 | 18.00 |
| Creamer, ftd | 25.00 | 25.00 | 25.00 | 24.00 |
| Jelly, 4-1/2" h, stemmed | 20.00 | 10.00 | 20.00 | 12.00 |
| Jelly, 4-1/2" h, stemmed, flared lid | 24.00 | 20.00 | 24.00 | 30.00 |
| Pitcher, 1 pt, 5-1/4" h | 95.00 | 115.00 | 125.00 | 115.00 |
| Plate, 7-3/4" sq | 20.00 | 7.50 | 20.00 | 10.00 |
| Plate, 8-3/4" | 30.00 | 24.00 | 30.00 | 30.00 |
| Sugar, ftd | 25.00 | 24.00 | 30.00 | 30.00 |
| Syrup | - | - | - | - |
| Vase, 6" h, ftd | 25.00 | 20.00 | 35.00 | 35.00 |

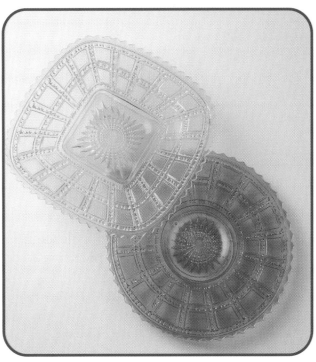

Beaded Block, cobalt blue bud vase and clear compote.

Beaded Block, Vaseline square plate and iridescent round plate.

| Item | Iridescent | Opal | Pink | Vaseline |
|------|-----------|------|------|----------|
| Bowl, 4-1/2" d, lily | 18.00 | 30.00 | 18.00 | 24.00 |
| Bowl, 4-1/2" d, 2 handles | 20.00 | 30.00 | 12.00 | 28.00 |
| Bowl, 5-1/2" sq | 10.00 | 15.00 | 10.00 | 12.00 |
| Bowl, 5 -/2 d, 1 handle | 10.00 | 15.00 | 20.00 | 12.00 |
| Bowl, 6" deep | 12.00 | 24.00 | 18.00 | 15.00 |
| Bowl, 6-1/4" d | 12.00 | 18.00 | 10.00 | 12.00 |
| Bowl, 6-1/2" d, 2 handles | 12.00 | 18.00 | 28.00 | 12.00 |
| Bowl, 6-3/4" d | 15.00 | 20.00 | 14.00 | 14.00 |
| Bowl, 7-1/4" d, flared | 15.00 | 20.00 | 14.00 | 14.00 |
| Bowl, 7-1/2" d, fluted | 20.00 | 24.00 | 24.00 | 24.00 |
| Bowl, 7-1/2" plain | 24.00 | 24.00 | 20.00 | 22.00 |
| Candy Dish, cov, pear shaped | - | - | - | 650.00 |
| Celery, 8-1/4" d | 18.00 | 30.00 | 16.50 | 18.00 |
| Creamer, ftd | 24.00 | 50.00 | 30.00 | 24.00 |
| Jelly, 4-1/2" h, stemmed | 12.00 | 15.00 | 12.00 | 12.00 |
| Jelly, 4-1/2" h, stemmed, flared lid | 15.00 | 24.00 | 15.00 | 12.00 |
| Pitcher, 1 pt, 5-1/4" h | 115.00 | 125.00 | 195.00 | 115.00 |
| Plate, 7-3/4" sq | 10.00 | 15.00 | 8.00 | 10.00 |
| Plate, 8-3/4" | 20.00 | 24.00 | 20.00 | 20.00 |
| Sugar, ftd | 20.00 | 60.00 | 30.00 | 20.00 |
| Syrup | - | - | - | 165.00 |
| Vase, 6" h, ftd | 25.00 | 110.00 | 36.00 | 30.00 |

# Beaded Edge

Made by Westmoreland Glass Co., late 1930s-1950s.
Made in white milk glass. Painted decorations add interesting variety to this pattern. Collectors can find eight different fruit patterns and eight different floral patterns; others include birds and Christmas designs. Another variation incorporates a red edge or band into the design.

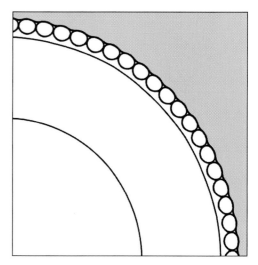

*Beaded Edge, luncheon plate, white.*

| Item | Decorated | Plain | Red edge |
| --- | --- | --- | --- |
| Creamer, cov, ftd | 35.00 | 20.00 | 25.00 |
| Creamer, open, ftd | 18.00 | 10.00 | 14.00 |
| Cup | 12.00 | 5.00 | 6.50 |
| Nappy, 5" d | 16.00 | 4.50 | 10.00 |
| Nappy, 6" d, crimped | 22.00 | 7.50 | 12.00 |
| Plate, 6" d, bread and butter | 19.00 | 5.00 | 7.00 |
| Plate, 7" d, salad | 12.00 | 6.00 | 8.00 |
| Plate, 7-1/2" d, coupe | 15.00 | 10.00 | 12.00 |
| Plate, 8-1/2" d, luncheon | 18.00 | 6.50 | 9.00 |
| Plate, 10-1/2" d, dinner | 45.00 | 12.00 | 20.00 |
| Platter, 12" l, tab handles | 90.00 | 75.00 | 45.00 |
| Relish, three-part | 90.00 | 25.00 | 50.00 |
| Salt and pepper shakers, pr | 75.00 | 30.00 | 35.00 |
| Saucer | 5.00 | 2.00 | 2.50 |
| Sherbet, ftd | 18.00 | 8.50 | 12.00 |
| Sugar, cov, ftd | 35.00 | 20.00 | 25.00 |
| Sugar, open, ftd | 18.00 | 10.00 | 14.00 |
| Torte plate, 15" d | 70.00 | 25.00 | 40.00 |
| Tumbler, ftd, 8 oz | 18.00 | 8.50 | 12.00 |

# Block Optic

## Block

Manufactured by Hocking Glass Company, Lancaster, Ohio, from 1929 to 1933.

Made in amber, crystal, green, pink, and yellow. Production in amber was very limited. A 11-3/4" d console bowl is valued at $50, while a pair of matching 1-3/4" h candlesticks is valued at $110.

* There are five styles of creamers and four styles of cups, each have a relative value.

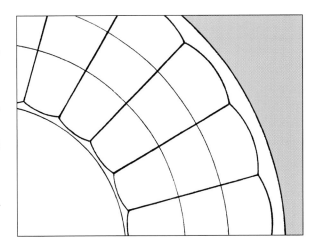

| Item | Crystal | Green | Pink | Yellow |
|---|---|---|---|---|
| Berry Bowl, 8-1/2" d | 20.00 | 35.00 | 40.00 | - |
| Bowl, 4-1/4" d, 1-3/8" h | 6.00 | 15.00 | 10.00 | - |
| Bowl, 4-1/2" d, 1-1/2" h | - | 28.00 | - | - |
| Bowl, 8-5/8" d, low, ruffled | - | 150.00 | - | - |
| Butter Dish, cov | - | 50.00 | - | - |
| Cake Plate, 10" d, ftd | 18.00 | - | - | - |
| Candlesticks, pr, 1-3/4" h | - | 120.00 | 100.00 | - |
| Candy Jar, cov, 2-1/4" h | 30.00 | 60.00 | 55.00 | 75.00 |
| Candy Jar, cov, 6-1/4" h | 40.00 | 80.00 | 60.00 | - |
| Cereal Bowl, 5-1/2" d | - | 20.00 | 30.00 | - |
| Champagne, 4-3/4" h | 10.00 | 27.50 | 16.50 | 20.00 |
| Cocktail, 4" h | - | 35.00 | 35.00 | - |
| Comport, 4" wide | - | 36.00 | 70.00 | - |
| Console Bowl, 11-3/4" d, rolled edge | 55.00 | 75.00 | 95.00 | - |
| Creamer* | 12.00 | 17.50 | 20.00 | 20.00 |
| Cup* | 7.50 | 9.00 | 7.00 | 10.00 |
| Goblet, 9 oz, 5-3/4" h | 12.00 | 40.00 | 45.00 | - |
| Goblet, 9 oz, 7-1/2" h, thin | 15.00 | - | 30.00 | 40.00 |
| Ice Bucket | - | 40.00 | 48.00 | - |
| Ice Tub, open | - | 60.00 | - | - |
| Mug | - | 35.00 | - | - |
| Pitcher, 54 oz, 7-5/8" h, bulbous | - | 75.00 | 75.00 | - |
| Pitcher, 54 oz, 8-1/2" h | - | 42.00 | 40.00 | - |
| Pitcher, 80 oz, 8" h | - | 90.00 | 85.00 | - |
| Plate, 6" d, sherbet | 1.50 | 5.00 | 5.00 | 6.50 |
| Plate, 8" d, luncheon | 3.50 | 8.00 | 7.50 | 8.50 |
| Plate, 9" d, dinner | 11.00 | 27.50 | 35.00 | 45.00 |
| Plate, 9" d, dinner, snowflake center | - | 16.50 | - | - |
| Plate, 9" d, grill | 15.00 | 27.50 | 30.00 | 60.00 |
| Salad Bowl, 7-1/4" d | - | 155.00 | - | - |

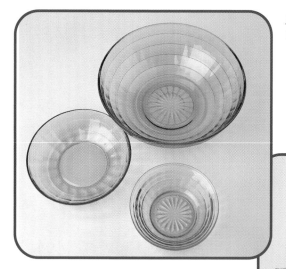

*Block Optic, green large and small berry bowl and salad bowl.*

*Block Optic, green sherbet, sugar and creamer, and Hazel Atlas look-alike covered candy dish.*

| Item | Crystal | Green | Pink | Yellow |
|---|---|---|---|---|
| Salad Bowl, 7-1/4" d | - | 155.00 | - | - |
| Salt and Pepper Shakers, pr, ftd | - | 42.00 | 90.00 | 95.00 |
| Salt and Pepper Shakers, pr, squatty | - | 100.00 | - | - |
| Sandwich Plate, 10-1/4" d | - | 27.50 | 30.00 | - |
| Sandwich Server, center handle | - | 65.00 | 50.00 | - |
| Saucer, 5-3/4" d | - | 12.00 | 10.00 | - |
| Saucer, 6-1/8" d | 2.00 | 10.00 | 10.00 | 3.50 |
| Sherbet, cone | - | 12.00 | 6.00 | - |
| Sherbet, 5-1/2 oz, 3-1/4" h | - | 12.00 | 9.50 | 7.50 |
| Sherbet, 6 oz, 4-3/4" h | 7.00 | 28.00 | 17.50 | 18.00 |
| Sugar, cone | - | 17.50 | 15.00 | 15.00 |
| Sugar, flat | - | 10.00 | 10.00 | - |
| Sugar, round, ftd | 10.00 | 12.00 | 18.00 | - |
| Tumbler, 3 oz, 2-5/8" h | - | 30.00 | 28.00 | - |
| Tumbler, 3 oz, 3-1/4" h, ftd | - | 27.50 | 25.00 | - |
| Tumbler, 5 oz, 3-1/2" h, flat | - | 20.00 | 17.50 | - |
| Tumbler, 5-3/8" h, ftd | - | - | 24.00 | 18.00 |
| Tumbler, 9" h, ftd | - | - | 17.50 | 22.00 |
| Tumbler, 9-1/2 oz, 3-13/16" h, flat | - | 17.50 | 15.00 | - |
| Tumbler, 10 oz, 6" h, ftd | 12.00 | - | - | - |
| Tumbler, 10 or 11 oz, 5" h, flat | - | 30.00 | 35.00 | - |
| Tumbler, 12 oz, 4-7/8" h, flat | - | 35.50 | 30.00 | - |
| Tumbler, 15 oz, 5-1/4" h, flat | - | 32.50 | 30.00 | - |
| Tumble-Up, 3" h tumbler and bottle | - | 90.00 | 75.00 | - |
| Vase, 5-3/4" h, blown | - | 350.00 | - | - |
| Whiskey, 1 oz, 1-5/8" h | 20.00 | 40.00 | 45.00 | - |
| Whiskey, 2 oz, 2-1/4" h | 15.00 | 35.00 | 30.00 | - |
| Wine, 3-1/2" h | - | 415.00 | 415.00 | - |
| Wine, 4-1/2" h | 15.00 | 35.00 | 32.00 | - |

# Bowknot

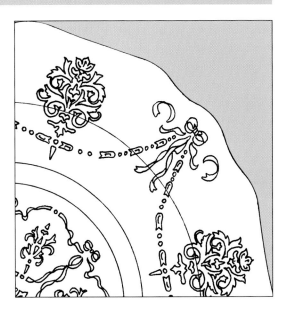

Unknown maker, late 1920s.
Made in green.

| Item | Green |
|---|---|
| Berry Bowl, 4-1/2" d | 25.00 |
| Cereal Bowl, 5-1/2" d | 30.00 |
| Cup | 20.00 |
| Plate, 7" d, salad | 15.00 |
| Sherbet, low, ftd | 25.00 |
| Tumbler, 10 oz, 5" h, flat | 20.00 |
| Tumbler, 10 oz, 5" h, ftd | 20.00 |

*Bowknot, green tumbler and footed berry bowl.*

# Bubble

## Bullseye, Provincial

Manufactured originally by Hocking Glass Company, and followed by Anchor Hocking Glass Corporation, Lancaster, Ohio, from 1937 to 1965.

Made in crystal (1937); forest green (1937); pink, Royal Ruby (1963); and sapphire blue (1937). Production in pink was limited. The current value for a pink cup and saucer is $175.

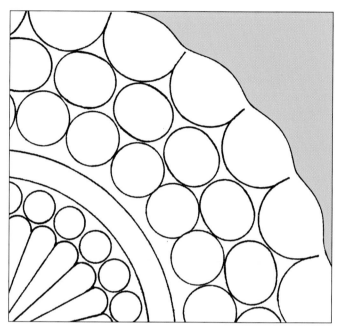

| Item | Crystal | Forest Green | Royal Ruby | Sapphire Blue |
|---|---|---|---|---|
| Berry Bowl, 4" d | 5.00 | - | 6.50 | 24.00 |
| Berry Bowl, 8-3/4" d | 12.00 | 15.00 | 18.00 | 20.00 |
| Bowl, 9" d, fanged | 8.00 | - | - | 335.00 |
| Candlesticks, pr | 24.00 | 40.00 | - | - |
| Cereal Bowl, 5-1/4" d | 8.00 | 20.00 | - | 17.50 |
| Cocktail, 3-1/2 oz | 4.50 | 10.00 | 10.00 | - |
| Cocktail, 4-1/2 oz | 4.50 | 12.50 | 12.50 | - |
| Creamer | 7.50 | 15.00 | 18.00 | 45.00 |
| Cup | 4.50 | 8.75 | 12.50 | 15.00 |
| Fruit Bowl, 4-1/2" d | 5.00 | 11.00 | 9.00 | 12.00 |
| Goblet, 9 oz, stem, 5-1/2" h | 7.50 | 15.00 | 15.00 | - |
| Goblet, 9-1/2 oz, stem | 7.50 | 15.00 | 15.00 | - |
| Iced Tea Goblet, 14 oz | 8.00 | 17.50 | - | - |
| Iced Tea Tumbler, 12 oz, 4-1/2" h | 12.50 | - | 19.50 | - |
| Juice Goblet, 4 oz | 3.00 | 14.00 | - | - |
| Juice Goblet, 5-1/2 oz | 5.00 | 12.50 | 12.50 | - |
| Juice Tumbler, 6 oz, ftd | 4.00 | 12.00 | 10.00 | - |
| Lamp, 3 styles | 42.00 | - | - | - |

| Item | Crystal | Forest Green | Royal Ruby | Sapphire Blue |
|---|---|---|---|---|
| Lemonade Tumbler, 16 oz, 5-7/8" h | 16.00 | - | 16.00 | - |
| Old Fashioned Tumbler, 8 oz, 3-1/4" h | 6.50 | 16.00 | 16.00 | - |
| Pitcher, 64 oz, ice lip | 60.00 | - | 65.00 | - |
| Plate, 6-3/4" d, bread and butter | 4.00 | 4.50 | - | 3.75 |
| Plate, 9-3/8" d, dinner | 7.50 | 28.00 | 27.50 | 8.00 |
| Plate, 9-3/8" d, grill | - | 20.00 | - | 22.00 |
| Platter, 12" l, oval | 10.00 | - | - | 18.00 |
| Sandwich Plate, 9-1/2" d | 7.50 | 25.00 | 22.00 | 8.00 |
| Saucer | 1.50 | 5.00 | 5.00 | 1.50 |
| Sherbet, 6 oz | 4.50 | 9.50 | 12.00 | - |
| Soup Bowl, flat, 7-3/4" d | 10.00 | - | - | 16.00 |
| Sugar | 6.00 | 14.50 | - | 30.00 |
| Tidbit, 2 tiers | - | - | 35.00 | - |
| Tumbler, 9 oz, water | 6.00 | - | 16.00 | - |

*Bubble, blue grill plate, platter, and bowls.*

# By Cracky

Manufactured by L.E. Smith Glass Company, Mount Pleasant, Pa., in the late 1920s.

Made in amber, canary, crystal, and green.

| Item | Amber | Canary | Crystal | Green |
|---|---|---|---|---|
| Cake plate, ftd | 35.00 | 40.00 | 30.00 | 30.00 |
| Candleholder, octagonal base | 7.50 | 10.00 | 5.00 | 5.00 |
| Candleholder, round base | 5.00 | 7.50 | 5.00 | 5.00 |
| Candy box, cov. | 17.50 | 20.00 | 15.00 | 17.50 |
| Candy jar, cov | 20.00 | 25.00 | 17.50 | 17.50 |
| Center bowl, 12", octagonal | 15.00 | 17.50 | 12.00 | 15.00 |
| Cup | 5.00 | 5.00 | 5.00 | 5.00 |
| Goblet | 18.00 | 18.00 | 10.00 | 15.00 |
| Flower block, 3" | 15.00 | 17.50 | 7.50 | 10.00 |
| Plate, 8", octagonal | 15.00 | 17.50 | 7.50 | 10.00 |
| Saucer | 3.00 | 5.00 | 2.00 | 2.00 |
| Sherbet | 7.50 | 10.00 | 5.00 | 5.00 |
| Sherbet plate | 12.00 | 15.00 | 5.00 | 7.50 |
| Vase, fan shape | 20.00 | 25.00 | 15.00 | 15.00 |
| Violet bowl | 20.00 | 25.00 | 15.00 | 15.00 |

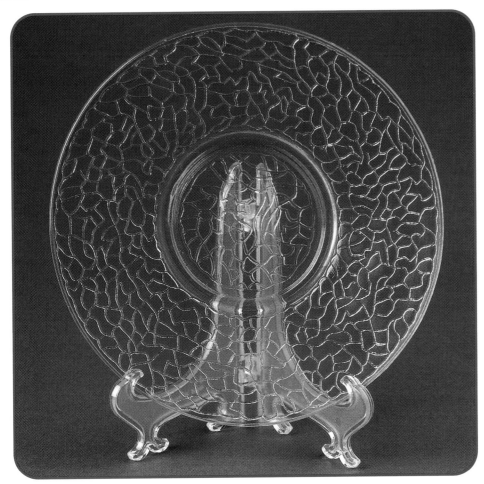

*By Cracky, clear sherbet plate.*

*By Cracky, green goblet.*

# Cameo

## Ballerina, Dancing Girl

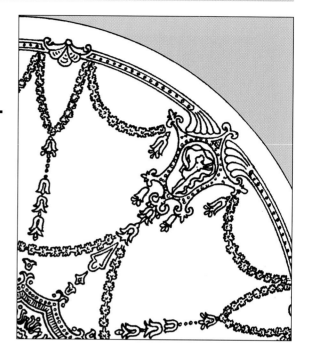

Manufactured by Hocking Glass Company, Lancaster, Ohio, from 1930 to 1934.

Made in crystal, green, pink, and yellow. Only the crystal has a platinum rim.

**Reproductions:** † Salt shakers made in blue, green and pink. Children's dishes have been made in green and pink, but were never part of the original pattern. Recently, a squatty candy dish in cobalt blue has also been made. This was not an original color.

| Item | Crystal | Green | Pink | Yellow |
|------|--------|-------|------|--------|
| Berry Bowl, 4-1/4" d | 15.00 | - | - | - |
| Berry Bowl, 8-1/4" d | - | 48.00 | 175.00 | - |
| Butter Dish, cov | - | 250.00 | - | 1,500.00 |
| Cake Plate, 10" d, 3 legs | - | 28.00 | - | - |
| Cake Plate, 10-1/2" d, flat | - | 120.00 | 165.00 | - |
| Candlesticks, pr, 4" h | - | 150.00 | - | - |
| Candy Jar, cov, 4" h | - | 100.00 | 495.00 | 125.00 |
| Candy Jar, cov, 6-1/2" h | - | 195.00 | - | - |
| Cereal Bowl, 5-1/2" d | 8.50 | 40.00 | 160.00 | 35.00 |
| Cocktail Shaker | 600.00 | - | - | - |
| Comport, 5" w | - | 50.00 | 200.00 | - |
| Console Bowl, 3 legs, 11" d | - | 90.00 | 45.00 | 125.00 |
| Cookie Jar, cov | - | 65.00 | - | - |
| Cream Soup, 4-3/4" d | - | 185.00 | - | - |
| Creamer, 3-1/4" h | - | 30.00 | 110.00 | 25.00 |
| Creamer, 4-1/4" h | - | 30.00 | 115.00 | - |
| Cup | 10.00 | 20.00 | 85.00 | 10.00 |
| Decanter, 10" h | 225.00 | 215.00 | - | - |
| Domino Tray, 7" l | 150.00 | 175.00 | 250.00 | - |
| Goblet, 6" h, water | - | 95.00 | 195.00 | - |
| Ice Bowl, 3" h, 5-1/2" d | 265.00 | 300.00 | 750.00 | - |
| Jam Jar, cov, 2" h | 175.00 | 225.00 | - | - |
| Juice Pitcher, 6" h, 36 oz | - | 110.00 | - | - |
| Juice Tumbler, 3 oz, ftd | - | 65.00 | 90.00 | - |
| Juice Tumbler, 5 oz, 3-3/4" h | - | 42.00 | - | - |
| Pitcher, 8-1/2" h, 56 oz | 550.00 | 70.00 | 1,450.00 | - |
| Plate, 6" d, sherbet | 6.00 | 12.50 | 90.00 | 4.00 |
| Plate, 7" d, salad | 12.00 | 13.50 | - | - |
| Plate, 8" d, luncheon | 8.00 | 18.00 | 36.00 | 12.50 |
| Plate, 8-1/2", luncheon, sq | - | 60.00 | - | 250.00 |

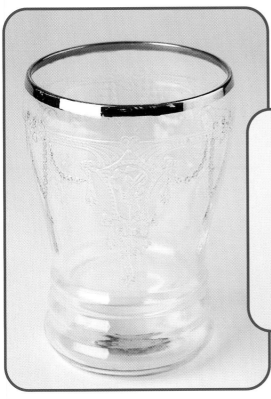

*Cameo, clear tumbler.*

*Cameo, green vegetable bowl.*

| *Item* | *Crystal* | *Green* | *Pink* | *Yellow* |
|---|---|---|---|---|
| Plate, 9-1/2" d, dinner | - | 28.00 | 85.00 | 15.00 |
| Plate, 10-1/2" d, dinner, rimmed | - | 115.00 | 175.00 | - |
| Plate, 10-1/2" d, grill | - | 20.00 | 55.00 | 10.00 |
| Platter, 12" l | - | 30.00 | - | 42.00 |
| Relish, 7-1/2" l, ftd, 3 parts | 175.00 | 35.00 | - | - |
| Salad Bowl, 7-1/4" d | - | 70.00 | - | - |
| Salt and Pepper Shakers, pr, ftd † | - | 95.00 | 90.00 | - |
| Sandwich Plate, 10" d | - | 18.00 | 45.00 | - |
| Sandwich Server, center handle | - | 6,500.00 | - | - |
| Saucer | 4.00 | 4.00 | 90.00 | 4.50 |
| Sherbet, 3-1/8" h, blown | - | 18.00 | 75.00 | - |
| Sherbet, 3-1/8" h, molded | - | 16.00 | 75.00 | 40.00 |
| Sherbet, 4-7/8" h | - | 40.00 | 100.00 | 45.00 |
| Soup Bowl, rimmed, 9" d | - | 95.00 | 135.00 | 85.00 |
| Sugar, 3-1/4" h | - | 24.00 | - | 22.00 |
| Sugar, 4-1/4" h | - | 32.50 | 125.00 | - |
| Syrup Pitcher, 20 oz, 5-3/4" h | - | 250.00 | - | 2,000.00 |
| Tumbler, 9 oz, 4" h | 16.00 | 32.00 | 80.00 | - |
| Tumbler, 9 oz, 5" h, ftd | - | 30.00 | 115.00 | 20.00 |
| Tumbler, 10 oz, 4-3/4" h, flat | - | 35.00 | 95.00 | - |
| Tumbler, 11" oz, 5" h, flat | - | 30.00 | 90.00 | 60.00 |
| Tumbler, 11 oz, 5-3/4" h, ftd | - | 75.00 | 135.00 | - |
| Tumbler, 15 oz, 5-1/4" h | - | 80.00 | 145.00 | - |
| Tumbler, 15 oz, 6-3/8" h, ftd | - | 495.00 | - | - |
| Vase, 5-3/4" h | - | 375.00 | - | - |
| Vase, 8" h | - | 70.00 | - | - |
| Vegetable, oval, 10" l | - | 50.00 | - | 45.00 |
| Wine, 3-1/2" h | - | 1,200.00 | 950.00 | - |
| Wine, 4" h | - | 95.00 | 250.00 | - |

# Candlewick

Manufactured by Imperial Glass Company from 1936 to 1984.

Made in black, blue, cobalt blue, crystal, green, pink, red, and yellow, with crystal being the most prevalent. Some etched designs are known.

**Reproductions:** † Reproduction Candlewick has been made in caramel slag and jadeite. Cobalt blue and red items were made by Dalzell Viking.

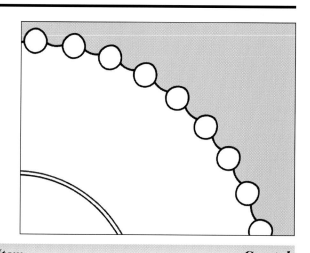

| Item | Crystal |
|---|---|
| After dinner cup and saucer, 400/77, 5-1/2" d beaded saucer | 20.00 |
| Ashtray, 400/118 | 18.00 |
| Ashtray, 400/150, 6" d, round, large beads | 8.00 |
| Ashtray, 400/176, 3-1/4" sq, large beads | 12.00 |
| Ashtray, 400/450, nested set, 4", 5", and 6" | 25.00 |
| Ashtray, 400/60, match holder center | 150.00 |
| Ashtray, 400/650, nested set, orig Imperial sticker | 135.00 |
| Atomizer, 400/96 shaker, atomizer top, made by DeVilbiss | 125.00 |
| Baked apple dish, 400/53X, 6-1/2" | 25.00 |
| Banana stand, 400/103E, 11" d, 2 turned-up sides, 4-bead stem | 1,500.00 |
| Basket, 400/273, 5" h | 300.00 |
| Basket, 400/273, 5", beaded top, beads on top of handle | 225.00 |
| Basket, 400/37/0, 11", applied handle | 200.00 |
| Basket, 400/40/0, 6-1/2", turned-up sides, applied handle | 50.00 |
| Bell, 400/108, 4", 4-bead handle | 60.00 |
| Bonbon, 400/51T, 6", heart shape, curved-over center handle, beaded edge | 30.00 |
| Bonbon, 400/149F, 7-1/2" | 225.00 |
| Bowl, 400/104B, 14" d, belled, large beads on sides | 75.00 |
| Bowl, 400/427B, 4-3/4" d, 6" d, 7" d and 8-1/2" d, nested | 75.00 |
| Bowl, 400/49H, 5" d, heart shaped | 175.00 |
| Bowl, 400/52, 6" d, divided | 20.00 |
| Bowl, 400/69B, 8-1/2" d | 35.00 |
| Bowl, 400/73H, 9" d, heart shape | 55.00 |
| Bowl, 400/74SC, 9" d, four ball toes, crimped | 60.00 |
| Bowl, 400/75B, 10-1/2" d | 40.00 |

| Item | Crystal |
|---|---|
| Bowl, 400/84, 6-1/2" d, divided | 20.00 |
| Bud vase, 400/107, 5-1/4" h, beaded foot, large beads, crimped top | 65.00 |
| Bud vase, 400/227, 8-1/2" h, beaded ball bottom, narrowed top slants, applied handle | 95.00 |
| Bud vase, 400/25, 3-3/4" h, beaded foot, ball shape, crimped top | 35.00 |
| Bud vase, 400/28C, 8-1/2", trumpet shaped top, crimped, beaded ball bottom | 75.00 |
| Buffet set, 400/9266, 14" d 400/92D plate, 5-1/2" d 400/66E cheese compote, plain stem, two pcs | 70.00 |
| Butter, cov, 400/161, quarter pound, graduated beads on cov | 25.00 |
| Butter, cov, 400/276, 6-3/4" x 4", California, beaded top, c1960 | 100.00 |
| Butter, cov, 400/276, 6-3/4" x 4", California, plain top, c1951 | 125.00 |
| Butter pat | 12.00 |
| Cake stand, 400/103D, 11" h, tall, three-bead stem | 95.00 |
| Cake stand, 400/160, 14" d, 72 candle holes | 400.00 |
| Cake stand, 400/67D, 10" d, wedge marks on plate, one-bead stem, dome foot, c1939 | 85.00 |
| Cake stand, 400/67D, 10" d, wedge marks on plate, one-bead stem, flat foot, c1943 | 70.00 |
| Candleholder, 400/115, 9" h, oval, beaded base, three candle cups | 125.00 |
| Candleholder, 400/115/2, 9" h, two eagle adapters | 350.00 |
| Candleholder, 400/175, 6-1/2" h, three-bead stem | 95.00 |
| Candleholder, 400/175, 9" h, three-bead stem, adapter, prisms | 250.00 |

Candleholder, 400/207, 4-1/2" h . . . . . . . . . 120.00

Candleholder, 400/224, 5-1/2" h, ftd, three sections of arched beads on stem . . . . . . . . . . . . . . 175.00

Candleholder, 400/40CV, 5" h, round bowl, beaded or fluted vase insert . . . . . . . . . . . . . . . . . . 75.00

Candleholder, 400/79R, 3-1/2" h, rolled saucer, small beads . . . . . . . . . . . . . . . . . . . . . . . . . . 15.00

Candleholder, 400/81, 3-1/2" h, dome ftd, small beads, round handle . . . . . . . . . . . . . . . . . . 75.00

Candleholders, pr, 400/147, three lite . . . . . 150.00

Candleholders, pr, 400/86, mushroom. . . . . . 92.00

Candy dish, cov, 400/110, three parts . . . . . 185.00

Candy dish, cov, 400/110, 7" d, three-part, two-bead finial. . . . . . . . . . . . . . . . . . . . . . . . . 195.00

Candy dish, cov, 400/140, 8" d, one-bead stem, domed beaded foot, c1942 . . . . . . . . . . . . 500.00

Candy dish, cov, 400/140, 8" d, one-bead stem, flat plain foot, c1944. . . . . . . . . . . . . . . . . . . 275.00

Candy dish, cov, 400/245, 6-1/2" d, round bowl, sq cov, two-bead finial. . . . . . . . . . . . . . . . . 300.00

Candy dish, cov, 400/259, 6-3/4" w, beaded rim, two-bead finial on cov. . . . . . . . . . . . . . . . 110.00

Candy dish, cov, 400/59, 5-1/2" d, two-bead finial . . . . . . . . . . . . . . . . . . . . . . . . . . . . . . . . 40.00

Candy dish, cov, 400/59, small . . . . . . . . . . 80.00

Celery tray, 400/105, 13" l, oval, two curved beaded handles . . . . . . . . . . . . . . . . . . . . . . . . . . 45.00

Celery tray, 400/46, 11" l, oval, scalloped edge . . . . . . . . . . . . . . . . . . . . . . . . . . . . . . . . . 75.00

Champagne, 3400, flared belled top, 5 oz, four graduated beads in stem . . . . . . . . . . . . . . . 24.00

Cheese and cracker set, 400/88, 5-1/2" ftd 400/88 cheese compote, 10-1/2" d 400/72D handled plate . . . . . . . . . . . . . . . . . . . . . . . . . . . . . . . . 65.00

Cheese, toast or butter dish, 400/123, 7-3/4" d plate with cupped edge, domed cov with bubble knob. . . . . . . . . . . . . . . . . . . . . . . . . . . . . 275.00

Chip and dip, 400/228. . . . . . . . . . . . . . . . 795.00

Cigarette set, 400/29/64/44 or 400/29/6, dome ftd 3" 400/44 cigarette holder, small beads, four nested 400/64 2-3/4" d ashtrays, 400/29 kidney-shaped tray. . . . . . . . . . . . . . . . . . . . . . . . . . . . . . . 95.00

Clock, 4", large beads, New Haven works . . 400.00

Cocktail, 4000/190, bell-shaped bowl, beads around foot, 4 oz, three-bead stem . . . . . . . . 18.00

Cocktail pitcher, 400/19, 40 ounce, 8-1/2". . 250.00

Cocktail set, 400/97, 6" d 400/39 plate with 2-1/2" off-center indent, #111 one-bead cocktail glass . . . . . . . . . . . . . . . . . . . . . . . . . . . . . . . . 35.00

Coffee cup and saucer, 400/37, slender 40/37 cup, 400/35 saucer . . . . . . . . . . . . . . . . . . . . . . 15.00

Compote, 400/103F, 10" d, crimped, three-bead stem, hp pink roses, blue ribbons . . . . . . . . 350.00

Compote, 400/220, 5" d, three-part, beaded edge, arched . . . . . . . . . . . . . . . . . . . . . . . . . . . 145.00

Compote, 400/220, 5", arch beaded trim-stem. . 150.00

Compote, 400/48F, 8" d, beaded edge, four-bead stem . . . . . . . . . . . . . . . . . . . . . . . . . . . . . 75.00

Compote, 400/48F, 8" d, beaded edge, five-bead stem . . . . . . . . . . . . . . . . . . . . . . . . . . . . 200.00

Compote, 400/67B, 9" d, flat, large bead stem, c1943 . . . . . . . . . . . . . . . . . . . . . . . . . . . 100.00

Compote, 400/67B, 9" d, ribbed bowl, dome ftd, large bead stem, c1937 . . . . . . . . . . . . . . . 225.00

Condiment set, 400/1589, jam set, two cov 400/89 marmalade jars, three-bead ladles, oval 400/159 tray. . . . . . . . . . . . . . . . . . . . . . . . . . . . . . 95.00

Condiment set, 400/1769, 6-ounce 400/119 cruet, pr 400/96 salt and pepper shakers, 8" 400/171 tray . . . . . . . . . . . . . . . . . . . . . . . . . . . . . . . 100.00

Condiment set, 400/2946, oil and vinegar, pr 400/164 and 400/166 beaded foot cruets, kidney-shaped 400/29 tray . . . . . . . . . . . . . . . . . . . . 90.00

Console set, 400/100, 12" 400/92F flat bowl, cupped edge, pr 400/100 two-lite candleholders, center circle of large beads . . . . . . . . . . . . . . . -

Console set, 400/8063B, bowl and pr candleholders . . . . . . . . . . . . . . . . . . . . . . . . . . . . . . . . . 95.00

Console set, 400/8692L, 13" 400/92L mushroom bowl on 400/127B 7-1/2" d base, pr 400/86 mushroom candleholders . . . . . . . . . . . . . . . . . . 125.00

Cordial bottle, 400/82, 15 oz, beaded foot, three-bead stopper, handle, c1938 . . . . . . . . . . . . 225.00

Cordial bottle, 400/82, 15 oz, beaded foot, c1941 . . . . . . . . . . . . . . . . . . . . . . . . . . . . . . . . 200.00

Cordial, 3400, flared belled top, four graduated beads stem . . . . . . . . . . . . . . . . . . . . . . . . . 48.00

Cream soup bowl . . . . . . . . . . . . . . . . . . . . 55.00

*Candlewick, crystal luncheon plate.*

Creamer and sugar, 400/122, individual, pr . . 22.00
Creamer and sugar, 400/18, domed foot, large beads, creamer with plain handle attached at bottom, no handle on sugar, 1954-55 . . . . . . . 125.00
Creamer and sugar, 400/29/30, flat base, beaded question mark handles, 400/30, 7" l 400/29 tray . . . . . . . . . . . . . . . . . . . . . . . . . . . . . . . . . 35.00
Creamer and sugar, 400/31, beaded foot, plain handles, c1937 . . . . . . . . . . . . . . . . . . . . . . . 45.00
Creamer and sugar, 400/31, plain foot, question mark handles, c1941. . . . . . . . . . . . . . . . . . . 50.00
Cruet, 400/119, orig stopper . . . . . . . . . . . 25.00
Cup and saucer, 400/35/252, no beads on question mark handle . . . . . . . . . . . . . . . . . . . . . . . . 25.00
Decanter, 400/163, beaded foot, round stopper . . . . . . . . . . . . . . . . . . . . . . . . . . . . . . . 195.00
Dessert tumbler, 400/18, domed beaded foot, rounded top, 6 oz . . . . . . . . . . . . . . . . . . . . 40.00
Dessert tumbler, 400/19, beaded base, straight sides, 5 oz. . . . . . . . . . . . . . . . . . . . . . . . . . . 14.00
Deviled egg server, 400/154, 11-1/2" d . . . . . 150.00
Deviled egg tray, 400/154, 11-1/2" d, 12 indents for eggs, heart-shaped center handle . . . . . . . 110.00
Dresser set, I. Rice Co., 400/151 round mirrored tray; powder jar, beaded base, three-bead cover; two round perfume bottles, beaded base, four-bead stoppers, 1942, four-pc set . . . . . . . . . . . 250.00
Epergne set, 400/196, 9" ftd 400/196FC flower candle holder, one-bead stem, 7-3/4" h two-bead peg vase, beaded top, peg to fit into candle cut . . 295.00
Float bowl, 400/92B, 11" d, cupped edge, fuchsia cutting . . . . . . . . . . . . . . . . . . . . . . . . . . . . 75.00
Float bowl, 400/92B, 11" d, cupped edge, plain . . . . . . . . . . . . . . . . . . . . . . . . . . . . . . . . . 55.00
Float bowl, 400/101, 13" d . . . . . . . . . . . . . 225.00
Fruit bowl, 400/103C, 10" d, ftd . . . . . . . . 185.00
Goblet, water, 3400 line, flared bell bowl, four graduated beads in stem, 9 oz . . . . . . . . . . . 15.00
Goblet, water, 400/190 Line, bell-shaped bowl, hollow trumpet-shaped stem with beads around foot, 10 oz . . . . . . . . . . . . . . . . . . . . . . . . 24.50
Gravy boat, liner. . . . . . . . . . . . . . . . . . . . 200.00
Hurricane lamp, 400/152R, candleholder, chimney, and 100/152 adapter, three pc. . . . . . . . . . 200.00
Hurricane lamp, 400/79R, 3-1/2" saucer candleholder, 9" chimney, two-pc set . . . . . . . . . 100.00
Iced tea tumbler, 12 oz, ftd, 3400 line . . . . . . 15.00
Iced tea tumbler, 12 oz, ftd, 400/18, domed beaded foot, rounded top . . . . . . . . . . . . . . . . . . . . . 50.00
Iced tea tumbler, 12 oz, ftd, 400/19, beaded base, straight sides. . . . . . . . . . . . . . . . . . . . . . . . 18.00
Ice tub, 400/63, 8" d . . . . . . . . . . . . . . . . . 110.00
Jelly server, 400/157, 4-3/4" d, ftd, one-bead stem, two-bead cov. . . . . . . . . . . . . . . . . . . . . . . . 65.00
Jelly server, 400/157, 4-3/4" d, ftd, one-bead stem, no cover . . . . . . . . . . . . . . . . . . . . . . . . . . . 35.00

Jelly server, 400/52, 6" d, divided dish, beaded edge, handles . . . . . . . . . . . . . . . . . . . . . . 20.00
Juice tumbler, 400/18, domed beaded foot, straight sides, 5 oz. . . . . . . . . . . . . . . . . . . . . . . . . . . 18.00
Ladle, 400/139, 6-3/8" l . . . . . . . . . . . . . . . . 42.00
Lemon tray, 400/221, 5-1/2" l, arched handle 35.00
Marmalade jar, 400/130, round 400/89 base, beaded cover with notch, two-bead finial, 400/130 3-bead ladle . . . . . . . . . . . . . . . . . . . . . . . . . 135.00
Marmalade jar, 400/8918, 400/18 old fashion tumbler, beaded notched cover with two-bead finial, 400/130 three-bead ladle. . . . . . . . . . . . . . . 175.00
Mayonnaise set, 400/52/3, 400/23D 7-1/2" d handled plate with indent, 400/52B 5-1/2" d handled bowl, 400/135 ladle . . . . . . . . . . . . . . . . . . . . 40.00
Mayonnaise set, 400/84, 6-1/4" divided bowl with silver overlay, 8-1/4" underplate . . . . . . . . . 85.00
Mint dish, 400/51F, 5" d, round, applied handle . . . . . . . . . . . . . . . . . . . . . . . . . . . . . . . . . 20.00
Mirror, domed beaded base, brass holder and frame, two-sided mirror flips on hinges, made for I. Rice Co., 1940s. . . . . . . . . . . . . . . . . . . . . . 250.00
Mustard jar, 400/156, beaded foot, notched beaded cov with two-bead finial, 3-1/2" glass spoon, fleur-de-lis handle . . . . . . . . . . . . . . . . . . . . . . . . 40.00
Nappy, 400/3F, 6" . . . . . . . . . . . . . . . . . . 12.00
Old fashion tumbler, 400/19, beaded base, straight sides, 7 oz. . . . . . . . . . . . . . . . . . . . . . . . . . . 20.00
Parfait, 3400, flared bell top, one-bead stem, 6 oz . . . . . . . . . . . . . . . . . . . . . . . . . . . . . . . . . 50.00
Pastry tray, 400/68D, 11-1/2" d beaded plate, center heart-shaped handle . . . . . . . . . . . . . . . . . 35.00
Pickle/celery, 400/57, 8-1/2" l, oval . . . . . . . 30.00
Pitcher, 400/16, 16 oz, beaded question mark handle, plain base. . . . . . . . . . . . . . . . . . . . . . 175.00
Pitcher, 400/18, 16 oz, plain handle, beaded base . . . . . . . . . . . . . . . . . . . . . . . . . . . . . . . 225.00
Pitcher, 400/18, 80 oz, plain handle, beaded base . . . . . . . . . . . . . . . . . . . . . . . . . . . . . . . 200.00
Pitcher, 400/24, 80 oz, beaded question mark handle, plain base. . . . . . . . . . . . . . . . . . . . . . 165.00
Plate, 400/1D, 6" d, bread and butter . . . . . . 10.00
Plate, 400/3D, 7" d, salad . . . . . . . . . . . . . 12.00
Plate, 400/5D, 8-1/2" d, salad/dessert. . . . . . 14.00
Plate, 400/7D, 9" d, luncheon . . . . . . . . . . . 18.00
Plate, 400/10D, 10-1/4" d, dinner . . . . . . . . 35.00
Plate, 400/42D, 7" w handle to handle. . . . . 45.00
Plate, 400/72C, 10" d, w handles, crimped . . 28.00
Plate, 400/145D, 12" d, two open handles . . . 30.00
Punch bowl set, 400/20, 13" d six-quart 400/20 bowl, 17" d 400/20V plate, 12 400/37 punch cups, 400/91 ladle, 15-pc set . . . . . . . . . . . . . . . 265.00
Punch bowl set, 400/210, 14-1/2" d 10-quart 400/210 bowl, 9" belled 400/210 base, 12 400/211 punch cups with round beaded handles, 400/91 ladle, 15-pc set . . . . . . . . . . . . . . . . . . . . . 800.00

Punch bowl, ladle. . . . . . . . . . . . . . . . . . 1,500.00
Punch bowl, set, 400/128, 13" d 400/20 bowl, 10" 400/128 belled base, 12 400/37 punch cups, 400/91 ladle . . . . . . . . . . . . . . . . . . . . . . . . . . . . 300.00
Relish and dressing set, 400/1112, 10-1/2" five-part 400/112 relish, 400/89 jar fits center well; long ladle, c1941 . . . . . . . . . . . . . . . . . . . . . 95.00
Relish and dressing set, 400/1112, 10-1/2" five-part 400/112 relish, 400/289 jar fits center well; three-bead ladle, c1945 . . . . . . . . . . . . . . . . . 70.00
Relish, 400/112, 10-1/2" d, three-part, well for mayonnaise jar . . . . . . . . . . . . . . . . . . . . . 75.00
Relish, 400/208, 10" l, three parts, three toes . . . . . . . . . . . . . . . . . . . . . . . . . . . . . . . 145.00
Relish, 400/213, 10" l, three parts. . . . . . . . . 95.00
Relish, 400/213, three-part, 10" l, handle . . . 75.00
Relish, 400/215, three-part on one side, one section on other, 5-1/2" l, two tab handles . . . . . 65.00
Relish, 400/234, two-part, 7" sq. . . . . . . . . . 140.00
Relish, 400/256, two-part, 10-1/2" l, oval, two tab handles. . . . . . . . . . . . . . . . . . . . . . . . . . . 25.00
Relish, 400/262, three-part, 10-1/2" l, two tab handles. . . . . . . . . . . . . . . . . . . . . . . . . . . 100.00
Relish, 400/54, two-part, 6-1/2" l, two tab handles . . . . . . . . . . . . . . . . . . . . . . . . . . . . . 15.00
Relish, five parts . . . . . . . . . . . . . . . . 130.00
Relish, cov, 400/214, 10" l, oblong, cover with beaded top handle. . . . . . . . . . . . . . . . . . . 250.00
Salad set, 400/106B/75, 12" d bell 400/106B bowl, graduated beads on both side, fork and spoon . . . . . . . . . . . . . . . . . . . . . . . . . . . 110.00
Salad set, 400/17, 14" 400/92D plate, 10-1/2" 400/17F bowl, Old-style ribbed fork and spoon . . . . . . . . . . . . . . . . . . . . . . . . . . . . . . . . 85.00
Salad set, 400/735, 9" d handled heart-shaped 400/73H bowl, 700/75 fork and spoon set . . 150.00
Salad set, 400/75B, 10-1/2" d beaded 400/75B bowl, 13" d cupped 400/75V plate, five-bead handles 400/75 fork and spoon set. . . . . . . . . . . . . . 110.00
Salt and pepper shakers, pr, 400/116, one-bead stem, no beads on foot, plastic or metal tops . . . . . . . . . . . . . . . . . . . . . . . . . . . . . . . . 75.00
Salt and pepper shakers, pr, 400/190, trumpet foot, chrome tops . . . . . . . . . . . . . . . . . . . . . . . . 65.00
Salt and pepper shakers, pr, 400/96, nine beads, flat bottom, plastic tops, c1941 . . . . . . . . . . 30.00
Salt and pepper shakers, pr, 400/96, bulbous, eight beads, chrome tops. . . . . . . . . . . . . . . . . . . 20.00
Salt dip, 400/61, 2" . . . . . . . . . . . . . . . . . 12.00
Sauce boat set, 400/169, oval gravy boat with handle, 9" oval plate with indent. . . . . . . . . . . . 125.00
Seafood icer, 400/190, one-pc coupette . . . . . 90.00
Sherbet, 3400 line, flared bell top, low, 5 oz . 24.00
Sherbet, 3400 line, flared bell top, tall, 5 oz . 24.00
Tea cup and saucer, 400/35, round 400/35 cup, 400/35 saucer . . . . . . . . . . . . . . . . . . . . . . 15.00

Tidbit server, 400/2701, two tiers, 7-1/2" d and 10-1/2" d plates joined by metal rod, round handle at top . . . . . . . . . . . . . . . . . . . . . . . . . . . . 60.00
Tidbit set, 400/750, three-pc nested hearts, 4-1/2", 5-1/2", 6-1/2", beaded edges. . . . . . . . . . . . . 40.00
Torte plate, 400/20D, 17" d, flat . . . . . . . . . 40.00
Torte plate, 400/20V, 17" d, cupped. . . . . . . 60.00
Tray, 400/159, 9" oval, concentric circles in bottom, rect Farberware chrome holder with cut-out lacy pattern on each corner . . . . . . . . . . . . . 75.00
Tumbler, 400/18, domed beaded foot, rounded top, 9 oz . . . . . . . . . . . . . . . . . . . . . . . . . . . . . 45.00
Tumbler, 400/19, beaded base, straight sides, ftd, 10 oz, 4-3/4" h . . . . . . . . . . . . . . . . . . . . . 18.00
Vase, 400/87C, 8" h, crimped beaded top . . . 35.00
Vase, 400/87F, 8" h, fan shaped . . . . . . . . . . 30.00
Vase, 400/87R, 7" h, rolled over beaded top. . 40.00
Wine, 3400 line, flared belled bowl, four graduated stems in base, 9 oz . . . . . . . . . . . . . . . . . . . 25.00
Wine, 400/190 line, belled bowl, hollow trumpet stem with beads, 5 oz . . . . . . . . . . . . . . . . . 25.00

Prices for colored pieces:

Ashtray, 400/150, 6" d, round, large beads: blue, $50; pink $15.
Ashtray, 400/450, nested set, 4", 5", and 6", patriotic dec: blue, yellow, pink, $75; red, white, and blue, $175.
Atomizer, 400/167 shaker, atomizer top: amethyst or aqua, $175.
Bonbon, 400/51T, 6", heart shape, curved-over center handle, beaded edge: blue, $90; ruby: $250.
Bowl, 400/74SC, 9" d, four ball toes, crimped: blue, $100; black with painted flowers, $250; ruby: $395.
Cordial bottle, 400/82, 15 oz, beaded foot, three-bead stopper, handle, c1938, ruby stopper: $275.
Creamer and sugar, 400/31, beaded foot, plain handles, c1937: blue, $60.
Cup and saucer, 400/35/252, no beads on question mark handle: blue, $40
Goblet, water, 3400 line, flared bell bowl, four graduated beads in stem, 9 oz, solid colors: Verde Green, Ultra Blue, Sunshine Yellow, Nut Brown, c1977-80, $40.
Iced tea tumbler, 12 oz, ftd, 3400 line, solid colors: Verde Green, Ultra Blue, Sunshine Yellow, Nut Brown, c1977-80, $40.
Tidbit server, 400/2701, two tiers, 7-1/2" d and 10-1/2" d plates joined by metal rod, round handle at top: emerald green, $750.
Wine, 3400 line, flared belled bowl, four graduated stems in base, 9 oz; solid colors: Verde Green, Ultra Blue, Sunshine Yellow, Nut Brown, c1977-80, $40 each; red: $125.

# Cape Cod

Manufactured by Imperial Glass Company, Bellaire, Ohio, from 1932 to 1984.

Made in amber, azalea (pink), black, blue, crystal, evergreen (dark green), milk glass, Ritz blue, ruby and Verde (green). The colored wares were manufactured in the late 1960s and 1970s. Values for most colors are about 50 percent higher than crystal, with Ritz Blue and ruby often commanding even higher values.

| Item | Crystal |
| --- | --- |
| Ashtray, 160/130, 5-1/2" d | 18.50 |
| Ashtray, 160/134/1, 4" d | 15.00 |
| Baked Apple, 160/53X, 6" d | 10.00 |
| Basket, 160/221/0, 9" | 200.00 |
| Basket, 160/40, 11" | 150.00 |
| Birthday Cake Plate, 160/72, 13" d | 375.00 |
| Bitters Bottle, 160/223, 4 oz | 60.00 |
| Bouillon Cup, 160/250 | 30.00 |
| Bowl, 160/10F, 7-3/4" d | 24.00 |
| Bowl, 160/137B, 10" d, ftd | 70.00 |
| Bowl, 160/199, 6-1/2" d, tab handle | 25.00 |
| Bowl, 160/62B, 7-1/2" d, 2 handles | 27.50 |
| Bowl, 160/75B, 12" d | 40.00 |
| Bread Plate, 160/222, 12-1/2" d | 65.00 |
| Butter Dish, cov, 1/4 pound | 48.00 |
| Butter Dish, cov, 160/144, handle | 32.00 |
| Cake Plate, 160/220, 10" d | 90.00 |
| Cake Stand, 160/67D, 10-1/2" d | 90.00 |
| Cake Stand, 160/103D, 11" d | 95.00 |
| Candlesticks, pr, 160/48BC, 6" h | 150.00 |
| Candlesticks, pr, 160/81, 4" h | 50.00 |
| Candlesticks, pr, 160/100, 2-lite | 145.00 |
| Candlesticks, pr, 160/170, 3" h | 35.00 |
| Candlesticks, pr, 160/175, 4-1/2" h, saucer base | 50.00 |
| Candy Jar, cov, 160/194, wicker band | 85.00 |
| Candy, cov, 160/110 | 65.00 |
| Celery Tray, 160/105, 8" l | 32.00 |
| Celery Tray, 160/189, 10-1/2" l | 45.00 |
| Cigarette Box, 160/134 | 45.00 |
| Cigarette Holder, 1602 | 14.00 |
| Cigarette Lighter, 1602 | 32.50 |
| Claret, 1602, 5 oz | 15.00 |
| Coaster, 160/1R, 4-1/2" d | 14.00 |
| Coaster, 160/76, spoon rest, 4" d | 12.50 |
| Coaster, 160/78, 4" d, round | 14.00 |
| Coaster, 160/85, 3" w, sq | 14.00 |
| Cocktail, 1602, 3-1/2 oz | 9.00 |
| Coffee Cup, 160/37 | 15.00 |
| Coffee Saucer, 160/37 | 3.50 |
| Cologne Bottle, stopper | 65.00 |
| Comport, 160/45, 6" | 27.50 |
| Comport, 160/48B, 7" | 35.00 |
| Comport, 160F, 5-1/4" | 30.00 |
| Comport, 160X, 5-3/4" | 32.00 |
| Comport, 1602, 11-1/4" d, 6-1/2" h | 175.00 |
| Comport, cov, 160/140, 6", ftd | 72.00 |
| Condiment Bottle, 160/224 | 68.00 |
| Console Bowl, 160/75L, 13" d | 45.00 |
| Console Bowl, 1601/0L, 15" d | 65.00 |
| Cookie Jar, 160/195, wicker band | 120.00 |
| Cordial, 1602, 1-1/2 oz | 12.00 |
| Cordial Bottle, 160/256, 18 oz | 120.00 |
| Creamer, 160/30 | 12.00 |
| Creamer, 160/31, ftd | 17.50 |
| Creamer, 160/190 | 32.00 |
| Cruet, stopper, 160/70, 5 oz | 30.00 |
| Cruet, stopper, 160/119, 4 oz | 30.00 |
| Cruet, stopper, 160/241, 6 oz | 40.00 |
| Decanter, 160/163, 30 oz | 70.00 |
| Decanter, 160/212, 24 oz | 75.00 |
| Decanter, 160/244 | 120.00 |
| Decanter, 160/260, bourbon | 85.00 |
| Decanter, 160/260, rye | 85.00 |
| Dessert Bowl, 160/197, 4-1/2" d, tab handle | 24.00 |
| Dessert Bowl, 160/49H, 5" d, heart shape | 20.00 |
| Egg Cup, 160/225 | 35.00 |
| Epergne, 160/196 | 225.00 |

| Item | Crystal |
|------|---------|
| Finger Bowl, 4" or 4-1/2" | 12.50 |
| Flower Bowl, 5" d | 24.00 |
| Fork, 160/701 | 12.00 |
| Fruit Bowl, 160/23B, 5-1/2" d | 10.00 |
| Fruit Bowl, 160/3F, 6" d | 10.00 |
| Fruit Bowl, 160/67/F, 9" d, ftd | 60.00 |
| Goblet, 1600, 10 oz | 28.00 |
| Goblet, 1602, 9 oz or 11 oz | 14.00 |
| Gravy Boat, 160/202 | 72.00 |
| Horseradish Jar, 160/226 | 80.00 |
| Ice Bucket, 160/63 | 185.00 |
| Iced Tea Tumbler, 1600, 12 oz | 15.00 |
| Iced Tea Tumbler, 1602, 12 oz, ftd | 30.00 |
| Jelly, 160/33, 3" | 15.00 |
| Juice Tumbler, 1602, 6 oz, ftd | 20.00 |
| Ketchup Bottle, 160/237 | 225.00 |
| Marmalade Ladle, 160/130 | 12.00 |
| Marmalade, 160/89/3, 3 pc set | 35.00 |
| Martini Pitcher, 160/178, blown, 40 oz | 200.00 |
| Mayonnaise Ladle, 160/165 | 12.00 |
| Mayonnaise, 160/52H, 3 pc set | 30.00 |
| Milk Pitcher, 160/240, 1 pint | 45.00 |
| Mint Bowl, 160/183, 3" d | 15.00 |
| Mint Bowl, 160/51F, 6" d, handle | 20.00 |
| Mug, 160/188, 12 oz | 48.00 |
| Mustard, cov, spoon, 160/156 | 24.00 |
| Nappy, 160/5F, 7" d | 24.00 |
| Nut Dish, 160/183, 3" d, handle | 27.50 |
| Nut Dish, 160/184, 4" d, handle | 27.50 |
| Old Fashioned Tumbler, 1600, 6 oz | 30.00 |
| Oyster Cocktail, 1602 | 12.00 |
| Parfait, 1602, 6 oz | 18.50 |
| Pastry Tray, 160/68D, 11" l | 72.00 |
| Peanut Jar, 160/210, 12 oz | 70.00 |
| Pepper Mill, 160/236 | 32.50 |
| Pitcher, 160/19, 40 oz, ice lip | 80.00 |
| Pitcher, 160/176, 5 pint | 150.00 |
| Pitcher, 160/239, 2 qt, ice lip | 100.00 |
| Plate, 4-1/2" d, butter | 8.50 |
| Plate, 6-1/2" d, bread and butter | 8.50 |
| Plate, 8" d, salad | 10.00 |
| Plate, 9" d, luncheon | 20.00 |
| Plate, 10" d, dinner | 40.00 |
| Platter, 160/124D, 13-1/2" l, oval | 60.00 |
| Puff Box, cov, 1601 | 48.00 |
| Punch Bowl, 160/20B, 12" d | 65.00 |
| Punch Ladle | 25.00 |
| Relish, 160/55, 9-1/2" l, oval, 3 part | 37.50 |
| Relish, 160/56, 9-1/2" d, 4-part | 35.00 |
| Relish, 160/102, 11" d, 5 part | 50.00 |
| Relish, 160/223, 8" d, 2-part, handle | 40.00 |
| Salad Bowl, 1608D, 11" d | 42.00 |
| Salad Crescent, 160/12, 8" | 50.00 |
| Salt and Pepper Shakers, pr, 160/96 | 20.00 |
| Salt and Pepper Shakers, pr, 160/109 | 24.00 |
| Salt and Pepper Shakers, pr, 160/116, ftd | 24.00 |

| Item | Crystal |
|------|---------|
| Salt and Pepper Shakers, pr, 160/243, stemmed | 42.00 |
| Salt and Pepper Shakers, pr, 160/251, individual size | 18.00 |
| Salt, open, 160/61 | 18.00 |
| Salt Spoon, 1600 | 10.00 |
| Sherbet, 1600, 6 oz | 30.00 |
| Sherbet, 1602, 6 oz, tall | 30.00 |
| Soup Bowl, 160/198, 5-1/2" d, tab handle | 20.00 |
| Spoon, 160/701 | 15.00 |
| Sugar, 160/30 | 8.50 |
| Sugar, 160/31, ftd | 18.00 |
| Sugar, 160/190 | 35.00 |
| Sundae, 1602, 6 oz, low | 8.50 |
| Tea Cup, 160/35 | 8.50 |
| Tea Saucer, 160/35 | 3.00 |
| Toast, cov, 160/123 | 165.00 |
| Tom and Jerry Bowl, 160/200 | 375.00 |
| Torte Plate, 1608F, 13" d | 40.00 |
| Torte Plate, 1608V, 13" d, cupped | 40.00 |
| Tray, 160/51T, 6" d, handle | 20.00 |
| Tumbler, 160, 10 oz | 12.00 |
| Tumbler, 1602, 10 oz, ftd | 22.50 |
| Urn, 160/186, 10-1/2" h, handle | 175.00 |
| Vase, 160/143, flip, 8-1/2" h | 55.00 |
| Vase, 160/192, 10" h | 80.00 |
| Vase, 160/21, 11-1/2" h, ftd | 65.00 |
| Vase, 160/22, 6-1/4" h, ftd | 35.00 |
| Vase, 160/22, 7-1/2" h, ftd | 42.00 |
| Vase, 160/87F, 8" h, fan | 200.00 |
| Vase, 1603, 11" h, flip | 175.00 |
| Whiskey, 160, 2-1/2 oz | 15.00 |
| Wine Carafe, 160/185 | 200.00 |
| Wine, 1602, 3 oz | 17.50 |

*Cape Cod, crystal mayonnaise underplate.*

# Capri

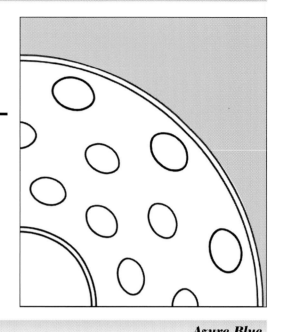

Manufactured by Hazel Ware, division of Continental Can, 1960s. Collectors are starting to divide these wares into several distinct patterns, based on the shape. All are the same pretty azure blue color and have the same market value. Original "Capri" paper labels are found on most of the styles.

Made in azure blue.

| Item | Azure Blue |
|---|---|
| Ashtray, 3-1/2" sq, emb flower center | 15.00 |
| Ashtray, 3-1/4" w, triangular or round | 5.00 |
| Ashtray, 5" d, round | 7.50 |
| Ashtray, 6-7/8" w, triangular | 10.00 |
| Bowl, 4-3/4" d, octagonal or swirled | 7.50 |
| Bowl, 4-7/8" d, round, Dots | 7.50 |
| Bowl, 5-3/4" w, sq | 9.50 |
| Bowl, 5-5/8", Colony Swirl | 8.50 |
| Bowl, 6" d, Dots, Colony Swirl | 8.00 |
| Bowl, 6" d, Tulip | 12.00 |
| Bowl, 7-3/4" l, oval | 12.00 |
| Bowl, 8-3/4" d, swirled | 12.00 |
| Bowl, 9-1/2" d | 18.00 |
| Candy jar, cov, ftd | 30.00 |
| Chip and dip set, metal rack | 30.00 |
| Creamer | 12.00 |
| Cup, octagonal | 6.50 |
| Cup, round | 5.00 |
| Iced tea tumbler, 5" h, 12 oz | 10.00 |

| Item | Azure Blue |
|---|---|
| Old fashioned tumbler, 3-5/8" h, Dots | 7.50 |
| Plate, 5-3/4" d, bread and butter | 5.00 |
| Plate, 7" d, salad | 6.50 |
| Plate, 8" w, sq | 7.50 |
| Plate, 9-3/4", dinner | 10.00 |
| Salad bowl, 5-3/8" d | 7.50 |
| Saucer, round, sq, or octagonal | 1.50 |
| Sherbet | 7.50 |
| Snack plate, fan shape | 12.00 |
| Snack plate, round | 9.50 |
| Sugar, cov | 20.00 |
| Tidbit, two bowl tiers, Colony Swirl | 45.00 |
| Tidbit, three-plate tiers | 20.00 |
| Tumbler, 2-3/4" h, Colony Swirl | 7.50 |
| Tumbler, 3" h, Dots | 7.50 |
| Tumbler, 3-1/16", Colony, Colony Swirl | 8.50 |
| Tumbler, 4-1/4" h, 9 oz | 7.50 |
| Vase, 8" h, Dots | 20.00 |
| Vase, 8-1/2" h, ruffled rim | 30.00 |

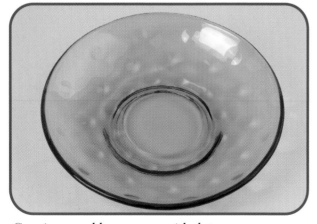

Capri, azure blue saucer with dots.

Capri, azure blue bowl with metal handle, 7-3/4 l".

# Cherryberry

Manufactured by U.S. Glass Company,
Pittsburgh, Pa., early 1930s.
Made in crystal, green, iridescent, and pink.

*Cherryberry, clear bowl.*

| Item | Crystal | Green | Iridescent | Pink |
|---|---|---|---|---|
| Berry Bowl, 4" d. | 7.00 | 8.75 | 7.00 | 8.75 |
| Berry Bowl, 7-1/2" d, deep | 17.50 | 20.00 | 20.00 | 20.00 |
| Bowl, 6-1/4" d, 2" deep | 50.00 | 55.00 | 40.00 | 55.00 |
| Butter Dish, cov | 150.00 | 175.00 | 150.00 | 175.00 |
| Comport, 5-3/4" | 17.50 | 25.00 | 17.50 | 25.00 |
| Creamer, large, 4-5/8" | 40.00 | 45.00 | 40.00 | 45.00 |
| Creamer, small | 15.00 | 20.00 | 15.00 | 20.00 |
| Olive Dish, 5" l, one handle | 10.00 | 15.00 | 10.00 | 15.00 |
| Pickle Dish, 8-1/4" l, oval | 10.00 | 15.00 | 10.00 | 15.00 |
| Pitcher, 7-3/4" h | 165.00 | 175.00 | 165.00 | 175.00 |
| Plate, 6" d, sherbet | 6.50 | 11.00 | 6.50 | 11.00 |
| Plate, 7-1/2" d, salad | 8.50 | 15.00 | 9.00 | 15.00 |
| Salad Bowl, 6-1/2" d, deep | 17.50 | 22.00 | 17.50 | 22.00 |
| Sherbet | 10.00 | 12.00 | 12.00 | 14.00 |
| Sugar, large, cov | 45.00 | 75.00 | 45.00 | 75.00 |
| Sugar, small, open | 15.00 | 20.00 | 15.00 | 20.00 |
| Tumbler, 9 oz, 3-5/8" h | 20.00 | 35.00 | 20.00 | 35.00 |

# Cherry Blossom

Manufactured by Jeannette Glass Company, Jeannette, Pa., from 1930 to 1939.

Made in Crystal, Delphite, green, jadite, pink, and red (production was very limited in crystal, jadite and red).

**Reproductions:** † Reproductions include: small berry bowl, 8-1/2" d bowl, covered butter dish, cake plate, cereal bowl, cup, pitcher, 6" and 9" plates, divided 13" platter, salt shaker, sandwich tray, saucer, and 3-3/4" and 4-1/2" h ftd tumblers. Reproductions have been made in cobalt blue, Delphite, green, pink, and red. A children's butter dish has also been made, which was never included in the original production.

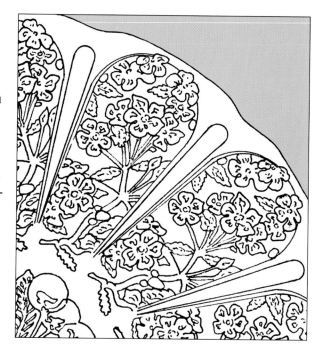

| Item | Delphite | Green | Pink |
|---|---|---|---|
| Berry Bowl, 4-3/4" d † | 17.50 | 25.00 | 22.50 |
| Berry Bowl, 8-1/2" d † | 55.00 | 50.00 | 65.00 |
| Bowl, 9" d, 2 handles | 27.50 | 95.00 | 48.00 |
| Butter Dish, cov † | - | 115.00 | 75.00 |
| Cake Plate, 10-1/4" d, 3 legs † | - | 38.00 | 25.00 |
| Cereal Bowl, 5-3/4" d † | - | 35.00 | 32.00 |
| Coaster | - | 20.00 | 15.00 |
| Creamer | 30.00 | 35.00 | 35.00 |
| Cup † | 28.00 | 25.00 | 28.00 |
| Fruit Bowl, 10-1/2" d | 32.00 | 90.00 | 90.00 |
| Juice Tumbler, 1 oz, 3-1/2" | - | 35.00 | 24.00 |
| Mug, 7 oz | - | 195.00 | 265.00 |
| Pitcher, 36 oz, 6-3/4" h, 36 oz † | 95.00 | 60.00 | 72.00 |
| Pitcher, 36 oz, 8", PAT, ftd | - | 65.00 | 60.00 |
| Pitcher, 42 oz, 8", PAT, flat | - | 65.00 | 60.00 |
| Plate, 6" d, sherbet † | 12.50 | 10.00 | 12.00 |
| Plate, 7" d, salad | - | 27.50 | 24.00 |
| Plate, 9" d, dinner † | 18.00 | 28.00 | 35.00 |
| Plate, 9" d, grill | - | 35.00 | 32.50 |
| Plate, 10" d, grill | - | 32.50 | - |
| Platter, 11" l, oval | 40.00 | 48.00 | 35.00 |
| Platter, 13" d | - | 72.00 | 100.00 |
| Platter, 13" divided † | - | 72.00 | 75.00 |
| Salt and Pepper Shakers, pr, scalloped base † | - | 995.00 | 1,250.00 |
| Sandwich Tray, 10-1/2" d † | 20.00 | 30.00 | 45.00 |

| Item | Delphite | Green | Pink |
|---|---|---|---|
| Saucer † | 6.00 | 7.50 | 6.00 |
| Sherbet | 18.00 | 30.00 | 19.50 |
| Soup, flat, 7-3/4" d | - | 90.00 | 80.00 |
| Sugar, cov | 24.00 | 37.50 | 35.00 |
| Tumbler, 3-3/4" h, AOP, ftd † | - | 22.00 | 24.00 |
| Tumbler, 5" h | 20.00 | 70.00 | 72.00 |
| Tumbler, 8 oz, 4-1/2" h, scalloped ftd base, AOP | - | 40.00 | 35.00 |
| Tumbler, 9 oz, 4-1/4" h | - | 24.00 | 22.00 |
| Tumbler, 9 oz, 4-1/2" h † | 20.00 | 30.00 | 32.00 |
| Vegetable Bowl, 9" l, oval | 45.00 | 42.00 | 40.00 |

# Children's

| Item | Delphite | Pink |
|---|---|---|
| Creamer | 50.00 | 50.00 |
| Cup † | 42.00 | 42.00 |
| Plate, 6" d | 15.00 | 15.00 |
| Saucer | 7.50 | 7.50 |
| Sugar | 50.00 | 50.00 |

*Cherry Blossom, delphite small bowls.*

# Chinex Classic

Manufactured by Macbeth-Evans Division of Corning Glass Works, from the late 1930s to early 1940s.

Made in Chinex (ivory) and Chinex with Classic Bouquet or Classic Castle decal.

| Item | Chinex | Chinex, Classic Bouquet decal | Chinex, Classic Castle decal |
|---|---|---|---|
| Bowl, 11" d | 20.00 | 36.00 | 48.00 |
| Butter Dish, cov | 55.00 | 80.00 | 135.00 |
| Cake Plate, 11-1/2" d | 10.00 | 15.00 | 25.00 |
| Cereal Bowl, 5- 3/4" d | 6.00 | 8.50 | 15.00 |
| Creamer | 8.50 | 12.00 | 20.00 |
| Cup | 6.00 | 9.50 | 17.50 |
| Plate, 6-1/4" d, sherbet | 8.00 | 6.50 | 10.00 |
| Plate, 9-3/4" d, dinner | 16.00 | 10.00 | 18.00 |
| Sandwich Plate, 11-1/2" d | 8.00 | 15.00 | 25.00 |
| Saucer | 2.00 | 4.00 | 7.00 |
| Sherbet, low, ftd. | 9.50 | 12.00 | 30.00 |
| Soup Bowl, 7-3/4" d | 14.00 | 25.00 | 40.00 |
| Sugar, open | 7.50 | 12.50 | 20.00 |
| Vegetable Bowl, 7" d | 15.00 | 25.00 | 35.00 |
| Vegetable Bowl, 9" d | 15.00 | 25.00 | 35.00 |

*Chinex Classic, plate with castle decal.*

# Christmas Candy

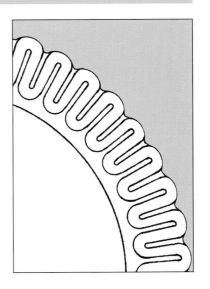

## No. 624

Manufactured by Indiana Glass Company, Dunkirk, Ind., 1950s.
Made in crystal and Terrace Green (teal).

| Item | Crystal | Terrace Green |
|---|---|---|
| Bowl, 5-3/4" d | 6.50 | - |
| Creamer | 15.00 | 30.00 |
| Cup | 8.00 | 35.00 |
| Mayonnaise, ladle, liner | 24.00 | - |
| Plate, 6" d, bread and butter | 6.00 | 16.00 |
| Plate, 8-1/4" d, luncheon | 8.00 | 28.00 |
| Plate, 9-5/8"d, dinner | 12.00 | 36.00 |
| Sandwich Plate, 11-1/4" d | 24.00 | 65.00 |
| Saucer | 5.00 | 15.00 |
| Soup Bowl, 7-3/8" d | 12.00 | 75.00 |
| Sugar | 15.00 | 35.00 |
| Tidbit, 2 tiers | 20.00 | - |
| Vegetable Bowl, 9-1/2" d | - | 235.00 |

*Christmas Candy, crystal sugar and creamer.*

# Circle

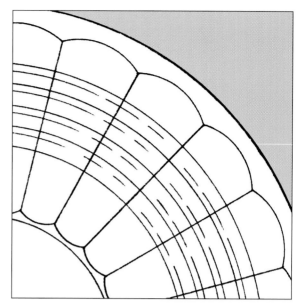

Manufactured by Hocking Glass Company, Lancaster, Ohio, in the 1930s.

Made in crystal, green, and pink. Crystal is listed in the original catalogs, but few pieces have surfaced to date. A 3-1/8" d sherbet is known and valued at $4.

| Item | Green | Pink |
|---|---|---|
| Bowl, 4-1/2" d | 15.00 | 15.00 |
| Bowl, 5-1/2" d, flared | 17.50 | 17.50 |
| Bowl, 8" d | 16.00 | 16.00 |
| Bowl, 9-3/8" d | 18.50 | 18.50 |
| Creamer, ftd | 9.00 | 16.00 |
| Cup | 6.00 | 7.50 |
| Goblet, 8 oz, 5-3/4" h | 16.50 | 15.00 |
| Iced Tea Tumbler, 10 oz | 17.50 | 17.50 |
| Juice Tumbler, 4 oz | 9.50 | 9.00 |
| Pitcher, 60 oz | 35.00 | 35.00 |
| Pitcher, 80 oz | 30.00 | 32.00 |
| Plate, 6" d, sherbet | 3.00 | 3.00 |
| Plate, 8-1/4"d, luncheon | 11.00 | 11.00 |
| Plate, 9-1/2" d, dinner | 12.00 | 12.00 |
| Sandwich Plate, 10" d | 15.00 | 17.50 |
| Saucer, 6" d | 2.50 | 2.50 |
| Sherbet, 3-1/8" | 5.00 | 5.00 |
| Sherbet, 4-3/4" | 12.00 | 12.00 |
| Sugar, ftd | 12.00 | 16.00 |
| Tumbler, 8 oz | 10.00 | 10.00 |
| Tumbler, 15 oz, flat | 17.50 | 17.50 |
| Wine, 4-1/2" h | 15.00 | 15.00 |

*Circle, green cup.*

# Cloverleaf

Manufactured by Hazel Atlas Glass Company, Clarksburg, W.V., and Zanesville, Ohio, from 1930 to 1936.

Made in black, crystal, green, pink, and yellow. Collector interest in crystal is minimal; prices would be about 50 percent of those listed for green.

| Item | Black | Green | Pink | Yellow |
|---|---|---|---|---|
| Ashtray, match holder in center, 4" d | 65.00 | - | - | - |
| Ashtray, match holder in center, 5-3/4" d | 90.00 | - | - | - |
| Bowl, 8" d | - | 95.00 | - | - |
| Candy Dish, cov | - | 65.00 | - | 130.00 |
| Cereal Bowl, 5" d | - | 50.00 | - | 55.00 |
| Creamer, 3-5/8" h, ftd | 25.00 | 12.00 | - | 24.00 |
| Cup | 18.50 | 9.00 | 8.00 | 12.00 |
| Dessert Bowl, 4" d | - | 30.00 | 30.00 | 35.00 |
| Plate, 6" d, sherbet | 40.00 | 6.50 | - | 10.00 |
| Plate, 8" d, luncheon | 16.00 | 9.00 | 12.00 | 18.00 |
| Plate, 10-1/4" d, grill | - | 25.00 | - | 40.00 |
| Salad Bowl, 7" d | - | 60.00 | - | 65.00 |
| Salt and Pepper Shakers, pr | 100.00 | 40.00 | - | 140.00 |
| Saucer | 7.00 | 6.00 | 6.00 | 5.00 |
| Sherbet, 3" h, ftd | 22.00 | 15.00 | 10.00 | 12.00 |
| Sugar, 3-5/8" h, ftd | 25.00 | 12.00 | - | 24.00 |
| Tumbler, 9 oz, 4" h, flat | - | 65.00 | 26.50 | 35.00 |
| Tumbler, 10 oz, 3-3/4" h, flat | - | 50.00 | 30.00 | - |
| Tumbler, 10 oz, 5-3/4" h, ftd | - | 30.00 | - | 42.00 |

*Cloverleaf, green saucer and pink plate and cup.*

# *Coin*

Manufactured by Fostoria Glass Company, Moundsville, Va., from 1958 to 1982.

Made in amber, blue, crystal, emerald green, olive green, and red.

**Reproductions:** † Reproductions have been made in colors similar to the original colors by Lancaster Colony, using original Fostoria molds.

| Item | Amber | Blue | Crystal | Emerald Green | Olive Green | Red |
|---|---|---|---|---|---|---|
| Ashtray, #110, cov, 3" | 20.00 | 24.00 | 24.00 | 30.00 | - | - |
| Ashtray, #114, 8" d | 25.00 | 40.00 | 24.00 | 42.00 | 30.00 | 45.00 |
| Ashtray, #115, 3" x 4" oblong | 25.00 | 22.00 | 12.00 | 25.00 | 25.00 | - |
| Ashtray, #119, 7-1/2" d, coin center | 25.00 | - | 35.00 | 95.00 | 35.00 | 25.00 |
| Ashtray, #123, 5" d | 25.00 | 27.50 | 20.00 | 30.00 | 20.00 | 25.00 |
| Ashtray, #124, 10" d | 35.00 | 30.00 | 40.00 | 65.00 | 35.00 | - |
| Bowl, #179, 7-1/2" d | 40.00 | 80.00 | 35.00 | 115.00 | 40.00 | 70.00 |
| Bowl, #189, 9" d, oval † | 45.00 | 55.00 | 30.00 | 105.00 | 35.00 | 65.00 |
| Bowl, #199, 8-1/2" d, ftd | 75.00 | 125.00 | 75.00 | 125.00 | 65.00 | 85.00 |
| Bowl, cov, #212, 8-1/2" d, ftd | 225.00 | 425.00 | 95.00 | 225.00 | - | - |
| Bud Vase, #799, 8" h | 35.00 | 85.00 | 25.00 | 125.00 | 35.00 | 70.00 |
| Cake Salver, #630, ftd † | 135.00 | 315.00 | 135.00 | 300.00 | 125.00 | - |
| Candlesticks, pr, #316, 4-1/2" h | 60.00 | 80.00 | 50.00 | 60.00 | 50.00 | 95.00 |
| Candlesticks, pr, #326, 8" h | 85.00 | - | 48.00 | - | 85.00 | 110.00 |
| Candy Box, cov, 4-1/8", #354 | 45.00 | 65.00 | 40.00 | 135.00 | 33.50 | 70.00 |
| Candy Jar, cov, #347, 6-1/2" † | 70.00 | 150.00 | 50.00 | 200.00 | 60.00 | 125.00 |
| Cigarette Box, cov, #374 † | 50.00 | 85.00 | 75.00 | 120.00 | - | - |
| Cigarette Holder, ash tray cover, #372 | 45.00 | 72.00 | 40.00 | 85.00 | - | - |
| Cigarette Urn, 3-1/2", #381 | 35.00 | 45.00 | 35.00 | 48.00 | 35.00 | 40.00 |
| Condiment Set, #737, salt & pepper, cruet, tray | 225.00 | 300.00 | 175.00 | - | 215.00 | - |
| Creamer, #680 † | 24.00 | 28.00 | 22.00 | 28.50 | 28.00 | 30.00 |
| Cruet, os, #531 | 115.00 | 195.00 | 115.00 | 250.00 | 115.00 | - |
| Decanter, os, #400, pint † | 135.00 | 250.00 | 100.00 | 350.00 | 175.00 | - |
| Goblet, water, #2, 6-1/2", 10-1/2" h | - | - | 40.00 | - | 95.00 | 95.00 |
| Iced Tea Tumbler, #58, 14 oz | - | - | 40.00 | - | - | - |
| Iced Tea Tumbler, #64, 12 oz | - | - | 45.00 | - | - | - |
| Jelly Compote, #448 † | 30.00 | 35.00 | 22.50 | 65.00 | 25.00 | 45.00 |
| Juice Tumbler, #81, 9 oz | - | - | 40.00 | - | - | - |
| Lamp Chimney, #461, patio | 50.00 | 60.00 | 40.00 | - | - | - |
| Lamp Chimney, #292, courting | 48.00 | 65.00 | - | - | - | - |
| Lamp, #310, courting, 9-3/4" h, oil, handle | 125.00 | 310.00 | - | - | - | - |

| Item | Amber | Blue | Crystal | Emerald Green | Olive Green | Red |
|---|---|---|---|---|---|---|
| Lamp, #311, courting, 10-3/4" h, electric | 135.00 | 315.00 | - | - | - | - |
| Lamp, #320, coach, 13-1/2" h, oil | 165.00 | 355.00 | 100.00 | - | - | |
| Lamp, #321, coach, 13-1/2" h, electric | 175.00 | 365.00 | 100.00 | - | | - |
| Lamp, #459, patio, 16-1/2", electric | 185.00 | 500.00 | 145.00 | - | - | - |
| Lamp, #466, patio, 16-1/2" h, oil | 195.00 | 490.00 | 145.00 | - | - | - |
| Nappy, #495, 4-1/2" d | - | - | 24.00 | - | - | |
| Nappy, handle, #499, 5-3/8" † | 25.00 | 50.00 | 25.00 | 95.00 | 25.00 | 40.00 |
| Old Fashioned Tumbler, #23, 10 oz | - | - | 45.00 | - | - | - |
| Pitcher, #453, 1 qt | 95.00 | 125.00 | 95.00 | 330.00 | 95.00 | 145.00 |
| Plate, 8" d, #550 | - | - | 45.00 | - | - | |
| Punch Bowl Set, punch bowl, base, 12 cups, #600/602, 615 | 650.00 | - | 675.00 | - | - | - |
| Salt and Pepper Shakers, pr, #652 | 45.00 | 85.00 | 35.00 | 125.00 | 45.00 | 60.00 |
| Sherbet, #7, 9 oz | - | - | 25.00 | - | 85.00 | 75.00 |
| Sugar, cov, #673 † | 30.00 | 45.00 | 30.00 | 60.00 | 35.00 | 40.00 |
| Tumbler, #73, 9 oz, water | - | - | 45.00 | - | - | - |
| Urn, cov, #829, 12-3/4" h † | 125.00 | 85.00 | 65.00 | 195.00 | 115.00 | 195.00 |
| Vase, #818, 10" h, ftd | - | - | 175.00 | - | - | - |
| Wedding Bowl, cov, #162, 8-1/4" d † | 70.00 | 125.00 | 55.00 | 125.00 | 65.00 | 95.00 |
| Wine, #26, 5 oz | - | - | 38.50 | - | 75.00 | 90.00 |

*Coin, red candy dish with cover.*

# Colonial

## Knife and Fork

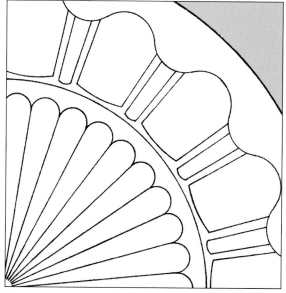

Manufactured by Hocking Glass Company, Lancaster, Ohio, from 1934 to 1938. Made in crystal, green, and pink.

| Item | Crystal | Green | Pink |
|---|---|---|---|
| Berry Bowl, 3-3/4" d | - | - | 60.00 |
| Berry Bowl, 4-1/2" | 12.00 | 22.00 | 18.00 |
| Berry Bowl, 9" d | 24.00 | 30.00 | 35.00 |
| Butter Dish, cov | 40.00 | 60.00 | 700.00 |
| Cereal Bowl, 5-1/2" d | 32.00 | 85.00 | 60.00 |
| Claret, 4 oz, 5-1/4" h | 20.00 | 25.00 | - |
| Cocktail, 3 oz, 4" h | 15.00 | 25.00 | - |
| Cordial, 1 oz, 3-3/4" h | 20.00 | 30.00 | - |
| Cream Soup Bowl, 4-1/2" d | 70.00 | 85.00 | 72.00 |
| Creamer, 8 oz, 5" h | 25.00 | 25.00 | 65.00 |
| Cup | 8.00 | 15.00 | 12.00 |
| Goblet, 8-1/2 oz, 5-3/4" h | 25.00 | 35.00 | 40.00 |
| Ice Tea Tumbler, 12 oz | 28.00 | 55.00 | 45.00 |
| Juice Tumbler, 5 oz, 3" h | 17.50 | 27.50 | 22.00 |
| Lemonade Tumbler, 15 oz | 47.50 | 75.00 | 65.00 |
| Milk Pitcher, 8 oz, 5" h | 25.00 | 25.00 | 65.00 |
| Mug, 12 oz, 5-1/2" h | - | 825.00 | 500.00 |
| Pitcher, 54 oz, 7" h, ice lip | 40.00 | 45.00 | 48.00 |
| Pitcher, 54 oz, 7" h, no lip | 40.00 | 45.00 | 48.00 |
| Pitcher, 68 oz, 7-3/4" h, ice lip | 35.00 | 72.00 | 65.00 |
| Pitcher, 68 oz, 7-3/4" h, no lip | 45.00 | 72.00 | 65.00 |
| Plate, 6" d, sherbet | 4.50 | 8.00 | 7.00 |
| Plate, 8-1/2" d, luncheon | 6.00 | 8.00 | 10.00 |
| Plate, 10" d, dinner | 35.00 | 65.00 | 55.00 |
| Plate, 10"d, grill | 17.50 | 27.00 | 27.50 |
| Plate, 12" d, oval | 17.50 | 25.00 | 30.00 |
| Platter, 12" l, oval | 17.50 | 25.00 | 35.00 |
| Salt and Pepper Shakers, pr | 65.00 | 160.00 | 150.00 |
| Saucer | 4.50 | 7.50 | 6.50 |
| Sherbet, 3" h | - | - | 24.00 |
| Sherbet, 3-3/8" h | 10.00 | 15.00 | 16.00 |
| Soup Bowl, 7" d | 30.00 | 85.00 | 85.00 |
| Spoon Holder or Celery Vase | 105.00 | 130.00 | 135.00 |
| Sugar, cov | 90.00 | 48.00 | 50.00 |
| Sugar, 5", open | 10.00 | 12.00 | 15.00 |

| Item | Crystal | Green | Pink |
|---|---|---|---|
| Tumbler, 3 oz, 3-1/4" h, ftd . . . . . . . . . . . . . . . . . . . . . . . . . . . . . . . 12.00 | | 25.00 | 20.00 |
| Tumbler, 5 oz, 4" h, ftd . . . . . . . . . . . . . . . . . . . . . . . . . . . . . . . . 20.00 | | 42.00 | 30.00 |
| Tumbler, 9 oz, 4" h . . . . . . . . . . . . . . . . . . . . . . . . . . . . . . . . . . . 15.00 | | 20.00 | 25.00 |
| Tumbler, 10 oz, 5-1/4" h, ftd . . . . . . . . . . . . . . . . . . . . . . . . . . . 30.00 | | 46.50 | 50.00 |
| Tumbler, 11 oz, 5-1/8" h . . . . . . . . . . . . . . . . . . . . . . . . . . . . . . . 25.00 | | 37.00 | 40.00 |
| Vegetable Bowl, 10" l, oval . . . . . . . . . . . . . . . . . . . . . . . . . . . . 18.00 | | 25.00 | 45.00 |
| Whiskey, 2-1/2" h, 1-1/2 oz . . . . . . . . . . . . . . . . . . . . . . . . . . . . 10.00 | | 20.00 | 15.00 |
| Wine, 4-1/2" h, 2-1/2 oz . . . . . . . . . . . . . . . . . . . . . . . . . . . . . . 17.00 | | 30.00 | 14.00 |

*Colonial, crystal wine and cocktail.*

*Colonial, green sugar and creamer.*

*Colonial, green saucer.*

# Colonial Block

Manufactured by Hazel Atlas Glass Company, Clarksburg, W.V., and Zanesville, Ohio, early 1930s.

Made in black, cobalt blue (rare), crystal, green, pink, and white (1950s).

| Item | Black | Crystal | Green | Pink | White |
|------|-------|---------|-------|------|-------|
| Bowl, 4" d. | - | 6.00 | 10.00 | 10.00 | - |
| Bowl, 7" d. | - | 16.00 | 20.00 | 20.00 | - |
| Butter Dish, cov | - | 35.00 | 50.00 | 45.00 | - |
| Butter Tub, cov | - | 35.00 | 40.00 | 40.00 | - |
| Candy Jar, cov | - | 30.00 | 40.00 | 40.00 | - |
| Compote, 4" h, 4-3/4" w | - | 12.00 | - | - | - |
| Creamer | - | 15.00 | 16.00 | 15.00 | 7.50 |
| Goblet, 5-3/4" h | - | 9.00 | 12.00 | 15.00 | - |
| Pitcher, 20 oz, 5-3/4" h | - | 40.00 | 50.00 | 50.00 | - |
| Powder Jar, cov | 30.00 | 20.00 | 24.00 | 24.00 | - |
| Sherbet | - | 6.00 | 10.00 | 9.50 | - |
| Sugar, cov | - | 20.00 | 25.00 | 25.00 | 20.00 |
| Sugar, open | - | 6.00 | 8.00 | 8.00 | 10.00 |

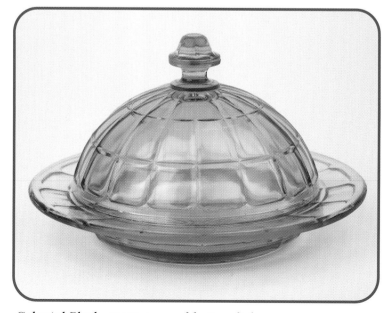

*Colonial Block, green covered butter dish.*

# Colonial Fluted

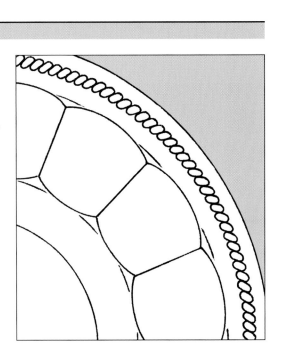

### Rope

Manufactured by Federal Glass Company, Columbus, Ohio, from 1928 to 1933.
Made in crystal and green.

| Item | Crystal | Green |
|---|---|---|
| Berry Bowl, 4" d. | 11.00 | 12.00 |
| Berry Bowl, 7-1/2" d. | 16.00 | 18.00 |
| Cereal Bowl, 6" d | 15.00 | 18.00 |
| Creamer, ftd. | 12.00 | 14.00 |
| Cup | 5.00 | 7.50 |
| Plate, 6" d, sherbet. | 2.50 | 4.00 |
| Plate, 8" d, luncheon | 5.00 | 10.00 |
| Salad Bowl, 6-1/2" d, 2-1/2" deep | 22.00 | 35.00 |
| Saucer | 2.50 | 4.00 |
| Sherbet | 6.00 | 8.50 |
| Sugar, cov | 21.00 | 25.00 |
| Sugar, open | 8.00 | 10.00 |

*Colonial Fluted, green sugar and creamer.*

# Colony

Manufactured by Fostoria Glass Company, Moundsville, Va., from the 1930s until 1983.

Made in crystal. The pattern was reissued as "Maypole" in the 1980s in the following colors: amber, blue, green, red, yellow, and white.

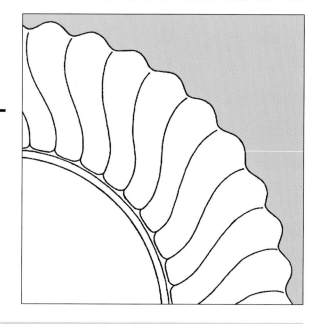

| Item | Crystal |
|---|---|
| Almond Bowl, ftd | 15.00 |
| Ashtray, 2-7/8" w, sq | 8.75 |
| Ashtray, 3" d, round | 7.50 |
| Ashtray, 3-1/2" w, sq | 12.00 |
| Ashtray, 4-1/2" d, round | 15.00 |
| Ashtray, 6" d, round | 18.00 |
| Bonbon, 5" d | 12.00 |
| Bonbon, 7" | 15.00 |
| Bowl, 4-1/2" d | 32.00 |
| Bowl, 5" d, handle | 40.00 |
| Bowl, 5-1/2" d, sq | 45.00 |
| Bowl, 8" d | 35.00 |
| Bowl, 10-1/2" d, high foot | 95.00 |
| Bowl, 10-1/2" d, low foot | 75.00 |
| Bowl, 11" l, flared | 35.00 |
| Bowl, 11" l, oval, ftd | 95.00 |
| Bud Vase, 6" h | 16.50 |
| Butter Dish, cov, quarter pound | 36.00 |
| Cake Plate, 10" d, handle | 24.00 |
| Candlesticks, pr, 3-1/2" h | 24.00 |
| Candlesticks, pr, 6-1/2" h, 2-lite | 50.00 |
| Candlesticks, pr, 7" h | 25.00 |
| Candlesticks, pr, 7-1/2" h, prisms | 150.00 |
| Candlesticks, pr, 9" h | 65.00 |
| Candlesticks, pr, 9-3/4" h, prisms | 172.00 |
| Candlesticks, pr, 14-1/2" h, prisms | 350.00 |
| Candy Dish, cov, 6-1/2" | 48.00 |
| Candy Dish, cov, ftd, half pound | 75.00 |
| Celery, 11-1/2" | 32.00 |
| Cheese and Cracker | 50.00 |
| Cigarette Box | 48.00 |
| Cocktail, 3-1/2 oz, 4" | 15.00 |
| Comport, 4" h | 18.00 |
| Comport, cov, 6-1/2" d | 38.00 |
| Console Bowl, 9" d or 13" d | 35.00 |
| Cornucopia, 9" h | 70.00 |

| Item | Crystal |
|---|---|
| Cream Soup, 5" d | 48.00 |
| Creamer | 6.50 |
| Creamer, individual size | 7.00 |
| Creamer and Sugar Tray, individual size | 9.00 |
| Cup | 8.00 |
| Finger Bowl | 45.00 |
| Fruit Bowl, 10" d | 36.00 |
| Fruit Bowl, 14" d | 45.00 |
| Goblet, 5-1/4" h | 18.00 |
| Ice Bucket | 150.00 |
| Iced Tea Tumbler, 12 oz | 28.50 |
| Juice Tumbler, 5 oz, ftd | 24.00 |
| Lamp, electric | 172.00 |
| Lemon Plate, 6-1/2" d, handle | 12.50 |
| Mayonnaise, 3 pcs | 36.00 |
| Milk Pitcher, 16 oz | 72.00 |
| Oil Bottle, orig stopper | 40.00 |
| Olive, 7" l, oblong | 18.00 |
| Oyster Cocktail, 4 oz | 14.00 |
| Pickle | 17.50 |
| Pitcher, 48 oz, ice lip | 215.00 |
| Plate, 6" d, bread and butter | 4.50 |
| Plate, 7" d, salad | 8.25 |
| Plate, 8" d, luncheon | 10.00 |
| Plate, 9" d, dinner | 27.50 |
| Platter, 12" l | 50.00 |
| Punch Bowl | 695.00 |
| Punch Cup | 12.00 |
| Relish, 10-1/2" d, 3-part | 20.00 |
| Rose Bowl | 145.00 |
| Salad Bowl, 7-3/4" d | 25.00 |
| Salad Bowl, 9-3/4" d | 40.00 |
| Salt & Pepper Shakers, pr, 2-1/2" h | 45.00 |
| Salt & Pepper Shakers, pr, 3-5/8" h | 15.00 |
| Salver, 12" d, ftd | 65.00 |
| Sandwich Plate, center handle | 32.00 |

| Item | Crystal |
|---|---|
| Saucer | 2.25 |
| Sherbet, 3-5/8" | 10.00 |
| Sugar | 6.50 |
| Sugar, individual | 7.50 |
| Torte Plate, 13" d | 32.00 |
| Torte Plate, 15" d | 60.00 |
| Torte Plate, 18" d | 100.00 |
| Tumbler, 5 oz, 4-1/2" h, ftd | 30.00 |
| Tumbler, 9 oz, 3-7/8" h | 30.00 |
| Tumbler, 12 oz, 5-3/4" h, ftd | 24.00 |
| Vase, 7" h | 35.00 |
| Vase, 7-1/2" h, flared | 42.00 |
| Vase, 12" h | 200.00 |
| Wine, 4-1/4" h | 32.00 |

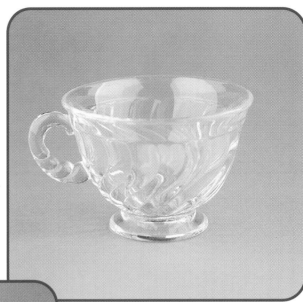

*Colony, crystal cup.*

*Colony, crystal plate.*

*Colony, crystal relish with two handles.*

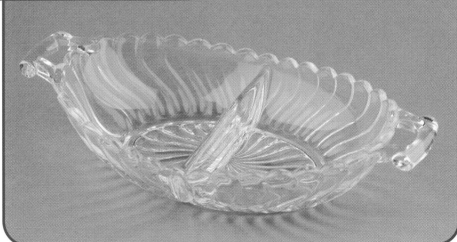

# Columbia

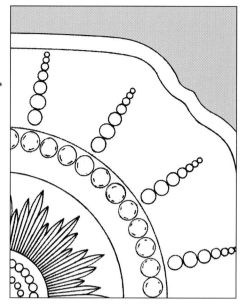

Manufactured by Federal Glass Company, Columbus, Ohio, from 1938 to 1942.

Made in crystal and pink. Several flashed (stained) colors are found, and some decaled pieces are known.

**Reproductions:** † The 2-7/8" h juice tumbler has been reproduced. Look for the "France" on the base to clearly identify the reproductions.

| Item | Crystal | Flashed | Pink |
|---|---|---|---|
| Bowl, 10-1/2" d, ruffled edge | 24.00 | 20.00 | - |
| Butter Dish, cov | 20.00 | 25.00 | - |
| Cereal Bowl, 5" d | 18.00 | - | - |
| Chop Plate, 11" d | 17.00 | 12.00 | - |
| Crescent Shaped Salad | 27.00 | - | - |
| Cup | 9.50 | 10.00 | 25.00 |
| Juice Tumbler, 4 oz, 2-3/4" h † | 30.00 | - | - |
| Plate, 6" d, bread & butter | 5.00 | 4.00 | 14.00 |
| Plate, 9-1/2" d, luncheon | 22.00 | 12.00 | 32.00 |
| Salad Bowl, 8-1/2" d | 20.00 | - | - |
| Saucer | 4.50 | 4.00 | 10.00 |
| Snack Tray, Cup | 35.00 | - | - |
| Soup Bowl, 8" d, low | 25.00 | - | - |
| Tumbler, 9 oz | 42.50 | - | - |

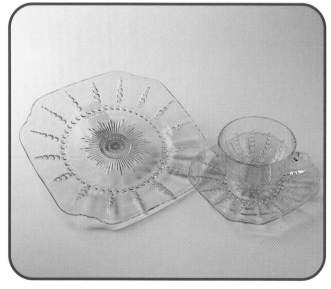

*Columbia, crystal plate, cup, and saucer.*

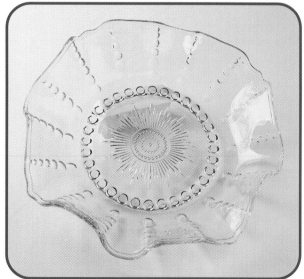

*Columbia, crystal ruffled bowl.*

# Constellation

## Pattern #300

Manufactured by Indiana Glass Company, Dunkirk, Ind., c1940. Later reissued as Sunset Constellation by Tiara Home products in the 1980s.

Made in crystal and amber by Indiana. Made in amberina, emerald green, red, and yellow mist by Tiara.

*Constellation, crystal nut bowl.*

| Item | Amber | Crystal | Tiara Colors |
|---|---|---|---|
| Basket, 11" | - | 30.00 | 25.00 |
| Bowl, 11" d, two handles | - | 25.00 | 12.00 |
| Buffet plate, 18" d | - | 40.00 | - |
| Cake stand | - | 50.00 | - |
| Candlesticks, pr | - | 45.00 | 15.00 |
| Candy dish, cov | - | 25.00 | 18.00 |
| Celery tray | - | 20.00 | - |
| Console bowl, 11-1/2" d | - | 25.00 | 20.00 |
| Cookie jar, cov | - | 28.00 | 24.00 |
| Creamer | - | 10.00 | - |
| Goblet, water | 15.00 | 15.00 | 12.00 |
| Mayonnaise bowl, ladle, underplate | - | 28.00 | - |
| Mug | - | 15.00 | - |
| Nappy, three toes | - | 15.00 | - |
| Nut bowl, 6" d, cupped | - | 12.00 | - |

| Item | Amber | Crystal | Tiara Colors |
|------|-------|---------|--------------|
| Pickle, oval | - | 15.00 | - |
| Pitcher, 7-1/2" d. | 65.00 | 45.00 | 60.00 |
| Plate, dessert | - | 5.00 | - |
| Plate, lunch | - | 8.00 | - |
| Plate, salad | - | 10.00 | - |
| Platter, oval | - | 20.00 | - |
| Punch bowl | - | 35.00 | - |
| Relish, three parts | - | 15.00 | - |
| Salad bowl | - | 22.00 | - |
| Serving plate, 13-1/2" d | - | 22.00 | 15.00 |
| Sugar | - | 10.00 | - |
| Tumbler, 8 oz | - | 15.00 | - |

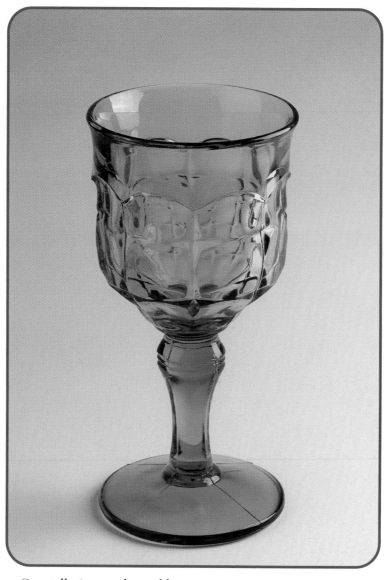

*Constellation, amber goblet.*

# Coronation

## Banded Fine Rib, Saxon

Manufactured by Hocking Glass Company, Lancaster, Ohio, from 1936 to 1940.

Made in crystal, green, pink, and Royal Ruby.

| Item | Crystal | Green | Pink | Royal Ruby |
|---|---|---|---|---|
| Berry Bowl, 4-1/4" d | - | 50.00 | 8.50 | 6.50 |
| Berry Bowl, 8" d, handle | - | - | 18.00 | 20.00 |
| Berry Bowl, 8" d | - | 195.00 | - | - |
| Cup | 5.00 | - | 6.00 | 7.50 |
| Nappy Bowl, 6-1/2" d | 15.00 | - | 7.50 | 15.00 |
| Pitcher, 68 oz, 7-3/4" h | - | - | 500.00 | - |
| Plate, 6" d, sherbet | 2.00 | - | 4.50 | - |
| Plate, 8-1/2" d, luncheon | 5.00 | 60.00 | 12.00 | 8.50 |
| Saucer | 2.00 | - | 4.00 | - |
| Sherbet | - | 85.00 | 7.00 | - |
| Tumbler, 10 oz, 5" h, ftd | - | 195.00 | 35.00 | - |

*Coronation, ruby handled bowl.*

# Cracked Ice

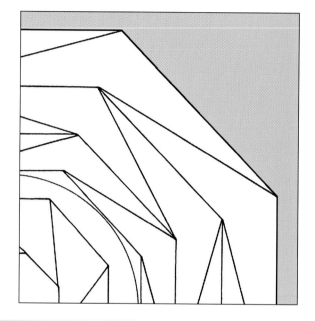

Manufactured by Indiana Glass, Dunkirk, Ind., in the 1930s.

Made in pink and green. Often mistaken for Tea Room, look for the additional diagonal line, giving it a more Art Deco style.

| Item | Green | Pink |
| --- | --- | --- |
| Creamer | 30.00 | 35.00 |
| Plate, 6-1/2" d | 15.00 | 18.00 |
| Sherbet | 12.00 | 15.00 |
| Sugar, cov | 30.00 | 35.00 |
| Tumbler | 30.00 | 32.50 |

*Cracked Ice, pink creamer and covered sugar.*

# *Cremax*

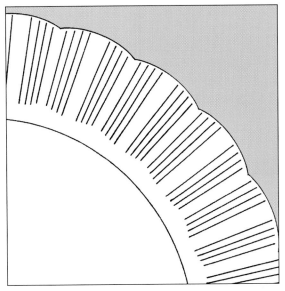

Manufactured by Macbeth-Evans Division of Corning Glass Works, late 1930s to early 1940s.

Made in Cremax, Cremax with fired-on colors, Delphite, and Robin's Egg Blue. One set is known as Bordette.

| Item | Bordette | Cremax | Cremax Fired-On | Delphite | Robin's Egg Blue |
|------|---------|--------|-----------------|----------|------------------|
| Cereal Bowl, 5-3/4" d . . . . . . . . . . . . . . . . 5.00 | | 6.00 | 9.00 | 10.00 | 10.00 |
| Creamer. . . . . . . . . . . . . . . . . . . . . . . . . . 6.00 | | 6.50 | 6.00 | 11.00 | 11.00 |
| Cup . . . . . . . . . . . . . . . . . . . . . . . . . . . . 5.00 | | 6.00 | 8.00 | 7.00 | 7.00 |
| Demitasse cup . . . . . . . . . . . . . . . . . . . . 10.00 | | 16.00 | 18.00 | 26.00 | 26.00 |
| Demitasse saucer . . . . . . . . . . . . . . . . . . 6.00 | | 7.00 | 8.00 | 12.00 | 20.00 |
| Egg cup, 2-1/4" h . . . . . . . . . . . . . . . . . . 12.00 | | - | - | - | - |
| Plate, 6-1/4" d, bread and butter. . . . . . . . 4.00 | | 4.50 | 5.50 | 7.00 | 7.00 |
| Plate, 9-3/4" d, dinner. . . . . . . . . . . . . . . 14.00 | | 7.00 | 11.00 | 12.00 | 12.00 |
| Sandwich plate, 11-1/2" d. . . . . . . . . . . . . 9.50 | | 10.00 | 15.00 | 17.00 | 17.00 |
| Saucer . . . . . . . . . . . . . . . . . . . . . . . . . . 3.50 | | 4.00 | 4.00 | 6.00 | 6.00 |
| Sugar, open . . . . . . . . . . . . . . . . . . . . . . 6.00 | | 6.50 | 6.00 | 11.00 | 11.00 |
| Vegetable bowl, 9" d . . . . . . . . . . . . . . . . 10.00 | | 11.00 | 10.00 | 20.00 | 20.00 |

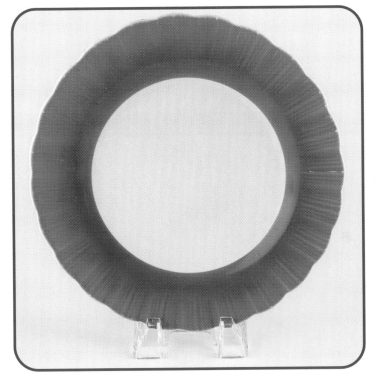

*Cremax, plate with blue edge.*

# Crocheted Crystal

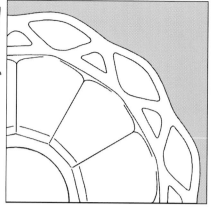

Manufactured by Imperial Glass Company, Bellaire, Ohio, from 1943 to the early 1950s.

Made exclusively for Sears, Roebuck. Made only in crystal.

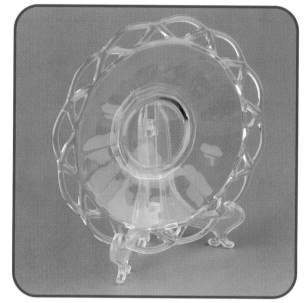

*Crocheted Crystal, plate.*

| Item | Crystal |
|---|---|
| Basket, 6" | 32.50 |
| Basket, 9" | 38.00 |
| Basket, 12" | 65.00 |
| Buffet Set, sauce bowl, ladle, 14" d plate | 48.00 |
| Cake Stand, 12" d, ftd | 42.00 |
| Candlesticks, pr, 4-1/2" h, 2 lite | 17.50 |
| Candlesticks, pr, 6" w | 20.00 |
| Celery Tray, 10" l, oval | 25.00 |
| Cheese and Cracker, 12" d plate, ftd dish | 42.00 |
| Cocktail, 3-1/2 oz, 4-1/2" h | 15.00 |
| Console Bowl, 12" d | 30.00 |
| Creamer, flat or footed | 25.00 |
| Epergne, 11" h, ftd | 140.00 |
| Goblet, 9 oz, 7-1/8" h | 15.00 |
| Hors d'oeuvre Dish, 10-1/2" d, 4 parts | 30.00 |
| Hurricane Lamp, 11" h | 48.00 |
| Iced Tea Tumbler, 12 oz, 7" h, ftd | 18.00 |
| Juice Tumbler, 6 oz, 6" h, ftd | 12.00 |
| Mayonnaise Bowl, 5-1/4" d | 15.00 |

| Item | Crystal |
|---|---|
| Mayonnaise Ladle | 7.50 |
| Mayonnaise Plate, 7-1/2" d | 8.00 |
| Narcissus Bowl, 7" d | 42.00 |
| Plate, 14" d | 25.00 |
| Plate, 17" d | 40.00 |
| Plate, 8" d, salad | 9.50 |
| Plate, 9-1/2" d, luncheon | 12.50 |
| Punch Bowl, 14" d | 70.00 |
| Punch Cup, closed handle | 5.50 |
| Punch Cup, open handle | 7.50 |
| Relish, 11-1/2" d, 3 parts | 27.50 |
| Salad Bowl, 10-1/2" d | 35.00 |
| Salad Bowl Liner, 13" d plate | 25.00 |
| Sherbet, 6 oz, 5" h | 12.00 |
| Sugar, flat or footed | 25.00 |
| Vase, 5" h, ftd | 35.00 |
| Vase, 8" h | 35.00 |
| Wine, 4-1/2 oz, 5-1/2" h | 24.00 |

# Crow's Foot

## Line #412 and Line #890

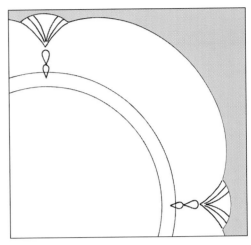

Manufactured by Paden City Glass Company, Paden City, W.V., 1930s. The square-shaped pieces are Line #412, the round line is Line #890.

Made in amber, amethyst, black, crystal, pink, Ritz blue, ruby red, white, and yellow.

| Item | Black Ritz Blue | Colors | Ruby Red |
|---|---|---|---|
| Bowl, 4-7/8" w, sq | 32.00 | 13.00 | 25.00 |
| Bowl, 6" d | 35.00 | 15.00 | 32.00 |
| Bowl, 6-1/2" d, round, 2-1/2" h, 3-1/2" d base | 50.00 | 24.00 | 45.00 |
| Bowl, 8-1/2" d, sq, 2 handles | 60.00 | 30.00 | 50.00 |
| Bowl, 8-3/4" w, sq | 55.00 | 25.00 | 45.00 |
| Bowl, 10" d, ftd | 75.00 | 35.00 | 70.00 |
| Bowl, 10" w, sq, 2 handles | 75.00 | 35.00 | 89.00 |
| Bowl, 11" l, oval | 45.00 | 20.00 | 40.00 |
| Bowl, 11" w, sq | 72.00 | 32.00 | 60.00 |
| Bowl, 11" w, sq, rolled edge | 75.00 | 35.00 | 70.00 |
| Cake Plate, sq, low pedestal foot | 95.00 | 45.00 | 135.00 |
| Candlesticks, pr, 5-3/4" h | 60.00 | 40.00 | 90.00 |
| Candlesticks, pr, round base, tall | 170.00 | 75.00 | 145.00 |
| Candlesticks, pr, sq, mushroom | 90.00 | 45.00 | 75.00 |
| Candy, 6-1/8" w, 3-1/4" h, 3 legs, round | 195.00 | 85.00 | 165.00 |
| Candy, cov, 6-1/2" d, 3 part | 95.00 | 25.00 | 55.00 |
| Cheese Stand, 5" h | 35.00 | 15.00 | 30.00 |
| Comport, 3-1/4" h, 6-1/4" w | 35.00 | 15.00 | 38.00 |
| Comport, 4-3/4" h, 7-3/8" w | 55.00 | 30.00 | 45.00 |
| Comport, 6-5/8" h, 7" w | 70.00 | 35.00 | 80.00 |
| Console Bowl, 11-1/2" d, 3 legs, round | 100.00 | 50.00 | 150.00 |
| Console Bowl, 11-1/2" w, sq | 95.00 | 40.00 | 80.00 |
| Cracker Plate, 11" d | 50.00 | 25.00 | 45.00 |
| Cream Soup Bowl, flat | 28.00 | 12.00 | 22.00 |
| Cream Soup Bowl, ftd | 28.00 | 12.00 | 22.00 |
| Creamer, flat | 17.50 | 10.00 | 15.00 |
| Creamer, footed | 17.50 | 10.00 | 15.00 |
| Cup, flat | 18.50 | 6.00 | 15.00 |
| Cup, ftd | 18.50 | 6.00 | 15.00 |
| Gravy Boat, flat | 100.00 | 45.00 | 85.00 |

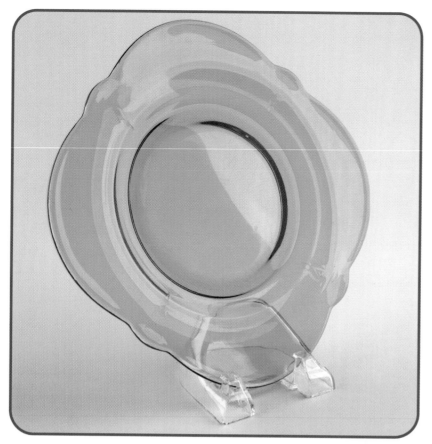

*Crow's Foot, amber plate.*

| Item | Black Ritz Blue | Colors | Ruby Red |
|---|---|---|---|
| Gravy Boat, ftd | 215.00 | 70.00 | 130.00 |
| Mayonnaise, 3 legs | 60.00 | 25.00 | 50.00 |
| Nasturium bowl, 3 legs | 200.00 | 100.00 | 175.00 |
| Plate, 5-3/4" d | 4.00 | 2.00 | 3.00 |
| Plate, 8" d, round | 12.00 | 5.00 | 10.00 |
| Plate, 8-1/2" w, sq | 10.00 | 7.00 | 8.00 |
| Plate, 9-1/4" d, round, dinner | 40.00 | 20.00 | 35.00 |
| Plate, 9-1/2" d, 2 handles | 75.00 | 35.00 | 65.00 |
| Plate, 10-3/8" d, round, 2 handles | 65.00 | 30.00 | 55.00 |
| Plate, 10-3/8" w, sq, 2 handles | 65.00 | 30.00 | 55.00 |
| Plate, 10-1/2" d, dinner | 100.00 | 45.00 | 90.00 |
| Platter, 12" l | 50.00 | 17.50 | 30.00 |
| Relish, 11" l, 3 parts | 100.00 | 48.00 | 85.00 |
| Sandwich Server, center handle, round | 75.00 | 50.00 | 70.00 |
| Sandwich Server, center handle, sq | 45.00 | 35.00 | 50.00 |
| Saucer, 6" d, round | 10.00 | 2.00 | 5.00 |
| Saucer, 6" w, sq | 10.00 | 2.00 | 5.00 |
| Sugar, flat | 17.50 | 10.00 | 15.00 |
| Sugar, ftd | 17.50 | 10.00 | 15.00 |
| Tumbler, 4-1/4" h | 80.00 | 35.00 | 75.00 |
| Vase, 4-5/8" h | 75.00 | 45.00 | 65.00 |
| Vases, 10-1/4" h, cupped | 110.00 | 50.00 | 90.00 |
| Vases, 10-1/4" h, flared | 85.00 | 35.00 | 70.00 |
| Vases, 11-3/4" h, flared | 185.00 | 125.00 | 240.00 |
| Whipped Cream Bowl, 3 legs | 70.00 | 30.00 | 60.00 |

# Cube

## Cubist

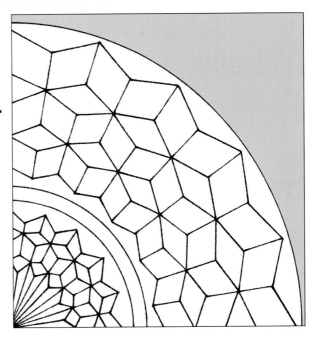

Manufactured by Jeannette Glass Company, Jeannette, Pa., from 1929 to 1933. Made in amber, crystal, green, pink, ultramarine, and white. Production in amber and white is limited to the 2-3/8" h sugar bowl, and is valued at $3.

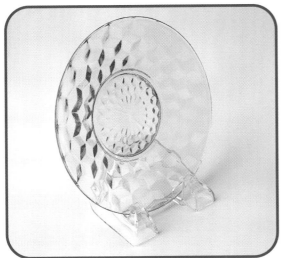

Cube, pink plate.

| Item | Crystal | Green | Pink | Ultramarine |
|------|---------|-------|------|-------------|
| Bowl, 4-1/2" d, deep | - | 7.00 | 9.50 | 35.00 |
| Butter Dish, cov | - | 60.00 | 65.00 | - |
| Candy Jar, cov, 6-1/2" h | - | 35.00 | 30.00 | - |
| Coaster, 3-1/4" d | - | 10.00 | 10.00 | - |
| Creamer, 2-5/8" h | 5.00 | 10.00 | 10.00 | 70.00 |
| Creamer, 3-9/16" h | - | 9.00 | 9.00 | - |
| Cup | - | 7.00 | 8.00 | - |
| Dessert Bowl, 4-1/2" d, pointed rim | 4.00 | 8.50 | 9.50 | - |
| Pitcher, 8-3/4" h, 45 oz | - | 235.00 | 215.00 | - |
| Plate, 6" d, sherbet | - | 11.00 | 3.50 | - |
| Plate, 8" d, luncheon | - | 8.50 | 7.50 | - |
| Powder Jar, cov, 3 legs | - | 30.00 | 35.00 | - |
| Salad Bowl, 6-1/2" d | 6.00 | 15.00 | 15.00 | - |
| Salt and Pepper Shakers, pr | - | 35.00 | 36.00 | - |
| Saucer | 1.50 | 3.00 | 3.50 | - |
| Sherbet, ftd | - | 8.50 | 12.00 | - |
| Sugar, cov, 2-3/8" h | 4.00 | 22.00 | 6.00 | - |
| Sugar, cov, 3" h | - | 25.00 | 25.00 | - |
| Sugar, open, 3" | 5.00 | 8.00 | 7.00 | - |
| Tray, 7-1/2" l | 9.00 | - | 5.00 | - |
| Tumbler, 9 oz, 4" h | - | 70.00 | 65.00 | - |

# *Cupid*

Manufactured by Paden City Glass Company, Paden City, W.V., 1930s.

Made in amber, black, canary yellow, crystal, green, light blue, peacock blue, and pink. Prices for colors like amber, black, canary yellow, and light blue are still being established as more pieces of this pattern arrive on the secondary market. This expensive pattern is one to keep your eyes open for while searching at flea markets and garage sales.

| Item | Crystal | Green | Peacock Blue | Pink |
|---|---|---|---|---|
| Bowl, 8-1/2" l, oval, ftd | - | 300.00 | - | 300.00 |
| Bowl, 9-1/4" d, center handle | - | 275.00 | - | 275.00 |
| Bowl, 10-1/2" d, rolled edge | - | 250.00 | - | 250.00 |
| Cake Plate, 11-3/4" h | - | 200.00 | - | 200.00 |
| Cake Stand, 2" h, ftd | - | 235.00 | - | 235.00 |
| Candlesticks, pr, 5" h | - | 245.00 | - | 245.00 |
| Candy, cov, 3 part | - | 385.00 | - | 385.00 |
| Candy, cov, 5-1/4" h | - | 295.00 | - | 295.00 |
| Champagne, 5-7/8" h | 35.00 | - | - | - |
| Cocktail, 5-1/8" h | 25.00 | - | - | - |
| Comport, 4-1/2" h, ftd | - | 175.00 | - | 175.00 |
| Comport, 6-1/4" h, ftd | - | 185.00 | 225.00 | 290.00 |
| Console Bowl, 11" d | - | 250.00 | - | 250.00 |
| Creamer, 4-1/2" h, ftd | 45.00 | 150.00 | - | 150.00 |
| Creamer, 5" h, ftd | - | 150.00 | - | 150.00 |
| Fruit Bowl, 9-1/4" d, ftd | - | 360.00 | - | 360.00 |
| Fruit Bowl, 10-1/4" d | - | 245.00 | - | 275.00 |
| Ice Bucket, 6" h | - | 325.00 | - | 325.00 |
| Ice Tub, 4-3/4" h | - | 325.00 | - | 325.00 |
| Mayonnaise, 6" d, spoon, 8" d plate | - | 275.00 | 295.00 | 275.00 |
| Plate, 10-1/2" d | - | 150.00 | 175.00 | 150.00 |
| Samovar | - | 990.00 | - | 990.00 |
| Sugar, 4-1/4" h, ftd | - | 150.00 | - | 150.00 |
| Sugar, 5" h, ftd | - | 150.00 | - | 150.00 |
| Tray, 10-3/4" d, center handle | - | 200.00 | - | 200.00 |
| Tray, 10-7/8" l, oval, ftd | - | 250.00 | - | 250.00 |
| Vase, 8-1/4" h, elliptical | - | 650.00 | - | 650.00 |
| Vase, 10" h | - | 315.00 | - | 315.00 |
| Wine, 5-1/8" h | 12.50 | - | - | - |

*Cupid, pink low pedestal-foot comport.*

# *Daisy*

### *No. 620*

Manufactured by Indiana Glass Company, Dunkirk, Ind., from late 1930s to 1980s.

Made in amber (1940s), crystal (1933-40), dark green (1960s-80s), fired-on red (late 1930s), and milk glass (1960s-80s).

| Item | Amber or Fired-On Red | Crystal | Dark Green or Milk White |
|---|---|---|---|
| Berry Bowl, 4-1/2" d | 11.00 | 6.00 | 6.00 |
| Berry Bowl, 7-3/8" d deep | 17.50 | 8.50 | 9.50 |
| Berry Bowl, 9-3/8" d, deep | 35.00 | 14.00 | 14.00 |
| Cake Plate, 11-1/2" d | 16.50 | 14.00 | 14.00 |
| Cereal Bowl, 6" d | 25.00 | 10.00 | 10.00 |
| Cream Soup Bowl, 4-1/2" d | 13.50 | 7.50 | 7.50 |
| Creamer, ftd | 10.00 | 8.00 | 8.00 |
| Cup | 8.00 | 6.00 | 6.00 |
| Plate, 6" d, sherbet | 5.00 | 4.50 | 5.00 |
| Plate, 7-3/8" d, salad | 8.50 | 8.50 | 9.00 |
| Plate, 8-3/8" d, luncheon | 10.00 | 10.00 | 12.00 |
| Plate, 9-3/8" d, dinner | 12.00 | 12.00 | 15.00 |
| Plate, 10-3/8" d, grill | 15.00 | 15.00 | 18.00 |
| Plate, 10-3/8" d, grill, indent for soup | 15.00 | 8.00 | 8.00 |
| Platter, 10-3/4" d | 18.00 | 11.00 | 11.00 |
| Relish Dish, 8-3/8" d, 3 part | 24.00 | 12.00 | 12.00 |
| Sandwich Plate, 11-1/2" d | 17.50 | 14.00 | 14.00 |
| Saucer | 2.00 | 6.00 | 2.00 |
| Sherbet, ftd | 9.00 | 5.00 | 5.00 |
| Sugar, ftd | 10.00 | 8.00 | 8.00 |
| Tumbler, 9 oz, ftd | 16.00 | 10.00 | 10.00 |
| Tumbler, 12 oz, ftd | 40.00 | 15.00 | 15.00 |
| Vegetable Bowl, 10" l, oval | 25.00 | 18.00 | 18.00 |

*Daisy, green luncheon plate.*

*Daisy, amber creamer.*

*Daisy, crystal sandwich plate.*

*Daisy, amber luncheon plate.*

# Delilah

## *Delilah Bird, Peacock Reverse, Line #412*

Manufactured by Paden City Glass Company, Paden City, W.V., 1930s.

Made in amber, black, cobalt blue, crystal, green, pink, red, and yellow.

*Delilah Bird, amber candle holders.*

| Item | Colors |
| --- | --- |
| Bowl, 4-7/8" w, sq | 50.00 |
| Bowl, 8-3/4" w, sq | 115.00 |
| Bowl, 8-3/4" w, sq, handles | 125.00 |
| Candlesticks, pr, 5-3/4" h, sq base | 90.00 |
| Candy dish, 6-1/2" w, sq | 200.00 |
| Comport, 3-1/4" h, 6-1/4" w | 90.00 |
| Comport, 4-1/4" h, 7-3/8" w | 95.00 |
| Console bowl, 11-3/4" d | 400.00 |
| Creamer, 2-3/4" h, flat | 95.00 |
| Cup | 95.00 |
| Plate, 5-3/4" d, sherbet | 25.00 |
| Plate, 8-1/2" d, luncheon | 70.00 |
| Plate, 10-3/8" d, 2 handles | 155.00 |
| Saucer | 25.00 |
| Server, center handle | 85.00 |
| Sherbet, two sizes | 75.00 |
| Tumbler, 10 oz, 4" h, flat | 95.00 |
| Vase, 6-3/4" h | 125.00 |
| Vase, 10" h | 100.00 |

*Delilah Bird, pink mayonnaise liner.*

# Della Robbia

## #1058

Manufactured by Westmoreland Glass Company, Grapeville, Pa., from late 1920s to 1940s.

Made in crystal, with applied luster colors and milk glass. Examples of milk white prices are: hand-painted decorated candy jar, $45; creamer, $18; goblet, $20; tumbler, $22.50; wine, $18.

| Item | Crystal |
|---|---|
| Basket, 9" | 210.00 |
| Basket, 12" | 300.00 |
| Bowl, 8" d, bell, handle | 48.00 |
| Bowl, 8"d, heart shape, handle | 95.00 |
| Bowl, 12" d, ftd | 12.00 |
| Bowl, 13" d, rolled edge | 115.00 |
| Bowl, 14" d, oval, flange | 155.00 |
| Bowl, 15" d. bell | 175.00 |
| Cake salver, 14" d, ftd | 120.00 |
| Candlesticks, pr, 4" h | 65.00 |
| Candlesticks, pr, 4" h, two-lite | 160.00 |
| Candy jar, cov, scalloped edge | 85.00 |
| Champagne, 6 oz. | 25.00 |
| Chocolate candy, round, flat | 75.00 |
| Cocktail, 3-1/4 oz. | 15.00 |
| Comport, 12" d, ftd, bell | 115.00 |
| Comport, 13" d, flanged | 125.00 |
| Creamer, ftd | 18.00 |
| Cup, coffee | 18.50 |
| Finger bowl, 5" d | 30.00 |
| Ginger ale tumbler, 5 oz | 25.00 |
| Goblet, 8 oz., 6" h. | 28.00 |
| Iced tea tumbler 11 oz., ftd. | 35.00 |
| Iced tea tumbler 12 oz., 5-3/16" h, straight | 40.00 |
| Iced tea tumbler 12 oz., bell | 32.00 |
| Iced tea tumbler, 12 oz., bell, ftd | 32.00 |
| Mint comport, 6-1/2" d, 3-5/8" h, ftd | 45.00 |

| Item | Crystal |
|---|---|
| Nappy, 7-1/2"d | 42.00 |
| Nappy, 8" d, bell | 45.00 |
| Nappy, 4-1/2" d | 30.00 |
| Nappy, 6" d, bell | 35.00 |
| Nappy, 6-1/2"d, one handle | 32.00 |
| Nappy, 9" d | 60.00 |
| Pitcher, 32 oz. | 200.00 |
| Plate, 6" d, finger bowl liner | 12.00 |
| Plate, 6-1/8" d, bread and butter | 14.00 |
| Plate, 7-1/4" d, salad | 22.00 |
| Plate, 9" d, luncheon | 35.00 |
| Plate, 10-1/2" d, dinner | 95.00 |
| Plate, 18" d | 195.00 |
| Platter, 14" l, oval | 195.00 |
| Punch bowl, 14"d | 225.00 |
| Punch bowl liner, 18" d plate, upturned edge | 200.00 |
| Punch cup | 15.00 |
| Salt and pepper shakers, pr | 55.00 |
| Saucer | 10.00 |
| Sherbet, 5 oz, low foot | 22.00 |
| Sherbet, 5 oz, 4-3/4" h, ftd | 24.00 |
| Sugar, ftd | 27.50 |
| Sweetmeat comport, 8" d | 115.00 |
| Torte plate, 14"d | 125.00 |
| Tumbler 8 oz., ftd | 30.00 |
| Tumbler, 8 oz, water | 32.00 |
| Wine, 3 oz | 25.00 |

*Della Robbia, clear plate.*

*Della Robbia, luster decorated compote.*

# Dewdrop

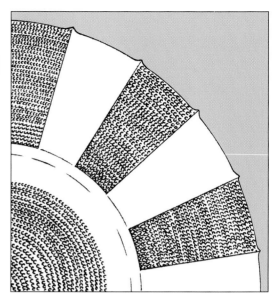

Manufactured by Jeannette Glass Company, Jeannette, Pa., from 1953 to 1956. Made in crystal.

| Item | Crystal |
|---|---|
| Bowl, 4-3/4" d | 9.00 |
| Bowl, 8-1/2" d | 22.00 |
| Bowl, 10-3/8" d | 24.00 |
| Butter, cov | 32.00 |
| Candy dish, cov, 7" d | 30.00 |
| Casserole, cov | 27.50 |
| Creamer | 8.50 |
| Iced tea tumbler, 15 oz | 17.50 |
| Lazy Susan, 13" d tray | 32.00 |
| Pitcher, 1/2 gallon, ftd | 48.00 |

| Item | Crystal |
|---|---|
| Plate, 11-1/2" d | 20.00 |
| Punch cup | 4.00 |
| Punch bowl set, bowl, 12 cups | 75.00 |
| Snack cup | 4.00 |
| Snack plate, indent for cup | 5.00 |
| Relish, leaf-shape, handle | 9.00 |
| Sugar, cov | 14.00 |
| Tray, 10" d | 22.00 |
| Tumbler, 9 oz | 15.00 |

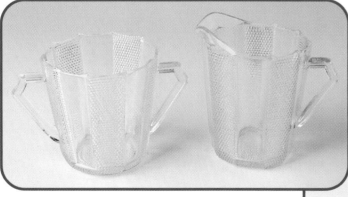

*Dewdrop, crystal sugar and creamer.*

*Dewdrop, clear tumbler and iridescent pitcher.*

# Diamond Quilted

### Flat Diamond

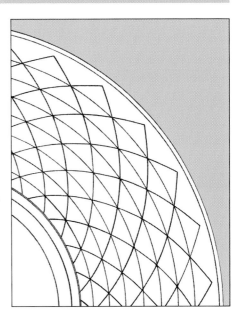

Manufactured by Imperial Glass Company, Bellaire, Ohio, from late 1920 to early 1930s.

Made in amber, black, blue, crystal, green, pink, and red. Amber and red prices would be valued slightly higher than black.

| Item | Black | Blue | Crystal |
|---|---|---|---|
| Bowl, 5-1/2" d, one handle | 20.00 | - | - |
| Bowl, 7" d, crimped edge | 22.00 | - | - |
| Cake Salver, 10" d, tall | - | - | - |
| Candlesticks, pr | 60.00 | - | 50.00 |
| Candy Jar, cov, ftd | - | - | 25.00 |
| Cereal Bowl, 5" d | 15.00 | - | 8.00 |
| Champagne, 9 oz, 6" h | - | - | - |
| Compote, 6" h, 7-1/4" w | - | - | - |
| Compote, cov, 11-1/2" d | - | - | - |
| Console Bowl, 10-1/2" d, rolled edge | 65.00 | 60.00 | 15.00 |
| Cordial, 1 oz | - | - | - |
| Cream Soup Bowl, 4-3/4" d | 22.00 | 20.00 | 20.00 |
| Creamer | 18.50 | 20.00 | 15.00 |
| Cup | 18.00 | 18.50 | 7.00 |
| Ice Bucket | 90.00 | 90.00 | - |
| Iced Tea Tumbler, 12 oz | - | - | - |
| Mayonnaise Set, comport, plate, ladle | 60.00 | 65.00 | 25.00 |
| Pitcher, 64 oz | - | - | - |
| Plate, 6" d, sherbet | 10.00 | 8.50 | 7.50 |
| Plate, 7" d, salad | 10.00 | 10.00 | 8.00 |
| Plate, 8" d, luncheon | 12.00 | 12.00 | 9.00 |
| Punch Bowl and Stand | - | - | - |
| Sandwich Plate, 14" d | - | - | - |
| Sandwich Server, center handle | 50.00 | 50.00 | 20.00 |
| Saucer | 5.00 | 5.00 | 2.00 |
| Sherbet | 16.00 | 16.00 | 14.00 |
| Sugar | 20.00 | 25.00 | 12.00 |
| Tumbler, 6 oz, ftd | - | - | - |
| Tumbler, 9 oz | - | - | - |
| Tumbler, 9 oz, ftd | - | - | - |
| Tumbler, 12 oz, ftd | - | - | - |
| Vase, fan | 80.00 | 75.00 | - |
| Whiskey, 1-1/2" oz | - | - | - |
| Wine, 2 oz | - | - | - |
| Wine, 3 oz | - | - | - |

| Item | Green | Pink |
|---|---|---|
| Bowl, 5-1/2" d, one handle | 15.00 | 18.00 |
| Bowl, 7" d, crimped edge | 18.00 | 20.00 |
| Cake Salver, 10" d, tall | 60.00 | 65.00 |
| Candlesticks, pr | 32.00 | 28.00 |
| Candy Jar, cov, ftd | 65.00 | 65.00 |
| Cereal Bowl, 5" d | 9.00 | 8.50 |
| Champagne, 9 oz, 6" h | 12.00 | - |
| Compote, 6" h, 7-1/4" w | 45.00 | 48.00 |
| Compote, cov, 11-1/2" d | 80.00 | 75.00 |
| Console Bowl, 10-1/2" d, rolled edge | 20.00 | 24.00 |
| Cordial, 1 oz | 12.00 | 15.00 |
| Cream Soup Bowl, 4-3/4" d | 12.00 | 14.00 |
| Creamer | 12.00 | 12.00 |
| Cup | 10.00 | 12.00 |
| Ice Bucket | 50.00 | 50.00 |
| Iced Tea Tumbler, 12 oz | 10.00 | 10.00 |
| Mayonnaise Set, comport, plate, ladle | 37.50 | 40.00 |
| Pitcher, 64 oz | 50.00 | 55.00 |
| Plate, 6" d, sherbet | 7.00 | 7.50 |
| Plate, 7" d, salad | 8.50 | 8.50 |
| Plate, 8" d, luncheon | 6.50 | 8.50 |
| Punch Bowl and Stand | 450.00 | 450.00 |
| Sandwich Plate, 14" d | 15.00 | 15.00 |
| Sandwich Server, center handle | 25.00 | 25.00 |
| Saucer | 4.00 | 4.00 |
| Sherbet | 12.00 | 10.00 |
| Sugar | 15.00 | 13.50 |
| Tumbler, 6 oz, ftd | 9.00 | 10.00 |
| Tumbler, 9 oz | 14.00 | 16.00 |
| Tumbler, 9 oz, ftd | 14.00 | 16.00 |
| Tumbler, 12 oz, ftd | 15.00 | 15.00 |
| Vase, fan | 50.00 | 50.00 |
| Whiskey, 1-1/2" oz | 10.00 | 12.00 |
| Wine, 2 oz | 12.50 | 12.50 |
| Wine, 3 oz | 15.00 | 15.00 |

Diamond Quilted, pink sugar and creamer.

# Diana

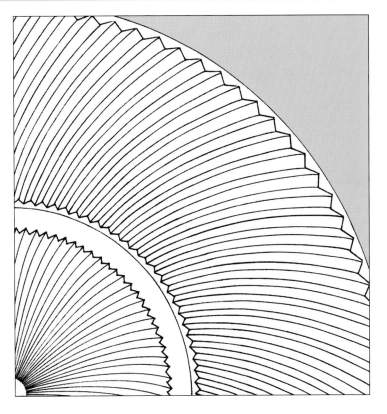

Manufactured by Federal Glass Company, Columbus, Ohio, from 1937 to 1941.

Made in amber, crystal, and pink.

**Reproductions:** † A 13-1/8" d scalloped pink bowl has been made, which was not original to the pattern.

| Item | Amber | Crystal | Pink |
|---|---|---|---|
| Ashtray, 3-1/2" d | - | 4.00 | 5.00 |
| Bowl, 12" d, scalloped edge | 20.00 | 10.00 | 32.00 |
| Candy jar, cov, round | 40.00 | 18.50 | 48.00 |
| Cereal bowl, 5" d | 15.00 | 6.50 | 13.00 |
| Coaster, 3-1/2" d | 12.00 | 4.00 | 7.00 |
| Console/fruit bowl, 11"d | 10.00 | 20.00 | 44.00 |
| Cream soup bowl, 5-1/2" d | 18.00 | 14.00 | 24.00 |
| Creamer, oval | 9.00 | 4.00 | 12.50 |
| Cup | 7.00 | 4.00 | 19.00 |
| Demitasse cup and saucer, 2 oz, 4-1/2" d saucer | - | 15.00 | 50.00 |
| Junior set, six cups and saucers, rack | - | 125.00 | 300.00 |
| Plate, 6" d, bread and butter | 3.50 | 3.00 | 5.50 |
| Plate, 9-1/2" d, dinner | 9.00 | 7.00 | 18.50 |
| Platter, 12" l, oval | 15.00 | 12.00 | 28.00 |
| Salad bowl, 9"d | 18.00 | 15.00 | 20.00 |
| Salt and pepper shakers, pr. | 100.00 | 30.00 | 75.00 |
| Sandwich plate, 11-3/4" d | 10.00 | 9.50 | 28.00 |
| Sandwich plate, 11-3/4" d, advertising in center | - | 15.00 | - |
| Saucer | 2.25 | 2.00 | 6.00 |
| Sherbet | 10.00 | 7.00 | 12.00 |
| Sugar, open, oval | 10.00 | 10.00 | 16.00 |
| Tumbler, 9 oz, 4-1/8" h | 27.50 | 18.00 | 45.00 |

*Diana, clear tumbler.*

*Diana, pink sherbet.*

*Diana, pink plate.*

# Dogwood

## Apple Blossom, Wild Rose

Manufactured by Macbeth-Evans Company, Charleroi, Pa., from 1929 to 1932.

Made in Cremax, crystal, green, Monax, pink and yellow. Yellow is rare; a cereal bowl is known and valued at $95. Crystal items are valued at 50 percent less than green.

Dogwood, pink sugar, creamer, and plate.

| Item | Cremax or Monax | Green | Pink |
|---|---|---|---|
| Berry bowl, 8-1/2" d | 40.00 | 100.00 | 65.00 |
| Cake plate, 11" d, heavy solid foot | - | - | 650.00 |
| Cake plate, 13" d, heavy solid foot | 185.00 | 135.00 | 165.00 |
| Cereal bowl, 5-1/2" d | 12.00 | 35.00 | 40.00 |
| Coaster, 3-1/4" d | - | - | 500.00 |
| Creamer, 2-1/2" h, thin | - | 48.00 | 30.00 |
| Creamer, 3-1/4" h, thick | - | - | 25.00 |
| Cup, thin | - | 32.00 | 24.00 |
| Cup, thick | 36.00 | 40.00 | 25.00 |
| Fruit bowl, 10-1/4" d | 100.00 | 250.00 | 600.00 |
| Pitcher, 8" h, 80 oz, (American Sweetheart style) | - | - | 1,350.00 |
| Pitcher, 8" h, 80 oz, decorated | - | 550.00 | 265.00 |
| Plate, 6" d, bread and butter | 25.00 | 10.00 | 9.50 |
| Plate, 8" d, luncheon | - | 12.00 | 12.00 |
| Plate, 9-1/4" d, dinner | - | - | 42.00 |
| Plates, 10-1/2" d, grill, AOP or border design only | - | 22.00 | 55.00 |
| Platter, 12" d, oval | - | - | 735.00 |
| Salver, 12"d | 185.00 | - | 40.00 |
| Saucer | 20.00 | 10.00 | 8.50 |
| Sherbet, low, ftd | - | 95.00 | 40.00 |
| Sugar, 2-1/2" h, thin | - | 50.00 | 22.50 |
| Sugar, 3-1/4" h, thick, ftd | - | - | 25.00 |
| Tidbit, 2 tier | - | - | 90.00 |
| Tumbler, 10 oz, 4" h, decorated | - | 100.00 | 55.00 |
| Tumbler, 11 oz, 4-3/4" h, decorated | - | 95.00 | 75.00 |
| Tumbler, 12 oz, 5" h, decorated | - | 125.00 | 75.00 |
| Tumbler, molded band | - | - | 25.00 |

# Doric

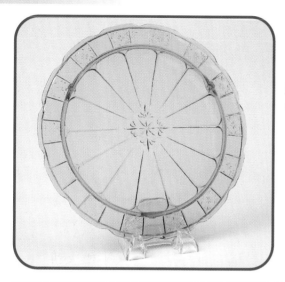

*Doric, green cake plate.*

Manufactured by Jeannette Glass Company, Jeannette, Pa., from 1935 to 1938. Made in Delphite, green, pink, and yellow. Yellow is rare.

| Item | Delphite | Green | Pink |
|------|---------|-------|------|
| Berry bowl, 4-1/2" d | 50.00 | 12.00 | 12.00 |
| Berry bowl, 8-1/4" d | 150.00 | 32.00 | 17.00 |
| Bowl, 9" d, two handles | - | 45.00 | 45.00 |
| Butter dish, cov | - | 90.00 | 75.00 |
| Cake plate, 10" d, three legs | - | 30.00 | 30.00 |
| Candy dish, cov, 8" d | - | 42.50 | 45.00 |
| Candy dish, three parts | 12.00 | 9.50 | 12.50 |
| Cereal bowl, 5-1/2" d | - | 65.00 | 90.00 |
| Coaster, 3" d | - | 28.00 | 20.00 |
| Cream soup, 5" d, two handles | - | 385.00 | - |
| Creamer, 4" h | - | 17.00 | 14.00 |
| Cup | - | 10.00 | 10.00 |
| Pitcher, 36 oz, 6" h, flat | 1,200.00 | 50.00 | 45.00 |
| Pitcher, 48 oz, 7-1/2" h, ftd | - | 1,000.00 | 750.00 |
| Plate, 6" d, sherbet | - | 7.50 | 7.50 |
| Plate, 7" d, salad | - | 20.00 | 18.00 |
| Plate, 9" d, dinner | - | 24.00 | 12.00 |
| Plate, 9" d, grill | - | 20.00 | 25.00 |
| Platter, 12" l, oval | - | 32.00 | 35.00 |
| Relish tray, 4" x 4" | - | 12.00 | 14.00 |
| Relish tray, 4" x 8" | - | 20.00 | 17.50 |
| Salt and pepper shakers, pr | - | 40.00 | 45.00 |
| Saucer | - | 7.00 | 7.00 |
| Sherbet, footed | 12.00 | 17.50 | 15.00 |
| Sugar, cov | - | 35.00 | 32.00 |
| Tray, 8" x 8", serving | - | 30.00 | 42.50 |
| Tray, 10" l, handle | - | 25.00 | 16.00 |
| Tumbler, 9 oz, 4-1/2" h, flat | - | 100.00 | 75.00 |
| Tumbler, 10 oz, 4" h, ftd | - | 90.00 | 65.00 |
| Tumbler, 12 oz, 5" h, ftd | - | 125.00 | 85.00 |
| Vegetable bowl, 9" l, oval | - | 45.00 | 40.00 |

# Doric & Pansy

Manufactured by Jeannette Glass Company, Jeannette, Pa., from 1937 to 1938.

Made in ultramarine, with limited production in pink and crystal.

*Doric and Pansy, pink plate.*

*Doric and Pansy, teal, child's sugar and creamer.*

| Item | Crystal | Pink | Ultramarine |
|---|---|---|---|
| Berry bowl, 4-1/2" d . . . . . . . | 12.00 | 12.00 | 24.00 |
| Berry bowl, 8" d. . . . . . . . . . . | - | 24.00 | 75.00 |
| Bowl, 9" d, handle . . . . . . . . | 15.00 | 20.00 | 35.00 |
| Butter dish, cov . . . . . . . . . . . | - | - | 600.00 |
| Candy, cov, three parts . . . . . . . | - | - | 22.50 |
| Cup. . . . . . . . . . . . . . . . . . | 12.00 | 14.00 | 20.00 |
| Creamer . . . . . . . . . . . . . . | 72.00 | 90.00 | 145.00 |
| Plate, 6" d, sherbet . . . . . . . . | 8.00 | 12.00 | 14.50 |
| Plate, 7" d, salad . . . . . . . . . . | - | - | 40.00 |
| Plate, 9" d, dinner . . . . . . . . . | 7.50 | 8.00 | 30.00 |
| Salt shaker, orig top. . . . . . . . . | - | - | 325.00 |
| Saucer . . . . . . . . . . . . . . . . | 4.50 | 4.50 | 5.50 |
| Sugar, open . . . . . . . . . . . . | 80.00 | 85.00 | 145.00 |
| Tray, 10" l, handles . . . . . . . | 45.00 | - | 25.00 |
| Tumbler, 9 oz, 4-1/2" h . . . . . . | - | - | 500.00 |

## Children's

| Item | Pink | Ultramarine |
|---|---|---|
| Creamer. . . . . . | 35.00 | 50.00 |
| Cup . . . . . . . . | 35.00 | 48.00 |
| Plate . . . . . . . . | 12.00 | 12.50 |
| Saucer . . . . . . . | 7.00 | 8.50 |
| Sugar . . . . . . . . | 35.00 | 50.00 |
| 14-pc set, orig box . . . | 400.00 | 425.00 |

# Early American Prescut

Manufactured by Anchor Hocking, Lancaster, Ohio, from 1960 and 1999. Made in crystal, with some limited production in colors.

*Early American Prescut, 11" d crystal cake plate.*

| Item | Crystal |
|---|---|
| Ashtray, 4" d | 4.00 |
| Ashtray, 5" d | 8.00 |
| Ashtray, 7-3/4" d. | 12.00 |
| Basket, 6" x 4-1/2" | 20.00 |
| Bowl, 4-1/4" d, plain rim | 20.00 |
| Bowl, 4-1/4" d, scalloped. | 7.50 |
| Bowl, 5-1/4" d, scalloped. | 7.50 |
| Bowl, 6-3/4" d, three legs | 5.00 |
| Bowl, 7-1/4" d, scalloped. | 20.00 |
| Bowl, 8-3/4" d. | 9.00 |
| Bowl, 9" d, oval. | 8.00 |
| Bowl, 11-3/4" d, paneled | 225.00 |
| Bud Vase, 5" h, ftd | 475.00 |
| Butter, cov, 1/4 lb. | 7.50 |
| Butter, cov, metal handle, knife | 15.00 |
| Cake plate | 25.00 |
| Candlesticks, pr, two-lite | 28.50 |
| Candy, cov, 5-1/4" | 12.00 |
| Candy, cov, 7-1/4" | 14.50 |
| Chip and dip, 10-1/4" bowl, metal holder | 25.00 |
| Coaster | 6.00 |
| Cocktail shaker, 30 oz | 300.00 |
| Console bowl, 9" d | 15.00 |
| Creamer. | 3.50 |
| Creamer and sugar tray | 3.00 |
| Cruet, os | 9.50 |
| Dessert bowl, 5-3/8" d. | 3.00 |
| Deviled egg plate, 11-3/4" d. | 42.00 |
| Gondola dish, 9-1/2" l. | 7.50 |
| Hostess tray, 6-1/2" x 12" | 14.00 |
| Iced tea tumbler, 15 oz, 6" h. | 20.00 |
| Juice tumbler, 5 oz, 4' h. | 5.00 |
| Lamp, oil | 315.00 |
| Lazy Susan, 9 pcs. | 60.00 |
| Pitcher, 18 oz. | 15.00 |
| Pitcher, 40 oz, sq | 60.00 |

| Item | Crystal |
|---|---|
| Pitcher, 60 oz. | 20.00 |
| Plate, 6-3/4" d, salad | 55.00 |
| Plate, 6-3/4" d, snack, ring for cup | 40.00 |
| Plate, 10" d, snack | 15.00 |
| Plate, 11" d. | 15.00 |
| Punch cup | 3.00 |
| Punch set, 15 pcs | 35.00 |
| Relish, two parts, 10" l, tab handle | 7.50 |
| Relish, three parts, 8-1/2" l, oval. | 6.50 |
| Relish, five parts, 13-1/2" d. | 30.00 |
| Salad bowl, 10-3/4" d | 15.00 |
| Salt and pepper shakers, pr, individual size | 72.00 |
| Salt and pepper shakers, pr, metal tops | 10.00 |
| Salt and pepper shakers, pr, plastic tops. | 12.00 |
| Serving plate, 11" d, four parts | 90.00 |
| Serving plate, 13-1/2" d | 15.00 |
| Sherbet, 6 oz | 90.00 |
| Snack cup | 3.00 |
| Sugar, cov. | 4.50 |
| Syrup pitcher, 12 oz. | 24.00 |
| Tumbler, 10 oz, 4-1/2" h. | 6.50 |
| Vase, 8-1/2" h. | 8.00 |
| Vase, 10" h. | 15.00 |

# English Hobnail

## Line #555

Manufactured by Westmoreland Glass Company, Grapeville, Pa., from the 1920s to 1983.

Made in amber, cobalt blue, crystal, crystal with various color treatments, green, ice blue, pink, red, and turquoise blue. Values for cobalt blue, red or turquoise blue pieces would be about 25 percent higher than ice blue values. Currently, a turquoise basket is valued at $150; a red basket at $100. Crystal pieces with a color accent would be slightly higher than crystal values.

**Reproductions:** † A creamer and sugar with a hexagonal foot have been reproduced, as well as a nut bowl and pickle dish.

English Hobnail, clear tumbler.

| Item | Amber | Crystal | Green | Ice Blue | Pink |
|---|---|---|---|---|---|
| Ashtray, 3" d | 20.00 | 20.00 | 22.00 | - | 22.00 |
| Ashtray, 4-1/2" d | 9.00 | 9.00 | 15.00 | 24.00 | 15.00 |
| Ashtray, 4-1/2" sq | 9.50 | 9.50 | 15.00 | - | 15.00 |
| Basket, 5" d, handle | 20.00 | 20.00 | - | - | - |
| Basket, 6" d, handle, tall | 40.00 | 40.00 | - | - | 43.00 |
| Bonbon, 6-1/2" h, handle | 15.00 | 17.50 | 30.00 | 40.00 | 30.00 |
| Bowl, 7" d, six parts | 17.50 | 17.50 | - | - | - |
| Bowl, 7" d, oblong spoon | 17.50 | 17.50 | - | - | - |
| Bowl, 8" d, ftd. | 30.00 | 30.00 | 48.00 | - | 48.00 |
| Bowl, 8" d, hexagonal foot, two handles | 38.00 | 38.00 | 75.00 | 115.00 | 75.00 |
| Bowl, 8", 6 pt | 24.00 | 24.00 | - | - | - |
| Bowl, 9-1/2" d, round, crimped | 30.00 | 30.00 | - | - | - |
| Bowl, 10" d, flared | 35.00 | 35.00 | 40.00 | - | 40.00 |

| Item | Amber | Crystal | Green | Ice Blue | Pink |
|---|---|---|---|---|---|
| Bowl, 10" l, oval, crimped | 40.00 | 40.00 | - | - | - |
| Bowl, 11" d, bell | 35.00 | 35.00 | - | - | - |
| Bowl, 11" d, rolled edge | 35.00 | 35.00 | 40.00 | 85.00 | 40.00 |
| Bowl, 12" d, flared | 32.00 | 32.00 | 40.00 | - | 95.00 |
| Bowl,12" l, oval crimped | 32.00 | 32.00 | - | - | - |
| Candelabra, two lite | 20.00 | 20.00 | - | - | - |
| Candlesticks, pr, 3-1/2" h, round base | 24.00 | 32.00 | 36.00 | - | 60.00 |
| Candlesticks, pr, 5-1/2" h, sq base | 30.00 | 32.00 | - | - | - |
| Candlesticks, pr, 9" h, round base | 50.00 | 40.00 | 72.00 | - | 125.00 |
| Candy dish, three feet | 45.00 | 38.00 | 50.00 | - | 50.00 |
| Candy dish, cov, 1/2 lb, cone shape | 45.00 | 40.00 | 55.00 | - | 90.00 |
| Celery, 12" l, oval | 24.00 | 45.00 | 36.00 | - | 36.00 |
| Celery, 9" d | 18.00 | 20.00 | 32.00 | - | 32.00 |
| Champagne, two ball, round foot | 8.00 | 7.00 | 20.00 | - | 20.00 |
| Chandelier, 17" shade, 200 prisms | 425.00 | 400.00 | - | - | - |
| Cheese, cov, 6" d | 40.00 | 42.00 | - | - | - |
| Cheese, cov, 8-3/4" d | 50.00 | 48.00 | - | - | - |
| Cigarette box, cov, 4-1/2 x 2-1/2" | 24.50 | 24.50 | 30.00 | - | 55.00 |
| Cigarette jar, cov, round | 16.00 | 18.00 | 25.00 | - | 65.00 |
| Claret, 5 oz, round | 15.00 | 17.50 | - | - | - |
| Coaster, 3" | 5.00 | 5.00 | - | - | - |
| Cocktail, 3 oz, round | 8.50 | 12.00 | - | - | 37.50 |
| Cocktail, 3-1/2 oz, round, ball | 15.00 | 17.50 | - | - | - |
| Compote, 5" d, round, round foot | 22.00 | 20.00 | 25.00 | - | 25.00 |
| Compote, 5" d, round, sq foot | 24.00 | 24.00 | - | - | - |
| Compote, 5-1/2" d, bell | 12.00 | 15.00 | - | - | - |
| Compote, 5-1/2" d, bell, sq foot | 20.00 | 20.00 | - | - | - |
| Console bowl, 12" d, flange | 30.00 | 30.00 | 40.00 | - | 40.00 |
| Cordial, 1 oz, round, ball | 16.50 | 17.50 | - | - | - |
| Cordial, 1 oz, round, foot | 16.50 | 16.50 | - | - | - |
| Cream soup bowl, 4-5/8" d | 15.00 | 15.00 | - | - | - |
| Cream soup liner, round, 6-1/2" d | 5.00 | 5.00 | - | - | - |
| Creamer, hexagonal foot † | 20.00 | 20.00 | 25.00 | - | 48.00 |
| Creamer, low, flat | 10.00 | 10.00 | - | - | - |
| Creamer, sq foot | 24.00 | 24.00 | 45.00 | - | 45.00 |
| Cruet, 12 oz | - | 25.00 | - | - | - |
| Cup | 8.00 | 12.00 | 18.00 | - | 25.00 |
| Decanter, 20 oz | 55.00 | 55.00 | - | - | - |
| Demitasse Cup | 17.50 | 17.50 | 55.00 | - | 55.00 |
| Dish, 6" d, crimped | 15.00 | 15.00 | - | - | - |
| Egg cup | 15.00 | 15.00 | - | - | - |
| Finger bowl, 4-1/2" d | 7.50 | 7.50 | 15.00 | 35.00 | 15.00 |
| Finger bowl, 4-1/2" sq, foot | 9.50 | 9.50 | 18.00 | 40.00 | 18.00 |
| Finger bowl liner, 6" sq | 6.50 | 7.00 | 20.00 | - | 20.00 |
| Finger bowl liner, 6-1/2" d, round | 12.00 | 12.00 | 10.00 | - | 10.00 |
| Ginger ale tumbler, 5 oz, flat | 10.00 | 10.00 | 18.00 | - | 20.00 |
| Ginger ale tumbler, 5 oz, round foot | 10.00 | 10.00 | - | - | - |
| Ginger ale tumbler, 5 oz, sq foot | 8.00 | 8.00 | 32.00 | - | 35.00 |
| Goblet, 8 oz, 6-1/4" h, round, water | 12.00 | 12.00 | - | 50.00 | 35.00 |
| Goblet, 8 oz, sq foot, water | 10.00 | 10.00 | - | - | 50.00 |
| Grapefruit bowl, 6-1/2" d | 12.00 | 12.00 | 22.00 | - | 24.00 |
| Hat, high | 18.00 | 18.00 | - | - | - |
| Hat, low | 15.00 | 15.00 | - | - | - |
| Honey compote, 6" d, round foot | 18.00 | 18.00 | 35.00 | - | 35.00 |
| Honey compote, 6" d, sq foot | 18.00 | 18.00 | - | - | - |
| Ice tub, 4" h | 18.00 | 18.00 | 50.00 | - | 85.00 |
| Ice tub, 5-1/2" h | 36.00 | 36.00 | 65.00 | - | 100.00 |
| Iced tea tumbler, 10 oz | 14.00 | 14.00 | 30.00 | - | 30.00 |

| Item | Amber | Crystal | Green | Ice Blue | Pink |
|---|---|---|---|---|---|
| Iced tea tumbler, 11 oz, round, ball | 12.00 | 12.00 | - | - | - |
| Iced tea tumbler, 11 oz, sq foot | 13.50 | 13.50 | - | - | - |
| Iced tea tumbler, 12-1/2 oz, round foot | 14.00 | 14.00 | - | - | - |
| Iced tea tumbler, 12 oz, flat | 14.00 | 14.00 | 32.00 | - | 32.00 |
| Icer, sq base, patterned insert | 45.00 | 45.00 | - | - | - |
| Ivy bowl, 6-1/2" d, sq foot, crimp top | 35.00 | 35.00 | - | - | - |
| Juice tumbler, 7 oz, round foot | 27.50 | 27.50 | - | - | - |
| Juice tumbler, 7 oz, sq foot | 6.50 | 6.50 | - | - | - |
| Lamp shade, 17" d | 175.00 | 165.00 | - | - | - |
| Lamp, 6-1/2" h, electric | 45.00 | 45.00 | 50.00 | - | 50.00 |
| Lamp, 9-1/2" d, electric | 45.00 | 45.00 | 115.00 | - | 115.00 |
| Lamp, candlestick | 32.00 | 32.00 | - | - | - |
| Marmalade, cov | 40.00 | 40.00 | 45.00 | - | 70.00 |
| Mayonnaise, 6" | 12.00 | 12.00 | 22.00 | - | 22.00 |
| Mustard, cov, sq, foot | 18.00 | 18.00 | - | - | - |
| Nappy, 4-1/2" d, round | 8.00 | 8.00 | 15.00 | 30.00 | 15.00 |
| Nappy, 4-1/2" w, sq. | 8.50 | 8.50 | - | - | - |
| Nappy, 5" d, round | 10.00 | 10.00 | 15.00 | 35.00 | 15.00 |
| Nappy, 5-1/2" d, bell | 12.00 | 12.00 | - | - | - |
| Nappy, 6" d, round | 10.00 | 10.00 | 17.50 | - | 17.50 |
| Nappy, 6" d, sq | 10.00 | 10.00 | 17.50 | - | 17.50 |
| Nappy, 6-1/2" d, round | 12.50 | 12.50 | 20.00 | - | 20.00 |
| Nappy, 6-1/2" d, sq | 14.00 | 14.00 | - | - | - |
| Nappy, 7" d, round | 14.00 | 14.00 | 24.00 | - | 24.00 |
| Nappy, 7-1/2" d, bell | 15.00 | 15.00 | - | - | - |
| Nappy, 8" d, cupped | 22.00 | 22.00 | 30.00 | - | 30.00 |
| Nappy, 8" d, round | 22.00 | 22.00 | 35.00 | - | 35.00 |
| Nappy, 9" d, bell | 25.00 | 25.00 | - | - | - |
| Nut, individual, ftd † | 6.00 | 6.00 | 14.50 | - | 14.50 |
| Oil bottle, 2 oz, handle | 25.00 | 25.00 | - | - | - |
| Oil bottle, 6 oz, handle | 27.50 | 27.50 | - | - | - |
| Old fashioned tumbler, 5 oz | 15.00 | 15.00 | - | - | - |
| Oyster cocktail, 5 oz, sq foot | 12.00 | 12.00 | 17.50 | - | 17.50 |
| Parfait, round foot | 17.50 | 17.50 | - | - | - |
| Pickle, 8" d † | 15.00 | 15.00 | - | - | - |
| Pitcher, 23 oz, rounded | 48.00 | 48.00 | 150.00 | - | 165.00 |
| Pitcher, 32 oz, straight side | 50.00 | 50.00 | 175.00 | - | 175.00 |
| Pitcher, 38 oz, rounded | 65.00 | 65.00 | 215.00 | - | 215.00 |
| Pitcher, 60 oz, rounded | 70.00 | 70.00 | 295.00 | - | 295.00 |
| Pitcher, 64 oz, straight side | 75.00 | 75.00 | 310.00 | - | 310.00 |
| Plate, 5-1/2" d, round | 7.00 | 7.00 | 10.00 | - | 10.00 |

*English Hobnail, crystal nappy with handle.*

| Item | Amber | Crystal | Green | Ice Blue | Pink |
|---|---|---|---|---|---|
| Plate, 6" w, sq. | 5.00 | 5.00 | - | - | - |
| Plate, 6-1/2" d, round | 6.25 | 6.25 | 10.00 | - | 10.00 |
| Plate, 6-1/2" d, round, depressed center | 6.00 | 6.00 | - | - | - |
| Plate, 8" d, round | 9.00 | 9.00 | 14.00 | - | 14.00 |
| Plate, 8" d, round, ftd | 13.00 | 13.00 | - | - | - |
| Plate, 8-1/2" d, plain edge | 9.00 | 9.00 | - | - | - |
| Plate, 8-1/2" d, round | 7.00 | 9.00 | 17.50 | - | 28.00 |
| Plate, 8-3/4" w, sq. | 9.25 | 9.25 | - | - | - |
| Plate, 10" d, round | 15.00 | 15.00 | 45.00 | - | 65.00 |
| Plate, 10" w, sq. | 15.00 | 15.00 | - | - | - |
| Plate, 10-1/2" d, round, grill | 18.00 | 18.00 | - | - | - |
| Plate, 12" w, sq. | 20.00 | 20.00 | - | - | - |
| Plate, 15" w, sq. | 28.00 | 28.00 | - | - | - |
| Preserve, 8" d. | 15.00 | 15.00 | - | - | - |
| Puff box, cov, 6" d, round | 20.00 | 20.00 | 47.50 | - | 80.00 |
| Punch bowl and stand | 215.00 | 215.00 | - | - | - |
| Punch cup | 7.00 | 7.00 | - | - | - |
| Relish, 8" d, three parts | 18.00 | 18.00 | - | - | - |
| Rose bowl, 4" d. | 17.50 | 17.50 | 48.00 | - | 50.00 |
| Rose bowl, 6" d. | 20.00 | 20.00 | - | - | - |
| Salt and pepper shakers, pr, round foot | 27.50 | 27.50 | 150.00 | - | 165.00 |
| Salt and pepper shakers, pr, sq, foot | 20.00 | 20.00 | - | - | - |
| Saucer, demitasse, round | 10.00 | 10.00 | 15.00 | - | 17.50 |
| Saucer, demitasse, sq | 10.00 | 10.00 | - | - | - |
| Saucer, round. | 2.00 | 2.00 | 6.00 | - | 6.00 |
| Saucer, sq | 2.00 | 2.00 | - | - | - |
| Sherbet, high, round foot | 7.00 | 7.00 | 18.00 | - | 37.50 |
| Sherbet, high, sq foot | 8.00 | 8.00 | 18.00 | - | - |
| Sherbet, high, two ball, round foot | 10.00 | 10.00 | - | - | - |
| Sherbet, low, one ball, round foot | 12.00 | 10.00 | - | - | 15.00 |
| Sherbet, low, round foot | 12.50 | 7.00 | - | - | - |
| Sherbet, low, sq foot | 6.50 | 6.00 | 15.00 | - | 17.50 |
| Straw jar, 10" h | 65.00 | 60.00 | - | - | - |
| Sundae. | 9.00 | 9.00 | - | - | - |
| Sugar, hexagonal, ftd † | 9.00 | 9.00 | 25.00 | - | 48.00 |
| Sugar, low, flat | 8.00 | 8.00 | 45.00 | - | - |
| Sugar, sq foot | 9.00 | 9.00 | 48.00 | - | 55.00 |
| Sweetmeat, 5-1/2" d, ball stem | 30.00 | 30.00 | - | - | - |
| Sweetmeat, 8" d, ball stem | 40.00 | 40.00 | 60.00 | - | 65.00 |
| Tidbit, two tiers | 27.50 | 27.50 | 65.00 | 85.00 | 80.00 |
| Toilet bottle, 5 oz | 25.00 | 25.00 | 40.00 | 65.00 | 40.00 |
| Torte plate, 14" d, round | 35.00 | 30.00 | 48.00 | - | 48.00 |
| Torte plate, 20-1/2" round | 55.00 | 50.00 | - | - | - |
| Tumbler, 8 oz, water | 10.00 | 10.00 | 24.00 | - | 24.00 |
| Tumbler, 9 oz, round, ball, water | 10.00 | 10.00 | - | - | - |
| Tumbler, 9 oz, round, ftd water | 10.00 | 10.00 | - | - | - |
| Tumbler, 9 oz, sq foot, water | 10.00 | 10.00 | - | - | - |
| Urn, cov, 11" h | 35.00 | 35.00 | 350.00 | - | 350.00 |
| Vase, 6-1/2" h, sq foot. | 24.00 | 24.00 | - | - | - |
| Vase, 7-1/2" h, flip | 27.50 | 27.50 | 70.00 | - | 70.00 |
| Vase, 7-1/2" h, flip jar with cov | 55.00 | 55.00 | 85.00 | - | 85.00 |
| Vase, 8" h, sq foot. | 35.00 | 35.00 | - | - | - |
| Vase, 8-1/2" h, flared top | 40.00 | 40.00 | 120.00 | - | 235.00 |
| Whiskey, 1-1/2 oz. | 10.00 | 10.00 | - | - | - |
| Whiskey, 3 oz. | 12.00 | 15.00 | - | - | - |
| Wine, 2 oz, round foot | 15.00 | 15.00 | - | - | - |
| Wine, 2 oz, sq ft. | 24.00 | 24.00 | 35.00 | - | 65.00 |
| Wine, 2-1/2 oz, ball, foot | 20.00 | 20.00 | - | - | - |

# Fairfax

## No.2375

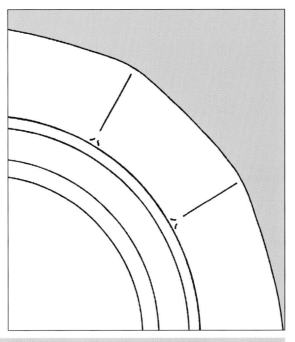

Manufactured by Fostoria Glass Company, Moundsville, Va., from 1927 to 1944. While this pattern is collected as Fairfax by many, the blanks were also used for some Fostoria etchings, such as June, Trojan, and Versailles. The values listed below are for the Fairfax pattern; expect to pay more for the etched patterns.

Made in amber, Azure blue, black, blue, green, orchid, rose, topaz, and wisteria, with limited production in ruby.

| Item | Amber | Azure Blue, Black, and Blue | Green | Orchid Rose, Wisteria | Topaz |
|---|---|---|---|---|---|
| After dinner cup and saucer | 15.00 | 30.00 | 18.00 | 30.00 | 18.00 |
| Ashtray, 2-1/2" d | 9.00 | 15.00 | 12.00 | 15.00 | 12.00 |
| Ashtray, 4" | 10.00 | 17.50 | 12.50 | 17.50 | 12.50 |
| Ashtray, 5-1/2" | 12.00 | 20.00 | 15.00 | 20.00 | 15.00 |
| Baker, oval, 9" l | 17.50 | 35.00 | 24.00 | 35.00 | 24.00 |
| Baker, oval, 10-1/2" l | 20.00 | 42.00 | 25.00 | 42.00 | 25.00 |
| Bonbon | 10.00 | 12.50 | 12.00 | 12.50 | 12.00 |
| Bouillon, ftd | 8.50 | 14.50 | 10.00 | 14.50 | 10.00 |
| Bowl, 7" d, three ftd | 10.00 | 15.00 | 14.00 | 15.00 | 14.00 |
| Bowl, 12" d | 22.00 | 42.00 | 24.00 | 42.00 | 24.00 |
| Bread plate, 12" d | 27.50 | 45.00 | 30.00 | 45.00 | 30.00 |
| Butter dish, cov | 80.00 | 140.00 | 100.00 | 140.00 | 100.00 |
| Cake plate, 10" d | 15.00 | 24.00 | 15.00 | 24.00 | 15.00 |
| Canapé plate | 12.00 | 20.00 | 15.00 | 20.00 | 15.00 |
| Candlesticks, pr, 3" h | 20.00 | 35.00 | 30.00 | 35.00 | 30.00 |
| Candy, cov, three parts | 40.00 | 65.00 | 50.00 | 65.00 | 50.00 |
| Candy, cov, ftd | 45.00 | 70.00 | 60.00 | 70.00 | 60.00 |
| Celery tray, 11-1/4" l | 12.00 | 25.00 | 17.50 | 25.00 | 17.50 |
| Centerpiece bowl, 12" d | 20.00 | 40.00 | 25.00 | 40.00 | 25.00 |
| Centerpiece bowl, 13" l, oval | 24.00 | 45.00 | 35.00 | 45.00 | 35.00 |
| Centerpiece bowl, 15" d | 27.50 | 48.00 | 37.50 | 48.00 | 40.00 |
| Cereal bowl, 6" d | 12.00 | 24.00 | 14.50 | 24.00 | 18.00 |
| Cheese and cracker set | 20.00 | 45.00 | 25.00 | 45.00 | 25.00 |
| Chop plate, 13" d | 15.00 | 25.00 | 17.50 | 25.00 | 17.50 |
| Cigarette box | 20.00 | 48.00 | 24.00 | 48.00 | 24.00 |
| Claret, 4 oz, 6" h | 25.00 | 40.00 | 35.00 | 40.00 | 35.00 |
| Cocktail, 3 oz, 5-1/4" h | 12.00 | 24.00 | 20.00 | 24.00 | 20.00 |
| Comport, 5" | 15.00 | 30.00 | 20.00 | 30.00 | 20.00 |
| Comport, 7" | 15.00 | 30.00 | 24.00 | 30.00 | 24.00 |
| Cordial, 3/4 oz, 4" h | 25.00 | 65.00 | 45.00 | 65.00 | 45.00 |
| Cream soup, ftd | 10.00 | 20.00 | 15.00 | 20.00 | 15.00 |
| Cream soup underplate | 5.00 | 8.00 | 5.00 | 8.00 | 5.00 |
| Creamer, flat | 12.00 | - | 15.00 | - | 15.00 |

| Item | Amber | Azure Blue, Black, and Blue | Green | Orchid Rose, Wisteria | Topaz |
|---|---|---|---|---|---|
| Creamer, ftd | 10.00 | 24.00 | 12.00 | 15.00 | 12.00 |
| Creamer, tea size | 9.00 | 18.50 | 12.50 | 18.50 | 12.50 |
| Cup, flat | 4.50 | - | 6.50 | - | 6.50 |
| Cup, ftd | 7.50 | 15.00 | 9.00 | 10.00 | 9.00 |
| Dessert bowl, large, handle | 15.00 | 40.00 | 24.00 | 40.00 | 24.00 |
| Flower holder, oval | 25.00 | 85.00 | 40.00 | 85.00 | 40.00 |
| Fruit bowl, 5" d | 8.00 | 15.00 | 9.00 | 15.00 | 9.00 |
| Goblet, 10 oz, 8-1/4" h | 17.50 | 32.00 | 22.00 | 35.00 | 22.00 |
| Grapefruit | 17.50 | 35.00 | 25.00 | 35.00 | 25.00 |
| Grapefruit liner | 15.00 | 32.00 | 20.00 | 32.00 | 22.00 |
| Ice bowl | 12.00 | 20.00 | 14.50 | 20.00 | 14.50 |
| Ice bowl liner | 12.00 | 22.00 | 12.00 | 22.00 | 14.50 |
| Ice bucket | 32.00 | 50.00 | 35.00 | 50.00 | 35.00 |
| Juice tumbler, 2-1/2 oz, ftd | 12.00 | 32.00 | 18.50 | 32.00 | 18.50 |
| Lemon bowl, two handles, ftd | 6.50 | 12.50 | 7.50 | 12.50 | 7.50 |
| Mayonnaise | 10.00 | 15.00 | 10.00 | 15.00 | 10.00 |
| Mayonnaise ladle | 20.00 | 30.00 | 24.00 | 30.00 | 24.00 |
| Mayonnaise underplate | 5.00 | 8.00 | 4.00 | 8.00 | 5.00 |
| Nappy, 8" d | 18.00 | 40.00 | 24.00 | 40.00 | 24.00 |
| Nut cup | 15.00 | 32.00 | 20.00 | 32.00 | 20.00 |
| Oil bottle, ftd, os | 85.00 | 150.00 | 110.00 | 150.00 | 110.00 |
| Pickle, 8-1/2" l | 10.00 | 25.00 | 15.00 | 25.00 | 15.00 |
| Pitcher | 115.00 | 200.00 | 145.00 | 200.00 | 145.00 |
| Plate, 6" d, bread and butter | 2.50 | 4.50 | 3.00 | 4.50 | 3.00 |
| Plate, 7-1/2" d, salad | 5.00 | 5.50 | 4.50 | 5.50 | 5.00 |
| Plate, 8-3/4" d, salad | 4.50 | 12.00 | 5.50 | 7.50 | 5.50 |
| Plate, 9-1/2" d, luncheon | 8.00 | 12.00 | 7.50 | 12.00 | 7.50 |
| Plate, 10-1/4" d, dinner | 18.00 | 40.00 | 30.00 | 40.00 | 30.00 |
| Plate, 10-1/4" d, grill | 17.50 | 40.00 | 27.50 | 40.00 | 27.50 |
| Platter, 10-1/2" l | 18.00 | 35.00 | 25.00 | 35.00 | 25.00 |
| Platter, 12" l | 20.00 | 40.00 | 32.00 | 40.00 | 32.00 |
| Platter, 15" l | 30.00 | 70.00 | 42.00 | 70.00 | 42.00 |
| Relish, three parts, 8-1/2" l | 12.00 | 22.00 | 14.00 | 22.00 | 14.00 |
| Relish, 11-1/2" l | 14.00 | 24.00 | 17.50 | 24.00 | 17.50 |
| Salad dressing bowl | 75.00 | 180.00 | 90.00 | 180.00 | 90.00 |
| Salt and pepper shakers, pr, ftd | 32.00 | 60.00 | 40.00 | 60.00 | 40.00 |
| Salt and pepper shakers, pr, individual size | 20.00 | - | 25.00 | - | 25.00 |
| Sauce boat and underplate | 30.00 | 65.00 | 38.00 | 65.00 | 40.00 |
| Saucer | 3.00 | 6.50 | 3.00 | 4.50 | 3.00 |
| Sherbet, 6 oz, 6" h | 10.00 | 20.00 | 12.50 | 20.00 | 12.50 |
| Soup bowl, 7" d | 18.00 | 40.00 | 24.00 | 40.00 | 24.00 |
| Sugar bowl, flat | 12.00 | - | 14.00 | - | 14.00 |
| Sugar bowl, ftd | 8.00 | 24.00 | 10.00 | 12.00 | 10.00 |
| Sugar bowl, tea size | 10.00 | 20.00 | 14.50 | 20.00 | 14.50 |
| Sugar bowl lid | 20.00 | 35.00 | 25.00 | 35.00 | 25.00 |
| Sugar pail | 25.00 | 60.00 | 40.00 | 60.00 | 40.00 |
| Sweetmeat | 12.00 | 17.50 | 15.00 | 17.50 | 15.00 |
| Tray, 11" d, center handle | 15.00 | 25.00 | 20.00 | 25.00 | 20.00 |
| Tumbler, 5 oz, 4-1/2" h, ftd | 10.00 | 17.50 | 12.00 | 17.50 | 12.00 |
| Tumbler, 9 oz, 5-1/4" h, ftd | 14.50 | 20.00 | 17.50 | 20.00 | 17.50 |
| Tumbler, 12 oz, 6", ftd | 17.50 | 27.50 | 25.00 | 27.50 | 25.00 |
| Vase, 8" h | 35.00 | 50.00 | 35.00 | 50.00 | 35.00 |
| Whipped cream pail | 25.00 | 55.00 | 40.00 | 55.00 | 40.00 |
| Whipped cream underplate | 9.00 | 12.00 | 10.00 | 12.00 | 10.00 |
| Wine, 3 oz, 5-1/2" h | 20.00 | 30.00 | 25.00 | 30.00 | 25.00 |

# Fire-King: Alice

Manufactured by Anchor Hocking Glass Co. Made in Jade-ite, white with blue trim, and white with red rim, early 1940s.

| Item | Jade-ite | White, blue trim | White, red trim |
| --- | --- | --- | --- |
| Cup | 8.00 | 12.00 | 15.00 |
| Cup and saucer | 12.00 | 15.00 | 20.00 |
| Plate, 9-1/2" d. | 25.00 | 28.00 | 30.00 |
| Saucer | 5.00 | 5.00 | 5.00 |

*Fire King Alice, Jade-ite cup and saucer.*

# Fire-King: Charm

Made by Anchor Hocking Glass Co. Made in Azure-ite and Jade-ite, 1950 to 1954.

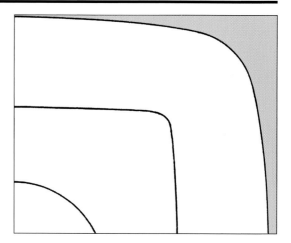

Fire King Charm, blue plate, cup and saucer.

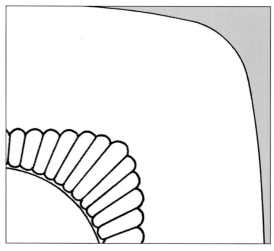

Fire King Charm, cup and saucer.

| Item | Azure-ite | Jade-ite |
|------|-----------|----------|
| Creamer | 6.50 | 17.00 |
| Cup | 4.50 | 15.00 |
| Cup and saucer | 6.00 | 15.00 |
| Dessert bowl, 4-3/4" d | 5.00 | 15.00 |
| Plate, 6-5/8" d, salad | 4.00 | 5.00 |
| Plate, 8-3/4" d, luncheon | 7.00 | 9.00 |
| Plate, 9-1/2" d, dinner | 20.00 | 25.00 |
| Platter, 11 x 8" | 15.00 | 30.00 |
| Salad bowl, 7-3/8" d | 15.00 | 30.00 |
| Saucer, 5-3/8" d | 2.50 | 3.50 |
| Soup bowl, 6" d | 20.00 | 24.00 |
| Sugar | 6.00 | 18.00 |

# Fire-King: Dinnerware

## *Jade-ite Restaurant Ware*

Made from 1950 to 1956 by Anchor Hocking.

*Fire-King Dinnerware, Jade-ite cup and saucer.*

| Item | Jade-ite |
|------|---------|
| Batter bowl | 45.00 |
| Bowl, 4-7/8" d | 15.00 |
| Bowl, 10 oz deep | 18.00 |
| Bowl, 15 oz, deep | 40.00 |
| Butter dish, cov | 150.00 |
| Cereal bowl, 8 oz, flanged rim | 28.00 |
| Chili bowl, 15 oz, 5-5/8" d, rolled rim | 24.00 |
| Coffee mug, 7 oz | 12.00 |
| Cup, 6 oz, straight | 10.00 |
| Cup, 7 oz, extra heavy | 12.00 |
| Cup, 7 oz, narrow rim | 10.00 |
| Demitasse cup and saucer | 85.00 |
| Egg cup, double | 65.00 |

| Item | Jade-ite |
|------|---------|
| Fruit bowl, 4-3/4" d | 8.50 |
| Plate, 5-1/2" d, bread and butter | 15.00 |
| Plate, 6-3/4" d, pie or salad | 18.00 |
| Plate, 8" d, luncheon | 20.00 |
| Plate, 8-7/8" d, oval, partitioned | 28.00 |
| Plate, 9" d, dinner | 24.00 |
| Plate, 9-3/4" l, oval, sandwich | 30.00 |
| Plate, 9-5/8" d, three sections | 24.00 |
| Plate, 9-5/8" d, five sections | 28.00 |
| Platter, 9-1/2" d, oval | 30.00 |
| Platter, 11-1/2" l, oval | 60.00 |
| Saucer, 6" d | 5.00 |

# Fire-King: Jane Ray

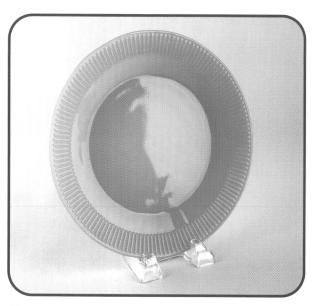

Made by Anchor Hocking in ivory, Jade-ite, Peach Lustre, white, and white with gold trim, from 1945 to 1963.

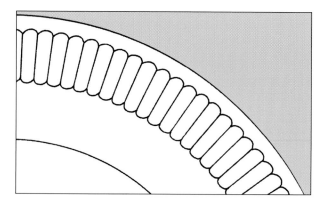

*Fire-King Jane Ray, Jade-ite plate.*

| Item | Ivory | Jade-ite | Peach Lustre | White |
|---|---|---|---|---|
| Berry bowl, 4-7/8" d | - | 12.00 | - | - |
| Cereal bowl | 8.00 | 30.00 | - | 8.00 |
| Chili bowl | 8.00 | 6.00 | - | 8.00 |
| Creamer | 9.00 | 10.00 | 15.00 | 9.00 |
| Cup | 5.00 | 7.00 | 6.00 | 5.00 |
| Cup, St. Denis | - | 7.50 | - | - |
| Demitasse cup | 18.00 | 45.00 | 30.00 | 18.00 |
| Demitasse saucer | 20.00 | 45.00 | 25.00 | 20.00 |
| Dessert bowl, 4-7/8" d | 4.00 | 7.50 | 6.00 | 4.00 |
| Egg cup, double | - | 18.50 | - | - |
| Mug | - | 8.00 | - | - |
| Oatmeal bowl, 5-7/8" d | 8.00 | 22.00 | - | 8.00 |
| Plate, 7-3/4" d, salad | 12.00 | 18.00 | 8.00 | 12.00 |
| Plate, 9-1/8" d, dinner | 15.00 | 20.00 | 10.00 | 15.00 |
| Platter, 9" x 12" | 15.00 | 35.00 | - | 15.00 |
| Saucer | 2.00 | 5.00 | 4.00 | 2.00 |
| Soup bowl | 8.00 | 35.00 | - | 8.00 |
| Soup plate, 7-5/8" d | 12.00 | 140.00 | 8.00 | 12.00 |
| Sugar, cov. | 15.00 | 42.00 | 15.00 | 15.00 |
| Sugar cover only | 5.00 | 6.00 | - | 5.00 |
| Sugar, no lid | 5.00 | 5.00 | - | 5.00 |
| Vegetable bowl, 8-1/4" d | 14.00 | 35.00 | - | 14.00 |

# Fire-King: Laurel Leaf

## Gray Laurel, Peach Lustre

Made from 1952 to 1963 by Anchor Hocking.

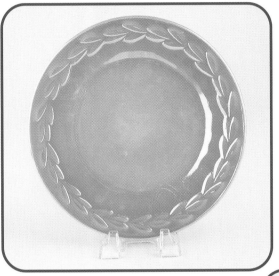

*Fire-King Peach Lustre, iridescent plate.*

**Reproductions:** †
Reproductions of the cup
and saucer have been found.

*Fire-King Peach Lustre, irides-cent sugar and creamer.*

| Item | Gray Laurel | Peach Lustre |
|---|---|---|
| Creamer | 10.00 | 8.00 |
| Cup † | 4.50 | 5.00 |
| Dessert bowl, 4-7/8" d | 7.00 | 5.00 |
| Plate, 7-3/8" d, salad | 7.00 | 6.50 |
| Plate, 9-1/8" d, dinner | 10.00 | 8.00 |
| Saucer, 5-3/4" d † | 2.00 | 1.50 |
| Serving plate, 11" d | 25.00 | 18.00 |
| Soup plate, 7-5/8" d | 15.00 | 10.00 |
| Sugar, ftd | 10.00 | 8.00 |
| Vegetable bowl, 8-1/4" d | 25.00 | 18.00 |

# Fire-King: Philbe

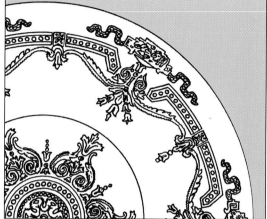

Made by Anchor Hocking Glass Co. in blue, crystal, green and pink, from 1937 to 1938.

*Fire-King Philbe, green creamer.*

| Item | Blue | Crystal | Green | Pink |
|---|---|---|---|---|
| Candy jar, cov, 4" d, low | 900.00 | 350.00 | 850.00 | 775.00 |
| Cereal bowl, 5-1/2" d | 70.00 | 25.00 | 45.00 | 45.00 |
| Cookie jar, cov | 1,850.00 | 650.00 | 995.00 | 995.00 |
| Creamer, 3-1/4", ftd | 145.00 | 50.00 | 135.00 | 135.00 |
| Cup | 160.00 | 85.00 | 115.00 | 115.00 |
| Goblet, 9 oz, 7-1/4" h | 225.00 | 80.00 | 175.00 | 175.00 |
| Iced tea tumbler, 15 oz, 6-1/2" h, ftd | 85.00 | 45.00 | 75.00 | 75.00 |
| Juice tumbler, 3-1/2" h, ftd | 175.00 | 45.00 | 150.00 | 150.00 |
| Pitcher, 36 oz, 6" h | 900.00 | 300.00 | 625.00 | 625.00 |
| Pitcher, 56 oz, 8-1/2" h | 1,450.00 | 625.00 | 1,200.00 | 1,200.00 |
| Plate, 6" d, sherbet | 75.00 | 35.00 | 60.00 | 60.00 |
| Plate, 8" d, luncheon | 50.00 | 22.00 | 40.00 | 40.00 |
| Plate, 10-1/2" d, grill | 75.00 | 25.00 | 65.00 | 65.00 |
| Platter, 12" l, closed handles | 200.00 | 65.00 | 175.00 | 175.00 |
| Refrigerator dish, 4" x 5" | 45.00 | - | - | - |
| Refrigerator dish, 5" x 9" | 50.00 | - | - | - |
| Salad bowl, 7-1/4" d | 85.00 | 30.00 | 50.00 | 50.00 |
| Salver, 10-1/2" d | 80.00 | 25.00 | 55.00 | 55.00 |
| Salver, 11-5/8" d | 95.00 | 25.00 | 65.00 | 65.00 |
| Sandwich plate, 10" d | 150.00 | 60.00 | 95.00 | 95.00 |
| Saucer, 6" d | 75.00 | 35.00 | 60.00 | 60.00 |
| Sugar, 3-1/4", ftd | 145.00 | 50.00 | 135.00 | 135.00 |
| Tumbler, 9 oz, 4" h, flat | 125.00 | 40.00 | 100.00 | 100.00 |
| Tumbler, 10 oz, 5-1/4" h | 95.00 | 35.00 | 75.00 | 75.00 |
| Vegetable bowl, 10" l, oval | 165.00 | 75.00 | 115.00 | 115.00 |

# Fire-King: Primrose

Manufactured by Anchor Hocking Glass Co., 1960 to 1962.

Made in white with a red, pink, and black floral decoration.

Fire-King Primrose, plate.

| Item | Decorated |
|---|---|
| Baking pan, 6-1/2" x 10-1/2" | 14.00 |
| Baking pan, 8" x 12-1/2" | 30.00 |
| Baking pan, cov, 5" x 9" | 18.00 |
| Cake pan, 8" d, round | 12.50 |
| Cake pan, 8" w, square | 12.50 |
| Casserole, cov, 1 pint | 9.50 |
| Casserole, cov, 1/2 quart, oval | 12.50 |
| Casserole, cov, 1 quart | 14.00 |
| Casserole, cov, 1-1/2 quart | 16.00 |
| Casserole, cov, 2 quart | 18.00 |
| Creamer | 5.00 |
| Cup, 8 oz | 3.50 |
| Custard cup | 3.50 |
| Dessert bowl, 4-5/8" d | 3.00 |

| Item | Decorated |
|---|---|
| Juice tumbler, 5 oz | 30.00 |
| Loaf pan, 5" x 9" | 15.00 |
| Plate, 7-3/8" d, salad | 5.00 |
| Plate, 9-1/8" d, dinner | 8.00 |
| Platter, 9" x 12" | 15.00 |
| Saucer, 5-3/4" d | 1.50 |
| Set, boxed, 19 pcs | 150.00 |
| Snack cup, 5 oz | 3.00 |
| Snack tray, 11" x 6" | 5.00 |
| Soup bowl, 6-5/8" d | 9.50 |
| Sugar, cov | 10.00 |
| Tumbler, 11 oz | 25.00 |
| Vegetable bowl, 8-1/4" d | 12.00 |

# Fire-King: Swirl

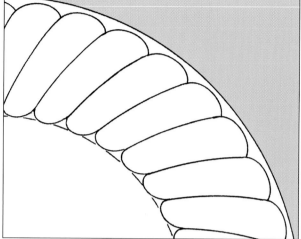

*Fire-King Swirl, pink plate.*

Made by Anchor Hocking Glass Co. in Azure-ite, ivory, ivory with gold trim, ivory with red trim, Jade-ite (1960s), pink, white, and white with gold trim,

| Item | Azure-ite | Ivory | Jade-ite | Pink | White | White/trim |
|------|-----------|-------|----------|------|-------|------------|
| Cereal bowl, 6-3/8" d | - | - | 16.00 | - | - | - |
| Creamer, flat | 6.00 | 4.00 | - | 9.00 | 4.50 | - |
| Creamer, ftd | - | 5.00 | 12.00 | - | 5.00 | 6.00 |
| Cup | 6.50 | 6.00 | 6.00 | 7.00 | 3.00 | 3.50 |
| Fruit or dessert bowl, 4-7/8" | 4.60 | 3.00 | 5.00 | 4.60 | 4.00 | 8.00 |
| Iced tea tumbler, 12 oz | 7.00 | - | - | 7.00 | - | - |
| Juice tumbler, 1 oz | 5.00 | - | - | 5.00 | - | - |
| Mixing bowl, 6" d | - | 8.00 | 12.00 | - | 9.00 | - |
| Mixing bowl, 7" d | - | 15.00 | 14.00 | - | 12.00 | - |
| Mixing bowl, 9" d | - | 18.00 | 16.00 | - | 16.00 | - |
| Plate, 7-1/8" d, salad | 8.00 | 6.50 | 12.00 | 8.00 | 6.50 | 10.00 |
| Plate, 9-1/8" d, dinner | 9.50 | 6.00 | 50.00 | 21.00 | 5.00 | 15.00 |
| Platter, 12" x 9" | 22.00 | 7.00 | - | 18.00 | 7.00 | 20.00 |
| Saucer, 5-3/4" d | 2.50 | 3.50 | 2.00 | 4.00 | 2.00 | 7.50 |
| Serving plate, 11" d | 18.00 | - | - | 20.00 | - | - |
| Soup plate, 7-5/8" d | 9.00 | 12.00 | 8.50 | 14.00 | 5.00 | 6.50 |
| Sugar lid for flat sugar | 6.00 | 3.00 | - | 6.00 | 3.00 | - |
| Sugar lid for ftd sugar | - | 3.00 | 20.00 | - | 3.00 | - |
| Sugar, flat, tab handles | 6.50 | 4.00 | - | 6.50 | 4.00 | - |
| Sugar, ftd, open handles | - | 3.50 | 30.00 | - | 4.00 | 6.00 |
| Tumbler, 9 oz, water | 15.00 | - | - | 15.00 | - | - |
| Vegetable bowl, 7-1/4" d | 15.00 | - | - | 15.00 | - | - |
| Vegetable bowl, 8-1/4" d | 15.00 | - | 18.00 | 15.00 | 7.50 | 15.00 |

# Fire-King: Turquoise Blue

Made from 1957 to 1958 by Anchor Hocking.

Fire-King Turquoise Blue, snack set in original box.

Fire-King Turquoise Blue, snack plate with indent for cup

| Item | Turquoise Blue |
|---|---|
| Ashtray, 3-1/2" d | 7.50 |
| Ashtray, 4-5/8" d | 8.50 |
| Ashtray, 5-3/4" d | 12.00 |
| Batter bowl, spout | 200.00 |
| Berry bowl, 4-1/2" d | 10.00 |
| Cereal bowl, 5" d | 15.00 |
| Creamer | 10.00 |
| Cup | 5.00 |
| Egg plate, 9-3/4" d | 18.00 |
| Mixing bowl, 1 pt, tear | 15.00 |
| Mixing bowl, 1 qt, round | 18.00 |
| Mixing bowl, 1 qt, tear | 20.00 |
| Mixing bowl, 2 qt, round | 24.00 |
| Mixing bowl, 2 qt, tear | 28.00 |

| Item | Turquoise Blue |
|---|---|
| Mixing bowl, 3 qt, round | 30.00 |
| Mixing bowl, 3 qt, tear | 30.00 |
| Mixing bowl, 4 qt, round | 35.00 |
| Mug, 8 oz | 15.00 |
| Plate, 6-1/8" d | 12.50 |
| Plate, 7" d | 12.00 |
| Plate, 9" d | 8.00 |
| Plate, 9" d, cup indent | 7.50 |
| Plate, 10" d, dinner | 30.00 |
| Relish, 11-1/8" l, three parts | 15.00 |
| Saucer | 2.00 |
| Soup/salad bowl, 6-5/8" ftd | 24.00 |
| Sugar | 10.00 |
| Vegetable bowl, 8" d | 18.00 |

# Floragold

Manufactured by Jeannette Glass Company, Jeannette, Pa., 1950s.

Made in iridescent. Some large comports were later made in ice blue, crystal, red-yellow, and shell pink.

*Floragold, iridescent plate and ruffled berry bowl.*

| Item | Iridescent |
| --- | --- |
| Ashtray, 4" d | 10.00 |
| Bowl, 4-1/2" sq | 6.50 |
| Bowl, 5-1/4" d, ruffled | 16.00 |
| Bowl, 8-1/2" d, sq | 22.00 |
| Bowl, 8-1/2" d, ruffled | 14.00 |
| Butter dish, cov, 1/4 pound, oblong | 30.00 |
| Butter dish, cov, round, 5-1/2" w sq base | 800.00 |
| Butter dish, cov, round, 6-1/4" w sq base | 55.00 |
| Candlesticks, pr, double branch | 60.00 |
| Candy dish, one handle | 16.50 |
| Candy or cheese dish, cov, 6-3/4" d | 130.00 |
| Candy, 5-3/4" l, four feet | 12.00 |
| Celery vase | 420.00 |
| Cereal bowl, 5-1/2" d, round | 40.00 |
| Coaster, 4" d | 10.00 |
| Comport, 5-1/4", plain top | 795.00 |
| Comport, 5-1/4", ruffled top | 895.00 |
| Creamer | 21.00 |
| Cup | 8.00 |
| Fruit bowl, 5-1/2" d, ruffled | 8.50 |

| Item | Iridescent |
| --- | --- |
| Fruit bowl, 12" d, ruffled, large | 15.00 |
| Nappy, 5" d, one handle | 12.00 |
| Pitcher, 64 oz | 45.00 |
| Plate, 5-1/4" d, sherbet | 15.00 |
| Plate, 8-1/2" d, dinner | 40.00 |
| Platter, 11-1/4" d | 30.00 |
| Salad bowl, 9-1/2" d, deep | 42.50 |
| Salt and pepper shakers, pr, plastic tops | 60.00 |
| Saucer, 5-1/4" d | 12.00 |
| Sherbet, low, ftd | 16.00 |
| Sugar | 22.00 |
| Sugar lid | 15.00 |
| Tidbit, wooden post | 35.00 |
| Tray, 13-1/2" d | 75.00 |
| Tray, 13-1/2" d, with indent | 65.00 |
| Tumbler, 11 oz, ftd | 20.00 |
| Tumbler, 10 oz, ftd | 20.00 |
| Tumbler, 15 oz, ftd | 110.00 |
| Vase | 420.00 |

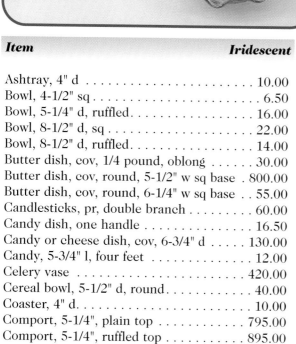

# Floral

## Poinsettia

Manufactured by Jeannette Glass Company, Jeannette, Pa., from 1931 to 1935.

Made in amber, crystal, Delphite, green, Jad-ite, pink, red, and yellow. Production in amber, crystal, red, and yellow was limited. A crystal 6-7/8" h vase would be valued at $295.

**Reproductions:** † Reproduction salt and pepper shakers have been made in cobalt blue, dark green, green, pink and red.

| Item | Delphite | Green | Jad-ite | Pink |
|---|---|---|---|---|
| Berry bowl, 4" d | 50.00 | 25.00 | - | 25.00 |
| Butter dish, cov | - | 95.00 | - | 90.00 |
| Candlesticks, pr, 4" h | - | 90.00 | - | 95.00 |
| Candy jar, cov | 80.00 | 45.00 | - | 45.00 |
| Canister set | - | - | 60.00 | - |
| Casserole, cov | - | 45.00 | - | 28.00 |
| Coaster, 3-1/4" d | - | 15.00 | - | - |
| Comport, 9" | - | 875.00 | - | 795.00 |
| Cream soup, 5-1/2" d | - | 735.00 | - | 735.00 |
| Creamer, flat | - | 24.00 | - | 24.00 |
| Cup | - | 15.00 | - | 15.00 |
| Dresser set | - | 1,350.00 | - | - |
| Dresser tray, 9-1/4" l, oval | - | 200.00 | - | - |
| Flower frog | - | 695.00 | - | - |
| Ice tub, 3-1/2" h, oval | - | 850.00 | - | 825.00 |
| Juice tumbler, ftd | - | 28.00 | - | 27.50 |
| Juice tumbler, 5 oz, 4" h, flat | - | 35.00 | - | 35.00 |
| Lamp | - | 295.00 | - | 260.00 |
| Lemonade pitcher, 48 oz, 10-1/4" h | - | 295.00 | - | 350.00 |
| Lemonade tumbler, 9 oz, 5-1/4" h, ftd | - | 60.00 | - | 55.00 |
| Pitcher, 23 or 24 oz, 5-1/2" h | - | 595.00 | - | - |
| Pitcher, 32 oz, ftd, cone, 8" h | - | 45.00 | - | 60.00 |
| Plate, 6" d, sherbet | - | 8.50 | - | 8.50 |
| Plate, 8" d, salad | - | 15.00 | - | 17.00 |
| Plate, 9" d, dinner | 145.00 | 30.00 | - | 27.50 |
| Plate, 9" d, grill | - | 185.00 | - | - |
| Plate, 10-3/4" l, oval | - | 20.00 | - | 17.50 |
| Platter, 11" l | 150.00 | 30.00 | - | 30.00 |
| Refrigerator dish, cov, 5" sq | - | - | 15.00 | - |
| Relish, two parts, oval | 165.00 | 24.00 | - | 20.00 |

| Item | Delphite | Green | Jad-ite | Pink |
|---|---|---|---|---|
| Rose bowl, three legs . . . . . . . . . . . . . . . . . . - | | 500.00 | - | - |
| Salad bowl, 7-1/2" d . . . . . . . . . . . . . . . . . - | | 40.00 | - | 40.00 |
| Salad bowl, 7-1/2" d, ruffled . . . . . . . . . . . 65.00 | | 125.00 | - | 120.00 |
| Salt and pepper shakers, pr, 4" h, ftd † . . . . . . - | | 60.00 | - | 50.00 |
| Salt and pepper shakers, pr, 6" flat . . . . . . . . - | | - | - | 60.00 |
| Saucer . . . . . . . . . . . . . . . . . . . . . . . . . . - | | 12.50 | - | 12.50 |
| Sherbet . . . . . . . . . . . . . . . . . . . . . . . . . 90.00 | | 20.00 | - | 20.00 |
| Sugar, cov . . . . . . . . . . . . . . . . . . . . . . . - | | 32.00 | - | 35.00 |
| Sugar, open . . . . . . . . . . . . . . . . . . . . . . 75.00 | | - | - | - |
| Tray, 6" sq, closed handles . . . . . . . . . . . . . - | | 195.00 | - | - |
| Tumbler, 3 oz, 3-1/2" h, ftd . . . . . . . . . . . . . - | | 18.00 | - | 25.00 |
| Tumbler, 7 oz, 4-1/2", ftd . . . . . . . . . . . . 175.00 | | 25.00 | - | 25.00 |
| Tumbler, 5-1/4" h, ftd . . . . . . . . . . . . . . . . . - | | 60.00 | - | 55.00 |
| Vase, flared, three legs . . . . . . . . . . . . . . . . - | | 485.00 | - | - |
| Vase, 6-7/8" h . . . . . . . . . . . . . . . . . . . . . - | | 475.00 | - | - |
| Vegetable bowl, 8" d, cov . . . . . . . . . . . . . . - | | 50.00 | - | 65.00 |
| Vegetable bowl, 8" d, open . . . . . . . . . . . 80.00 | | - | - | 40.00 |
| Vegetable bowl, 9" l, oval . . . . . . . . . . . . . . - | | 35.00 | - | 35.00 |

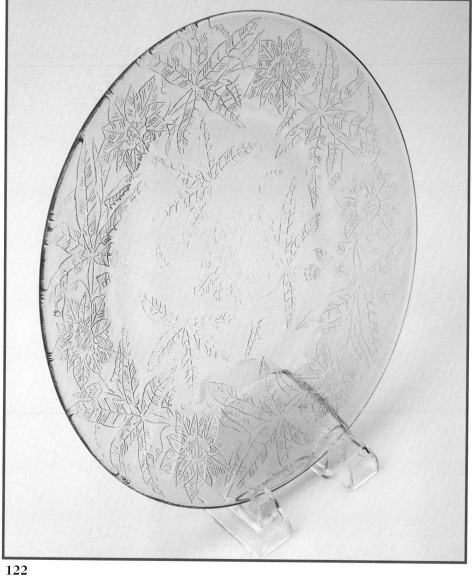

*Floral, pink plate.*

# Floral and Diamond Band

Manufactured by U.S. Glass Company, Pittsburgh, Pa., in the late 1920s.

Made in pink and green with limited production in black, crystal, and iridescent.

*Floral and Diamond Band, green plate.*

| Item | Green | Pink |
|---|---|---|
| Berry bowl, 4-1/2" d | 12.00 | 15.00 |
| Berry bowl, 8" d | 15.00 | 18.00 |
| Butter dish, cov | 140.00 | 175.00 |
| Compote, 5-1/2" h | 18.00 | 17.50 |
| Creamer, 4-3/4" | 20.00 | 17.50 |
| Iced tea tumbler, 5" h | 45.00 | 50.00 |

| Item | Green | Pink |
|---|---|---|
| Nappy, 5-3/4" d, handle | 12.00 | 11.00 |
| Pitcher, 42 oz, 8" h | 95.00 | 90.00 |
| Plate, 8" d, luncheon | 40.00 | 40.00 |
| Sherbet | 8.00 | 9.50 |
| Sugar, 5-1/4" | 15.00 | 15.00 |
| Tumbler, 4" h, water | 25.00 | 25.00 |

# Florentine No. 1

Manufactured by Hazel Atlas Glass Company, Clarksburg, W.V., and Zanesville, Ohio, from 1932 to 1935.

Made in crystal, green, pink, yellow, and limited production in cobalt blue.

**Reproductions:** † Salt and pepper shakers have been reproduced in cobalt blue, pink, and red.

*Florentine No. 1, green creamer and covered sugar.*

| Item | Cobalt Blue | Crystal | Green | Pink | Yellow |
|---|---|---|---|---|---|
| Ashtray, 5-1/2" d | - | 24.00 | 24.00 | 28.00 | 28.00 |
| Berry bowl, 5" d | 24.00 | 12.00 | 12.00 | 15.00 | 15.00 |
| Berry bowl, 8-1/2" d | - | 24.00 | 25.00 | 28.00 | 28.00 |
| Butter dish, cov | - | 110.00 | 115.00 | 165.00 | 160.00 |
| Cereal bowl, 6" d | - | 32.00 | 32.00 | 35.00 | 35.00 |
| Coaster/ashtray, 3-3/4" d | - | 18.00 | 20.00 | 25.00 | 25.00 |
| Comport, 3-1/2" h, ruffled | 60.00 | 25.00 | 25.00 | 15.00 | - |
| Cream soup, 5" d, ruffled | 50.00 | 12.00 | 14.00 | 20.00 | - |
| Creamer | - | 10.00 | 12.00 | 25.00 | 20.00 |
| Creamer, ruffled | 65.00 | 45.00 | 35.00 | 37.00 | - |
| Cup | 85.00 | 10.00 | 8.00 | 12.00 | 10.00 |
| Iced tea tumbler, 12 oz, 5-1/4" h, ftd | - | 28.00 | 28.00 | 30.00 | 24.00 |
| Juice tumbler, 5 oz, 3-3/4" h, ftd | - | 16.00 | 16.00 | 20.00 | 22.00 |
| Lemonade tumbler, 9 oz, 5-1/4" h | - | - | - | 100.00 | - |
| Pitcher, 36 oz, 6-1/2", ftd | 850.00 | 45.00 | 45.00 | 65.00 | 50.00 |
| Pitcher, 48 oz, 7-1/2", flat, with or without ice lip | - | 75.00 | 75.00 | 135.00 | 195.00 |
| Plate, 6" d, sherbet | - | 7.50 | 9.00 | 7.50 | 9.00 |
| Plate, 8-1/2" d, salad | - | 8.00 | 10.00 | 12.00 | 12.00 |
| Plate, 10" d, dinner | - | 16.00 | 16.00 | 22.00 | 24.00 |
| Plate, 10" d, grill | - | 12.00 | 12.50 | 20.00 | 22.00 |
| Platter, 11-1/2" l, oval | - | 19.00 | 10.00 | 22.00 | 28.00 |
| Salt and pepper shakers, pr, ftd † | - | 22.00 | 32.00 | 55.00 | 58.00 |
| Saucer | 18.00 | 3.50 | 3.50 | 4.00 | 3.00 |
| Sherbet, 3 oz, ftd | - | 10.00 | 10.00 | 13.00 | 16.00 |
| Sugar, cov | - | 10.00 | 12.50 | 25.00 | 12.00 |
| Sugar, ruffled | 55.00 | 35.00 | 30.00 | 42.50 | - |
| Tumbler, 4 oz, 3-1/4" h, ftd | - | 15.00 | 16.00 | - | - |
| Tumbler, 9 oz, 4" h, ribbed | - | 14.00 | 14.00 | 22.00 | - |
| Tumbler, 10 oz, 4-3/4" h, ftd | - | 22.00 | 20.00 | 22.00 | 24.00 |
| Vegetable bowl, cov, 9-1/2" l, oval | - | 42.00 | 42.00 | 60.00 | 60.00 |

# Florentine No.2

## Poppy No. 2

Manufactured by Hazel Atlas Glass Company, Clarksburg, W.V., and Zanesville, Ohio, from 1932 to 1935.

Made in amber, cobalt blue, crystal, green, ice blue, pink, and yellow. Ice blue production is limited to 7-1/2" h pitcher, valued at $525. Amber production is limited to 9 oz and 12 oz tumblers, both currently valued at $80; cup and saucer, valued at $75; and sherbet, valued at $45. Cobalt blue production is limited to 3-1/2" comport, valued at $60, and 9 oz tumbler, valued at $80.

**Reproductions:** † 7-1/2" h cone-shaped pitcher and 4" h footed tumbler. Reproductions are found in amber, cobalt blue, crystal, deep green, and pink.

| Item | Crystal | Green | Pink | Yellow |
|---|---|---|---|---|
| Ashtray, 3-1/2" d | 18.50 | 18.50 | - | 25.00 |
| Ashtray, 5-1/2" d | 20.00 | 25.00 | - | 35.00 |
| Berry bowl, 4-1/2" d | 14.50 | 16.50 | 17.50 | 22.50 |
| Berry bowl, 8" d | 24.00 | 26.00 | 30.00 | 35.00 |
| Bowl, 5-1/2" d | 32.00 | 35.00 | - | 42.00 |
| Bowl, 7-1/2" d, shallow | - | - | - | 85.00 |
| Bowl, 9" d, flat | 27.50 | 27.50 | - | - |
| Butter dish, cov | 115.00 | 125.00 | - | 165.00 |
| Candlesticks, pr, 2-3/4" h | 45.00 | 48.00 | - | 70.00 |
| Candy dish, cov | 110.00 | 100.00 | 150.00 | 165.00 |
| Cereal bowl, 6" d | 28.00 | 28.00 | - | 40.00 |
| Coaster, 3-1/4" d | - | - | - | 25.00 |
| Coaster, 3-3/4" d | 18.50 | 18.50 | - | 25.00 |
| Coaster, 5-1/2" d | 20.00 | 25.00 | - | 35.00 |
| Cocktail, 3-1/4" h, ftd | - | - | - | 14.50 |
| Comport, 3-1/2" d, ruffled | 25.00 | 25.00 | 25.00 | - |
| Condiment tray, round | - | - | - | 65.00 |
| Cream soup, 4-3/4" d, two handles | 16.50 | 16.00 | 18.50 | 20.00 |
| Creamer | 8.00 | 12.00 | - | 14.50 |
| Cup | 7.50 | 8.00 | - | 12.00 |
| Custard cup | 60.00 | 60.00 | - | 85.00 |
| Gravy boat | - | - | - | 65.00 |
| Gravy boat underplate, 11-1/2" l | - | - | - | 115.00 |
| Iced tea tumbler, 12 oz, 5" h | 35.00 | 35.00 | - | 45.00 |
| Juice tumbler, 5 oz, 3-1/8" h, flat | 14.50 | 14.50 | 14.50 | 22.00 |

| Item | Crystal | Green | Pink | Yellow |
|---|---|---|---|---|
| Juice tumbler, 5 oz, 3-1/8" h, ftd | 13.00 | 15.00 | - | 21.00 |
| Parfait, 6" h | 30.00 | 32.00 | - | 65.00 |
| Pitcher, 24 oz, cone, ftd, 6-1/4" h | - | - | - | 35.00 |
| Pitcher, 28 oz, cone ftd, 7-1/2" h † | 60.00 | 40.00 | - | 50.00 |
| Pitcher, 48 oz, 7-1/2" h | 60.00 | 70.00 | 120.00 | 32.00 |
| Pitcher, 76 oz, 8-1/4" h | 90.00 | 95.00 | 225.00 | 400.00 |
| Plate, 6" d, sherbet | 6.00 | 6.00 | - | 7.50 |
| Plate, 6-1/2" d, indent | 16.00 | 17.50 | - | 30.00 |
| Plate, 8-1/2" d, salad | 8.50 | 9.50 | 9.00 | 10.00 |
| Plate, 10" d, dinner | 16.50 | 16.00 | - | 19.00 |
| Plate, 10-1/4" d, grill | 15.00 | 15.00 | - | 14.50 |
| Plate, 10-1/4" d, grill, cream soup ring | 35.00 | 35.00 | - | - |
| Platter, 11" oval | 15.00 | 16.00 | 18.50 | 24.00 |
| Relish, 10" d, divided, three parts | 22.50 | 24.00 | 26.00 | 32.00 |
| Relish, 10" d, plain | 22.50 | 24.00 | 26.00 | 32.00 |
| Salt and pepper shakers, pr | 48.00 | 48.00 | - | 65.00 |
| Saucer | 5.00 | 4.00 | - | 3.50 |
| Sherbet, ftd | 10.00 | 12.50 | - | 14.50 |
| Sugar, cov | 8.50 | 9.00 | - | 38.00 |
| Tumbler, 5 oz, 3-1/4" h, ftd | 18.00 | 15.00 | 15.00 | - |
| Tumbler, 5 oz, 4" h, ftd † | 15.00 | 15.00 | 18.00 | 20.00 |
| Tumbler, 5 oz, 3-5/16" h, blown | 18.50 | 18.50 | - | - |
| Tumbler, 6 oz, 3-9/16" h, blown | 16.00 | 18.50 | - | - |
| Tumbler, 9 oz, 4" h | 14.50 | 18.50 | 16.00 | 22.50 |
| Tumbler, 9 oz, 4-1/2" h, ftd | 25.00 | 25.00 | - | 38.00 |
| Tumbler, 10 oz, 4-11/16, blown | 19.00 | 19.00 | - | - |
| Tumbler, 12 oz, 5" h, blown | 20.00 | 20.00 | - | 20.00 |
| Vase, 6" h | 30.00 | 32.00 | - | 65.00 |
| Vegetable bowl, cov, 9" l, oval | 55.00 | 60.00 | - | 85.00 |

*Florentine No. 2, yellow cup.*

*REPRODUCTION! Florentine No. 2, green pitcher and tumbler.*

# Flower Garden with Butterflies

## Butterflies and Roses

Manufactured by U.S. Glass Company, Pittsburgh, Pa., in the late 1920s.

Made in amber, black, blue, blue-green, canary yellow, crystal, green, and pink.

| Item | Amber or Crystal | Black | Blue-Green, Green or Pink | Blue or Canary Yellow |
|---|---|---|---|---|
| Ashtray | 175.00 | - | 185.00 | 225.00 |
| Bonbon, cov, 6-5/8" d | - | 265.00 | - | - |
| Bowl, 9" d, rolled edge | - | 225.00 | - | - |
| Candlesticks, pr, 4" h | 50.00 | - | 60.00 | 100.00 |
| Candlesticks, pr, 8" h | 90.00 | 325.00 | 145.00 | 145.00 |
| Candy, cov, 6" d, flat | 135.00 | - | 165.00 | - |
| Candy, cov, 7-1/2" cone shape | 90.00 | 100.00 | 165.00 | 175.00 |
| Candy, cov, heart shape | - | - | 1,250.00 | 1,500.00 |
| Cologne bottle, 7-1/2" h | - | - | 225.00 | 365.00 |
| Comport, 2-7/8" h | - | 250.00 | 40.00 | 45.00 |
| Comport, 3" h | 25.00 | - | 30.00 | 35.00 |
| Comport, 4-1/4" h, 4-3/4" w | - | - | - | 65.00 |
| Comport, 4-3/4" h, 10-1/4" w | 50.00 | 250.00 | 70.00 | 90.00 |
| Comport, 5-7/8" h, 11" w | 60.00 | - | - | 95.00 |
| Comport, 7-1/4" h, 8-1/4" w | 65.00 | 175.00 | 85.00 | - |
| Creamer | - | - | 75.00 | - |
| Cup | - | - | 70.00 | - |

*Flower Garden with Butterflies, blue compote.*

| Item | Amber or Crystal | Black | Blue-Green, Green or Pink | Blue or Canary Yellow |
|---|---|---|---|---|
| Mayonnaise, ftd, 4-3/4" h, 6-1/4" w, 7" d plate, ladle | 70.00 | - | 95.00 | 145.00 |
| Orange bowl, 11" d, ftd | - | 250.00 | - | - |
| Plate, 7" d | 20.00 | - | 25.00 | 30.00 |
| Plate, 8" d | 17.50 | - | 20.00 | 27.50 |
| Plate, 10" d | - | - | 45.00 | 50.00 |
| Plate, 10" d, indent | 35.00 | 150.00 | 45.00 | 50.00 |
| Powder jar, 3-1/2", flat | - | - | 75.00 | - |
| Powder jar, 6-1/4" h, ftd | 225.00 | - | 130.00 | 175.00 |
| Powder jar, 7-1/2" h, ftd | 85.00 | - | 135.00 | 195.00 |
| Sandwich server, center handle | 55.00 | 135.00 | 75.00 | 100.00 |
| Saucer | - | - | 30.00 | - |
| Tray, 5-1/2" x 10", oval | 50.00 | - | 75.00 | 9.00 |
| Tray, 11-3/4" x 7-3/4", rect | 50.00 | - | 75.00 | 90.00 |
| Tumbler, 7-1/2 oz | 175.00 | - | - | - |
| Vase, 6-1/4" h | 75.00 | 145.00 | 135.00 | 145.00 |
| Vase, 8" h, Dahlia, cupped | - | 275.00 | - | - |
| Vase, 10" h, two handles | - | 250.00 | - | - |
| Vase, 10-1/2" h | - | - | 150.00 | 225.00 |
| Wall pocket, 9" l | - | 365.00 | - | - |

# *Forest Green*

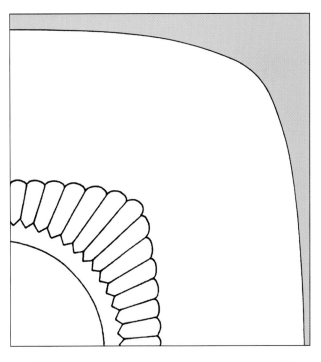

Manufactured by Anchor Hocking Glass Company, Lancaster, Ohio, and Long Island City, N.Y., from 1950 to 1957. Made only in forest green.

| Item | Forest Green |
|---|---|
| Ashtray, 3-1/2" sq | 5.00 |
| Ashtray, 4-5/8" sq | 5.50 |
| Ashtray, 5-3/4" hexagon | 8.00 |
| Ashtray, 5-3/4" sq | 7.50 |
| Batter bowl, spout | 25.00 |
| Berry bowl, large | 15.00 |
| Berry bowl, small | 7.50 |
| Bonbon, 6-1/4" w, tricorn | 12.00 |
| Bowl, 4-1/2" w, sq | 7.00 |
| Bowl, 5-1/4" deep | 8.50 |
| Bowl, 6" w, sq | 18.00 |
| Bowl, 6-1/2" d, scalloped | 9.00 |
| Bowl, 6-3/8" d, three toes | 15.00 |
| Bowl, 7-3/8" w, sq | 30.00 |
| Bowl, 7-1/2" d, crimped | 10.00 |
| Cocktail, 3-1/2 oz | 12.00 |
| Cocktail, 4-1/2 oz | 14.00 |
| Creamer, flat | 7.50 |
| Cup, sq | 7.00 |
| Dessert bowl, 4-3/4" d | 7.00 |
| Goblet, 9 oz | 10.00 |
| Goblet, 9-1/2 oz | 14.00 |
| Iced tea tumbler, 13 oz | 8.00 |
| Iced tea tumbler, 14 oz, Boopie | 8.00 |
| Iced tea tumbler, 15 oz, tall | 10.00 |
| Iced tea tumbler, 32 oz, giant | 18.00 |
| Ivy ball, 4" h | 5.00 |
| Juice tumbler, 4 oz | 10.00 |
| Juice tumbler, 5-1/2 oz | 12.50 |
| Juice Roly Poly tumbler, 3-3/8" h | 6.00 |
| Ladle, all green glass | 80.00 |
| Mixing bowl, 6" d | 9.50 |

*Forest Green, tumbler.*

*Forest Green, cup and saucer.*

| Item | Forest Green |
|------|-------------:|
| Pitcher, 22 oz | 22.50 |
| Pitcher, 36 oz | 25.00 |
| Pitcher, 86 oz, round | 45.00 |
| Plate, 6-3/4" d, salad | 7.50 |
| Plate, 7" w, sq | 6.75 |
| Plate, 8-3/8" d, luncheon | 9.00 |
| Plate, 9-1/4" d, dinner | 33.50 |
| Platter, 11" l, rect | 22.00 |
| Popcorn bowl, 5-1/4" d | 10.00 |
| Punch bowl | 25.00 |
| Punch bowl and stand | 60.00 |
| Punch cup | 4.25 |
| Relish tray, 4-3/4" x 6-3/4" l, two handles | 25.00 |
| Roly Poly tumbler, 5 1/8" h | 7.50 |
| Salad bowl, 7-3/8" d | 15.00 |
| Sandwich plate, 13-3/4" d | 45.00 |
| Saucer, 5-3/8" w | 3.00 |
| Sherbet, 6 oz | 9.00 |
| Sherbet, 6 oz, Boopie | 7.00 |
| Sherbet, flat | 7.50 |
| Soup bowl, 6" d | 17.00 |
| Sugar, flat | 7.00 |
| Tray, 6" x 10", two handles | 30.00 |
| Tumbler, 5 oz, 3-1/2" h | 4.00 |
| Tumbler, 7 oz | 4.50 |
| Tumbler, 5-1/4" h | 4.00 |
| Tumbler, 9-1/2 oz, tall | 8.00 |
| Tumbler, 9 oz, fancy | 7.00 |
| Tumbler, 9 oz, table | 5.00 |
| Tumbler, 10 oz, 4-1/2" h, ftd | 7.50 |
| Tumbler, 11 oz | 7.00 |
| Tumbler, 14 oz, 5" h | 8.00 |
| Tumbler, 15 oz, long boy | 10.00 |
| Vase, 6-3/8" h, Harding | 10.00 |
| Vase, 7" h, crimped | 15.00 |
| Vase, 9" h | 12.00 |
| Vegetable bowl, 8-1/2" l, oval | 24.00 |

# Fortune

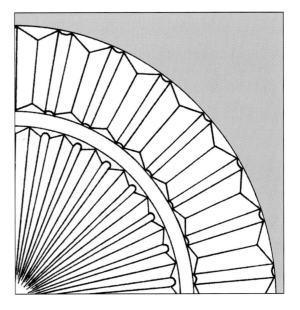

Manufactured by Hocking Glass Company, Lancaster, Ohio, from 1937 to 1938. Made in crystal and pink.

*Fortune, pink berry bowl.*

| Item | Crystal | Pink |
|---|---|---|
| Berry bowl, 4" d. | 10.00 | 12.00 |
| Berry bowl, 7-3/4" d. | 25.00 | 28.00 |
| Bowl, 4-1/2" d, handle | 12.00 | 15.00 |
| Bowl, 5-1/4" d, rolled edge | 20.00 | 22.00 |
| Candy dish, cov, flat | 28.00 | 30.00 |
| Cup | 12.00 | 15.00 |
| Dessert bowl, 4-1/2" d | 12.00 | 15.00 |
| Juice tumbler, 5 oz, 3-1/2" h | 12.00 | 12.00 |
| Plate, 6" d, sherbet | 8.00 | 15.00 |
| Plate, 8" d, luncheon | 25.00 | 25.00 |
| Salad bowl, 7-3/4" d | 25.00 | 25.00 |
| Saucer | 5.00 | 8.50 |
| Tumbler, 9 oz, 4" h | 15.00 | 18.50 |

# Fruits

Manufactured by Hazel Atlas Company, and several other small glass companies, from 1931 to 1935.

Made in crystal, green, iridized, and pink. Iridized production includes only a 4" tumbler, valued at $10.

Fruits, green cup and saucer.

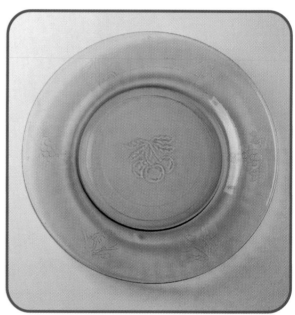

Fruits, green plate.

| Item | Crystal | Green | Pink |
|---|---|---|---|
| Berry bowl, 5" d | 17.50 | 32.00 | 28.00 |
| Berry bowl, 8" d | 40.00 | 85.00 | 45.00 |
| Cup | 5.00 | 10.00 | 7.00 |
| Juice tumbler, 5 oz, 3-1/2" h | 20.00 | 60.00 | 22.00 |
| Pitcher, 7" h | 50.00 | 95.00 | - |
| Plate, 8" d, luncheon | 12.00 | 15.00 | 12.00 |
| Saucer | 2.50 | 5.00 | 4.50 |
| Sherbet | 10.00 | 15.00 | 12.00 |
| Tumbler, 4" h, multiple fruits | 15.00 | 24.00 | 22.00 |
| Tumbler, 4" h, single fruit | 20.00 | 30.00 | 25.00 |
| Tumbler, 12 oz, 5" h | 70.00 | 200.00 | 95.00 |

# Georgian

Manufactured by Federal Glass Company, Columbus, Ohio, from 1931 to 1936.

Made in green. A crystal hot plate is valued at $25.

*Georgian, green sherbet.*

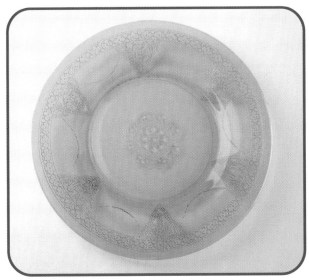

*Georgian, green plate.*

| Item | Green |
| --- | --- |
| Berry bowl, 4-1/2" d | 10.00 |
| Berry bowl, 7-1/2" d, large | 65.00 |
| Bowl, 6-1/2" d, deep | 65.00 |
| Butter dish, cov | 80.00 |
| Cereal bowl, 5-3/4" d | 30.00 |
| Cold cuts server, 18-1/2" d, wood, seven openings for 5" d coasters | 875.00 |
| Creamer, 3" d, ftd | 16.00 |
| Creamer, 4" d, ftd | 16.50 |
| Cup | 10.00 |
| Hot plate, 5" d, center design | 48.00 |
| Plate, 6" d, sherbet | 6.50 |
| Plate, 8" d, luncheon | 10.00 |
| Plate, 9-1/4" d, center design only | 25.00 |
| Plate, 9-1/4" d, dinner | 36.00 |
| Platter, 11-1/2" l, closed handle | 70.00 |
| Saucer | 4.00 |
| Sherbet, ftd | 16.00 |
| Sugar cover, 3" d | 12.00 |
| Sugar cover, 4" d | 12.00 |
| Sugar, 3" d, ftd | 15.00 |
| Sugar, 4" d, ftd | 15.00 |
| Tumbler, 9 oz, 4" h, flat | 80.00 |
| Tumbler 12 oz, 5-1/4" h, flat | 135.00 |
| Vegetable bowl, 9" l, oval | 65.00 |

# Golf Ball

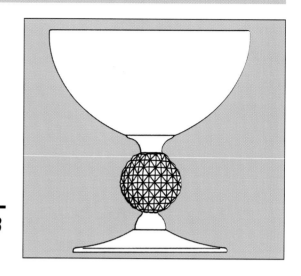

## #7643

Manufactured by Morgantown Glass, Morgantown, W.V., from 1928 to 1971.

Made in Anna Rose (Pink Champagne), Azure (Gloria Blue), Caramel, Cobalt, Copen Blue, crystal, 14K Topaz (Topaz Mist), India Black, Light Amethyst, Meadow Green (crystal ball and foot), Mission Gold, Old Amethyst, Peach (non-opaque), Ritz Blue, Ruby, Smoke, Spanish Red, Stiegel Green, and Venetian Green (Shamrock). There was some production in all-Alabaster (opalescent milk glass) in stemware and vases during the late 1920s and early 1930s.

Decorations include gold and platinum #769 Sparta etching, Berne (platinum #12 border) on Spanish Red; Vernay (platinum #12 border) on Ritz Blue; Avon, Chateau, Eton, Gorton and Toland cuttings; special crest, logo and slogan cuttings, Lotus Decorating Co. silver overlay Hunt Scene. To calculate values for etched pieces, increase crystal by 35% and colors as much as 100 percent higher. Values for pieces with cuttings, increase value of crystal by 25 percent and colored wares about 50 percent higher.

| Item | Crystal | India Black | Pastels | Ritz Blue | Spanish Red | Stiegel Green |
|---|---|---|---|---|---|---|
| Bell, 5-1/2" h . . . . . . . . . . . . . . . . . . . . . . . - | | - | - | 225.00 | - | - |
| Bonbon, #2938, Helga, 5-1/4" d . . . . . . . . . - | | 375.00 | 500.00 | 415.00 | 415.00 | 375.00 |
| Bonbon, #7758, Leora, 5" d . . . . . . . . . . . . - | | 360.00 | - | 495.00 | 495.00 | 360.00 |
| Bonbon, #9074, Maureen, 4-1/2" d . . . . . . . - | | 365.00 | 365.00 | 495.00 | 495.00 | 365.00 |
| Box, cov, #1212, Michael, 7" d . . . . . . . . . . - | | - | - | 375.00 | 375.00 | - |
| Brandy snifter, 21 oz, 6-1/2" h . . . . . . . . . . - | | - | - | 165.00 | 185.00 | 145.00 |
| Cafe parfait, 5 oz, 6-1/4" h . . . . . . . . . . 50.00 | | - | 50.00 | 72.00 | 65.00 | 60.00 |
| Candleholder, 4" h, Jacobi, price for pr . . . - | | 255.00 | 235.00 | 265.00 | 265.00 | 255.00 |
| Candleholder, 4-5/8" h, Dupont, price for pr . . . . . . . . . . . . . . . . . . . . . . . - | | - | 285.00 | - | - | - |
| Candleholder, 6" h, torch, single . . . . . . . . - | | - | - | 280.00 | 225.00 | 200.00 |
| Candy jar, cov, Fairway, 22 oz, #14-1/2 . . . - | | 325.00 | - | 345.00 | 325.00 | 325.00 |
| Champagne, 5-1/2 oz, 5" h . . . . . . . . . . 45.00 | | - | 50.00 | 60.00 | 55.00 | 52.00 |
| Claret, 4-1/2 oz, 5-1/4" h . . . . . . . . . . . . 48.00 | | - | 52.00 | 68.00 | 55.00 | 55.00 |
| Compote, cov, Celeste, 6" d . . . . . . . . . . . . - | | 285.00 | 285.00 | 285.00 | 285.00 | 260.00 |
| Compote, open, Celeste, 6" d . . . . . . . . . . - | | 190.00 | 175.00 | 21.00 | 190.00 | 175.00 |
| Cordial, 1-1/2 oz, 3-1/2" h . . . . . . . . . . . . 40.00 | | - | 55.00 | 58.00 | 55.00 | 55.00 |
| Creamer and sugar . . . . . . . . . . . . . . . . . . - | | - | 255.00 | 285.00 | 285.00 | 285.00 |
| Goblet, 9 oz, 6-3/4" h . . . . . . . . . . . . . . . 38.00 | | - | 55.00 | 58.00 | 55.00 | 55.00 |
| Iced tea tumbler, 12 oz, 6-3/4" h, ftd . . . . 35.00 | | - | 45.00 | 50.00 | 55.00 | 45.00 |
| Irish coffee, 6 oz, 5-1/4" h . . . . . . . . . . . . - | | - | - | 95.00 | - | - |
| Ivy ball, #7643, Kennon, 4" d . . . . . . . . . . - | | - | - | 85.00 | 85.00 | 85.00 |

| Item | Crystal | India Black | Pastels | Ritz Blue | Spanish Red | Stiegel Green |
|---|---|---|---|---|---|---|
| Ivy ball, #7643, Kimball, 4" d. . . . . . . . . . . - | | - | - | 85.00 | 85.00 | 85.00 |
| Juice tumbler, 5 oz, 5" h, ftd . . . . . . . . . 32.00 | | - | 45.00 | 45.00 | 45.00 | 42.00 |
| Lamp, Amherst water . . . . . . . . . . . . . . . . - | | - | - | - | - | 625.00 |
| Liquor cocktail, 3-1/2 oz, 4-1/8" h . . . . . . 35.00 | | - | 42.00 | 42.00 | 42.00 | 42.00 |
| Luncheon tumbler/goblet, 9 oz, 6-1/8" h, ftd . . . . . . . . . . . . . . . . . . . . . . . . . . 30.00 | | - | 42.00 | 55.00 | 48.00 | 45.00 |
| Oyster cocktail, 4 oz, 4-1/4" h, flared . . . 40.00 | | - | - | 55.00 | 50.00 | 48.00 |
| Oyster cocktail, 4-1/2 oz, 4-3/8" h, cupped . . . . . . . . . . . . . . . . . . . . . . . 40.00 | | - | - | 55.00 | 50.00 | 48.00 |
| Pilsner, 11 oz, 9-1/8" h . . . . . . . . . . . . 100.00 | | - | - | 125.00 | - | - |
| Schooner, 32 oz . . . . . . . . . . . . . . . . . 245.00 | | - | - | - | - | - |
| Sherbet/sundae, 5-1/2 oz, 4-1/8" h . . . . . 30.00 | | - | 40.00 | 50.00 | 40.00 | 40.00 |
| Sherry, 2-1/2" oz, 4-5/8" h . . . . . . . . . . 40.00 | | - | 45.00 | 60.00 | 55.00 | 50.00 |
| Vase, 6-1/2" h, #7643, Urn . . . . . . . . . . . . - | | - | - | 125.00 | 125.00 | 110.00 |
| Vase, 6-1/2" h, #7643-1/2, urn, Stephanie . . . . . . . . . . . . . . . . . . . . . . . - | | - | - | 165.00 | 165.00 | 145.00 |
| Vase, 8" h, #7643, Charlotte . . . . . . . . . . . - | | - | 175.00 | 165.00 | 165.00 | 165.00 |
| Vase, 9-1/2" h, #79, Montague . . . . . . . . . . - | | - | - | 255.00 | 255.00 | 240.00 |
| Vase, 10-1/2" h, #78, Lancaster . . . . . . . . . - | | - | - | 245.00 | 245.00 | 245.00 |
| Wine tumbler, 2-1/2 oz, 4-3/8" h, ftd . . . . 35.00 | | - | 48.00 | 48.00 | 45.00 | 45.00 |
| Wine, 3 oz, 4-3/4" h . . . . . . . . . . . . . . . 45.00 | | - | 55.00 | 65.00 | 60.00 | 55.00 |

*Golf Ball, Spanish Red goblet.*

# Harp

Manufactured by Jeannette Glass Company, Jeannette, Pa., from 1954 to 1957.

Made in crystal and crystal with gold trim; limited pieces made in ice blue, iridescent white, pink, and shell pink.

| Item | Crystal | Ice Blue | Shell Pink |
|------|---------|----------|------------|
| Ashtray | 6.00 | - | - |
| Cake stand, 9" d | 35.00 | 45.00 | 45.00 |
| Coaster | 6.00 | - | - |
| Cup | 30.00 | - | - |
| Parfait | 20.00 | - | - |
| Plate, 7" d | 20.00 | 25.00 | - |
| Saucer | 12.00 | - | - |
| Snack set, cup, saucer, 7" plate | 48.00 | - | - |
| Tray, two handles, rectangular | 35.00 | 35.00 | 65.00 |
| Vase, 7-1/2" h | 35.00 | - | - |

*Harp, crystal, gold-edge plate and cake stand.*

# Heritage

Manufactured by Federal Glass Company, Columbus, Ohio, from 1940 to 1955.

Made in blue, crystal, green, and pink.

**Reproductions:** † Bowls have been reproduced in amber, crystal, and green. Some are marked with N or MC.

| Item | Blue | Crystal | Green | Pink |
|------|------|---------|-------|------|
| Berry bowl, 5" d † | 80.00 | 12.00 | 75.00 | 75.00 |
| Berry bowl, 8-1/2" d † | 250.00 | 48.00 | 200.00 | 195.00 |
| Creamer, ftd. | - | 32.00 | - | - |
| Cup | - | 8.00 | - | - |
| Fruit bowl, 10-1/2" d | - | 18.00 | - | - |
| Plate, 8" d, luncheon | - | 10.00 | - | - |
| Plate, 9-1/4" d, dinner | - | 12.00 | - | - |
| Sandwich plate, 12" d. | - | 18.00 | - | - |
| Saucer | - | 5.00 | - | - |
| Sugar, open, ftd | - | 25.00 | - | - |

*Heritage, crystal cup and saucer.*

*Heritage, crystal plate.*

# Hex Optic

## Honeycomb

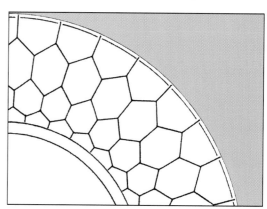

Manufactured by Jeannette Glass Company, Jeannette, Pa., from 1928 to 1932.

Made in green and pink. Ultramarine tumblers have been found. Iridescent tumblers and pitchers were made about 1960 and it is assumed that they were made by Jeannette.

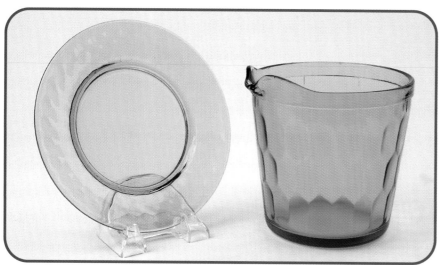

*Hex Optic, green plate and ice tub.*

| Item | Green | Pink |
|---|---|---|
| Berry bowl, 4-1/4" d, ruffled | 9.50 | 8.50 |
| Berry bowl, 7-1/2" d | 15.00 | 12.00 |
| Bucket reamer | 65.00 | 60.00 |
| Butter dish, cov, rect, 1-lb size | 90.00 | 90.00 |
| Creamer, two style handles | 8.00 | 7.00 |
| Cup, two style handles | 5.00 | 5.00 |
| Ice bucket, metal handle | 30.00 | 30.00 |
| Mixing bowl, 7-1/4" d | 15.00 | 15.00 |
| Mixing bowl, 8-1/4" d | 18.00 | 18.00 |
| Mixing bowl, 9" d | 20.00 | 20.00 |
| Mixing bowl, 10" d | 20.00 | 20.00 |
| Pitcher, 32 oz, 5" h | 25.00 | 25.00 |
| Pitcher, 48 oz, 9" h, ftd | 48.00 | 50.00 |
| Pitcher, 96 oz, 8" h | 235.00 | 245.00 |
| Plate, 6" d, sherbet | 3.00 | 3.00 |

| Item | Green | Pink |
|---|---|---|
| Plate, 8" d, luncheon | 6.00 | 6.00 |
| Platter, 11" d, round | 14.00 | 16.00 |
| Refrigerator dish, 4" x 4" | 20.00 | 18.00 |
| Refrigerator stack set, 4 pcs | 75.00 | 75.00 |
| Salt and pepper shakers, pr | 30.00 | 30.00 |
| Saucer | 4.00 | 4.00 |
| Sherbet, 5 oz, ftd | 5.00 | 5.00 |
| Sugar, two styles of handles | 6.00 | 6.00 |
| Sugar shaker | 225.00 | 225.00 |
| Tumbler, 12 oz, 5" h | 8.00 | 8.00 |
| Tumbler, 5-3/4" h, ftd | 10.00 | 10.00 |
| Tumbler, 7" h, ftd | 12.00 | 12.00 |
| Tumbler, 7 oz, 4-3/4" h, ftd | 8.00 | 8.00 |
| Tumbler, 9 oz, 3-3/4" h | 5.00 | 5.00 |
| Whiskey, 1 oz, 2" h | 8.50 | 8.50 |

# Hobnail

Manufactured by Hocking Glass Company, Lancaster, Ohio, from 1934 to 1936.

Made in crystal, crystal with red trim, and pink.

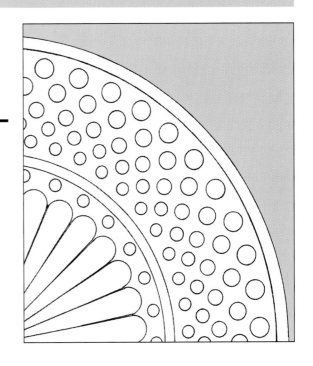

*Hobnail, pink sherbet.*

| Item | Crystal | Crystal, red trim | Pink |
|---|---|---|---|
| Cereal bowl, 5-1/2" d | 4.25 | 4.25 | - |
| Cordial, 5 oz, ftd | 6.00 | 6.00 | - |
| Creamer, ftd | 4.00 | 4.00 | - |
| Cup | 5.00 | 5.00 | 6.00 |
| Decanter and stopper, 32 oz | 27.50 | 27.50 | - |
| Goblet, 10 oz | 7.50 | 7.50 | - |
| Iced tea goblet, 13 oz | 8.50 | 8.50 | - |
| Iced tea tumbler, 15 oz | 8.50 | 8.50 | - |
| Juice tumbler, 5 oz | 4.00 | 4.00 | - |
| Milk pitcher, 18 oz | 22.00 | 22.00 | - |
| Pitcher, 67 oz | 25.00 | 25.00 | - |
| Plate, 6" d, sherbet | 2.50 | 2.50 | 3.50 |
| Plate, 8-1/2" d, luncheon | 5.50 | 5.50 | 7.50 |
| Salad bowl, 7" d | 5.00 | 5.00 | - |
| Saucer | 2.00 | 2.00 | 3.00 |
| Sherbet | 4.00 | 4.00 | 5.00 |
| Sugar, ftd | 4.00 | 4.00 | - |
| Tumbler, 9 oz, 4-3/4" h, flat | 5.00 | 5.00 | - |
| Whiskey, 1-1/2 oz | 5.00 | 5.00 | - |
| Wine, 3 oz, ftd | 6.50 | 6.50 | - |

# Holiday

### Button and Bows

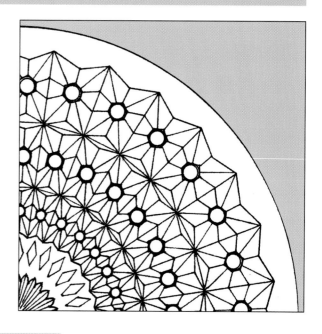

Manufactured by Jeannette Glass Company, Jeannette, Pa., from 1947 to the 1950s.

Made in crystal, iridescent, pink, and shell pink. Shell pink production was limited to the console bowl, valued at $48.

| Item | Crystal | Iridescent | Pink |
|---|---|---|---|
| Berry bowl, 5-1/8" d | - | - | 16.00 |
| Berry bowl, 8-1/2" d | - | - | 55.00 |
| Butter dish, cov | - | - | 60.00 |
| Cake plate, 10-1/2" d, three legs | - | - | 220.00 |
| Candlesticks, pr, 3" h | - | - | 125.00 |
| Chop plate, 13-3/4" d | - | - | 140.00 |
| Console bowl, 10-1/4" d | - | - | 225.00 |
| Creamer, ftd | - | - | 20.00 |
| Cup, plain | - | - | 15.00 |
| Cup, rayed bottom, 2" d base | - | - | 12.00 |
| Cup, rayed bottom, 2-3/8" d base | - | - | 16.00 |
| Juice tumbler, 5 oz, 4" h, ftd | - | - | 60.00 |
| Pitcher, 16 oz, 4-3/4" h | 17.50 | 35.00 | 85.00 |
| Pitcher, 52 oz, 6-3/4" h | - | - | 45.00 |
| Plate, 6" d, sherbet | - | - | 8.50 |
| Plate, 9" d, dinner | - | - | 25.00 |
| Platter, 11-3/8" l, oval | - | 17.50 | 30.00 |
| Sandwich tray, 10-1/2" l | - | 20.00 | 28.00 |
| Saucer, plain center | - | - | 5.00 |
| Saucer, rayed center, 2-1/8" d ring | - | - | 7.50 |
| Saucer, rayed center, 2-1/2" d ring | - | - | 7.50 |
| Sherbet | - | - | 12.00 |
| Soup bowl, 7-3/4" d | - | - | 82.00 |
| Sugar, cov | - | - | 30.00 |
| Sugar lid | - | - | 20.00 |
| Tumbler, 5 oz, 4" h, ftd | - | 15.00 | 35.00 |
| Tumbler, 5-1/4 oz, 4-1/4" h, ftd | 8.00 | - | 45.00 |
| Tumbler, 6" h, ftd | - | - | 195.00 |
| Tumbler, 9 oz, 4" h, ftd | - | - | 55.00 |
| Tumbler, 10 oz, 4" h, flat | - | - | 28.00 |
| Vegetable bowl, 9-1/2" l, oval | - | - | 36.00 |

*Holiday, pink water pitcher.*

# Homespun

## Fine Rib

Manufactured by Jeannette Glass Company, Jeannette, Pa., from 1939 to 1949. Made in crystal and pink.

| Item | Crystal | Pink |
|---|---|---|
| Ashtray | 6.00 | 6.00 |
| Berry bowl, 4-1/2" d, closed handles | 15.00 | 15.00 |
| Berry bowl, 8-1/4" d | 20.00 | 20.00 |
| Butter dish, cov | 55.00 | 60.00 |
| Cereal bowl, 5" d, closed handles | 30.00 | 30.00 |
| Coaster | 6.00 | 6.00 |
| Creamer, ftd | 12.50 | 12.50 |
| Cup | 12.00 | 12.00 |
| Iced tea tumbler, 13 oz, 5-1/4" h | 32.00 | 32.00 |
| Plate, 6" d, sherbet | 7.50 | 7.50 |
| Plate, 9-1/4" d, dinner | 18.00 | 18.00 |
| Platter, 13" d, closed handles | 20.00 | 20.00 |
| Saucer | 5.50 | 5.50 |
| Sherbet, low, flat | 17.50 | 19.00 |
| Sugar, ftd | 12.50 | 12.50 |
| Tumbler, 5 oz, 4" h, ftd | 8.00 | 8.00 |
| Tumbler, 6 oz, 3-7/8" h, straight | 7.00 | 7.00 |
| Tumbler, 9 oz, 4" h, flared top | 17.50 | 17.50 |
| Tumbler, 9 oz, 4-1/4" h, top band | 17.50 | 17.50 |
| Tumbler, 15 oz, 6-1/4" h, ftd | 38.00 | 38.00 |
| Tumbler, 15 oz, 6-3/8" h, ftd | 36.00 | 36.00 |

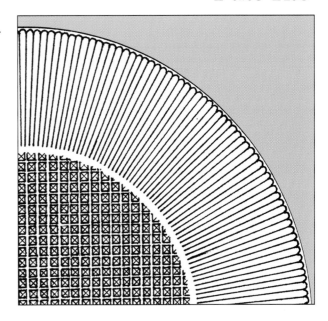

## Children's

| Item | Crystal | Pink |
|---|---|---|
| Cup | 25.00 | 35.00 |
| Plate | 10.00 | 15.00 |
| Saucer | 9.00 | 12.00 |
| Teapot | - | 125.00 |

*Homespun, pink sugar and look-alike tumbler.*

# Horseshoe

## No. 612

Manufactured by Indiana Glass Company, Dunkirk, Ind., from 1930 to 1933.

Made in crystal, green, pink, and yellow. There is limited collector interest in crystal and pink at the current time.

| Item | Green | Yellow |
|------|-------|--------|
| Berry bowl, 4-1/2" d | 30.00 | 25.00 |
| Berry bowl, 9-1/2" d | 40.00 | 35.00 |
| Butter dish, cov | 750.00 | - |
| Candy dish, metal holder | 175.00 | - |
| Cereal bowl, 6-1/2" d | 25.00 | 35.00 |
| Creamer, ftd | 18.00 | 20.00 |
| Cup and saucer | 20.00 | 24.00 |
| Pitcher, 64 oz, 8-1/2" h | 295.00 | 350.00 |
| Plate, 6" d, sherbet | 9.00 | 9.00 |
| Plate, 8-3/8" d, salad | 10.00 | 10.00 |
| Plate, 9-3/8" d, luncheon | 15.00 | 20.00 |
| Plate, 10-3/8" d, grill | 125.00 | 150.00 |
| Platter, 10-3/4" l, oval | 25.00 | 25.00 |
| Relish, three parts, ftd | 20.00 | 24.00 |
| Salad bowl, 7-1/2" d | 24.00 | 24.00 |
| Sandwich plate, 11-1/2" d | 24.00 | 27.50 |
| Saucer | 6.00 | 6.50 |
| Sherbet | 16.00 | 18.50 |
| Sugar, open | 16.50 | 17.00 |
| Tumbler, 9 oz, ftd | 25.00 | 28.00 |
| Tumbler, 9 oz, 4-1/4" h | 150.00 | - |

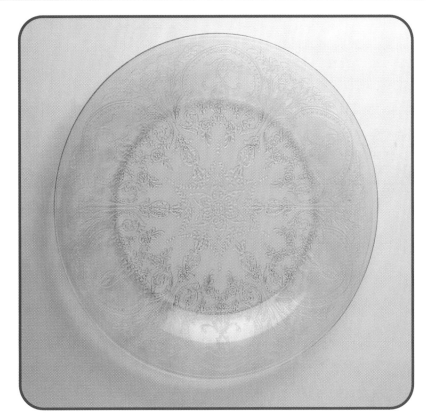

*Horseshoe, No. 612 yellow plate.*

*Horseshoe, No. 612 yellow cup.*

| Item | Green | Yellow |
|---|---|---|
| Tumbler, 12 oz, ftd . . . . . . . . . . . . . . . . . . . . . . . . . . . . . . . . . . . . . 140.00 | | 150.00 |
| Tumbler, 12 oz, 4-3/4" h . . . . . . . . . . . . . . . . . . . . . . . . . . . . . 150.00 | | - |
| Vegetable bowl, 8-1/2" d . . . . . . . . . . . . . . . . . . . . . . . . . . . . . . 30.00 | | 30.00 |
| Vegetable bowl, 10-1/2" d, oval . . . . . . . . . . . . . . . . . . . . . . . . 25.00 | | 28.50 |

# Indiana Custard

## Flower and Leaf Band

Manufactured by Indiana Glass Company, Dunkirk, Ind., in the 1930s and in the 1950s. Made in custard color, known as French Ivory.

| Item | French Ivory |
|---|---|
| Berry bowl, 5-1/2" d | 16.50 |
| Berry bowl, 9" d, 1-3/4" deep | 36.00 |
| Butter dish, cov | 68.00 |
| Cereal bowl, 6-1/2" d | 8.00 |
| Creamer | 20.00 |
| Cup | 38.00 |
| Plate, 5-3/4" d, bread and butter | 7.00 |
| Plate, 7-1/2" d, salad | 16.00 |
| Plate, 8-7/8" d, luncheon | 18.00 |
| Plate, 9-3/4" d, dinner | 28.00 |
| Platter, 11-1/2" l, oval | 30.00 |
| Saucer | 12.00 |
| Sherbet | 90.00 |
| Soup bowl, 7-1/2" d, flat | 32.00 |
| Sugar, cov | 35.00 |

*Indiana Custard, covered sugar.*

# Iris

## Iris and Herringbone

Manufactured by Jeannette Glass Company, Jeannette, Pa., from 1928 to 1932 and in the 1950s and 1970s.

Made in crystal, iridescent, some green, and pink. Recent color combinations of yellow and red and blue and green and white have been made. A record price of $495 is noted for a rare amethyst demitasse cup and saucer.

**Reproductions:** † Some collectors and dealers feel strongly that the newer re-issues of this pattern are actually reproductions. Forms that have the potential to fool buyers are the 4-1/2" berry bowl, covered candy jar, 10" d dinner plate, 6-1/2" h footed tumbler, and vase. Careful examination of the object, plus careful consideration of the color, should help determine age.

| Item | Crystal | Green | Iridescent | Pink |
|---|---|---|---|---|
| Berry bowl, 4-1/2" d, beaded edge † | 50.00 | - | 20.00 | - |
| Berry bowl, 8" d, beaded edge | 135.00 | - | 30.00 | - |
| Bowl, 5-1/2" d, scalloped | 10.00 | - | 23.00 | - |
| Bowl, 9-1/2" d, scalloped | 17.50 | - | 14.00 | - |
| Bread plate, 11-3/4" d | 20.00 | - | 38.00 | - |
| Butter dish, cov. | 60.00 | - | 65.00 | - |
| Candlesticks, pr | 50.00 | - | 55.00 | - |
| Candy jar, cov † | 195.00 | - | - | - |
| Cereal bowl, 5" d | 150.00 | - | - | - |
| Coaster † | 120.00 | - | - | - |
| Cocktail, 4 oz, 4-1/4" h | 32.00 | - | - | - |
| Creamer, ftd | 25.00 | 150.00 | 17.50 | 150.00 |
| Cup | 22.00 | - | 20.00 | - |
| Demitasse cup and saucer | 225.00 | - | 350.00 | - |
| Fruit bowl, 11" d, straight edge | 75.00 | - | - | - |
| Fruit bowl, 11-1/2" d, ruffled | 25.00 | - | 18.00 | - |
| Fruit set | 110.00 | - | - | - |
| Goblet, 4 oz, 5-3/4" h | 30.00 | - | 135.00 | - |
| Goblet, 8 oz, 5-3/4" h | 35.00 | - | 175.00 | - |
| Iced tea tumbler, 6-1/2" h, ftd | 42.00 | - | - | - |
| Lamp shade, 11-1/2" | 100.00 | - | - | - |
| Nut set | 115.00 | - | - | - |
| Pitcher, 9-1/2" h, ftd | 50.00 | - | 50.00 | - |

| Item | Crystal | Green | Iridescent | Pink |
|---|---|---|---|---|
| Plate, 5-1/2" d, sherbet | 16.00 | - | 15.00 | - |
| Plate, 7" d | 95.00 | - | - | - |
| Plate, 8" d, luncheon | 130.00 | - | 115.00 | - |
| Plate, 9" d, dinner † | 65.00 | - | 48.00 | - |
| Salad bowl, 9-1/2" d, ruffled | 20.00 | 150.00 | 20.00 | 135.00 |
| Sandwich plate, 11-3/4" d | 55.00 | - | 40.00 | - |
| Sauce, 5" d, ruffled | 12.50 | - | 30.00 | - |
| Saucer | 15.00 | - | 11.00 | - |
| Sherbet, 2-1/2" h, ftd | 35.00 | - | 15.50 | - |
| Sherbet, 4" h, ftd | 30.00 | - | 15.50 | - |
| Soup bowl, 7-1/2" d | 185.00 | - | 90.00 | - |
| Sugar, cov | 32.00 | 150.00 | 23.00 | 150.00 |
| Tumbler, 4" h, flat † | 150.00 | - | 18.00 | - |
| Tumbler, 6" h, ftd † | 30.00 | - | 25.00 | - |
| Tumbler, 6-1/2" h, ftd † | 40.00 | - | - | - |
| Tumbler, flat, water † | 135.00 | - | - | - |
| Vase, 9" h † | 38.00 | - | 35.00 | 225.00 |
| Wine, 4" h | 20.00 | - | 33.50 | - |
| Wine, 4-1/4" h, 3 oz | 24.00 | - | - | - |
| Wine, 5-1/2" h | 27.50 | - | - | - |

*Iris, crystal candlesticks and iridescent plate.*

# Jamestown

Manufactured by Fostoria Glass Company, Moundsville, Va., from 1958 to 1982.

Made in amber, amethyst, blue, brown, crystal, green, pink, and red.

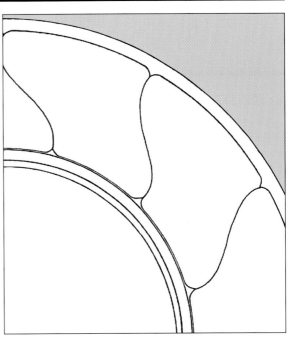

*Jamestown, 8" d amber plate.*

| Item | Amber or Brown | Amethyst | Blue or Red | Crystal or Green | Pink |
|---|---|---|---|---|---|
| Butter, cov. | 25.00 | 48.00 | 60.00 | 48.00 | 60.00 |
| Cake plate | 25.00 | 45.00 | 60.00 | 45.00 | 60.00 |
| Celery | 20.00 | 35.00 | 40.00 | 35.00 | 40.00 |
| Creamer, ftd | 12.00 | 20.00 | 25.00 | 20.00 | 25.00 |
| Dessert bowl, 4-1/2" d | 8.50 | 14.00 | 17.50 | 13.50 | 15.00 |
| Goblet, 9 oz or 10 oz | 12.00 | 17.50 | 20.00 | 21.00 | 24.50 |
| Iced tea tumbler, 11 or 12 oz | 12.00 | 20.00 | 24.00 | 22.00 | 24.00 |
| Jelly, cov | 35.00 | 60.00 | 80.00 | 60.00 | 80.00 |
| Juice tumbler, 5 oz | 12.00 | 24.00 | 30.00 | 24.00 | 30.00 |
| Muffin tray. | 30.00 | 45.00 | 55.00 | 45.00 | 55.00 |
| Pickle | 20.00 | 40.00 | 48.00 | 40.00 | 48.00 |
| Pitcher, 48 oz, ice lip | 48.00 | 95.00 | 145.00 | 95.00 | 145.00 |
| Plate, 8" d | 9.50 | 17.50 | 25.00 | 17.50 | 25.00 |
| Relish, 2 parts | 18.00 | 35.00 | 40.00 | 35.00 | 40.00 |
| Salad bowl, 10" d | 24.00 | 40.00 | 50.00 | 40.00 | 50.00 |
| Salt and pepper shakers, pr, chrome top | 30.00 | 42.00 | 55.00 | 42.00 | 55.00 |
| Salver, 10" d, 7" h | 60.00 | 120.00 | 125.00 | 135.00 | 125.00 |
| Sauce dish, cov | 20.00 | 35.00 | 42.00 | 35.00 | 42.00 |
| Serving bowl, two handles, 10" d | 22.00 | 45.00 | 60.00 | 45.00 | 60.00 |
| Sherbet, 6 oz or 7 oz | 7.50 | 15.00 | 17.50 | 15.00 | 17.50 |
| Sugar, ftd. | 12.00 | 17.50 | 25.00 | 17.50 | 25.00 |
| Torte plate, 14" d | 30.00 | 45.00 | 60.00 | 45.00 | 60.00 |
| Tumbler, 9 oz | 7.50 | 18.00 | 25.00 | 18.00 | 25.00 |
| Tumbler, 12 oz. | 7.50 | 20.00 | 25.00 | 20.00 | 25.00 |
| Wine, 4 oz | 12.00 | 25.00 | 30.00 | 35.00 | 33.50 |

# Jubilee

Manufactured by Lancaster Glass Company, Lancaster, Ohio, early 1930s. Made in pink and yellow.

| Item | Pink | Yellow |
|---|---|---|
| Bowl, 8" d, 5-1/8" h, three legs | 275.00 | 225.00 |
| Bowl, 11-1/2" d, three legs | 265.00 | 250.00 |
| Bowl, 11-1/2" d, three legs, curved in | - | 250.00 |
| Bowl, 13" d, three legs | 250.00 | 245.00 |
| Cake tray, 11" d, two handles | 75.00 | 85.00 |
| Candlesticks, pr | 190.00 | 195.00 |
| Candy jar, cov, three legs | 325.00 | 325.00 |
| Cheese and cracker set | 265.00 | 255.00 |
| Cordial, 1 oz, 4" h | - | 245.00 |
| Creamer | 45.00 | 30.00 |
| Cup | 40.00 | 17.50 |
| Fruit bowl, 9" d, handle | - | 125.00 |
| Fruit bowl, 11-1/2" h, flat | 200.00 | 165.00 |
| Goblet, 3 oz, 4-7/8" h | - | 150.00 |
| Goblet, 11 oz, 7-1/2" h | - | 75.00 |
| Iced tea tumbler, 12-1/2 oz, 6 1/8" h | - | 135.00 |
| Juice tumbler, 6 oz, 5" h, ftd | - | 100.00 |
| Mayonnaise, plate, orig ladle | 315.00 | 285.00 |
| Mayonnaise underplate | 125.00 | 110.00 |
| Plate, 7" d, salad | 25.00 | 14.00 |
| Plate, 8-3/4" d, luncheon | 30.00 | 16.50 |
| Plate, 14" d, three legs | - | 210.00 |
| Sandwich plate, 13-1/2" d | 95.00 | 85.00 |
| Sandwich tray, 11" d, center handle | 215.00 | 250.00 |
| Saucer | 15.00 | 8.00 |
| Sherbet, 8 oz, 3" h | - | 75.00 |
| Sherbet/champagne, 7 oz, 5-1/2" h | - | 75.00 |
| Sugar | 40.00 | 24.00 |
| Tumbler, 10 oz, 6" h, ftd | 75.00 | 35.00 |
| Vase, 12" h | - | 385.00 |

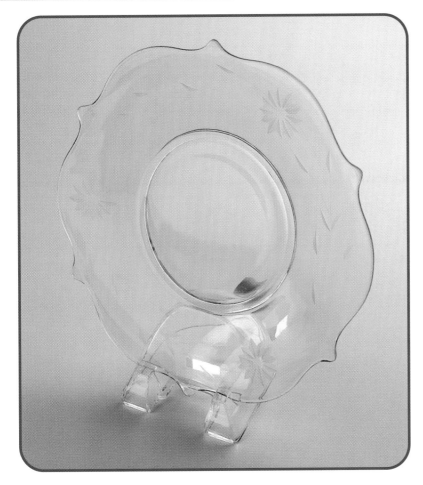

*Jubilee, yellow serving plate with handles.*

*Jubilee, yellow cup and saucer.*

*Jubilee, yellow goblet.*

149

# Laced Edge

Manufactured by Imperial Glass Company, Bellaire, Ohio, early 1930s.
Made in blue and green with opalescent edges.

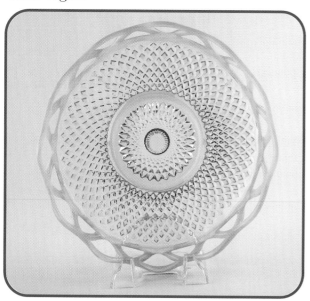

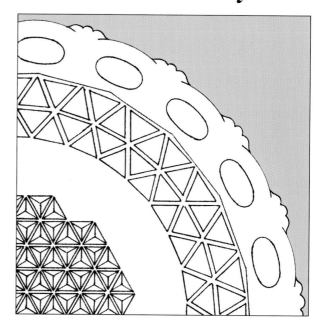

*Laced Edge, blue-opalescent bowl.*

| Item | Blue | Green |
|------|------|-------|
| Basket, 9" d | 265.00 | - |
| Bowl, 5" d | 40.00 | 40.00 |
| Bowl, 5-1/2" d | 42.00 | 42.00 |
| Bowl, 5-7/8" d | 42.00 | 42.00 |
| Bowl, 11" l, oval | 295.00 | 285.00 |
| Bowl, 11" l, oval, divided | 165.00 | 165.00 |
| Candlesticks, pr, double lite | 175.00 | 180.00 |
| Creamer | 45.00 | 40.00 |
| Cup | 35.00 | 35.00 |
| Fruit bowl, 4-1/2" d | 32.00 | 30.00 |
| Mayonnaise, three pieces | 100.00 | 125.00 |
| Plate, 6-1/2" d, bread and butter | 24.00 | 24.00 |
| Plate, 8" d, salad | 35.00 | 35.00 |
| Plate, 10" d, dinner | 95.00 | 95.00 |
| Plate, 12" d, luncheon | 90.00 | 90.00 |
| Platter, 13" l | 185.00 | 165.00 |
| Saucer | 18.00 | 15.00 |
| Soup bowl, 7" d | 85.00 | 80.00 |
| Sugar | 45.00 | 40.00 |
| Tidbit, two tiers, 8" and 10" plates | 110.00 | 100.00 |
| Tumbler, 9 oz | 60.00 | 60.00 |
| Vegetable bowl, 9"d | 95.00 | 95.00 |

# *Lake Como*

Manufactured by Hocking Glass Company, Lancaster, Ohio, from 1934 to 1937.
Made in opaque white with a blue scene.

| Item | White |
|---|---|
| Cereal bowl, 6" d | 30.00 |
| Creamer, ftd | 35.00 |
| Cup, regular | 32.00 |
| Cup, St. Denis | 35.00 |
| Plate, 7-1/4" d, salad | 30.00 |
| Plate, 9-1/4" d, dinner | 35.00 |
| Platter, 11" d | 70.00 |
| Salt and pepper shakers, pr | 48.00 |
| Saucer | 12.00 |
| Saucer, St. Denis | 12.00 |
| Soup bowl, flat | 100.00 |
| Sugar, ftd | 35.00 |
| Vegetable bowl, 9-3/4" l | 65.00 |

*Lake Como, blue and white plate.*

# Laurel

Manufactured by McKee Glass Company, Pittsburgh, Pa., 1930s.
Made in French Ivory, Jade Green, Poudre Blue, and White Opal.

| Item | French Ivory | Jade Green | Poudre Blue | White Opal |
|---|---|---|---|---|
| Berry bowl, 4-3/4" d | 9.00 | 15.00 | 16.00 | 14.00 |
| Berry bowl, 9" d | 28.50 | 40.00 | 55.00 | 30.00 |
| Bowl, 6" d, three legs | 15.00 | 25.00 | - | 15.00 |
| Bowl, 10-1/2" d, three legs | 37.50 | 50.00 | 68.00 | 45.00 |
| Bowl, 11" d | 40.00 | 55.00 | 85.00 | 37.50 |
| Candlesticks, pr, 4" h | 50.00 | 65.00 | - | 45.00 |
| Cereal bowl, 6" d | 12.00 | 25.00 | 28.00 | 20.00 |
| Cheese dish, cov | 60.00 | 95.00 | - | 75.00 |
| Creamer, short | 12.00 | 25.00 | - | 18.00 |
| Creamer, tall | 15.00 | 28.00 | 40.00 | 24.00 |
| Cup | 9.50 | 15.00 | 20.00 | 12.00 |
| Plate, 6" d, sherbet | 6.00 | 15.00 | 10.00 | 8.00 |
| Plate, 7-1/2" d, salad | 10.00 | 20.00 | 17.50 | 12.00 |
| Plate, 9-1/8" d, dinner | 15.00 | 25.00 | 30.00 | 18.50 |
| Plate, 9-1/8" d, grill, round | 15.00 | 25.00 | - | 18.50 |
| Plate, 9-1/8" d, grill, scalloped | 15.00 | 25.00 | - | 18.50 |
| Platter, 10-3/4" l, oval | 32.00 | 48.00 | 45.00 | 30.00 |
| Salt and pepper shakers, pr | 60.00 | 85.00 | - | 65.00 |
| Saucer | 3.25 | 4.50 | 7.50 | 3.50 |
| Sherbet | 12.50 | 20.00 | - | 18.00 |
| Sherbet/champagne, 5" | 50.00 | 72.00 | - | 60.00 |
| Soup bowl, 7-7/8" d | 35.00 | 40.00 | - | 40.00 |
| Sugar, short | 12.00 | 25.00 | - | 18.00 |
| Sugar, tall | 15.00 | 28.00 | 40.00 | 24.00 |
| Tumbler, 9 oz, 4-1/2" h, flat | 40.00 | 60.00 | - | 60.00 |
| Tumbler, 12 oz, 5" h, flat | 60.00 | - | - | - |
| Vegetable bowl, 9-3/4" l, oval | 18.50 | 480.00 | 45.00 | 20.00 |

# Children's

| Item | Plain | Green or Decorated | Scotty Dog Green | Scotty Dog Ivory |
|---|---|---|---|---|
| Creamer | 30.00 | 100.00 | 250.00 | 125.00 |
| Cup | 25.00 | 50.00 | 100.00 | 50.00 |
| Plate | 15.00 | 20.00 | 75.00 | 40.00 |
| Saucer | 12.00 | 14.00 | 75.00 | 40.00 |
| Sugar | 30.00 | 100.00 | 250.00 | 125.00 |

*Laurel, green plate.*

# Lincoln Inn

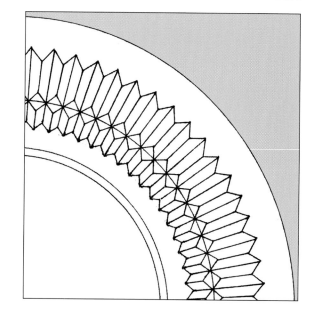

Manufactured by Fenton Art Glass Company, Williamstown, W.V., late 1920s.

Made in amber, amethyst, black, cobalt blue, crystal, green, green opalescent, light blue, opaque jade, pink, and red. Production in black was limited to salt and pepper shakers, valued at $325. Some rare pieces have been identified in several other colors.

| Item | Cobalt Blue | Crystal | Other Colors | Red |
|---|---|---|---|---|
| Ashtray | 17.50 | 12.00 | 12.00 | 17.50 |
| Bonbon, oval, handle | 17.50 | 12.00 | 14.00 | 18.00 |
| Bonbon, sq, handle | 15.00 | 12.00 | 14.00 | 15.00 |
| Bowl, 6" d, crimped | 14.50 | 7.50 | 10.00 | 14.50 |
| Bowl, 9" d, shallow | - | 9.00 | - | - |
| Bowl, 9-1/4" d, ftd | 42.00 | 18.00 | 20.00 | 45.00 |
| Bowl, 10-1/2" d, ftd | 50.00 | 28.00 | 30.00 | 50.00 |
| Candy dish, ftd, oval | 24.00 | 14.50 | 14.50 | 24.00 |
| Cereal bowl, 6" d | 12.50 | 7.50 | 9.50 | 12.50 |
| Comport | 25.00 | 14.00 | 15.00 | 25.00 |
| Creamer | 24.00 | 12.00 | 15.00 | 24.00 |
| Cup | 17.50 | 8.50 | 9.50 | 18.00 |
| Finger bowl | 20.00 | 14.00 | 14.50 | 20.00 |
| Fruit bowl, 5" d | 14.00 | 7.00 | 9.00 | 14.00 |
| Goblet, 6" h | 30.00 | 18.50 | 16.00 | 30.00 |
| Iced tea tumbler, 12 oz, ftd | 40.00 | 22.00 | 24.00 | 40.00 |
| Juice tumbler, 4 oz, flat | 27.50 | 9.00 | 14.00 | 27.50 |
| Nut dish, ftd | 20.00 | 14.50 | 16.00 | 20.00 |
| Olive bowl, handle | 15.00 | 8.50 | 12.00 | 15.00 |
| Pitcher, 46 oz, 7-1/4" h | 820.00 | 700.00 | 715.00 | 820.00 |
| Plate, 6" d | 19.50 | 12.00 | 12.50 | 19.50 |
| Plate, 8" d | 27.50 | 15.00 | 14.00 | 27.50 |
| Plate, 9-1/4" d | 30.00 | 15.00 | 16.50 | 30.00 |
| Plate, 12" d | 35.00 | 16.00 | 18.00 | 35.00 |
| Salt and pepper shakers, pr | 265.00 | 175.00 | 175.00 | 265.00 |
| Sandwich server, center handle | 175.00 | 110.00 | 110.00 | 175.00 |
| Saucer | 5.00 | 4.00 | 4.50 | 5.00 |
| Sherbet, 4-1/2" h, cone shape | 18.00 | 12.00 | 14.00 | 18.00 |
| Sherbet, 4-3/4" h | 20.00 | 14.00 | 14.50 | 20.00 |
| Sugar | 24.00 | 12.00 | 15.00 | 24.00 |

| Item | Cobalt Blue | Crystal | Other Colors | Red |
|---|---|---|---|---|
| Tumbler, 5 oz, ftd | 24.00 | 14.00 | 14.50 | 24.00 |
| Tumbler, 9 oz, flat | - | 14.00 | 15.00 | 15.00 |
| Tumbler, 9 oz, ftd | 28.00 | 32.00 | 35.00 | 30.00 |
| Vase, 9-3/4" h | 160.00 | 85.00 | 95.00 | 145.00 |
| Vase, 12" h, ftd | 225.00 | 115.00 | 125.00 | 175.00 |
| Wine | 35.00 | 20.00 | 24.00 | 40.00 |

*Lincoln Inn, pink plate.*

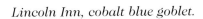

*Lincoln Inn, cobalt blue goblet.*

# *Lorain*

### *Basket, No. 615*

Manufactured by Indiana Glass Company, Dunkirk, Ind., from 1929 to 1939.

Made in crystal, green, and yellow.

**Reproductions:** † A fantasy sherbet has been reported in both milk white and avocado green.

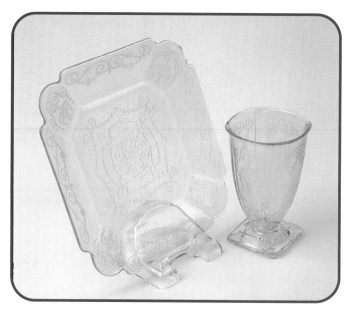

*Lorain, yellow plate and tumbler.*

| Item | Crystal | Green | Yellow |
|---|---|---|---|
| Berry bowl, 8" d | 125.00 | 190.00 | 250.00 |
| Cereal bowl, 6" d | 45.00 | 50.00 | 65.00 |
| Creamer, ftd | 20.00 | 20.00 | 30.00 |
| Cup and saucer | 32.00 | 32.00 | 25.00 |
| Plate, 5-1/2" d, sherbet | 10.00 | 12.00 | 15.00 |
| Plate, 7-3/4" d, salad | 15.00 | 18.00 | 24.00 |
| Plate, 8-3/4" d, luncheon | 20.00 | 24.00 | 32.50 |
| Plate, 10-1/4" d, dinner | 30.00 | 40.00 | 90.00 |
| Platter, 11-1/2" l | 32.50 | 32.50 | 48.00 |
| Relish, 8" d, four parts | 32.00 | 32.00 | 40.00 |
| Salad bowl, 7-3/4" d | 40.00 | 40.00 | 75.00 |
| Saucer | 6.00 | 6.00 | 8.00 |
| Sherbet, ftd † | 32.00 | 20.00 | 40.00 |
| Snack tray, crystal trim | 32.00 | 37.50 | - |
| Sugar, ftd | 20.00 | 24.00 | 30.00 |
| Tumbler, 9 oz, 4-3/4" h, ftd | 32.00 | 35.00 | 40.00 |
| Vegetable bowl, 9-3/4" l, oval | 5000 | 60.00 | 75.00 |

# Madrid

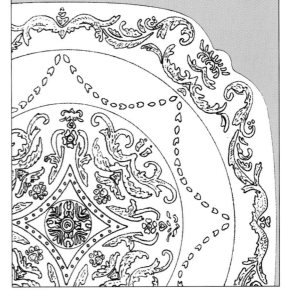

Manufactured by Federal Glass Company, Lancaster, Ohio, from 1932 to 1939.

Made in amber, blue, crystal, green, iridescent, and pink. Iridized pieces are limited to a console set, consisting of a low bowl and pair of candlesticks, valued at $40.

**Reproductions:** † Reproductions include candlesticks, cups, saucers and vegetable bowl. Reproductions are found in amber, blue, crystal, and pink. Federal Glass Company reissued this pattern under the name "Recollection." Some of these pieces were dated 1976. When Federal went bankrupt, the molds were sold to Indiana Glass, which removed the date and began production of crystal, then pink. Several pieces were made recently that were not part of the original production and include a footed cake stand, goblet, two-section grill plate, preserves stand, squatty salt and pepper shakers, 11-oz tumbler and vase.

| Item | Amber | Blue | Crystal | Green | Pink |
|---|---|---|---|---|---|
| Ashtray, 6" sq | 300.00 | - | - | 295.00 | - |
| Berry bowl, small | 7.50 | - | 6.50 | - | - |
| Berry bowl, 9-3/8" d | 25.00 | - | 25.00 | - | 25.00 |
| Bowl, 7" d | 17.50 | - | 12.00 | 17.50 | - |
| Butter dish, cov | 80.00 | - | 65.00 | 90.00 | - |
| Cake plate, 11-1/4" d | 24.00 | - | 20.00 | - | 28.00 |
| Candlesticks, 2-1/4" h, pr † | 18.50 | - | 14.50 | - | 28.00 |
| Coaster, 5" d | 40.00 | - | 40.00 | 35.00 | - |
| Console bowl, 11" d | 20.00 | - | 18.00 | - | 36.00 |
| Cookie jar | 50.00 | - | 45.00 | - | 40.00 |
| Creamer | 12.00 | 18.00 | 7.00 | 10.00 | - |
| Cream soup, 4 3/4" d | 18.00 | - | 15.50 | - | - |
| Cup † | 14.00 | 20.00 | 6.50 | 12.00 | 8.50 |
| Gelatin mold, 2-1/2" h | 25.00 | - | 20.00 | - | - |
| Gravy boat | 1,950.00 | - | 900.00 | - | - |
| Gravy boat platter | 900.00 | - | 900.00 | - | - |
| Hot dish coaster, 3-1/2" d | 95.00 | - | 40.00 | 45.00 | - |
| Iced tea tumbler, round | 24.00 | - | 24.00 | 22.00 | - |
| Jam dish, 7" d | 24.00 | 35.00 | 12.00 | 25.00 | - |
| Juice pitcher | 50.00 | - | 45.00 | - | - |
| Juice tumbler, 5 oz, 3-7/8" h, ftd | 16.50 | 40.00 | 35.00 | 30.00 | - |
| Pitcher, jug-type | 60.00 | - | 24.00 | 190.00 | - |
| Pitcher, 60 oz, 8" h, sq | 50.00 | 225.00 | 150.00 | 145.00 | 50.00 |
| Pitcher, 80 oz, 8-1/2" h, ice lip | 75.00 | - | 30.00 | 225.00 | - |

| Item | Amber | Blue | Crystal | Green | Pink |
|---|---|---|---|---|---|
| Plate, 6" d, sherbet | 5.50 | 12.00 | 4.00 | 4.50 | 4.00 |
| Plate, 7-1/2" d, salad | 12.00 | 17.00 | 12.00 | 9.00 | 9.00 |
| Plate, 8-7/8" d, luncheon | 10.00 | 20.00 | 7.50 | 12.00 | 10.00 |
| Plate, 10-1/2" d, dinner | 48.00 | 60.00 | 24.00 | 45.00 | - |
| Plate, 10-1/2" d, grill | 12.00 | - | 10.00 | 18.50 | - |
| Platter, 11-1/2" oval | 20.00 | 32.00 | 20.00 | 18.00 | 18.00 |
| Relish dish, 10-1/2" d | 14.50 | - | 7.00 | 16.00 | 20.00 |
| Salad bowl, 8" d | 17.00 | - | 9.50 | 15.50 | - |
| Salad bowl, 9-1/2" d | 32.00 | - | 30.00 | - | - |
| Salt and pepper shakers, 3-1/2" h | 135.00 | 145.00 | 95.00 | 110.00 | - |
| Sauce bowl, 5" d | 9.00 | - | 7.50 | 8.50 | 11.00 |
| Saucer † | 5.00 | 8.00 | 4.00 | 7.00 | 5.00 |
| Sherbet, cone | 7.50 | 18.00 | 6.50 | 14.00 | - |
| Sherbet, ftd | 8.50 | 15.00 | 6.00 | 11.00 | - |
| Soup bowl, 7" d † | 15.00 | 20.00 | 6.00 | 15.50 | - |
| Sugar, cov † | 46.00 | 175.00 | 32.50 | 48.00 | - |
| Sugar, open † | 10.00 | 15.00 | 8.00 | 10.00 | - |
| Tumbler, 9 oz, 4-1/2" h | 20.00 | 40.00 | 17.50 | 25.00 | 25.00 |
| Tumbler, 12 oz, 5-1/4" h, ftd or flat | 35.00 | - | 30.00 | 40.00 | - |
| Vegetable bowl, 10" l, oval † | 28.00 | 35.00 | 24.00 | 24.00 | 30.00 |

*Madrid, amber sugar and creamer.*

*Madrid, amber bowl.*

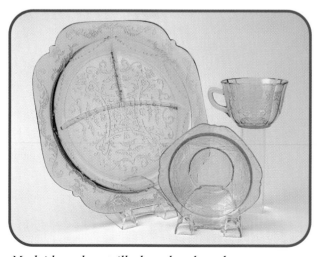

*Madrid, amber grill plate, bowl, and cup.*

# Manhattan

## Horizontal Ribbed

Manufactured by Anchor Hocking Glass Company, from 1938 to 1943.

Made in crystal, green, iridized, pink, and ruby. Ruby pieces are limited to relish tray inserts, currently valued at $8 each. Green and iridized production was limited to footed tumblers, currently valued at $17.50.

Anchor Hocking introduced a similar pattern, Park Avenue, in 1987. Anchor Hocking was careful to preserve the Manhattan pattern. Collectors should pay careful attention to measurements if they are uncertain of the pattern.

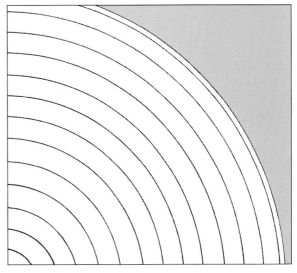

| Item | Crystal | Pink |
|---|---|---|
| Ashtray, 4" d, round | 12.00 | 10.00 |
| Ashtray, 4-1/2" w, sq | 25.00 | - |
| Berry bowl, 5-3/8" d, handles | 24.00 | 24.00 |
| Berry bowl, 7-1/2" d | 28.00 | - |
| Bowl, 4-1/2" d | 9.00 | - |
| Bowl, 8" d, closed handles | 28.00 | 25.00 |
| Bowl, 8" d, metal handle | 25.00 | - |
| Bowl, 9-1/2" d, handle | - | 45.00 |
| Candlesticks, pr, 4-1/2" h | 25.00 | - |
| Candy dish, three legs | - | 16.00 |
| Candy dish, cov | 40.00 | - |
| Cereal bowl, 5-1/4" d, no handles | 95.00 | - |
| Coaster, 3-1/2" | 20.00 | - |
| Cocktail | 18.00 | - |
| Comport, 5-3/4" h | 35.00 | 65.00 |
| Creamer, oval | 9.00 | 20.00 |
| Cup | 20.00 | 160.00 |
| Fruit bowl, 9-1/2" d, two open handles | 40.00 | 50.00 |
| Juice pitcher, 24 oz | 40.00 | - |
| Pitcher, 80 oz, tilted | 55.00 | 85.00 |
| Plate, 6" d, sherbet | 7.00 | 50.00 |
| Plate, 8-1/2" d, salad | 24.00 | - |
| Plate, 10-1/4" d, dinner | 30.00 | 120.00 |
| Relish tray insert | 2.50 | 6.00 |
| Relish tray, 14" d, inserts | 85.00 | 50.00 |
| Relish tray, 14" d, four parts | 65.00 | - |

| Item | Crystal | Pink |
|---|---|---|
| Salad bowl, 9" d. | 20.00 | - |
| Salt and pepper shakers, pr, 2" h, sq | 50.00 | 60.00 |
| Sandwich plate, 14" d | 22.00 | - |
| Sauce bowl, 4-1/2" d, handles | 12.00 | - |
| Saucer | 7.00 | 50.00 |
| Sherbet | 14.00 | 20.00 |
| Sugar, oval | 12.00 | 17.50 |
| Tumbler, 10 oz, 5-1/4" h, ftd | 22.00 | 25.00 |
| Vase, 8" h | 30.00 | - |
| Wine, 3-1/2" h | 15.00 | - |

Manhattan, relish tray with ruby inserts and crystal base; and crystal compote, vase, and bowl.

Manhattan, small crystal bowl (on pedestal); pink creamer and sugar; crystal salt and pepper shakers; crystal cereal bowl, crystal iced tea tumbler, pitcher, relish with metal stand; and pink footed bowl.

# Mayfair
## Federal

Manufactured by Federal Glass Company, Columbus, Ohio, 1934.
  Made in amber, crystal, and green.

*Mayfair Federal, amber plate.*

| Item | Amber | Crystal | Green |
|---|---|---|---|
| Cereal Bowl, 6" d | 18.50 | 15.00 | 22.00 |
| Cream Soup, 5" d | 22.00 | 12.00 | 20.00 |
| Creamer, ftd | 17.50 | 14.00 | 16.00 |
| Cup | 8.50 | 5.00 | 8.50 |
| Plate, 6-3/4" d, salad | 7.00 | 4.50 | 8.50 |
| Plate, 9-1/2" d, dinner | 14.00 | 12.00 | 14.50 |
| Plate, 9-1/2" d, grill | 17.50 | 15.00 | 17.50 |
| Platter, 12" l, oval | 27.50 | 22.00 | 30.00 |
| Sauce Bowl, 5" d | 8.50 | 7.00 | 12.00 |
| Saucer | 4.50 | 2.50 | 4.50 |
| Sugar, ftd | 14.00 | 12.00 | 14.00 |
| Tumbler, 9 oz, 4-1/2" h | 27.50 | 16.50 | 32.00 |
| Vegetable, 10" l, oval | 32.00 | 32.00 | 32.00 |

# Mayfair

## Open Rose

Manufactured by Hocking Glass Company, Lancaster, Ohio, from 1931 to 1937.

Made in crystal, green, ice blue, pink, and yellow.

**Reproductions:** † This pattern has been plagued with reproductions since 1977. Items reproduced include cookie jars, salt and pepper shakers, juice pitchers, and whiskey glasses. Reproductions are found in amethyst, blue, cobalt blue, green, pink, and red.

| Item | Crystal | Green | Ice Blue | Pink | Pink Satin | Yellow |
|---|---|---|---|---|---|---|
| Bowl, 11-3/4" l, flat . . . . . . . . . . . . . . . | - | 35.00 | 75.00 | 65.00 | 70.00 | 195.00 |
| Butter dish, cov. . . . . . . . . . . . . . . . . . | - | 1,295.00 | 325.00 | 80.00 | 95.00 | 1,295.00 |
| Cake plate, 10" d, ftd. . . . . . . . . . . . | - | 115.00 | 75.00 | 40.00 | 45.00 | - |
| Cake plate, 12" d, handles . . . . . . . . . | - | 40.00 | 95.00 | 65.00 | 50.00 | - |
| Candy dish, cov . . . . . . . . . . . . . . . | - | 575.00 | 325.00 | 70.00 | 85.00 | 475.00 |
| Celery dish, 9" l, divided . . . . . . . . . . . | - | 155.00 | 60.00 | - | - | 150.00 |
| Celery dish, 10" l, divided . . . . . . . . . . | - | - | 90.00 | 295.00 | - | - |
| Celery dish, 10" l, not divided . . . . . . . | - | 115.00 | 80.00 | 55.00 | 50.00 | 115.00 |
| Cereal bowl, 5-1/2" d . . . . . . . . . . . . . | - | 24.00 | 48.00 | 30.00 | 35.00 | 75.00 |
| Claret, 4-1/2 oz, 5-1/4" h . . . . . . . . . . | - | 950.00 | - | 1,150.00 | - | - |
| Cocktail, 3 oz, 4" h . . . . . . . . . . . . . | - | 975.00 | - | 125.00 | - | - |
| Console bowl, 9" d, 3-1/8" h, three legs | - | 5,000.00 | - | 5,000.00 | - | - |
| Cookie jar, cov † . . . . . . . . . . . . . . . | - | 575.00 | 295.00 | 75.00 | 37.00 | 860.00 |
| Cordial, 1 oz, 3-3/4" h . . . . . . . . . . . | - | 950.00 | - | 1,100.00 | - | - |
| Cream soup, 5" d . . . . . . . . . . . . . . . | - | - | - | 65.00 | 68.00 | - |
| Creamer, ftd . . . . . . . . . . . . . . . . . | - | | | 35.00 | 30.00 | |
| Cup. . . . . . . . . . . . . . . . . . . . . . . | - | 150.00 | 55.00 | 24.00 | 27.50 | 150.00 |
| Decanter, stopper, 32 oz . . . . . . . . . . . | - | - | - | 225.00 | - | - |
| Fruit bowl, 12" d, scalloped . . . . . . . . . | - | 50.00 | 125.00 | 90.00 | 75.00 | 215.00 |
| Goblet, 2-1/2 oz, 4-1/8" . . . . . . . . . . . | - | 950.00 | - | 950.00 | - | - |
| Goblet, 9 oz, 5-3/4" h . . . . . . . . . . . . | - | 465.00 | - | 90.00 | - | - |
| Goblet, 9 oz, 7-1/4" h, thin . . . . . . . . | - | - | 225.00 | 250.00 | - | - |
| Iced tea tumbler, 13-1/2 oz, 5-1/4" h . . . . . . . . . . . . . . | - | - | 225.00 | 70.00 | - | - |
| Iced tea tumbler, 15 oz, 6-1/2" h, ftd . . | - | 250.00 | 285.00 | 65.00 | 65.00 | - |
| Juice pitcher, 37oz, 6" h † . . . . . . . . | 24.50 | 525.00 | 150.00 | 70.00 | 65.00 | 525.00 |
| Juice tumbler, 3 oz, 3-1/4" h, ftd . . . . . | - | - | - | 80.00 | - | - |
| Juice tumbler, 5 oz, 3-1/2" . . . . . . . . . . | - | - | 225.00 | 80.00 | - | - |
| Pitcher, 60 oz, 8" h . . . . . . . . . . . . . | - | 475.00 | 195.00 | 95.00 | 100.00 | 425.00 |
| Pitcher, 80 oz, 8-1/2" h . . . . . . . . . . . | - | 725.00 | 295.00 | 130.00 | 135.00 | 725.00 |
| Plate, 5-3/4" d . . . . . . . . . . . . . . . . | - | 90.00 | 25.00 | 15.00 | 15.00 | 90.00 |
| Plate, 6-1/2" d, off-center indent . . . . . | - | 115.00 | 42.00 | 30.00 | 35.00 | - |

| Item | Crystal | Green | Ice Blue | Pink | Pink Satin | Yellow |
|---|---|---|---|---|---|---|
| Plate, 6-1/2" d, sherbet . . . . . . . . . . . . - | | - | 24.00 | 14.50 | - | - |
| Plate, 8-1/2" d, luncheon . . . . . . . . . . . - | | 85.00 | 55.00 | 40.00 | 35.00 | 80.00 |
| Plate, 9-1/2" d, dinner . . . . . . . . . . . . . - | | 150.00 | 90.00 | 65.00 | 62.00 | 150.00 |
| Plate, 9-1/2" d, grill . . . . . . . . . . . . . . - | | 75.00 | 70.00 | 50.00 | 35.00 | 80.00 |
| Plate, 11-1/2" d, grill, handles . . . . . . . - | | - | - | - | - | 100.00 |
| Platter, 12" l, oval, open handles . . . . 17.50 | | 175.00 | 60.00 | 40.00 | 35.00 | 115.00 |
| Platter, 12-1/2" oval, 8" wide, closed handles . . . . . . . . . . . . . . . . - | | 245.00 | - | - | - | 245.00 |
| Relish, 8-3/8" d, four parts . . . . . . . . . - | | 160.00 | 65.00 | 37.50 | 37.50 | 160.00 |
| Relish, 8-3/8" d, non-partitioned . . . . . - | | 275.00 | - | 200.00 | - | 275.00 |
| Salt and pepper shakers, pr, flat † . . . 20.00 | | 1,000.00 | 295.00 | 65.00 | 70.00 | 800.00 |
| Sandwich server, center handle. . . . . . - | | 48.00 | 85.00 | 65.00 | 50.00 | 130.00 |
| Saucer. . . . . . . . . . . . . . . . . . . . . . . . - | | 90.00 | 30.00 | 45.00 | 35.00 | 140.00 |
| Sherbet, 2-1/4" flat . . . . . . . . . . . . . . - | | - | 135.00 | 185.00 | - | - |
| Sherbet, 3" ftd. . . . . . . . . . . . . . . . . . - | | - | - | 20.00 | - | - |
| Sherbet, 4-3/4" ftd . . . . . . . . . . . . . . - | | 150.00 | 75.00 | 75.00 | 75.00 | 150.00 |
| Sugar, ftd. . . . . . . . . . . . . . . . . . . . . - | | 195.00 | 85.00 | 35.00 | 40.00 | 185.00 |
| Sweet pea vase . . . . . . . . . . . . . . . . . - | | 285.00 | 135.00 | 250.00 | 145.00 | - |
| Tumbler, 9 oz, 4-1/4" h . . . . . . . . . . . - | | - | 100.00 | 30.00 | - | - |
| Tumbler, 10 oz, 5-1/4" h . . . . . . . . . . - | | - | 145.00 | 65.00 | - | 185.00 |
| Tumbler, 11 oz, 4-3/4" h . . . . . . . . . . - | | 200.00 | 250.00 | 225.00 | 225.00 | 215.00 |
| Vegetable bowl, 7" d, two handles . . . . - | | 33.00 | 75.00 | 65.00 | 70.00 | 195.00 |
| Vegetable bowl, 9-1/2" l, oval . . . . . . . - | | 110.00 | 70.00 | 40.00 | 30.00 | 125.00 |
| Vegetable bowl, 10" d cov . . . . . . . . . - | | - | 120.00 | 120.00 | 120.00 | 900.00 |
| Vegetable bowl, 10" d open . . . . . . . . . - | | - | 85.00 | 20.00 | 19.00 | 200.00 |
| Whiskey, 1-1/2 oz, 2-1/4" h † . . . . . . . - | | - | - | 58.00 | - | - |
| Wine, 3 oz, 4-1/2" h. . . . . . . . . . . . . . - | | 450.00 | - | 120.00 | - | - |

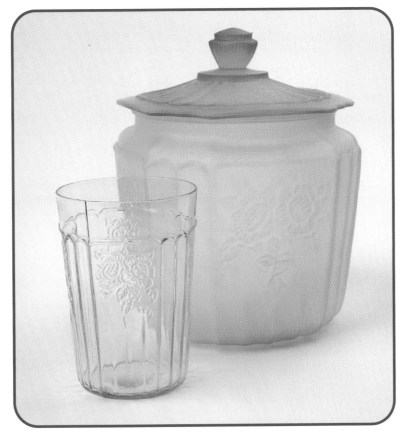

*Mayfair Open Rose, pink tumbler and pink satin-finish covered cookie jar.*

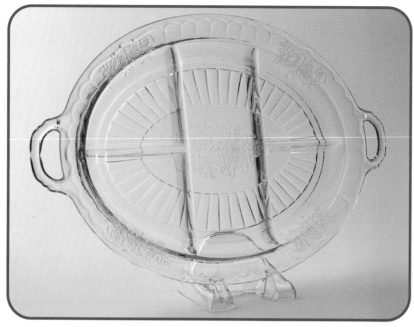

*Mayfair Open Rose, divided crystal celery dish.*

*REPRODUCTION! Mayfair Open Rose, green and blue cookie jars.*

*Mayfair Open Rose, blue vegetable bowl.*

# Melba

### Line #707

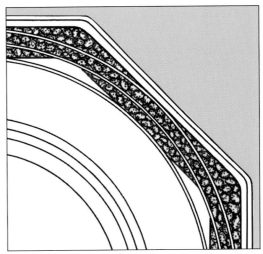

Manufactured by L.E. Smith Glass Company, Mount Pleasant, Pa., in the early 1930s.

Made in amethyst, black, green, and pink.

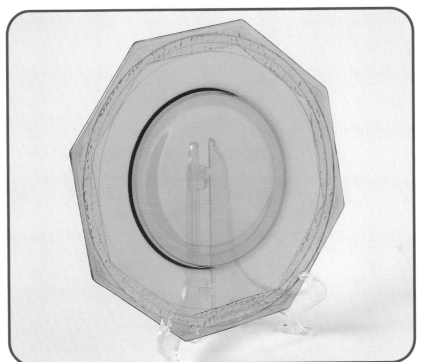

*Melba, amethyst luncheon plate.*

| Items | Amethyst | Black | Green | Pink |
|---|---|---|---|---|
| Baker, oval | 20.00 | 22.00 | 18.00 | 18.00 |
| Bowl, 10-1/2" d, ruffled | 18.00 | 20.00 | 15.00 | 15.00 |
| Candleholder | 15.00 | 17.00 | 12.00 | 12.00 |
| Creamer | 15.00 | 18.00 | 12.00 | 12.00 |
| Cup | 6.50 | 8.50 | 5.00 | 5.00 |
| Dessert bowl | 4.50 | 5.00 | 3.50 | 3.50 |
| Plate, 6" d, bread and butter | 5.00 | 7.50 | 4.00 | 4.00 |
| Plate, 7" d, salad | 7.00 | 9.50 | 6.00 | 6.00 |
| Plate, 9" d, luncheon | 9.00 | 12.00 | 8.00 | 8.00 |
| Platter | 15.00 | 18.00 | 12.00 | 12.00 |
| Salad bowl | 18.00 | 20.00 | 15.00 | 15.00 |
| Saucer | 3.50 | 4.50 | 3.00 | 3.00 |
| Serving plate, 9" d, handles | 15.00 | 18.00 | 12.00 | 12.00 |
| Sugar | 15.00 | 18.00 | 12.00 | 12.00 |
| Vegetable bowl, 9-1/2" l | 18.00 | 20.00 | 15.00 | 15.00 |

# Miss America

## Diamond Pattern

Manufactured by Hocking Glass Company, Lancaster, Ohio, from 1935 to 1938.

Made in crystal, green, ice blue, jade-ite, pink, and royal ruby.

**Reproductions:** † Reproductions include the butter dish (including a new importer), creamer, 8" pitcher, salt and pepper shakers, sugar, and tumbler. Reproductions are found in amberina, blue, cobalt blue, crystal, green, pink, and red.

| Item | Crystal | Green | Ice Blue | Pink | Royal Ruby |
|---|---|---|---|---|---|
| Berry bowl, 4-1/2" d | - | 15.00 | - | - | - |
| Bowl, 8" d, curved at top | 48.00 | - | - | 95.00 | - |
| Bowl, 8" d, straight sides | - | - | - | 85.00 | - |
| Bowl, 11" d, shallow | - | - | - | - | 850.00 |
| Butter dish, cov † | 200.00 | - | - | 550.00 | - |
| Cake plate, 12" d, ftd | 27.50 | - | - | 45.00 | - |
| Candy jar, cov, 11-1/2" | 65.00 | - | - | 200.00 | - |
| Celery dish, 10-1/2" l, oval | 19.50 | - | 160.00 | 42.00 | - |
| Cereal bowl, 6-1/4" d | 12 | 18.00 | - | 35.00 | - |
| Coaster, 5-3/4" d | 19.50 | - | - | 45.00 | - |
| Comport, 5" d | 20.00 | - | - | 40.00 | - |
| Creamer, ftd † | 12.50 | - | - | 24.00 | 215.00 |
| Cup | 12.50 | 12.00 | 14.00 | 30.00 | 235.00 |
| Fruit bowl, 8-3/4" d | 39.50 | - | - | 60.00 | 450.00 |
| Goblet, 10 oz, 5-1/2" h | 22.50 | - | - | 70.00 | 250.00 |
| Iced tea tumbler, 14 oz, 5-3/4" h | 25.00 | - | - | 85.00 | - |
| Juice goblet, 5 oz, 4-3/4" h | 27.50 | - | - | 125.00 | 250.00 |
| Juice tumbler, 5 oz, 4" h | 27.50 | - | 150.00 | 60.00 | 200.00 |
| Pitcher, 65 oz, 8" h † | 45.00 | - | - | 175.00 | - |
| Pitcher, 65 oz, 8-1/2" h, ice lip | 75.00 | - | - | 135.00 | 50.00 |
| Plate, 5-3/4" d, sherbet | 7.50 | 9.00 | 55.00 | 18.00 | - |
| Plate, 6-3/4" d | - | 12.00 | - | - | - |
| Plate, 8-1/2" d, salad | 9.00 | 14.00 | - | 32.00 | 150.00 |
| Plate, 10-1/4" d, dinner | 16.50 | - | 150.00 | 45.00 | - |
| Plate, 10-1/4" d, grill | 15.00 | - | - | 37.50 | - |
| Platter, 12-1/4" l, oval | 18.00 | - | - | 50.00 | - |
| Relish, 8-3/4" l, 4 part | 30.00 | - | - | 40.00 | - |
| Relish, 11-3/4" d, divided | 35.00 | - | - | 40.00 | - |
| Salt and pepper shakers, pr † | 35.00 | 300.00 | - | 65.00 | - |
| Saucer | 4.00 | - | - | 10.00 | 60.00 |

| Item | Crystal | Green | Ice Blue | Pink | Royal Ruby |
|---|---|---|---|---|---|
| Sherbet | 10.00 | - | 60.00 | 20.00 | 175.00 |
| Sugar † | 12.00 | - | - | 25.00 | 225.00 |
| Tumbler, 10 oz, 4-1/2" h, flat † | 20.00 | 45.00 | - | 40.00 | - |
| Tumbler, 14 oz, 5-3/4" h | 28.00 | - | - | - | - |
| Vegetable bowl, 10" l, oval | 18.00 | - | - | 47.50 | - |
| Whiskey | 24.00 | - | - | - | - |
| Wine, 3 oz, 3-3/4" h | 25.00 | - | - | 85.00 | 250.00 |

*Miss America, pink goblet, comport, and tumbler with original label.*

*Miss America, close-up view of original label on pink tumbler.*

*Miss America, green plate and bowl.*

**167**

# Moderntone

Manufactured by Hazel Atlas Glass Company, Clarksburg, W.V., and Zanesville, Ohio, from 1934 to 1942; also, in the late 1940s to early 1950s.

Made in amethyst, cobalt blue, crystal, pink, and Platonite fired-on colors. Later period production saw plain white, as well as white with blue or red stripes, a Willow-type design in blue or red on white. Collector interest in crystal is limited and prices remain low, less than 50 percent of Platonite.

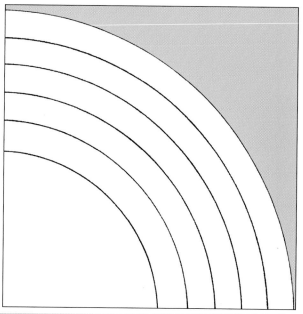

| Item | Amethyst | Cobalt Blue | Platonite, Darker Shades | Platonite, Pastel Shades | White or White with Dec | Willow-Type Dec |
|---|---|---|---|---|---|---|
| Ashtray, 7-3/4" d, match holder center. . | - | 225.00 | - | - | - | - |
| Berry bowl, 5" d, rim . . . . . . . . . . . . . | 25.00 | 27.50 | - | 7.00 | 5.00 | 15.00 |
| Berry bowl, 5" d, without rim . . . . . . . . | - | - | 12.50 | 25.00 | - | - |
| Berry bowl, 8-3/4" d . . . . . . . . . . . . . | 42.00 | 55.00 | - | - | 7.50 | 28.00 |
| Bowl, 8" d, no rim . . . . . . . . . . . . . . . | - | - | 40.00 | 50.00 | - | - |
| Bowl, 8" d, rim . . . . . . . . . . . . . . . . . | - | - | - | 15.00 | 6.00 | 28.00 |
| Butter dish, metal cov . . . . . . . . . . . . | - | 98.00 | - | - | - | - |
| Cereal bowl, 5" d, deep, no white . . . . . . | - | - | 17.50 | 10.00 | - | - |
| Cereal bowl, 5" d, deep, with white . . . . | - | - | - | 9.00 | 4.50 | - |
| Cereal bowl, 6-1/2" d . . . . . . . . . . . . . | 70.00 | 70.00 | - | - | - | - |
| Cheese dish, 7" d, metal cov . . . . . . . . . | - | 475.00 | - | - | - | - |
| Cream soup, 4-3/4" d . . . . . . . . . . . . . | 22.00 | 24.00 | - | 12.00 | 7.00 | 24.00 |
| Cream soup, 5" d, ruffled. . . . . . . . . . . | 30.00 | 85.00 | - | - | - | - |
| Creamer . . . . . . . . . . . . . . . . . . . . . | 18.00 | 15.00 | 12.00 | 5.50 | 4.50 | 20.00 |
| Cup. . . . . . . . . . . . . . . . . . . . . . . . . | 12.00 | 16.00 | 9.00 | 6.50 | 2.50 | 22.00 |
| Custard cup . . . . . . . . . . . . . . . . . . . | 18.00 | 24.00 | - | - | - | - |
| Mug, 4" h, 8 oz. . . . . . . . . . . . . . . . . | - | - | - | - | 8.50 | - |
| Mustard, metal lid . . . . . . . . . . . . . . . | - | 25.00 | - | - | - | - |
| Plate, 5-7/8" d, sherbet . . . . . . . . . . . | 10.00 | 12.50 | - | - | - | - |
| Plate, 6-3/4" d, salad . . . . . . . . . . . . . | 12.50 | 15.00 | 12.00 | 9.00 | 6.00 | 10.00 |
| Plate, 7-3/4" d, luncheon . . . . . . . . . . | 10.00 | 18.00 | - | - | - | - |
| Plate, 8-7/8" d, dinner . . . . . . . . . . . . | 13.50 | 22.00 | 15.00 | 12.00 | 4.00 | 20.00 |
| Platter, 11" l, oval . . . . . . . . . . . . . . | 40.00 | 55.00 | - | - | 14.00 | 30.00 |
| Platter, 12" l, oval . . . . . . . . . . . . . . | 48.00 | 165.00 | 32.00 | 15.00 | 10.00 | 35.00 |
| Salt and pepper shakers, pr. . . . . . . . . | 45.00 | 50.00 | - | 10.00 | 12.00 | - |
| Sandwich plate, 10-1/2" d . . . . . . . . . | 35.00 | 75.00 | - | 20.00 | 12.50 | - |

| Item | Amethyst | Cobalt Blue | Platonite, Darker Shades | Platonite, Pastel Shades | White or White with Dec | Willow-Type Dec |
|---|---|---|---|---|---|---|
| Saucer | 4.50 | 5.00 | 7.50 | 2.50 | 2.50 | 4.50 |
| Sherbet | 13.00 | 18.00 | 12.00 | 8.00 | 4.50 | 14.00 |
| Soup bowl, 7-1/2" d | 95.00 | 225.00 | - | - | - | - |
| Sugar | 18.00 | 12.50 | 12.00 | 6.00 | 4.50 | 20.00 |
| Tumbler, 5 oz | 40.00 | 55.00 | - | - | - | - |
| Tumbler, 9 oz | 30.00 | 40.00 | 45.00 | 12.00 | - | - |
| Tumbler, 12 oz | 85.00 | 95.00 | - | - | - | - |
| Tumbler, cone, ftd | - | - | - | - | 4.00 | - |
| Whiskey, 1-1/2 oz | - | 45.00 | - | 18.50 | - | - |

# Children's

Hazel Atlas also manufactured children's sets in the early 1950s, known as Little Hostess Party Dishes. The original box adds to the value. Colorful combinations were found.

| Item | Gray/ Rust/ Gold | Green/ Gray/ Chartreuse | Lemon/ Beige/ Pink/Aqua | Pastel Pink/ Green/Blue/ Yellow | Pink/ Black/ White |
|---|---|---|---|---|---|
| Creamer, 1-3/4" | 17.50 | 16.00 | 15.00 | 15.00 | 15.00 |
| Cup, 3/4" | 15.00 | 12.00 | 12.00 | 12.00 | 12.00 |
| Plate, 5-1/4" d | 15.00 | 12.00 | 12.00 | 12.00 | 12.00 |
| Saucer, 3-7/8" d | 8.00 | 7.00 | 12.50 | 7.00 | 7.00 |
| Sugar, 1-3/4" | 12.00 | 15.00 | 20.00 | 15.00 | 18.00 |
| Teapot, 3-1/2" d | 125.00 | 115.00 | 95.00 | - | 95.00 |

*Moderntone, cobalt blue cup and saucer, sherbet (on pedestal), salad plate, dinner plate, and cream soup.*

# Monticello

## *Waffle, #698*

Manufactured by Imperial Glass Company, c1920 to 1950s.

Made in crystal, Rubigold (Imperial's trademarked name for marigold carnival glass), teal, and white milk glass. Some other colors are known in very limited production runs, such as a basket in Rose Marie. Collector interest is highest for crystal.

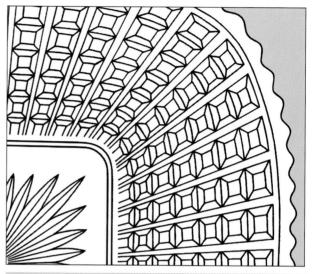

| Item | Crystal |
| --- | --- |
| Basket, 10" h | 25.00 |
| Bonbon, 5-1/2" d, handle | 15.00 |
| Bowl, 6" d | 10.00 |
| Bowl, 6-1/2" d or 7-1/2" d, belled | 15.00 |
| Bowl, 8-1/2" d or 10" d, belled | 18.00 |
| Bowl, 9" d | 18.00 |
| Bowl, 10" d | 20.00 |
| Butter tub, 5-1/2" d | 35.00 |
| Cake plate, 12" d | 35.00 |
| Celery tray, 9" l | 20.00 |
| Cheese dish, cov | 75.00 |
| Coaster, 3-1/4" d | 7.50 |
| Cocktail | 15.00 |
| Compote, 5-1/4" d | 12.50 |
| Compote, 5-3/4" d, belled rim | 15.00 |
| Cream soup bowl, 5-1/2" d | 12.50 |
| Creamer | 18.00 |
| Cup | 10.00 |
| Finger bowl, 4-1/2" d | 10.00 |
| Fruit bowl, 4-1/2" d or 5" d | 10.00 |
| Goblet | 15.00 |
| Iced tea tumbler, 12 oz | 15.00 |
| Lily bowl, 5" d | 20.00 |
| Lily bowl, 6" d | 25.00 |
| Lily bowl, 7" d | 30.00 |
| Lily bowl, 8" d, cupped | 35.00 |
| Mayonnaise, three pcs | 32.50 |
| Nappy, 7" d | 15.00 |
| Pickle dish, 6" l, oval | 15.00 |
| Pitcher, 52 oz, ice lip | 60.00 |
| Plate, 6" d, bread and butter | 5.00 |
| Plate, 8" d, salad | 8.00 |
| Plate, 9" d, dinner | 18.00 |
| Plate, 10-1/2" w, sq | 25.00 |

| Item | Crystal |
| --- | --- |
| Punch bowl | 65.00 |
| Punch cup | 8.50 |
| Relish, 8-1/4" l, divided | 18.00 |
| Salad bowl, 7-1/2" sq | 30.00 |
| Salt and pepper shakers, pr, glass tops | 24.00 |
| Saucer | 4.50 |
| Serving plate, 16" d, cupped | 50.00 |
| Sherbet | 13.00 |
| Sugar | 18.00 |
| Tidbit, two tiers | 45.00 |
| Tumbler, 9 oz | 12.00 |
| Vase, 6" h | 25.00 |
| Vase, 10-1/2" h | 35.00 |
| Vegetable bowl, 8" d | 25.00 |

*Monticello, crystal compote.*

# Moondrops

Manufactured by New Martinsville Glass Company, New Martinsville, W.V., from 1932 to 1940.

Made in amber, amethyst, black, cobalt blue, crystal, dark green, green, ice blue, jadeite, light green, pink, red, and smoke.

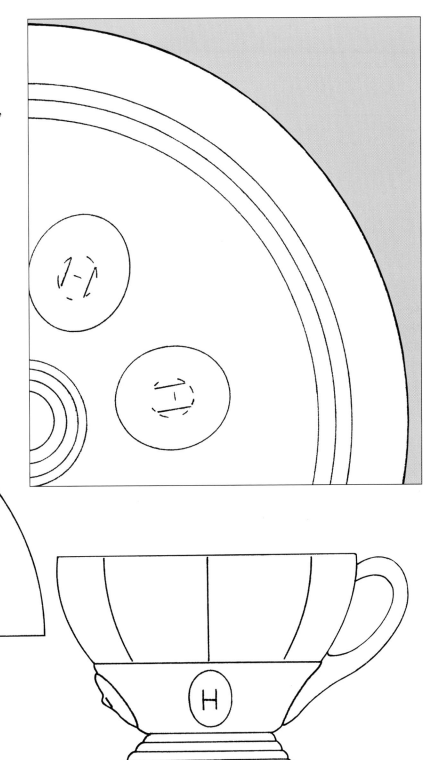

| Item | Cobalt Blue | Crystal | Other Colors | Red |
|---|---|---|---|---|
| Ashtray | 30.00 | - | 18.00 | 30.00 |
| Berry bowl, 5-1/4" d | 20.00 | - | 12.00 | 20.00 |
| Bowl, 8-1/2" d, ftd, concave top | 40.00 | - | 25.00 | 40.00 |
| Bowl, 9-1/2" d, three legs, ruffled | 60.00 | - | - | 60.00 |
| Bowl, 9-3/4" l, oval, handles | 50.00 | - | 30.00 | 50.00 |
| Butter dish, cov | 425.00 | - | 275.00 | 295.00 |
| Candlesticks, pr, 2" h, ruffled | 40.00 | - | 25.00 | 40.00 |
| Candlesticks, pr, 4" h, sherbet style | 30.00 | - | 18.00 | 30.00 |
| Candlesticks, pr, 5" h, ruffled | 32.00 | - | 22.00 | 32.00 |
| Candlesticks, pr, 5" h, wings | 90.00 | - | 60.00 | 90.00 |
| Candlesticks, pr, 5-1/4" h, triple light | 100.00 | 65.00 | 65.00 | 100.00 |
| Candlesticks, pr, 8-1/2" h, metal stem | 40.00 | - | 32.00 | 40.00 |
| Candy dish, 8" d, ruffled | 40.00 | - | 20.00 | 40.00 |
| Casserole, cov, 9-3/4" d | 185.00 | - | 100.00 | 185.00 |
| Celery bowl, 11" l, boat-shape | 30.00 | - | 24.00 | 30.00 |
| Cocktail shaker, metal top | 60.00 | - | 35.00 | 60.00 |
| Comport, 4" d | 25.00 | - | 15.00 | 25.00 |
| Comport, 11-1/2" d | 60.00 | - | 30.00 | 60.00 |
| Console bowl, 12" d, round, three ftd | - | - | 40.00 | |
| Console bowl, 13" d, wings | - | - | 80.00 | 120.00 |
| Cordial, 3/4 oz, 2-7/8" h | 55.00 | - | 25.00 | 48.00 |
| Cream soup, 4-1/4" d | 90.00 | - | 35.00 | 90.00 |
| Creamer, 2-3/4" h | 15.00 | - | 10.00 | 20.00 |
| Creamer, 3-3/4" h | 12.00 | - | 12.00 | 16.00 |
| Cup | 14.00 | 8.00 | 10.00 | 16.00 |
| Decanter, 7-3/4" h | 70.00 | - | 40.00 | 70.00 |
| Decanter, 8-1/2" h | 72.00 | - | 45.00 | 72.00 |
| Decanter, 10-1/4" h, rocket-shape | 425.00 | - | 375.00 | 425.00 |
| Decanter, 11-1/4" h | 100.00 | - | 50.00 | 110.00 |
| Goblet, 5 oz, 4-3/4" h | 25.00 | - | 15.00 | 22.00 |
| Goblet, 8 oz, 5-3/4" h | 35.00 | - | 20.00 | 33.00 |
| Goblet, 9 oz, 6-1/4" h, metal stem | 15.00 | - | 17.50 | 15.00 |
| Gravy boat | 120.00 | - | 90.00 | 125.00 |
| Juice tumbler, 3 oz, 3-1/4" h, ftd | 15.00 | - | 10.00 | 15.00 |
| Mayonnaise, 5-1/4" h | 32.50 | - | 30.00 | 32.50 |
| Mug, 12 oz, 5-1/8" h | 40.00 | - | 24.00 | 42.00 |
| Perfume bottle, rocket-shape | 200.00 | - | 150.00 | 210.00 |
| Pickle, 7-1/2" d | 25.00 | - | 15.00 | 25.00 |
| Pitcher, 22 oz, 6-7/8" h | 175.00 | - | 90.00 | 175.00 |
| Pitcher, 32 oz, 8-1/8" h | 195.00 | - | 110.00 | 195.00 |
| Pitcher, 50 oz, 8" h, lip | 200.00 | - | 115.00 | 200.00 |
| Pitcher, 53 oz, 8-1/8" h | 195.00 | - | 120.00 | 195.00 |
| Plate, 5-7/8" d | 12.00 | - | 7.50 | 12.00 |
| Plate, 6" d, round, off center indent | 12.50 | - | 10.00 | 12.50 |
| Plate, 6-1/8" d, sherbet | 8.00 | - | 6.00 | 8.00 |
| Plate, 7-1/8" d, salad | 12.00 | - | 10.00 | 12.00 |
| Plate, 8-1/2" d, luncheon | 15.00 | - | 12.00 | 15.00 |
| Plate, 9-1/2" d, dinner | 25.00 | - | 15.00 | 25.00 |
| Platter, 12" l, oval | 35.00 | - | 20.00 | 35.00 |
| Powder jar, three ftd | 175.00 | - | 100.00 | 185.00 |
| Relish, 8-1/2" d, 3 ftd, divided | 30.00 | - | 20.00 | 30.00 |
| Sandwich plate, 14" d | 40.00 | - | 20.00 | 40.00 |
| Sandwich plate, 14" d, with handles | 44.00 | - | 24.00 | 45.00 |
| Saucer | 6.00 | 2.00 | 4.00 | 6.50 |
| Sherbet, 2-5/8" h | 15.00 | 10.00 | 11.00 | 20.00 |

| Item | Cobalt Blue | Crystal | Other Colors | Red |
|---|---|---|---|---|
| Sherbet, 3-1/2" h. | 25.00 | - | 15.00 | 25.00 |
| Shot glass, 2 oz, 2-3/4" h | 17.50 | - | 12.00 | 17.50 |
| Shot glass, 2 oz, 2-3/4" h, handle. | 17.50 | - | 15.00 | 17.50 |
| Soup bowl, 6-3/4" d | 80.00 | - | - | 80.00 |
| Sugar, 2-3/4" h | 10.00 | - | 10.00 | 18.00 |
| Tray, 7-1/2" l | 15.00 | - | 20.00 | 16.00 |
| Tumbler, 5 oz, 3-5/8" h | 15.00 | - | 10.00 | 15.00 |
| Tumbler, 7 oz, 4-3/8" h | 17.50 | - | 10.00 | 18.00 |
| Tumbler, 8 oz, 4-3/8" h | 17.50 | - | 12.00 | 22.00 |
| Tumbler, 9 oz, 4-7/8" h, handle | 30.00 | - | 15.00 | 28.00 |
| Tumbler, 9 oz, 4-7/8" h | 20.00 | - | 15.00 | 19.00 |
| Tumbler, 12 oz, 5-1/8" h | 30.00 | - | 15.00 | 33.00 |
| Vase, 7-1/4" h, flat, ruffled | 60.00 | - | 60.00 | 60.00 |
| Vase, 8-1/2" h, bud, rocket-shape | 245.00 | - | 185.00 | 245.00 |
| Vase, 9-1/4" h, rocket-shape | 240.00 | - | 125.00 | 240.00 |
| Vegetable bowl, 9-3/4" l, oval | 48.00 | - | 24.00 | 48.00 |
| Wine, 3 oz, 5-1/2" h, metal stem | 17.50 | - | 12.00 | 16.00 |
| Wine, 4-3/4" h, rocket-shape | 27.50 | - | 30.00 | 85.00 |
| Wine, 4 oz, 4" h | 24.00 | - | 12.00 | 25.00 |
| Wine, 4 oz, 5-1/2" h, metal stem | 20.00 | - | 12.00 | 20.00 |

Moondrops, ruby sugar and creamer.

Moondrops, pink cup and saucer.

# Moonstone

Manufactured by Anchor Hocking Glass Company, Lancaster, Ohio, from 1941 to 1946.

Made in crystal with opalescent hobnails and Ocean Green with opalescent hobnails.

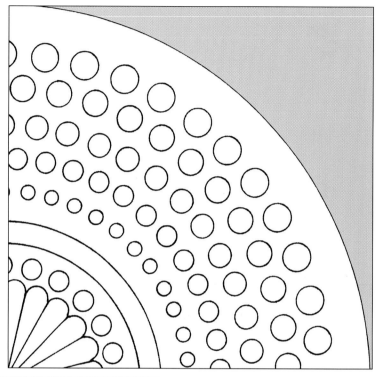

| Item | Crystal | Ocean Green |
|------|---------|-------------|
| Berry bowl, 5-1/2" d | 25.00 | - |
| Bonbon, heart shape, handle | 16.00 | - |
| Bowl, 6-1/2" d, crimped, handle | 20.00 | - |
| Bowl, 7-1/4" d, flat | 25.00 | - |
| Bowl, 9-1/2" d, crimped | 30.00 | - |
| Bud vase, 5-1/2" h | 15.00 | - |
| Candleholder, pr. | 25.00 | - |
| Candy jar, cov, 6" h | 30.00 | - |
| Cigarette box, cov | 25.00 | - |
| Creamer | 10.00 | 9.50 |
| Cup | 10.00 | 10.00 |
| Dessert bowl, 5-1/2" d, crimped | 12.50 | - |
| Goblet, 10 oz | 28.00 | 24.00 |
| Plate, 6-1/4" d, sherbet | 7.00 | 9.00 |
| Plate, 8-3/8" d, luncheon | 17.50 | 17.50 |
| Puff box, cov, 4-3/4" d, round | 25.00 | - |
| Relish, 7-1/4" d, divided | 12.50 | - |
| Relish, cloverleaf | 14.00 | - |
| Sandwich plate, 10-3/4" d | 45.00 | - |
| Saucer | 6.00 | 6.00 |
| Sherbet, ftd | 8.00 | 7.00 |
| Sugar, ftd | 10.00 | 12.50 |
| Vase, 6-1/2" h, ruffled | 12.00 | - |

*Moonstone, crystal luncheon plate with opalescent hobnails.*

*Moonstone, crystal ruffled plate with opalescent hobnails.*

# Moroccan Amethyst

Manufactured by Hazel Ware, division of Continental Can, 1960s.

Made in amethyst.

*Moroccan Amethyst, cup and saucer.*

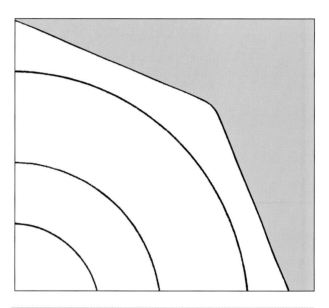

| Item | Amethyst |
|---|---|
| Ashtray, 3-1/4" d, round | 5.75 |
| Ashtray, 3-1/4" w, triangular | 5.75 |
| Ashtray, 6-7/8" w, triangular | 12.50 |
| Ashtray, 8" w, square | 14.00 |
| Bowl, 5-3/4" w, deep, square | 12.00 |
| Bowl, 6" d, round | 12.50 |
| Bowl, 7-3/4" l, oval | 18.50 |
| Bowl, 7-3/4" l, rectangular | 15.00 |
| Bowl, 7-3/4" l, rectangular, metal handle | 17.50 |
| Bowl, 10-3/4" d | 30.00 |
| Candy, cov, short | 35.00 |
| Candy, cov, tall | 32.00 |
| Chip and dip, 10-3/4" and 5-3/4" bowls in metal frame | 40.00 |
| Cocktail shaker, chrome lid | 30.00 |
| Cocktail, stirrer, 16 oz, 6-1/4" h, lip | 30.00 |
| Cup | 7.50 |
| Fruit bowl, 4-3/4" d, octagonal | 9.50 |
| Goblet, 9 oz, 5-1/2" h | 12.50 |

| Item | Amethyst |
|---|---|
| Ice bucket, 6" h | 35.00 |
| Iced tea tumbler, 16 oz, 6-1/2" h | 18.50 |
| Juice goblet, 5-1/2 oz, 4-3/8" h | 12.00 |
| Juice tumbler, 4 oz, 2-1/2" h | 12.50 |
| Old fashioned tumbler, 8 oz, 3-1/4" h | 15.00 |
| Plate, 5-3/4" d, sherbet | 4.50 |
| Plate, 7-1/4" d, salad | 4.75 |
| Plate, 9-3/4" d, dinner | 7.00 |
| Punch bowl | 85.00 |
| Punch cup | 6.00 |
| Relish, 7-3/4" l | 14.00 |
| Salad fork and spoon | 12.00 |
| Sandwich plate, 12" d, metal handle | 15.00 |
| Saucer | 3.00 |
| Sherbet, 7-1/2 oz, 4-1/4" h | 8.00 |
| Snack plate, 10" l, fan shaped, cup rest | 8.00 |
| Snack set, square plate, cup | 12.00 |
| Tidbit, three tiers | 75.00 |
| Tumbler, 9 oz | 12.50 |
| Tumbler, 11 oz, 4-1/4" h, crinkled bottom | 12.00 |
| Tumbler, 11 oz, 4-5/8" h | 12.00 |
| Vase, 8-1/2" h, ruffled | 40.00 |
| Wine, 4-1/2 oz, 4" h | 12.50 |

# Mt. Pleasant

## Double Shield

Manufactured by L.E. Smith, Mt. Pleasant, Pa., from the 1920s to 1934.
Made in amethyst, black, cobalt blue, crystal, green, pink, and white.

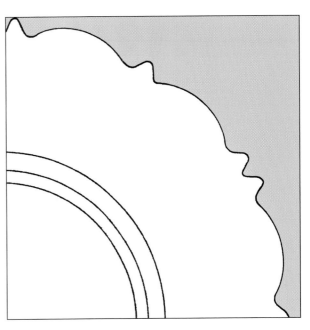

| Item | Amethyst | Black | Cobalt Blue | Green | Pink |
|---|---|---|---|---|---|
| Bonbon, 7" d, rolled edge | 24.00 | 24.50 | 24.00 | 16.00 | 16.00 |
| Bowl, 6" d, three legs | - | 25.00 | - | - | - |
| Bowl, 6" w, sq, two handles | 27.50 | 18.00 | 24.00 | 15.00 | 15.00 |
| Bowl, 7" d, three ftd, rolled out edge | 18.50 | 24.50 | 18.50 | 17.50 | 17.50 |
| Bowl, 8" d, scalloped, two handles | 37.50 | 35.00 | 37.50 | 20.00 | 20.00 |
| Bowl, 8" d, sq, two handles | 38.00 | 40.00 | 38.00 | 20.00 | 20.00 |
| Bowl, 9" d, scalloped, 1-3/4" deep, ftd | 28.00 | 32.00 | 30.00 | - | - |
| Bowl, 10" d, two handles, turned-up edge | 30.00 | 34.00 | 32.00 | - | - |
| Cake plate, 10-1/2" d, 1-1/4" h, ftd | 45.00 | 47.00 | 40.00 | - | - |
| Cake plate, 10-1/2" d, two handles | 26.00 | 40.00 | 28.00 | 17.50 | 17.50 |
| Candlesticks, pr, single lite | 28.00 | 42.50 | 30.00 | 24.00 | 28.00 |
| Candlesticks, pr, two lite | 48.00 | 55.00 | 50.00 | 30.00 | 32.00 |
| Creamer | 21.00 | 20.00 | 22.50 | 20.00 | 24.00 |
| Cup | 15.00 | 15.00 | 14.00 | 12.50 | 12.50 |
| Fruit bowl, 4-7/8" sq | 16.00 | 20.00 | 18.00 | 12.00 | 12.50 |
| Fruit bowl, 9-1/4" sq | 30.00 | 50.00 | 35.00 | 20.00 | 20.00 |
| Fruit bowl, 10" d, scalloped | 40.00 | 40.00 | 40.00 | - | - |
| Leaf, 8" l | 12.50 | 17.50 | 16.00 | - | - |
| Leaf, 11-1/4" l | 25.00 | 30.00 | 28.00 | - | - |
| Mayonnaise, 5-1/2" h, three ftd | 25.00 | 28.00 | 25.00 | 17.50 | 17.50 |
| Mint, 6" d, center handle | 25.00 | 26.50 | 25.00 | 16.00 | 16.00 |
| Plate, 7" h, two handles, scalloped | 15.00 | 16.00 | 16.50 | 12.50 | 12.50 |
| Plate, 8" d, scalloped | 16.00 | 15.00 | 16.00 | 12.50 | 12.50 |
| Plate, 8" d, scalloped, three ftd | 17.50 | 27.00 | 17.50 | 12.50 | 12.50 |
| Plate, 8" w, sq | 17.50 | 25.00 | 17.50 | 12.50 | 12.50 |

| Item | Amethyst | Black | Cobalt Blue | Green | Pink |
|---|---|---|---|---|---|
| Plate, 8-1/4" w, sq, indent for cup | 17.50 | 19.00 | 17.50 | - | - |
| Plate, 9" d, grill | 20.00 | 20.00 | 20.00 | - | - |
| Plate, 12" d, two handles | 35.00 | 35.00 | 35.00 | 20.00 | 20.00 |
| Rose bowl, 4" d | 25.00 | 30.00 | 27.50 | 20.00 | 20.00 |
| Salt and pepper shakers, pr | 50.00 | 50.00 | 45.00 | 25.00 | 25.00 |
| Sandwich server, center handle | 40.00 | 37.50 | 40.00 | - | - |
| Saucer | 5.00 | 5.00 | 5.00 | 3.50 | 3.50 |
| Sherbet | 15.00 | 16.50 | 16.50 | 12.50 | 12.50 |
| Sugar | 9.00 | 20.00 | 15.00 | 20.00 | 20.00 |
| Tumbler, ftd | 25.00 | 27.50 | 27.50 | - | - |
| Vase, 7-1/4" h | 30.00 | 35.00 | 40.00 | - | 35.00 |

*Mt. Pleasant, black creamer, sugar (on pedestal), cup, and bowl.*

*Mt. Pleasant, black scalloped fruit bowl.*

# National

Manufactured by Jeannette Glass Company, Jeannette, Pa., from the late 1940s to the mid-1950s.

Made in crystal, pink, and shell pink. Collector interest is primarily with crystal. Prices for pink and shell pink are not yet firmly established, but usually command slightly higher than crystal.

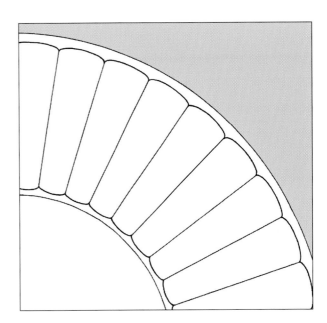

*National, crystal candleholders.*

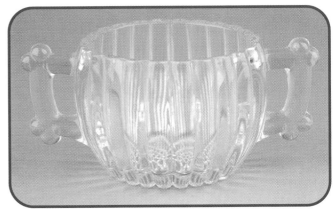

*National, crystal sugar bowl.*

| Item | Crystal |
| --- | --- |
| Ashtray | 4.50 |
| Berry bowl, 4-1/2" d | 4.00 |
| Berry bowl, 8-1/2" d | 8.00 |
| Bowl, 12" d | 15.00 |
| Candleholders, pr | 30.00 |
| Candy dish, cov, ftd | 20.00 |
| Cigarette box | 15.00 |
| Creamer | 6.50 |
| Creamer and sugar tray | 6.00 |
| Cup | 4.00 |
| Jar, cov | 15.00 |
| Lazy Susan | 40.00 |
| Milk pitcher, 20 oz | 20.00 |

| Item | Crystal |
| --- | --- |
| Plate, 8" d | 6.50 |
| Punch bowl stand | 10.00 |
| Punch bowl, 12" d | 25.00 |
| Punch cup | 3.50 |
| Relish, three parts | 15.00 |
| Salt and pepper shakers, pr | 10.00 |
| Saucer | 1.00 |
| Sugar, open | 6.50 |
| Serving plate, 15" d | 17.50 |
| Tray, two handles | 17.50 |
| Tumbler, ftd | 8.50 |
| Vase, 9" | 20.00 |
| Water pitcher, 64 oz | 30.00 |

# New Century

Manufactured by Hazel Atlas Company, Clarksburg, W.V., and Zanesville, Ohio, from 1930 to 1935.

Made in crystal and green, with limited production in amethyst, cobalt blue, and pink.

| Item | Amethyst | Cobalt Blue | Crystal | Green | Pink |
|---|---|---|---|---|---|
| Ashtray/coaster, 5-3/8" d | - | - | 30.00 | 30.00 | - |
| Berry bowl, 4-1/2" d | - | - | 35.00 | 35.00 | - |
| Berry bowl, 8" d | - | - | 30.00 | 30.00 | - |
| Butter dish, cov. | - | - | 75.00 | 75.00 | - |
| Casserole, cov, 9" d | - | - | 115.00 | 115.00 | - |
| Cocktail, 3-1/4 oz | - | - | 42.00 | 42.00 | - |
| Cream soup, 4-3/4" d | - | - | 25.00 | 25.00 | - |
| Creamer | - | - | 12.00 | 14.00 | - |
| Cup | 20.00 | 20.00 | 10.00 | 12.00 | 20.00 |
| Decanter, stopper | - | - | 90.00 | 90.00 | - |
| Pitcher, with or without ice lip, 60 oz | 55.00 | 55.00 | 45.00 | 48.00 | 50.00 |
| Pitcher, with or without ice lip, 80 oz | 55.00 | 55.00 | 45.00 | 48.00 | 50.00 |
| Plate, 6" d, sherbet | - | - | 5.50 | 6.50 | - |
| Plate, 7-1/8" d, breakfast | - | - | 12.00 | 12.00 | - |
| Plate, 8-1/2" d, salad | - | - | 12.00 | 12.00 | - |
| Plate, 10" d, dinner | - | - | 24.00 | 24.00 | - |
| Plate, 10" d, grill | - | - | 15.00 | 18.00 | - |
| Platter, 11" l, oval | - | - | 30.00 | 30.00 | - |
| Salt and pepper shakers, pr | - | - | 45.00 | 45.00 | - |
| Saucer | 7.50 | 7.50 | 5.00 | 6.50 | 8.00 |
| Sherbet, 3" h | - | - | 9.00 | 9.00 | - |
| Sugar, cov | - | - | 40.00 | 45.00 | - |
| Tumbler, 5 oz, 3-1/2" h | 12.00 | 16.50 | 15.00 | 18.00 | 18.00 |
| Tumbler, 5 oz, 4" h, ftd | - | - | 30.00 | 32.50 | - |
| Tumbler, 8 oz, 3-1/2" h | - | - | 25.00 | 27.50 | - |
| Tumbler, 9 oz, 4-1/4" h | 15.00 | 15.00 | 18.00 | 20.00 | 15.00 |
| Tumbler, 9 oz, 4-7/8" h, ftd | - | - | 25.00 | 25.00 | - |

| Item | Amethyst | Cobalt Blue | Crystal | Green | Pink |
|------|----------|-------------|---------|-------|------|
| Tumbler, 10 oz, 5" h | 16.00 | 30.00 | 20.00 | 17.50 | 16.00 |
| Tumbler, 12 oz, 5-1/4" h | 25.00 | 25.00 | 30.00 | 32.50 | 20.00 |
| Whiskey, 2-1/2" h, 1-1/2 oz | - | - | 18.00 | 20.00 | - |
| Wine, 2-1/2 oz | - | - | 35.00 | 40.00 | - |

New Century, green plate.

New Century, green salt and pepper shakers.

# Newport

Manufactured by Hazel Atlas Glass Company, Clarksburg, W.V., and Zanesville, Ohio, from 1936 to the early 1950s.

Made in amethyst, cobalt blue, pink (from 1936 to 1940), Platonite white, and fired-on colors (from the 1940s to early 1950s).

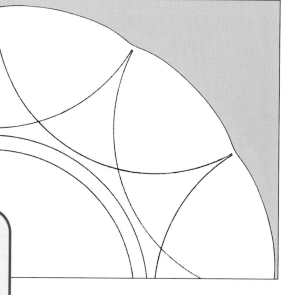

*Newport, amethyst plate, sugar, creamer, and soup bowl.*

| Item | Amethyst | Cobalt Blue | Fired-On Color | Pink | Platonite |
|---|---|---|---|---|---|
| Berry bowl, 4-3/4" d . . . . . . . . . . 20.00 | | 25.00 | 9.00 | 12.50 | 5.00 |
| Berry bowl, 8-1/4" d . . . . . . . . . . 50.00 | | 50.00 | 16.00 | 25.00 | 10.00 |
| Cereal bowl, 5-1/4" d . . . . . . . . . 42.00 | | 45.00 | - | 20.00 | - |
| Cream soup, 4-3/4" d . . . . . . . . . 25.00 | | 25.00 | 10.00 | 17.50 | 8.50 |
| Creamer. . . . . . . . . . . . . . . . . . 20.00 | | 22.00 | 8.50 | 10.00 | 3.00 |
| Cup . . . . . . . . . . . . . . . . . . . . 12.00 | | 15.00 | 9.00 | 6.00 | 4.50 |
| Plate, 6" d, sherbet. . . . . . . . . . . 7.50 | | 10.00 | 5.00 | 3.50 | 2.00 |
| Plate, 8-1/2" d, luncheon . . . . . . 15.00 | | 22.00 | 9.00 | 8.00 | 4.50 |
| Plate, 8-13/16" d, dinner. . . . . . . 32.00 | | 35.00 | 15.00 | 15.00 | 12.00 |
| Platter, 11-3/4" l, oval . . . . . . . . . 42.00 | | 48.00 | 18.00 | 20.00 | 12.00 |
| Salt and pepper shakers, pr . . . . . 60.00 | | 65.00 | 32.00 | 30.00 | 18.00 |
| Sandwich plate, 11-1/2" d. . . . . . . 48.00 | | 50.00 | 15.00 | 24.00 | 10.00 |
| Saucer . . . . . . . . . . . . . . . . . . . 5.25 | | 6.00 | 3.00 | 2.50 | 2.00 |
| Sherbet . . . . . . . . . . . . . . . . . . 15.00 | | 18.50 | 10.00 | 8.00 | 4.00 |
| Sugar . . . . . . . . . . . . . . . . . . . . 20.00 | | 22.00 | 9.50 | 10.00 | 5.00 |
| Tumbler, 9 oz, 4-1/2" h . . . . . . . . 40.00 | | 48.00 | 15.00 | 20.00 | - |

# Nora Bird

## Line#300

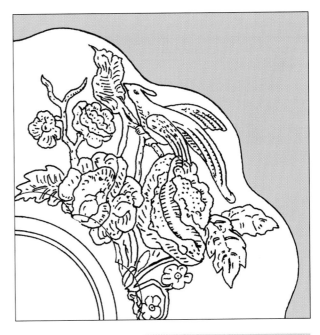

Manufactured by Paden City Glass Company, Paden City, W.V., from 1929 to 1930s.

Made in amber, crystal, green and pink. Amber production is limited; a pair of candlesticks is valued at $150.

| Item | Green | Pink |
|---|---|---|
| Candlesticks, pr | 220.00 | 155.00 |
| Candy dish, cov, 5-1/4" h, ftd | 325.00 | 325.00 |
| Candy dish, cov, 6-1/2" d, three parts | 350.00 | 350.00 |
| Creamer, 4-1/2" h, round handle | 75.00 | 85.00 |
| Creamer, 5" h, pointed handle | 75.00 | 85.00 |
| Cup | 60.00 | 60.00 |
| Ice tub, 6" d | 125.00 | 125.00 |
| Mayonnaise and liner | 150.00 | 165.00 |
| Plate, 8" d | 45.00 | 50.00 |
| Saucer | 15.00 | 15.00 |
| Sugar, 4-1/2" h, round handle | 75.00 | 85.00 |
| Sugar, 5" h, pointed handle | 75.00 | 85.00 |
| Tumbler, 2-1/4" h, 3 oz | 45.00 | 45.00 |
| Tumbler, 3" h | 42.00 | 42.00 |
| Tumbler, 4" h | 50.00 | 50.00 |
| Tumbler, 4-3/4" h, ftd | 60.00 | 60.00 |
| Tumbler, 5-1/4" h, 10 oz | 65.00 | 65.00 |

# Normandie

## Bouquet and Lattice

Manufactured by Federal Glass Company, Columbus, Ohio, from 1933 to 1940.

Made in amber, crystal, iridescent, and pink.

| Item | Amber | Crystal | Iridescent | Pink |
|------|-------|---------|------------|------|
| Berry bowl, 5" d | 9.50 | 6.00 | 6.50 | 12.00 |
| Berry bowl, 8-1/2" d | 35.00 | 24.00 | 30.00 | 80.00 |
| Cereal bowl, 6-1/2" d | 30.00 | 20.00 | 10.00 | 35.00 |
| Creamer, ftd | 20.00 | 10.00 | 8.00 | 18.00 |
| Cup | 8.00 | 4.00 | 6.00 | 9.50 |
| Iced tea tumbler, 12 oz, 5" h | 40.00 | - | - | - |
| Juice tumbler, 5 oz, 4" h | 38.00 | - | - | - |
| Pitcher, 80 oz, 8" h | 115.00 | - | - | 245.00 |
| Plate, 6" d, sherbet | 4.50 | 2.00 | 3.50 | 5.00 |
| Plate, 7-3/4" d, salad | 10.00 | 5.00 | 55.00 | 14.00 |
| Plate, 9-1/4" d, luncheon | 12.50 | 6.00 | 16.50 | 100.00 |
| Plate, 11" d, dinner | 32.00 | 15.00 | 10.00 | 18.00 |
| Plate, 11" d, grill | 15.00 | 8.00 | 10.00 | 25.00 |
| Platter, 11-3/4" l | 24.00 | 10.00 | 12.00 | 80.00 |
| Salt and pepper shakers, pr | 50.00 | 20.00 | - | 4.00 |
| Saucer | 4.00 | 1.50 | 3.50 | 10.00 |
| Sherbet | 7.50 | 6.50 | 9.00 | 9.00 |
| Sugar | 8.00 | 6.00 | 7.00 | 12.00 |
| Tumbler, 9 oz, 4-1/4" h | 25.00 | 10.00 | - | 50.00 |
| Vegetable bowl, 10" l, oval | 27.50 | 12.00 | 25.00 | 45.00 |

*Normandie, iridescent cup.*

*Normandie, iridescent plate.*

# Old Café

Manufactured by Hocking Glass Company,
Lancaster, Ohio, from 1936 to 1940.
Made in crystal, pink, and royal ruby.

*Old Café, ruby bowl.*

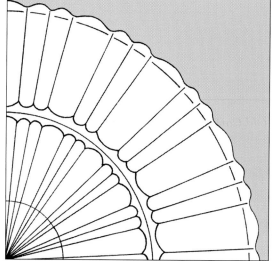

| Item | Crystal | Pink | Royal Ruby |
|---|---|---|---|
| Berry bowl, 3-3/4" d | 9.50 | 10.00 | 9.00 |
| Bowl, 6-1/2" d | 15.00 | 18.00 | - |
| Bowl, 9" d, closed handles | 10.00 | 10.00 | 15.00 |
| Candy dish, 8" d, low | 18.00 | 15.00 | 20.00 |
| Candy jar, 5-1/2" d, crystal with ruby cover | - | - | 25.00 |
| Cereal bowl, 5-1/2" d | 30.00 | 30.00 | 15.00 |
| Cup | 12.00 | 12.00 | 15.00 |
| Juice tumbler, 3" h | 18.00 | 18.00 | 20.00 |
| Lamp | 100.00 | 100.00 | 150.00 |
| Olive dish, 6" l, oblong | 7.50 | 8.50 | - |
| Pitcher, 36 oz, 6" h | 125.00 | 145.00 | - |
| Pitcher, 80 oz | 150.00 | 165.00 | - |
| Plate, 6" d, sherbet | 5.00 | 5.00 | - |
| Plate, 10" d, dinner | 60.00 | 65.00 | - |
| Saucer | 5.00 | 5.00 | - |
| Sherbet, low, ftd | 15.00 | 12.00 | 12.00 |
| Tumbler, 4" h | 18.00 | 20.00 | 18.00 |
| Vase, 7-1/4" h | 40.00 | 45.00 | 50.00 |

*Old Café, clear vase and bowl with handles.*

*Old Café, close-up view of original label on ruby bowl with handles.*

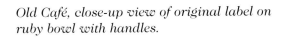

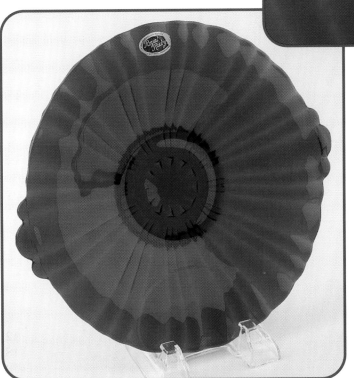

*Old Café, ruby bowl with handles and original label.*

# Old Colony

Manufactured by Hocking Glass Company, Lancaster, Ohio, from 1935 to 1938.

Made in crystal and pink.

Crystal Old Colony pieces are valued at about 50 percent of pink, as are frosted or satin finish prices. Many other companies made a look-alike to Old Colony, so care must be exercised.

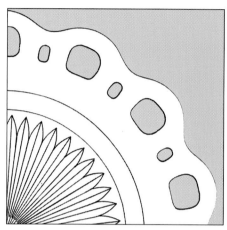

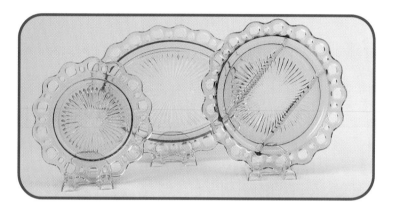

Old Colony Lace Edge, pink plate, platter, and divided relish.

Old Colony Lace Edge, pink satin-finish candleholder.

| Item | Pink |
|---|---|
| Bonbon, cov | 65.00 |
| Bowl, 9-1/2" d, plain | 40.00 |
| Bowl, 9-1/2" d, ribbed | 35.00 |
| Butter dish, cov | 70.00 |
| Candlesticks, pr | 350.00 |
| Candy jar, cov, ribbed | 65.00 |
| Cereal bowl, 6-3/8" d | 24.00 |
| Comport, 7" d, cov | 60.00 |
| Comport, 9" d | 950.00 |
| Console bowl, 10-1/2" d, three legs | 250.00 |
| Cookie jar, cov | 75.00 |
| Creamer | 25.00 |
| Cup | 24.00 |
| Flower bowl, crystal frog | 30.00 |
| Plate, 7-1/4" d, salad | 27.50 |
| Plate, 8-1/4" d, luncheon | 32.00 |

| Item | Pink |
|---|---|
| Plate, 10-1/2" d, dinner | 36.00 |
| Plate, 10-1/2" d, grill | 28.00 |
| Plate, 13" d, four parts, solid lace | 65.00 |
| Plate, 13" d, solid lace | 65.00 |
| Platter, 12-3/4" l | 42.00 |
| Platter, 12-3/4" l, five parts | 40.00 |
| Relish dish, 7-1/2" d, three parts, deep | 60.00 |
| Relish plate, 10-1/2" d, three parts | 25.00 |
| Salad bowl, 7-3/4" d, ribbed | 60.00 |
| Saucer | 15.00 |
| Sherbet, ftd | 112.00 |
| Sugar | 25.00 |
| Tumbler, 5 oz, 3-1/2" h, flat | 120.00 |
| Tumbler, 9 oz, 4-1/2" h, flat | 22.00 |
| Tumbler, 10-1/2 oz, 5" h, ftd | 95.00 |
| Vase, 7" h | 650.00 |

# Old English

## Threading

Manufactured by Indiana Glass Company, Dunkirk, Ind., late 1920s.

Made in amber, crystal, green, and pink.

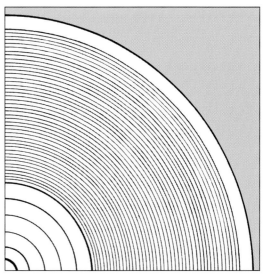

Old English, green compote.

| Item | Amber | Crystal | Green | Pink |
|---|---|---|---|---|
| Bowl, 4" d, flat | 20.00 | 18.00 | 22.00 | 20.00 |
| Bowl, 9-1/2" d, flat | 35.00 | 25.00 | 35.00 | 35.00 |
| Candlesticks, pr, 4" h | 35.00 | 25.00 | 35.00 | 35.00 |
| Candy dish, cov, flat | 50.00 | 40.00 | 50.00 | 50.00 |
| Candy jar, cov | 55.00 | 45.00 | 55.00 | 55.00 |
| Cheese compote, 3-1/2" h | 17.50 | 12.00 | 17.50 | 17.50 |
| Cheese plate, indent | 20.00 | 10.00 | 20.00 | 20.00 |
| Compote, 3-1/2" h, 6-3/8" w, two handles | 24.00 | 12.00 | 24.00 | 24.00 |
| Compote, 3-1/2" h, 7" w | 24.00 | 12.00 | 24.00 | 24.00 |
| Creamer | 18.00 | 10.00 | 18.00 | 18.00 |
| Egg cup | - | 10.00 | - | - |
| Fruit bowl, 9" d, ftd | 30.00 | 20.00 | 30.00 | 30.00 |
| Fruit stand, 11" h, ftd | 40.00 | 18.00 | 40.00 | 40.00 |
| Goblet, 8 oz, 5-3/4" h | 30.00 | 15.00 | 30.00 | 30.00 |
| Pitcher | 70.00 | 35.00 | 70.00 | 70.00 |
| Pitcher, cov | 125.00 | 55.00 | 125.00 | 125.00 |
| Sandwich server, center handle | 60.00 | - | 60.00 | 60.00 |
| Sherbet | 20.00 | 10.00 | 20.00 | 20.00 |
| Sugar, cov | 38.00 | 14.00 | 38.00 | 38.00 |
| Tumbler, 4-1/2" h, ftd | 24.00 | 12.00 | 28.00 | 24.00 |
| Tumbler, 5-1/2" h, ftd | 40.00 | 20.00 | 40.00 | 40.00 |
| Vase, 5-3/8" h, 7" w, fan-shape | 48.00 | 24.00 | 48.00 | 48.00 |
| Vase, 8" h, 4-1/2" w, ftd | 45.00 | 20.00 | 45.00 | 45.00 |
| Vase, 8-1/4" h, 4-1/4" w, ftd | 45.00 | 20.00 | 45.00 | 45.00 |
| Vase, 12" h, ftd | 72.00 | 35.00 | 72.00 | 72.00 |

# *Orange Blossom*

Manufactured by Indiana Glass Company, Dunkirk, Ind., in 1957. This pattern was originally made in a custard color in the 1930s. That pattern is known as Indiana Custard.

Made in milk white. Some plates have a decaled Currier and Ives type scene in the center.

*Orange Blossom, milk white sugar.*

| Item | Milk White |
| --- | --- |
| Creamer, ftd | 5.00 |
| Cup | 4.50 |
| Dessert bowl, 5-1/2" d | 5.00 |
| Plate, 5-3/8" d, sherbet | 3.50 |
| Plate, 8-7/8" d, lunch | 8.50 |
| Saucer | 2.00 |
| Sugar, ftd | 5.00 |

*Orange Blossom, milk white creamer.*

# Orchid

Manufactured by Paden City Glass Company, Paden City, W.V., early 1930s.

Made in amber, black, cobalt blue, green, pink, red, and yellow.

| Item | Amber | Black | Cobalt Blue | Green | Pink | Red | Yellow |
|------|------|-------|-------------|-------|------|-----|--------|
| Bowl, 4-1/2" sq. | 40.00 | 50.00 | 50.00 | 40.00 | 55.00 | 50.00 | 55.00 |
| Bowl, 8-1/2" d, two handles | 60.00 | 95.00 | 95.00 | 60.00 | 100.00 | 95.00 | 100.00 |
| Bowl, 8-3/4" w, sq | 50.00 | 85.00 | 85.00 | 50.00 | 90.00 | 85.00 | 90.00 |
| Bowl, 10" d, ftd | 85.00 | 165.00 | 165.00 | 75.00 | 150.00 | 165.00 | 150.00 |
| Bowl, 11" d, sq. | 60.00 | 115.00 | 115.00 | 60.00 | 120.00 | 115.00 | 120.00 |
| Candlesticks, pr, 5-3/4" h | 110.00 | 195.00 | 195.00 | 95.00 | 225.00 | 195.00 | 215.00 |
| Candy, cov, 6-1/2" w, sq, three parts | 70.00 | 145.00 | 145.00 | 70.00 | 150.00 | 145.00 | 150.00 |
| Comport, 3-1/4" h, 6-1/4" w | 30.00 | 48.00 | 48.00 | 30.00 | 50.00 | 48.00 | 50.00 |
| Comport, 6-5/8" h, 7" w | 42.00 | 95.00 | 95.00 | 42.00 | 115.00 | 95.00 | 100.00 |
| Creamer | 60.00 | 95.00 | 95.00 | 60.00 | 75.00 | 95.00 | 75.00 |
| Ice bucket, 6" h | 95.00 | 195.00 | 195.00 | 95.00 | 185.00 | 195.00 | 200.00 |
| Mayonnaise, three pcs | 85.00 | 165.00 | 165.00 | 85.00 | 150.00 | 150.00 | 165.00 |
| Plate, 8-1/2" w, sq. | - | 135.00 | 135.00 | - | - | 135.00 | - |
| Sandwich server, center handle | 85.00 | 125.00 | 125.00 | 125.00 | 125.00 | 125.00 | 135.00 |
| Sugar | 48.00 | 95.00 | 95.00 | 50.00 | 95.00 | 95.00 | 95.00 |
| Vase, 8" h | 95.00 | 275.00 | 275.00 | 95.00 | 95.00 | 275.00 | 95.00 |
| Vase, 10" h. | 125.00 | 295.00 | 295.00 | 125.00 | 145.00 | 295.00 | 150.00 |

*Orchid, yellow comport.*

# Ovide

Manufactured by Hazel Atlas Glass Company, Clarksburg, W.V., and Zanesville, Ohio, 1930-35 and in the 1950s.

Made in black, green, and white Platonite with fired-on colors in the 1950s.

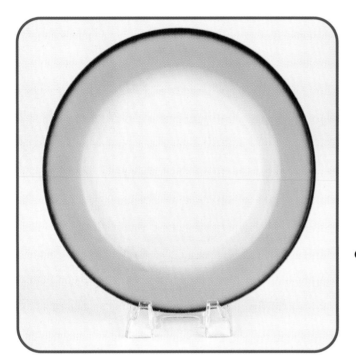

*Ovide, informal pink and gray plate.*

| Item | Black | Green | Platonite |
|---|---|---|---|
| Berry bowl, 4-3/4" d | - | - | 10.00 |
| Berry bowl, 8" d | - | - | 22.00 |
| Candy dish, cov | 45.00 | 24.00 | 35.00 |
| Cereal bowl, 5-1/2" d | 10.00 | - | 12.00 |
| Creamer | 7.00 | 6.00 | 18.00 |
| Cup | 6.50 | 4.50 | 15.00 |
| Egg cup | - | - | 22.00 |
| Fruit cocktail, ftd | 5.00 | 4.50 | - |
| Plate, 6" d, sherbet | - | 2.50 | 6.00 |
| Plate, 8" d, luncheon | - | 3.50 | 15.00 |
| Plate, 9" d, dinner | - | - | 25.00 |
| Platter, 11" d | - | - | 24.00 |
| Salt and pepper shakers, pr | 28.00 | 28.00 | 25.00 |
| Saucer | 3.50 | 4.50 | 6.00 |
| Sherbet | 6.50 | 3.50 | 15.00 |
| Sugar, open | 9.00 | 7.00 | 20.00 |
| Tumbler | 18.00 | - | 20.00 |

# Oyster & Pearl

Manufactured by Anchor Hocking Glass Corporation, from 1938 to 1940.

Made in crystal, pink, royal ruby, and white with fired-on green or pink.

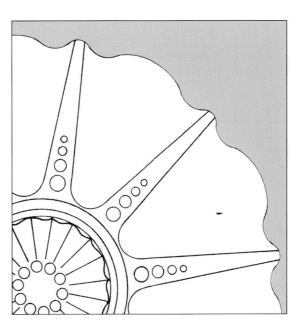

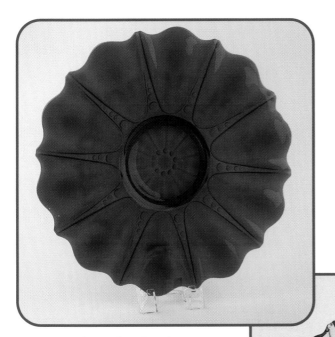

*Oyster and Pearl, ruby plate.*

*Oyster and Pearl, pink relish.*

| Item | Crystal | Pink | Royal Ruby | White, Fired-On Green | White, Fired-On Pink |
|---|---|---|---|---|---|
| Bowl, 5-1/2" d, handle | 8.00 | 15.00 | 20.00 | - | - |
| Bowl, 5-1/4" w, handle, heart-shape | 12.00 | 21.00 | - | 12.00 | - |
| Bowl, 6-1/2" d, handle | 12.00 | 15.00 | 28.00 | - | - |
| Candle holders, pr, 3-1/2" h | 35.00 | 45.00 | 65.00 | 25.00 | 25.00 |
| Fruit bowl, 10-1/2" d, deep | 20.00 | 25.00 | 50.00 | 30.00 | 30.00 |
| Relish dish, 10-1/4" l, divided | 10.00 | 35.00 | - | - | - |
| Sandwich plate, 13-1/2" d | 20.00 | 40.00 | 50.00 | - | - |

# Paneled Grape

## Pattern #1881

Manufactured by Westmoreland Glass Company, from 1950 to the 1970s.

Made in milk white glass. Some pieces were decorated. A limited production in mint green occurred in 1979. Decorated pieces are usually valued the same as the white pieces, providing the painted decoration is in very good condition. The re-sale market on green is very limited at the present time.

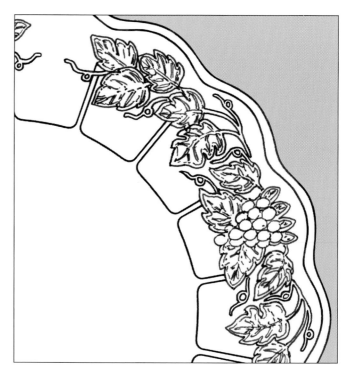

| Item | Milk White |
| --- | --- |
| Appetizer set, three pcs | 60.00 |
| Banana bowl, 12" d, ftd | 175.00 |
| Basket, 5-1/2", ruffled | 50.00 |
| Basket, 6-1/2", oval | 30.00 |
| Basket, 8" | 70.00 |
| Bowl, 4" d, crimped | 22.00 |
| Bowl, 6" d, crimped, stemmed | 30.00 |
| Bowl, 6" d, ruffled, stemmed | 30.00 |
| Bowl, 6-1/2" d, oval | 30.00 |
| Bowl, 8" d, cupped | 35.00 |
| Bowl, 9" d, ftd, skirted base | 50.00 |
| Bowl, 9-1/2" d, bell shape | 45.00 |
| Bowl, 9-1/2" d, bell shape, ftd | 90.00 |
| Bowl, 10-1/2" d | 70.00 |
| Bowl, 11" l, oval, ftd | 125.00 |
| Bowl, 12" d, flat | 120.00 |
| Bowl, 12" d, ftd | 125.00 |
| Bowl, cov, 9" d, ftd | 75.00 |
| Bowl, cov, 9" w, sq | 85.00 |
| Bud vase, 10" h | 30.00 |
| Butter, cov, 1/4 pound | 25.00 |
| Cake plate, 10-1/2" d | 65.00 |
| Cake plate, 11" d, ftd, skirt | 70.00 |
| Candelabra, three-lite | 225.00 |
| Candleholder, 4", octagonal | 15.00 |
| Candleholder, 5" h, handle | 40.00 |
| Candleholder, 9" h, two-lite | 30.00 |
| Candy jar, cov, 6-1/4" | 40.00 |
| Canister, cov, 7" h | 175.00 |
| Canister, cov, 9-1/2" h | 185.00 |
| Canister, cov, 11" h | 195.00 |
| Celery vase, 6-1/2" h | 40.00 |
| Cheese, cov, 7" d | 60.00 |
| Chocolate box, cov, 6-1/2" l | 55.00 |
| Chop plate, 14" d | 125.00 |
| Cigarette lighter, goblet or toothpick shape | 25.00 |

| Item | Milk White |
|---|---|
| Cologne, gold trim | 60.00 |
| Compote, cov, 7" d, ftd | 45.00 |
| Compote, cov, 9" d, ftd, crimped | 48.00 |
| Compote, open, 4-1/2" d, crimped | 30.00 |
| Condiment set, five pcs | 130.00 |
| Cordial, 2 oz | 20.00 |
| Creamer, individual | 12.00 |
| Creamer, table | 15.00 |
| Creamer, tall | 30.00 |
| Cruet, stopper | 40.00 |
| Cup, flared | 15.00 |
| Decanter | 165.00 |
| Dresser set, four pcs | 215.00 |
| Egg plate, 10" d, center handle | 75.00 |
| Egg plate, 12" d | 70.00 |
| Epergne, 8-1/2" h | 60.00 |
| Epergne, 9" d bowl, two pcs | 175.00 |
| Flower pot | 45.00 |
| Fruit cocktail, 3-1/2" or 4-1/2" | 12.00 |
| Goblet, 8 oz | 25.00 |
| Iced tea tumbler, 12 oz | 28.00 |
| Ivy ball | 65.00 |
| Jardinière, 5", cupped or straight, ftd | 25.00 |
| Jardinière, 6-1/2" h, cupped or straight, ftd | 35.00 |
| Jelly, cov, 4-1/2" d | 25.00 |
| Juice tumbler, 5 oz | 24.00 |
| Ladle | 10.00 |
| Marmalade | 55.00 |
| Mayonnaise, 4" d, ftd | 35.00 |
| Napkin ring | 12.00 |
| Nappy, 4-1/2" d | 20.00 |
| Nappy, 5" d, bell shape | 22.00 |
| Nappy, 5" d, round, handle | 24.00 |
| Nappy, 7" d | 26.00 |
| Nappy, 8-1/2" d | 28.00 |
| Nappy, 9" d | 30.00 |
| Nappy, 10" d | 35.00 |
| Oil or vinegar bottle, stopper | 40.00 |
| Old fashioned tumbler, 6 oz | 28.00 |
| Parfait, 6" h | 25.00 |
| Pickle dish, oval | 20.00 |
| Pitcher, 16 oz | 50.00 |
| Pitcher, 32 oz | 45.00 |
| Planter, 3" x 8-1/2" | 30.00 |
| Planter, 4-1/2" x 4-1/2" | 35.00 |
| Planter, 5" x 9" | 38.00 |
| Plate, 6" d, bread and butter | 8.00 |
| Plate, 7" d, salad | 25.00 |
| Plate, 8-1/2" d, luncheon | 25.00 |

| Item | Milk White |
|---|---|
| Plate, 10-1/2" d, dinner | 40.00 |
| Puff box, cov | 35.00 |
| Punch bowl, 13" d, bell or flared | 300.00 |
| Punch cup | 15.00 |
| Punch ladle | 65.00 |
| Relish, three parts, 9" l | 40.00 |
| Rose bowl, 4" d | 20.00 |
| Rose bowl, 4-1/2" d, cupped, ftd | 35.00 |
| Salt and pepper shakers, pr, ftd, three sizes | 45.00 |
| Sauce boat | 40.00 |
| Sauce boat underplate | 20.00 |
| Saucer | 8.50 |
| Serving plate, 18" d | 165.00 |
| Sherbet, 3-3/4" h | 15.00 |
| Sherbet, 4-3/4" h | 17.50 |
| Soap dish | 100.00 |
| Spooner, 6" h | 40.00 |
| Sugar, cov, individual | 15.00 |
| Sugar, cov, large | 25.00 |
| Sugar, cov, table | 20.00 |

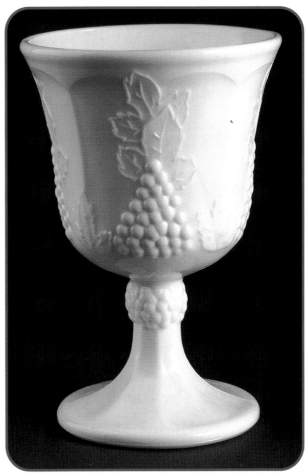

*Paneled Grape, milk white goblet.*

| Item | Milk White |
|---|---|
| Sugar, open, 4-1/4" | 15.00 |
| Tidbit tray, metal handle, 8-1/2" d | 30.00 |
| Tidbit tray, metal handle, 10-1/2" d | 50.00 |
| Toothpick holder | 25.00 |
| Tray, 9" l, oval | 55.00 |
| Tray, 13-1/2" l, oval | 90.00 |
| Tumbler, 8 oz | 20.00 |
| Vase, 6" h, bell shape | 20.00 |

| Item | Milk White |
|---|---|
| Vase, 8-1/2" h or 9" h, bell shape | 35.00 |
| Vase, 9-1/2" h, straight sides | 30.00 |
| Vase, 11-1/2" h, bell or straight sides | 35.00 |
| Vase, 14" h, 16" h, 18" h, swung | 35.00 |
| Wall pocket, 6" | 85.00 |
| Wall pocket, 8" | 95.00 |
| Wine, 3 oz | 24.00 |

*Paneled Grape, milk white dinner plate.*

# Park Avenue

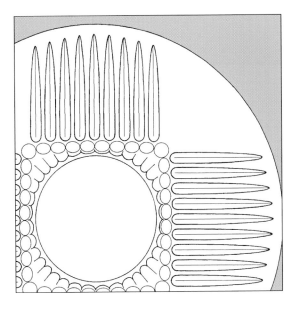

Manufactured by Federal Glass Company, Columbus, Ohio, 1941 to the early 1970s.

Made in amber, crystal, and crystal with gold trim. Values for crystal and crystal with gold trim are the same.

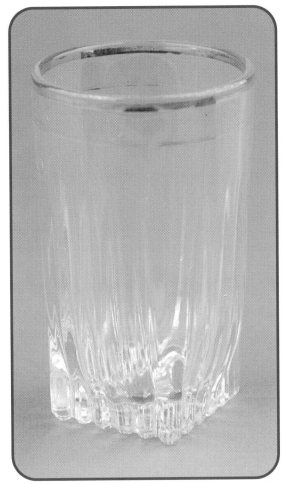

| Item | Amber | Crystal |
|------|-------|---------|
| Ashtray, 3-1/2" sq. | - | 5.00 |
| Ashtray, 4-1/2" sq. | - | 6.50 |
| Candleholder, pr, 5" d | - | 9.00 |
| Dessert bowl, 5" d | 6.50 | 3.00 |
| Iced tea tumbler, 12 oz | 12.00 | 6.50 |
| Juice tumbler, 4-1/2 oz | 5.00 | 5.00 |
| Tumbler, 9 oz | 8.00 | 6.00 |
| Tumbler, 10 oz | 9.00 | 6.00 |
| Vegetable bowl, 8-1/2" d | 18.00 | 10.00 |
| Whiskey tumbler, 1-1/4 oz | - | 4.50 |

*Park Avenue, juice tumbler, crystal with gold band.*

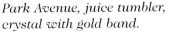

# Parrot
## Sylvan

Manufactured by Federal Glass Company, Columbus, Ohio, from 1931 to 1932.

Made in amber and green, with limited production in blue and crystal.

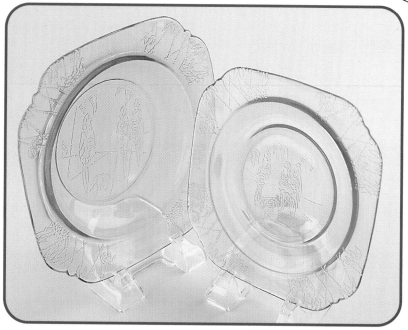

Parrot, amber jam dish and green sherbet plate.

| Item | Amber | Green |
|------|-------|-------|
| Berry bowl, 5" d | 22.50 | 30.00 |
| Berry bowl, 8" d | 75.00 | 80.00 |
| Butter dish, cov | 1,250.00 | 475.00 |
| Creamer, ftd | 65.00 | 55.00 |
| Cup | 35.00 | 35.00 |
| Hot plate, 5" d, pointed | 875.00 | 900.00 |
| Hot plate, round | - | 950.00 |
| Jam dish, 7" d | 35.00 | - |
| Pitcher, 80 oz, 8-1/2" h | - | 2,500.00 |
| Plate, 5-3/4" d, sherbet | 24.00 | 35.00 |
| Plate, 7-1/2" d, salad | - | 40.00 |
| Plate, 9" d, dinner | 50.00 | 50.00 |
| Plate, 10-1/2" d, grill, round | 35.00 | - |
| Plate, 10-1/2" d, grill, square | - | 30.00 |
| Platter, 11-1/4" l, oblong | 65.00 | 70.00 |
| Salt and pepper shakers, pr | - | 270.00 |
| Saucer | 18.00 | 18.00 |
| Sherbet, ftd, cone | 30.00 | 27.50 |
| Soup bowl, 7" d | 35.00 | 45.00 |
| Sugar, cov | 450.00 | 175.00 |
| Tumbler, 10 oz, 4-1/4" h | 100.00 | 130.00 |
| Tumbler, 10 oz, 5-1/2" h, ftd, Madrid mold | 145.00 | - |
| Tumbler, 12 oz, 5-1/2" h | 115.00 | 160.00 |
| Tumbler, 5-3/4" h, ftd, heavy | 100.00 | 120.00 |
| Vegetable bowl, 10" l, oval | 75.00 | 65.00 |

# Patrician

### Spoke

Manufactured by Federal Glass Company, Columbus, Ohio, from 1933 to 1937.

Made in amber (also called Golden Glo), crystal, green, and pink.

*Patrician, amber bowl, sherbet, and cup.*

| Item | Amber | Crystal | Green | Pink |
|---|---|---|---|---|
| Berry bowl, 5" d. | 12.50 | 10.00 | 12.50 | 18.50 |
| Berry bowl, 8-1/2" d. | 50.00 | 15.00 | 37.50 | 35.00 |
| Butter dish, cov. | 95.00 | 100.00 | 215.00 | 225.00 |
| Cereal bowl, 6" d. | 32.00 | 27.50 | 27.50 | 25.00 |
| Cookie jar, cov | 90.00 | 80.00 | 500.00 | - |
| Cream soup, 4-3/4" d. | 28.00 | 25.00 | 24.50 | 22.00 |
| Creamer, ftd | 12.50 | 9.00 | 12.50 | 12.50 |
| Cup | 12.50 | 12.00 | 15.00 | 12.50 |
| Jam dish | 30.00 | 25.00 | 35.00 | 30.00 |
| Mayonnaise, three toes | - | - | - | 165.00 |
| Pitcher, 75 oz, 8" h, molded handle | 120.00 | 125.00 | 125.00 | 115.00 |
| Pitcher, 75 oz, 8-1/4" h, applied handle | 150.00 | 140.00 | 150.00 | 145.00 |
| Plate, 6" d, sherbet | 10.00 | 8.50 | 10.00 | 10.00 |
| Plate, 7-1/2" d, salad | 17.50 | 15.00 | 12.50 | 15.00 |
| Plate, 9" d, luncheon | 14.00 | 12.50 | 12.00 | 12.50 |
| Plate, 10-1/2" d, grill | 15.00 | 13.50 | 20.00 | 20.00 |
| Plate, 10-1/2 d, dinner | 10.00 | 12.75 | 32.00 | 36.00 |
| Platter, 11-1/2" l, oval | 32.50 | 30.00 | 30.00 | 28.00 |
| Salt and pepper shakers, pr | 65.00 | 65.00 | 65.00 | 85.00 |
| Saucer | 10.00 | 9.25 | 9.50 | 9.50 |
| Sherbet | 15.00 | 10.00 | 14.00 | 16.00 |
| Sugar | 12.50 | 9.00 | 12.50 | 12.50 |
| Sugar lid | 55.00 | 50.00 | 75.00 | 60.00 |
| Tumbler, 5 oz, 4" h | 40.00 | 28.50 | 30.00 | 32.00 |
| Tumbler, 8 oz, 5-1/4" h, ftd | 50.00 | 42.00 | 50.00 | - |
| Tumbler, 9 oz, 4-1/4" h | 32.00 | 28.50 | 25.00 | 28.00 |
| Tumbler, 12 oz | 45.00 | - | - | - |
| Tumbler, 14 oz, 5-1/2" h | 42.00 | 38.00 | 40.00 | 46.00 |
| Vegetable bowl, 10" l, oval | 38.00 | 30.00 | 38.50 | 30.00 |

# Patrick

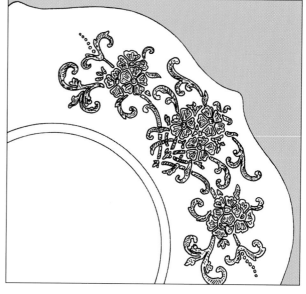

Manufactured by Lancaster Glass Company, Lancaster, Ohio, early 1930s. Made in pink and yellow.

| Item | Pink | Yellow |
|---|---|---|
| Candlesticks, pr | 200.00 | 160.00 |
| Candy dish, three ftd | 175.00 | 175.00 |
| Cheese and cracker set | 150.00 | 130.00 |
| Cocktail, 4" h | 85.00 | 85.00 |
| Console bowl, 11" d | 150.00 | 150.00 |
| Creamer | 75.00 | 40.00 |
| Cup | 70.00 | 40.00 |
| Fruit bowl, 9" d, handle | 175.00 | 130.00 |
| Goblet, 10 oz, 6" h | 85.00 | 75.00 |
| Juice goblet, 6 oz, 4-3/4" h | 85.00 | 75.00 |

| Item | Pink | Yellow |
|---|---|---|
| Mayonnaise, three pieces | 200.00 | 140.00 |
| Plate, 7" d, sherbet | 20.00 | 15.00 |
| Plate, 7-1/2" d, salad | 25.00 | 20.00 |
| Plate, 8" d, luncheon | 45.00 | 30.00 |
| Saucer | 20.00 | 12.00 |
| Sherbet, 4-3/4" d | 72.00 | 60.00 |
| Sugar | 75.00 | 40.00 |
| Tray, 11" d, center handle | 165.00 | 120.00 |
| Tray, 11" d, two handles | 80.00 | 65.00 |

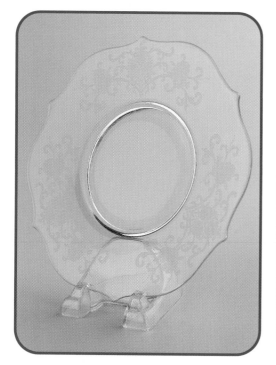

Patrick, yellow luncheon plate.

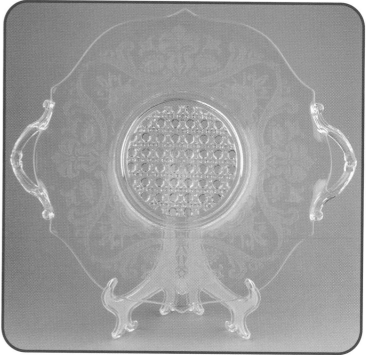

Patrick, yellow tray with caned center.

# Peacock & Wild Rose

## *Line #1300*

Manufactured by Paden City Glass Company, Paden City, W.V., 1930s.

Made in amber, black, cobalt blue, crystal, green, light blue, pink and red.

A black 6-1/4" vase is valued at $100; a black 10" vase is valued at $165.

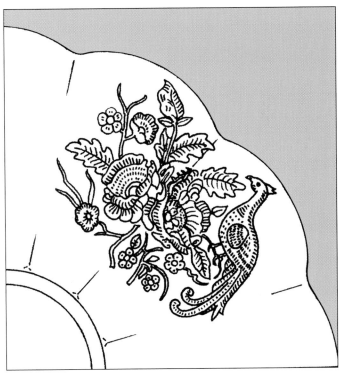

| Item | Amber, Cobalt Blue, Crystal Light Blue, Red | Green | Pink |
|---|---|---|---|
| Bowl, 8-1/2" d, flat | 110.00 | 175.00 | 185.00 |
| Bowl, 8-3/4" d, ftd | 115.00 | 125.00 | 135.00 |
| Bowl, 9-1/2" d, center handle | 175.00 | 185.00 | 195.00 |
| Bowl, 9-1/2" d, ftd | 85.00 | 95.00 | 95.00 |
| Bowl, 10-1/2" d, center handle | 85.00 | 115.00 | 195.00 |
| Bowl, 10-1/2" d, ftd | 95.00 | 165.00 | 195.00 |
| Cake plate, low foot | 195.00 | 195.00 | 150.00 |
| Candlesticks, pr, 5" h | 145.00 | 165.00 | 165.00 |
| Candy dish, cov, 7" | 250.00 | 250.00 | 250.00 |
| Cheese and cracker set | 195.00 | 225.00 | 225.00 |
| Comport, 3-1/4" h, 6-1/4" w | 75.00 | 100.00 | 115.00 |
| Console bowl, 11" d | 165.00 | 175.00 | 175.00 |

| Item | Amber, Cobalt Blue, Crystal Light Blue, Red | Green | Pink |
|---|---|---|---|
| Console bowl, 14" d | 80.00 | 120.00 | 120.00 |
| Fruit bowl, 8-1/2" l, oval, ftd | 165.00 | 175.00 | 185.00 |
| Fruit bowl, 10-1/2" d | 175.00 | 185.00 | 185.00 |
| Ice bucket | 175.00 | 175.00 | 200.00 |
| Ice Tub, 4-3/4" | 185.00 | 195.00 | 195.00 |
| Mayonnaise | 115.00 | 120.00 | 125.00 |
| Pitcher, 5" h | 250.00 | 250.00 | 265.00 |
| Relish, three parts | 75.00 | 90.00 | 90.00 |
| Sandwich tray, 10" | 125.00 | 125.00 | 150.00 |
| Tumbler, 3" h | 55.00 | 60.00 | 65.00 |
| Tumbler, 4" h | 65.00 | 70.00 | 75.00 |
| Tumbler 5-1/4" h | 75.00 | 75.00 | 75.00 |
| Vase, 8-1/4" h, elliptical | 200.00 | 350.00 | 375.00 |
| Vase, 10" h | 250.00 | 145.00 | 225.00 |
| Vase, 12" h | 250.00 | 200.00 | 200.00 |

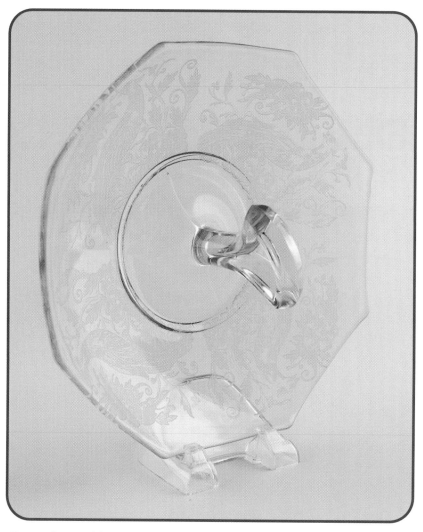

*Peacock & Wild Rose, pink bowl with center handle.*

# Peanut Butter

Unknown maker, 1950s.
Made in crystal and milk glass.
Some pieces were originally filled with
Big Top Peanut Butter.

*Peanut Butter, clear tumbler.*

| Item | Crystal | Milk Glass |
| --- | --- | --- |
| Cup . . . . . . . . . . . . . . . . . . . . . | 6.50 | - |
| Juice tumbler, 5-1/4" h . . . . . . . . | 10.00 | 12.00 |
| Plate, 8" d . . . . . . . . . . . . . . . . | 7.50 | - |
| Saucer . . . . . . . . . . . . . . . . . . . | 3.50 | - |
| Sherbet, ftd. . . . . . . . . . . . . . . . | 5.00 | 5.00 |
| Tumbler, 5-3/4" h . . . . . . . . . . . . | 8.50 | 7.50 |

# Petalware

Manufactured by Macbeth-Evans Glass Company, Charleroi, Pa., from 1930 to 1940.

Made in cobalt blue, Cremax, crystal, fired-on red, blue, green and yellow, Monax and pink. Florette is the name given to a floral decorated with a pointed petal. There are other patterns, such as red flower with a red rim, fruit and other floral patterns.

Crystal values are approximately 50 percent less than those listed for Cremax. Cobalt blue production was limited and the mustard is currently valued at $15 when complete with its metal lid. Monax Regency is priced the same as Monax Florette.

| Item | Cremax | Cremax, Gold Trim | Fired-On Colors | Monax, Florette | Monax, Plain | Pink |
|---|---|---|---|---|---|---|
| Berry bowl, 9" d | 30.00 | 32.00 | - | 35.50 | 18.00 | 25.00 |
| Cereal bowl, 5-1/4" d | 15.00 | 17.50 | 8.50 | 15.50 | 9.00 | 15.00 |
| Cream soup liner | - | - | - | - | 18.75 | - |
| Cream soup, 4-1/2" d | 12.50 | 12.00 | 12.00 | 15.00 | 11.25 | 17.00 |
| Creamer, ftd | 12.50 | 15.00 | 8.50 | 12.00 | 10.00 | 10.00 |
| Cup | 8.00 | 10.00 | 9.50 | 12.00 | 4.50 | 10.00 |
| Lamp shade, 9" d | 17.00 | - | - | 14.00 | 18.00 | - |
| Plate, 6" d, sherbet | 4.50 | 50.00 | 6.00 | 6.00 | 2.50 | 4.50 |
| Plate, 8" d, salad | 8.00 | 8.00 | 7.50 | 10.00 | 4.50 | 10.00 |
| Plate, 9" d, dinner | 15.50 | 14.00 | 8.50 | 16.50 | 10.00 | 16.00 |
| Platter, 13" l, oval | 25.00 | 20.00 | 20.00 | 25.00 | 20.00 | 17.50 |
| Salver, 11" d | 14.00 | 17.00 | 14.00 | 27.50 | 14.00 | 20.00 |
| Salver, 12" d | - | - | - | - | 24.00 | 22.50 |
| Saucer | 3.50 | 4.00 | 4.00 | 5.00 | 4.50 | 5.00 |
| Sherbet, 4" h, low ftd | - | - | - | - | 32.00 | - |
| Sherbet, 4-1/2" h, low ftd | 15.00 | 12.00 | 8.00 | 12.00 | 10.00 | 8.50 |
| Soup bowl, 7" d | 65.00 | 60.00 | 70.00 | 65.00 | 60.00 | - |
| Sugar, ftd | 7.50 | 11.00 | 12.00 | 12.00 | 10.00 | 10.00 |
| Tumbler, 12 oz, 4-5/8" h | - | - | - | - | - | 25.00 |

*Petalware, Monax plate.*

*Petalware, pink sugar, creamer, and two plates.*

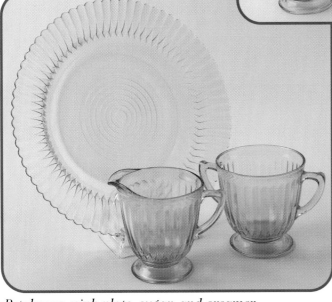

*Petalware, pink plate, sugar, and creamer.*

# Pineapple & Floral

### No. 618

Manufactured by Indiana Glass Company, Dunkirk, Ind., from 1932 to 1937.

Made in amber, avocado (late 1960s), cobalt blue (1980s), crystal, fired-on green, fired-on red, and pink (1980s).

**Reproductions:** † Salad bowl and diamond-shaped comport have been reproduced in several different colors, including crystal, pink, and avocado green.

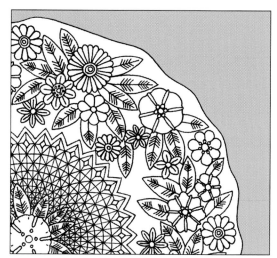

| Item | Amber | Crystal | Red |
|---|---|---|---|
| Ashtray, 4-1/2" d . . . . . . . . . . . . . . . . . . . . . . . . . . . . 20.00 | | 17.50 | 20.00 |
| Berry bowl, 4-3/4" d . . . . . . . . . . . . . . . . . . . . . . . . . . 24.00 | | 20.00 | 22.00 |
| Cereal bowl, 6" d . . . . . . . . . . . . . . . . . . . . . . . . . . . . 24.00 | | 30.00 | 22.00 |
| Comport, diamond-shape . . . . . . . . . . . . . . . . . . . . . . 10.00 | | 5.00 | 10.00 |
| Creamer, diamond-shape . . . . . . . . . . . . . . . . . . . . . . 10.00 | | 7.50 | 10.00 |
| Cream soup . . . . . . . . . . . . . . . . . . . . . . . . . . . . . . . . 16.50 | | 18.00 | 16.50 |
| Cup . . . . . . . . . . . . . . . . . . . . . . . . . . . . . . . . . . . . . 10.00 | | 12.00 | 10.00 |
| Plate, 6" d, sherbet . . . . . . . . . . . . . . . . . . . . . . . . . . . 8.00 | | 6.50 | 8.00 |
| Plate, 8-3/8" d, salad . . . . . . . . . . . . . . . . . . . . . . . . . 12.00 | | 10.00 | 12.00 |
| Plate, 9-3/8" d, dinner . . . . . . . . . . . . . . . . . . . . . . . . 17.50 | | 18.00 | 17.50 |
| Plate, 9-3/4" d, indentation . . . . . . . . . . . . . . . . . . . . . . - | | 25.00 | - |
| Plate, 11" d, closed handles . . . . . . . . . . . . . . . . . . . . 24.00 | | 20.00 | 24.00 |
| Plate, 11-1/2" d, indentation . . . . . . . . . . . . . . . . . . . . . - | | 25.00 | - |
| Platter, 11" l, closed handles . . . . . . . . . . . . . . . . . . . . 20.00 | | 18.00 | 20.00 |
| Relish, 11-1/2" d, divided . . . . . . . . . . . . . . . . . . . . . 28.00 | | 24.00 | 28.00 |
| Salad bowl, 7" d † . . . . . . . . . . . . . . . . . . . . . . . . . . . 10.00 | | 5.00 | 10.00 |
| Sandwich plate, 11-1/2" d . . . . . . . . . . . . . . . . . . . . . 24.00 | | 20.00 | 24.00 |
| Saucer . . . . . . . . . . . . . . . . . . . . . . . . . . . . . . . . . . . . 7.50 | | 6.00 | 7.50 |
| Sherbet, ftd . . . . . . . . . . . . . . . . . . . . . . . . . . . . . . . 28.00 | | 24.00 | 28.00 |
| Sugar, diamond-shape . . . . . . . . . . . . . . . . . . . . . . . . 10.00 | | 7.50 | 10.00 |
| Tumbler, 8 oz, 4-1/4" h . . . . . . . . . . . . . . . . . . . . . . . 40.00 | | 40.00 | 40.00 |
| Tumbler, 12 oz, 5" h . . . . . . . . . . . . . . . . . . . . . . . . . 48.00 | | 47.50 | 48.00 |
| Vase, cone shape . . . . . . . . . . . . . . . . . . . . . . . . . . . . 45.00 | | 42.50 | 45.00 |
| Vegetable bowl, 10" l, oval . . . . . . . . . . . . . . . . . . . . 32.00 | | 30.00 | 32.00 |

*Pineapple & Floral, clear sugar and creamer.*

*Pineapple & Floral, amber cream soup.*

# Pioneer

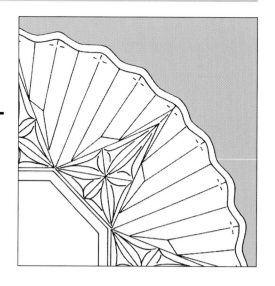

Manufactured by Federal Glass Co., Columbus, Ohio, starting in the 1940s.

Originally made in pink, crystal was added later. The crystal 11" fluted bowl and 12" dinner plate were made until 1973.

| Item | Crystal | Pink |
|---|---|---|
| Bowl, 7" d, low, fruits center | 8.00 | 10.00 |
| Bowl, 7-3/4" d, ruffled, fruits center | 10.00 | 12.00 |
| Bowl, 10-1/2" d, fruits center | 12.00 | 14.00 |
| Bowl, 10-1/2" d, plain center | 10.00 | 12.00 |
| Bowl, 11" d, ruffled, fruits center | 15.00 | 18.00 |
| Bowl, 11" d, ruffled, plain center | 12.00 | 15.00 |
| Nappy, 5-3/8" d, fruits center | 8.00 | 10.00 |
| Nappy, 5-3/8" d, plain center | 6.00 | 8.00 |
| Plate, 8" d, luncheon, fruits center | 6.00 | 8.00 |
| Plate, 8" d, luncheon, plain center | 6.00 | 8.00 |
| Plate, 12" d, fruits center | 10.00 | 12.00 |
| Plate, 12" d, plain center | 10.00 | 12.00 |

*Pioneer, pink plate with fruit center.*

# *Pretzel*

## *No. 622*

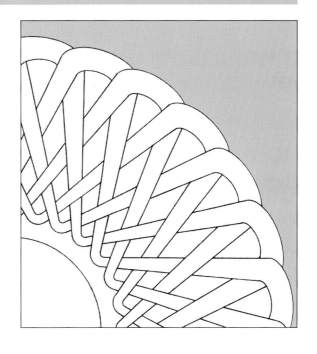

Manufactured by Indiana Glass Company, Dunkirk, Ind., from late 1930s to 1960s.

Made in avocado, crystal, and teal. Some crystal pieces have a fruit decoration. Recent amber, blue, and opaque white issues. A teal cup and saucer is valued at $165.

| Item | Crystal, Plain | Crystal, Fruits |
|---|---|---|
| Berry bowl, 9-3/8" d | 18.00 | - |
| Bowl, 8" d | 7.00 | - |
| Celery tray, 10-1/4" l | 7.50 | - |
| Creamer | 7.00 | - |
| Cup | 7.50 | - |
| Fruit cup, 4-1/2" d | 7.50 | - |
| Iced tea tumbler, 12 oz, 5-1/2" h | 70.00 | - |
| Juice tumbler | 35.00 | - |
| Olive, 7" l, leaf-shape | 7.00 | - |
| Pickle, 8-1/2" d, two handles | 4.00 | - |
| Pitcher, 39 oz | 250.00 | - |
| Plate, 6" d | 3.50 | 5.00 |
| Plate, 6" d, tab handle | 7.00 | - |
| Plate, 7" sq, wings | 9.00 | - |
| Plate, 7-1/4" w, sq, indent | 8.00 | - |
| Plate, 7-1/4" w, sq, indent, three parts | 10.00 | - |
| Plate, 8-3/8" d, salad | 7.50 | 4.00 |
| Plate, 9-3/8" d, dinner | 10.00 | 12.00 |
| Plate, 10" d, dinner | 12.00 | 15.00 |
| Relish, 7", three parts | 10.00 | - |
| Sandwich plate, 11-1/2" d | 12.50 | 12.00 |
| Saucer | 1.50 | - |
| Soup bowl, 7-1/2" d | 15.00 | 10.00 |
| Sugar | 8.00 | - |
| Tumbler, 5 oz, 3-1/2" h | 50.00 | - |
| Tumbler, 9 oz, 4-1/2" h | 70.00 | - |

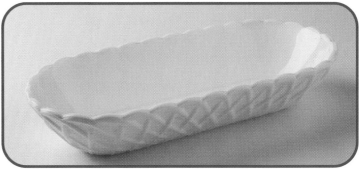

*Pretzel, creamer and clear sugar.*

*Pretzel, milk white celery tray.*

# *Primo*

## *Paneled Aster*

Manufactured by U.S. Glass Company, Pittsburgh, Pa., early 1930s. Made in green and yellow.

*Primo, yellow cup.*

| Item | Green | Yellow |
| --- | --- | --- |
| Bowl, 4-1/2" d. | 20.00 | 25.00 |
| Bowl, 7-3/4" d. | 38.00 | 40.00 |
| Cake plate, 10" d, 3 ftd. | 40.00 | 45.00 |
| Coaster/ashtray | 8.75 | 8.75 |
| Creamer | 12.00 | 15.00 |
| Cup | 14.50 | 14.50 |
| Hostess tray, 5-3/4" d, handles | 42.00 | 45.00 |
| Plate, 7-1/2" d. | 10.25 | 12.00 |
| Plate, 10" d, dinner | 27.50 | 30.00 |
| Plate, 10" d, grill | 18.00 | 20.00 |
| Saucer | 3.25 | 3.25 |
| Sherbet | 14.25 | 14.50 |
| Sugar | 12.00 | 12.00 |
| Tumbler, 9 oz, 5-3/4" h, ftd. | 22.00 | 45.00 |

# Princess

Manufactured by Hocking Glass Company, Lancaster, Ohio, from 1931 to 1935.

Made in apricot yellow, blue, green, pink, and topaz yellow.

**Reproductions:** † The candy dish and salt and pepper shakers have been reproduced in blue, green and pink.

| Item | Apricot Yellow | Blue | Green | Pink | Topaz Yellow |
|---|---|---|---|---|---|
| Ashtray, 4-1/2" d | 110.00 | - | 72.00 | 90.00 | 110.00 |
| Berry bowl, 4-1/2" d | 55.00 | - | 40.00 | 32.00 | 55.00 |
| Butter dish, cov | 700.00 | - | 110.00 | 115.00 | 700.00 |
| Cake plate, 10" d, ftd | - | - | 37.50 | 100.00 | - |
| Candy dish, cov † | - | - | 75.00 | 85.00 | - |
| Cereal bowl, 5" d | - | - | 48.00 | 45.00 | - |
| Coaster | 100.00 | - | 65.00 | 65.00 | 100.00 |
| Cookie jar, cov | - | 875.00 | 65.00 | 75.00 | - |
| Creamer, oval | 25.00 | - | 15.00 | 17.50 | 22.50 |
| Cup | 7.50 | 120.00 | 14.00 | 15.50 | 10.00 |
| Hat-shaped bowl, 9-1/2" d | 125.00 | - | 45.00 | 50.00 | 125.00 |
| Iced tea tumbler, 13 oz, 5-1/2" h | 45.00 | - | 125.00 | 115.00 | 40.00 |
| Juice tumbler, 5 oz, 3" h | 28.00 | - | 25.00 | 28.00 | 28.00 |
| Pitcher, 24 oz, 7-3/8" h, ftd | - | - | 550.00 | 475.00 | - |
| Pitcher, 37 oz, 6" h | 775.00 | - | 60.00 | 75.00 | 775.00 |
| Pitcher, 60 oz, 8" h | 95.00 | - | 65.00 | 80.00 | 95.00 |
| Plate, 5-1/2" d, sherbet | 4.75 | 65.00 | 12.00 | 12.00 | 4.75 |
| Plate, 8" d, salad | 10.00 | - | 15.00 | 15.00 | 10.00 |
| Plate, 9-1/2" d, dinner | 25.00 | - | 33.50 | 45.00 | 25.00 |
| Plate, 9-1/2" d, grill | 10.00 | 175.00 | 15.00 | 15.00 | 10.00 |
| Plate, 10-1/2" d, grill, closed handles | 10.00 | - | 15.00 | 15.00 | 10.00 |
| Platter, 12" l, closed handles | 60.00 | - | 25.00 | 25.00 | 60.00 |
| Relish, 7-1/2" l, divided, four parts | 100.00 | - | 35.00 | 30.00 | 100.00 |
| Relish, 7-1/2" l, plain | 225.00 | - | 195.00 | 195.00 | 225.00 |
| Salad bowl, 9" d, octagonal | 125.00 | - | 55.00 | 40.00 | 125.00 |
| Salt and pepper shakers, pr, 4-1/2" h † | 75.00 | - | 60.00 | 65.00 | 85.00 |
| Sandwich plate, 10-1/4" d, two closed handles | 175.00 | - | 30.00 | 35.00 | 175.00 |
| Saucer, 6" sq | 2.75 | 65.00 | 10.00 | 10.00 | 3.75 |
| Sherbet, ftd | 40.00 | - | 28.00 | 25.00 | 40.00 |
| Spice shakers, pr, 5-1/2" h | - | - | 20.00 | - | - |
| Sugar, cov | 30.00 | - | 35.00 | 65.00 | 30.00 |
| Tumbler, 9 oz, 4" h | 25.00 | - | 28.00 | 25.00 | 25.00 |
| Tumbler, 9 oz, 4-3/4" h, sq, ftd | - | - | 65.00 | 25.00 | - |

| Item | Apricot Yellow | Blue | Green | Pink | Topaz Yellow |
|---|---|---|---|---|---|
| Tumbler, 10 oz, 5-1/4" h, ftd. . . . . . . . . . . . . . | 28.00 | - | 35.00 | 32.00 | 30.00 |
| Tumbler, 12-1/2 oz, 6-1/2" h, ftd. . . . . . . . . . . | 25.00 | - | 180.00 | 95.00 | 25.00 |
| Vase, 8" h . . . . . . . . . . . . . . . . . . . . . . . . . . . | - | - | 45.00 | 50.00 | - |
| Vegetable bowl, 10" l, oval . . . . . . . . . . . . . . . | 60.00 | - | 30.00 | 30.00 | 65.00 |

*Princess, green cookie jar.*

*Princess, green bowl.*

# Pyramid

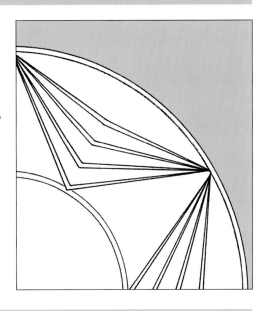

## No. 610

Manufactured by Indiana Glass Company, Dunkirk, Ind., from 1926 to 1932.

Made in crystal, green, pink, white, and yellow. Later production in 1974 to 1975 by Tiara produced black and blue pieces. Production limited in blue and white. Prices for black not firmly established in secondary market at this time.

| Item | Crystal | Green | Pink | Yellow |
|---|---|---|---|---|
| Berry bowl, 4-3/4" d. | 20.00 | 35.00 | 35.00 | 55.00 |
| Berry bowl, 8-1/2" d. | 30.00 | 65.00 | 55.00 | 75.00 |
| Bowl, 9-1/2" l, oval | 30.00 | 45.00 | 40.00 | 65.00 |
| Creamer | 20.00 | 35.00 | 35.00 | 40.00 |
| Ice tub | 95.00 | 145.00 | 155.00 | 225.00 |
| Pickle dish, 9-1/2" l, 5-3/4" w | 30.00 | 35.00 | 35.00 | 65.00 |
| Pitcher | 395.00 | 265.00 | 400.00 | 550.00 |
| Relish, four parts, handles | 25.00 | 65.00 | 60.00 | 70.00 |
| Sugar | 20.00 | 35.00 | 35.00 | 40.00 |
| Tray for creamer and sugar | 25.00 | 30.00 | 30.00 | 35.00 |
| Tumbler, 8 oz, ftd. | 55.00 | 50.00 | 55.00 | 75.00 |
| Tumbler, 11 oz, ftd. | 70.00 | 75.00 | 50.00 | 95.00 |

*Pyramid, green pickle dish.*

# Queen Mary

### Prismatic Line, Vertical Ribbed

Manufactured by Hocking Glass Company, Lancaster, Ohio, from 1936 to 1948.

Made in crystal, pink, and royal ruby.

| Item | Crystal | Pink | Royal Ruby |
|---|---|---|---|
| Ashtray, 2" x 3-3/4" l, oval | 4.00 | 5.50 | 5.00 |
| Ashtray, 3-1/2" d, round | 4.00 | - | - |
| Berry bowl, 4-1/2" d | 3.00 | 5.00 | - |
| Berry bowl, 5" d | 5.00 | 10.00 | - |
| Berry bowl, 8-3/4" d | 10.00 | 17.50 | - |
| Bowl, 4" d, one handle | 4.00 | 12.50 | - |
| Bowl, 5-1/2" d, two handles | 6.00 | 15.00 | - |
| Bowl, 7" d | 7.50 | 35.00 | - |
| Butter dish, cov | 42.00 | 125.00 | - |
| Candlesticks, pr, two lite, 4-1/2" h | 24.00 | - | 70.00 |
| Candy dish, cov | 30.00 | 42.00 | - |
| Celery tray, 5" x 10" | 10.00 | 24.00 | - |
| Cereal bowl, 6" d | 8.00 | 24.00 | - |
| Cigarette jar, 2" x 3" oval | 6.50 | 7.50 | - |
| Coaster, 3-1/2" d | 4.00 | 5.00 | - |
| Coaster/ashtray, 4-1/4" sq | 4.00 | 6.00 | - |
| Comport, 5-3/4" | 9.00 | 14.00 | - |
| Creamer, ftd | 6.00 | 40.00 | - |
| Creamer, oval | 6.00 | 12.00 | - |
| Cup, large | 6.50 | 10.00 | - |
| Cup, small | 8.50 | 12.50 | - |
| Juice tumbler, 5 oz, 3-1/2" h | 9.50 | 15.00 | - |
| Pickle dish, 5" x 10" | 10.00 | 24.00 | - |
| Plate, 6" d, sherbet | 4.00 | 5.00 | - |
| Plate, 6-1/2" d, bread and butter | 6.00 | - | - |
| Plate, 8-1/4" d, salad | 6.00 | - | - |
| Plate, 9-1/2" d, dinner | 15.00 | 65.00 | - |
| Preserve, cov | 30.00 | 125.00 | - |
| Relish, clover-shape | 15.00 | 17.50 | - |

| Item | Crystal | Pink | Royal Ruby |
|------|---------|------|------------|
| Relish, 12" d, three parts | 10.00 | 15.00 | - |
| Relish, 14" d, four parts | 15.00 | 17.50 | - |
| Salt and pepper shakers, pr | 25.00 | - | - |
| Sandwich plate, 12" d | 20.00 | 17.50 | - |
| Saucer | 2.00 | 5.00 | - |
| Serving tray, 14" d | 15.00 | 9.00 | - |
| Sherbet, ftd | 6.50 | 10.00 | - |
| Sugar, ftd | - | 40.00 | - |
| Sugar, oval | 6.00 | 12.00 | - |
| Tumbler, 9 oz, 4" h | 6.00 | 19.50 | - |
| Tumbler, 10 oz, 5" h, ftd | 35.00 | 70.00 | - |

*Queen Mary, crystal bowl and candlesticks.*

# *Radiance*

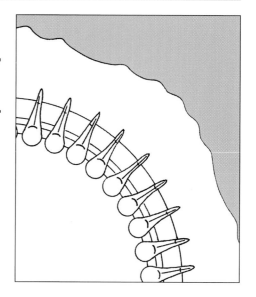

Manufactured by New Martinsville Glass Company, New Martinsville, W.V., from 1936 to 1939.

Made in amber, cobalt blue, crystal, emerald green, ice blue, pink, and red. Some pieces are found with an etched design. This adds slightly to the value.

| Item | Amber | Cobalt Blue | Crystal | Emerald Green | Ice Blue | Pink | Red |
|---|---|---|---|---|---|---|---|
| Bonbon, 6" d | 16.00 | - | 8.00 | - | 32.00 | - | 32.00 |
| Bonbon, 6" d, cov | 48.00 | - | 24.00 | - | 95.00 | - | 95.00 |
| Bonbon, 6" d, ftd | 18.00 | - | 9.00 | - | 35.00 | - | 35.00 |
| Bowl, 6" d, ruffled | - | - | - | - | 35.00 | - | - |
| Bowl, 6-1/2" d, ftd, metal holder | - | - | - | - | - | - | 32.00 |
| Bowl, 10" d, crimped | 28.00 | - | 14.00 | - | 48.00 | - | 48.00 |
| Bowl, 10" d, flared | 22.00 | - | 11.00 | - | 48.00 | - | 48.00 |
| Bowl, 12" d, crimped | 30.00 | - | 15.00 | - | 50.00 | - | 50.00 |
| Bowl, 12" d, flared | 28.00 | - | 14.00 | - | 50.00 | - | 50.00 |
| Butter dish, cov | 210.00 | - | 100.00 | - | 460.00 | - | 460.00 |
| Butter dish, chrome lid | 40.00 | - | 37.50 | - | - | - | - |
| Cake salver | - | - | - | - | 175.00 | - | 175.00 |
| Candlesticks, pr, two lite | 75.00 | - | 37.50 | - | 120.00 | - | 120.00 |
| Candlesticks, pr, 6" h, ruffled | 85.00 | - | 40.00 | - | 175.00 | - | 175.00 |
| Candlesticks, pr, 8" h | 60.00 | - | 30.00 | - | 110.00 | - | 110.00 |
| Candy dish, cov, three parts | - | 125.00 | - | - | 125.00 | - | 125.00 |
| Celery tray, 10" l | 18.00 | - | 9.00 | - | 32.00 | - | 32.00 |
| Cheese and cracker set, 11" d plate | 45.00 | - | 20.00 | - | 195.00 | - | 65.00 |
| Comport, 5" h | 18.00 | - | 9.00 | - | 30.00 | - | 30.00 |
| Comport, 6" h | 24.00 | - | 12.00 | - | 35.00 | - | 35.00 |
| Condiment set, four pcs, tray | 160.00 | - | 85.00 | - | 295.00 | - | 295.00 |
| Cordial, 1 oz | 30.00 | 55.00 | 15.00 | - | 45.00 | - | 45.00 |
| Creamer | 15.00 | 25.00 | 10.00 | - | 35.00 | 32.00 | 35.00 |
| Cruet, individual | 40.00 | - | 20.00 | - | 26.00 | - | 27.50 |
| Cup, ftd | 15.00 | 18.00 | 8.00 | - | 18.00 | 20.00 | 20.00 |
| Decanter, stopper, handle | 90.00 | 195.00 | 45.00 | - | 225.00 | - | 225.00 |
| Lamp, 12" h | 60.00 | - | 30.00 | - | 115.00 | - | 115.00 |
| Mayonnaise, three-pc set | 37.50 | - | 19.00 | - | 85.00 | - | 85.00 |
| Nut bowl, 5" d, two handles | 12.00 | - | 6.50 | - | 20.00 | - | 24.00 |
| Pickle, 7" d | 16.00 | - | 8.00 | - | 25.00 | - | 27.50 |
| Pitcher, 64 oz | 175.00 | 350.00 | 95.00 | - | 375.00 | - | 375.00 |
| Pitcher, silver overlay | - | - | - | - | - | - | 125.00 |
| Plate, 8" d, luncheon | 10.00 | - | 5.00 | - | 12.00 | - | 12.00 |
| Punch bowl, 9" d | 110.00 | - | 65.00 | 135.00 | 185.00 | - | 185.00 |

| Item | Amber | Cobalt Blue | Crystal | Emerald Green | Ice Blue | Pink | Red |
|---|---|---|---|---|---|---|---|
| Punch bowl liner, 14" d. | 48.00 | - | 24.00 | 35.00 | 85.00 | - | 85.00 |
| Punch cup | 8.00 | - | 5.00 | - | 15.00 | - | 15.00 |
| Punch ladle | 100.00 | - | 45.00 | - | 120.00 | - | 120.00 |
| Relish, 7"d, two parts | 18.00 | - | 9.00 | - | 32.00 | - | 32.00 |
| Relish, 8" d, three parts | 28.00 | - | 14.00 | - | 35.00 | - | 35.00 |
| Salt and pepper shakers, pr | 50.00 | - | 25.00 | - | 90.00 | 95.00 | 95.00 |
| Saucer | 6.00 | 7.50 | 3.50 | - | 7.50 | 8.00 | 8.00 |
| Sugar | 16.00 | - | 8.00 | - | 30.00 | 32.00 | 32.00 |
| Tray, oval | 25.00 | - | 15.00 | - | 32.00 | 32.00 | 32.00 |
| Tumbler, 9" oz | 22.50 | 35.00 | 12.00 | - | 30.00 | - | 35.00 |
| Vase, 10" h, crimped | 48.00 | 75.00 | 24.00 | - | 60.00 | - | 70.00 |
| Vase, 10" h, flared | 48.00 | 75.00 | 24.00 | - | 60.00 | - | 70.00 |
| Vase, 12" h, crimped | 60.00 | 50.00 | 30.00 | - | 55.00 | - | 85.00 |
| Vase, 12" h, flared | 70.00 | - | 50.00 | - | 175.00 | - | 175.00 |

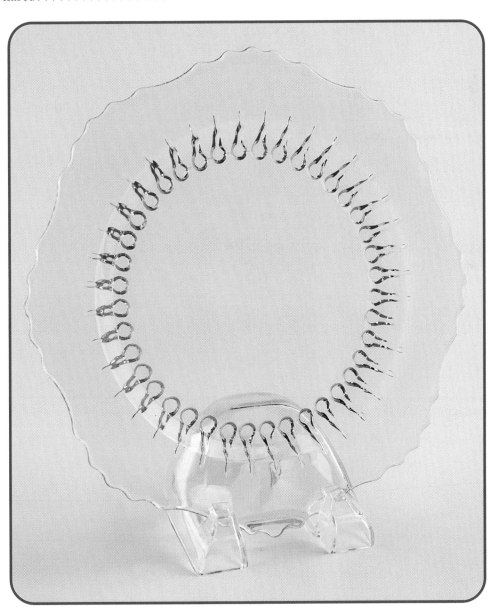

*Radiance, blue plate.*

# Raindrops

Manufactured by Federal Glass Company, Columbus, Ohio, from 1929 to 1933. Made in crystal and green.

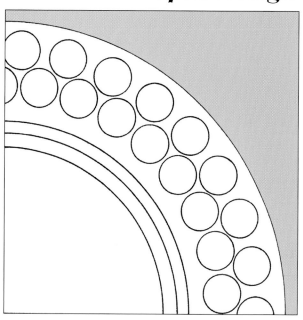

| Item | Crystal | Green |
|---|---|---|
| Berry bowl, 7-1/2" d | 30.00 | 45.00 |
| Cereal bowl, 6" d | 10.00 | 15.00 |
| Creamer | 8.00 | 10.00 |
| Cup | 8.50 | 6.50 |
| Fruit bowl, 4-1/2" d | 5.00 | 11.00 |
| Plate, 6" d, sherbet | 1.50 | 3.00 |
| Plate, 8" d, luncheon | 4.00 | 7.50 |
| Salt and pepper shakers, pr | 200.00 | 350.00 |
| Saucer | 3.00 | 3.50 |
| Sherbet | 4.50 | 7.50 |
| Sugar, cov | 7.50 | 15.00 |
| Tumbler, 2 oz, 2-1/8" h | 4.00 | 7.00 |
| Tumbler, 4 oz, 3" h | 4.00 | 7.00 |
| Tumbler, 5 oz, 3-7/8" h | 5.50 | 9.50 |
| Tumbler, 9-1/2 oz, 4-1/8" h | 6.00 | 12.00 |
| Tumblers, 10 oz, 5" h | 6.00 | 12.00 |
| Tumblers, 14 oz, 5-3/8" h | 7.50 | 15.00 |
| Whiskey, 1 oz, 1-7/8" h | 7.50 | 10.00 |

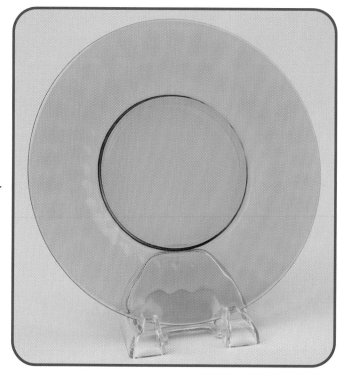

*Raindrops, green salad plate.*

# Ribbon

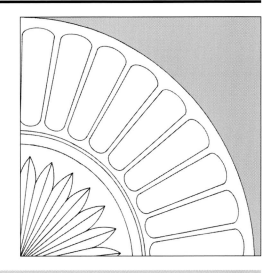

Manufactured by Hazel Atlas Glass Company, Clarksburg, W.V., and Zanesville, Ohio, early 1930s.

Made in black, crystal, green, and pink. Production in pink was limited to salt and pepper shakers, valued at $40.

| Item | Black | Crystal | Green |
| --- | --- | --- | --- |
| Berry bowl, 4" d | - | 20.00 | 22.00 |
| Berry bowl, 8" d | - | 27.50 | 30.00 |
| Bowl, 9" d, wide bands | - | - | 35.00 |
| Candy dish, cov | 45.00 | 35.00 | 45.00 |
| Cereal bowl, 5" d | - | 20.00 | 25.00 |
| Creamer, ftd | - | 10.00 | 15.00 |
| Cup | - | 4.50 | 6.50 |
| Plate, 6-1/4" d, sherbet | - | 3.50 | 4.50 |
| Plate, 8" d, luncheon | 15.00 | 7.00 | 10.00 |
| Salt and pepper shakers, pr | 45.00 | 22.00 | 32.00 |
| Saucer | - | 2.00 | 3.50 |
| Sherbet | - | 6.00 | 8.00 |
| Sugar, ftd | - | 12.00 | 16.50 |
| Tumbler, 10 oz, 6" h | - | 28.00 | 30.00 |

*Ribbon, green cup and creamer.*

# Ring

### Banded Rings

Manufactured by Hocking Glass Company, Lancaster, Ohio, from 1927 to 1933.

Made in crystal, crystal with rings of black, blue, pink, red, orange, silver and yellow; and green, Mayfair blue, pink and red. Prices for decorated pieces are quite similar to each other.

| Item | Crystal | Decorated | Green |
|---|---|---|---|
| Berry bowl, 5" d. | 4.00 | 9.00 | 8.00 |
| Berry bowl, 8" d. | 7.50 | 16.00 | 16.00 |
| Bowl, 5-1/4" d, divided | 12.50 | - | - |
| Butter tub | 24.00 | 25.00 | 20.00 |
| Cereal bowl | - | 5.00 | 8.00 |
| Cocktail shaker | 20.00 | 30.00 | 27.50 |
| Cocktail, 3-1/2 oz, 3-3/4" h | 12.00 | 18.00 | 18.00 |
| Creamer, ftd | 5.00 | 10.00 | 10.00 |
| Cup | 5.00 | 3.00 | 5.00 |
| Decanter, stopper | 30.00 | 35.00 | 32.00 |
| Goblet, 9 oz, 7-1/4" h | 7.00 | 14.00 | 14.00 |
| Ice bucket | 24.00 | 33.00 | 30.00 |
| Ice tub | 24.00 | 25.00 | 20.00 |
| Iced tea tumbler, 6-1/2" h | 10.00 | 15.00 | 15.00 |
| Juice tumbler, 3-1/2" h, ftd | 6.50 | 10.00 | 15.00 |
| Old fashioned tumbler, 8 oz, 4" h | 15.00 | 17.50 | 17.50 |
| Pitcher, 60 oz, 8" h | 22.00 | 25.00 | 25.00 |
| Pitcher, 80 oz, 8-1/2" h | 25.00 | 30.00 | 36.00 |
| Plate, 6-1/2" d, off-center ring | 6.50 | 8.50 | 8.00 |
| Plate, 6-1/4" d, sherbet | 3.00 | 4.50 | 4.00 |
| Plate, 8" d, luncheon | 3.00 | 7.00 | 9.00 |
| Salt and pepper shakers, pr, 3" h | 20.00 | 40.00 | 42.00 |
| Sandwich plate, 11-3/4" d | 8.00 | 15.00 | 15.00 |
| Sandwich server, center handle | 15.00 | 27.50 | 27.50 |
| Saucer | 1.50 | 2.50 | 2.50 |
| Sherbet, 4-3/4" h | 6.50 | 10.00 | 12.00 |
| Sherbet, flat, 6-1/2" d underplate | 12.00 | 18.00 | 21.00 |
| Soup bowl, 7" d | 10.00 | 9.00 | 8.00 |
| Sugar, ftd | 5.00 | 10.00 | 3.00 |
| Tumbler, 4 oz, 3" h | 4.00 | 6.50 | 6.00 |
| Tumbler, 5-1/2" h, ftd | 6.00 | 10.00 | 10.00 |
| Tumbler, 5 oz, 3-1/2" h | 6.50 | 6.50 | 12.00 |
| Tumbler, 9 oz, 4-1/4" h | 7.50 | 7.00 | 9.00 |

| Item | Crystal | Decorated | Green |
|---|---|---|---|
| Tumbler, 10 oz, 4-3/4" h | 8.50 | - | 9.00 |
| Tumbler, 12 oz, 5-1/8" h, ftd | 10.00 | 12.00 | 20.00 |
| Vase, 8" h | 20.00 | 35.00 | 37.50 |
| Whiskey, 1-1/2 oz, 2" h | 8.50 | 10.00 | 12.00 |
| Wine, 3-1/2 oz, 4-1/2" h | 17.50 | 20.00 | 24.00 |

*Ring, green ice tub.*

*Ring, crystal sandwich server.*

# Ripple

### Crinoline, Petticoat, Pie Crust, Lasagna, No. 6091, No. 6040

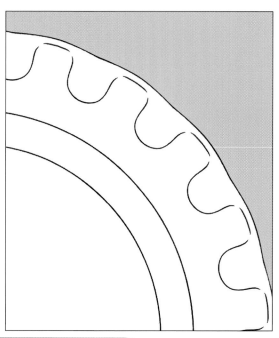

Manufactured by Hazel Atlas Glass Company, Clarksburg, W.V., in the early 1950s.

Made in Platonite white, Jewel Turquoise (white with turquoise trim), and Princess Pink (white with pink trim). All the colors have a similar value.

*Ripple, Jewel Turquoise luncheon plate.*

| Item | Platonite white |
|---|---|
| Berry bowl, 5" d | 12.00 |
| Cereal bowl, 5-5/8" d | 8.50 |
| Creamer | 7.50 |
| Cup | 4.50 |
| Juice tumbler, 5 oz | 7.50 |
| Plate, 6-7/8" d, salad | 5.00 |
| Plate, 8-7/8" d, luncheon | 6.00 |

| Item | Platonite white |
|---|---|
| Sandwich plate, 10-1/2" d | 18.00 |
| Saucer, 5-3/8" d | 2.00 |
| Sugar | 7.50 |
| Tidbit, three tiers | 35.00 |
| Tumbler, 6" h, 16 oz | 12.00 |
| Tumbler, 6-3/4" h, 20 oz | 15.00 |

# Rock Crystal

## Early American Rock Crystal

Manufactured by McKee Glass Company, Pittsburgh, Pa., in the 1920s and colors in 1930s.

Made in amber, amberina red, amethyst, aquamarine, blue frosted, cobalt blue, crystal, crystal with goofus decoration, crystal with gold decoration, dark red, four shades of green, milk glass, pink and frosted pink, red, red slag, Vaseline, and yellow.

| Item | Crystal | Colors | Red |
|---|---|---|---|
| Banana split dish | 75.00 | - | - |
| Bonbon, 7-1/2"d, scalloped edge | 22.00 | 35.00 | 55.00 |
| Bowl, 4" d, scalloped edge | 15.00 | 24.00 | 35.00 |
| Bowl, 4-1/2" d, scalloped edge | 15.00 | 24.00 | 35.00 |
| Bowl, 5" d, plain edge | 20.00 | 26.00 | 45.00 |
| Bowl, 5" d, scalloped edge | 20.00 | 26.00 | 45.00 |
| Bowl, 8-1/2" d, center handle | - | - | 150.00 |
| Bowl, 12-1/2" d, pedestal | 80.00 | 125.00 | 300.00 |
| Butter dish, cov | 345.00 | - | - |
| Cake stand, 11" d, 2-3/4" h, ftd | 40.00 | 55.00 | 135.00 |
| Candelabra, pr, two-lite | 50.00 | 110.00 | 250.00 |
| Candelabra, pr, three-lite | 70.00 | 135.00 | 350.00 |
| Candlesticks, pr, 5-1/2" h, low | 45.00 | 70.00 | 175.00 |
| Candlesticks, pr, 8" h | 95.00 | 70.00 | 400.00 |
| Candy dish, cov, ftd, 9-1/2" d | 55.00 | 95.00 | 225.00 |
| Candy dish, cov, round | 50.00 | 75.00 | 175.00 |
| Celery tray, 12" l, oblong | 30.00 | 40.00 | 85.00 |
| Center bowl, 12-1/2" d, ftd | 98.00 | 135.00 | 310.00 |
| Champagne, 6 oz, ftd | 20.00 | 25.00 | 35.00 |
| Claret, 3 oz | - | 65.00 | - |
| Cocktail, 3-1/2 oz, ftd | 17.50 | 24.00 | 45.00 |
| Comport, 7" d | 35.00 | 50.00 | 90.00 |
| Cordial, 1 oz, ftd | 25.00 | 45.00 | 65.00 |
| Creamer, 9 oz, ftd | 20.00 | 35.00 | 75.00 |
| Creamer, flat, scalloped edge | 40.00 | - | - |

| Item | Crystal | Colors | Red |
|---|---|---|---|
| Cruet, stopper, 6 oz, | 95.00 | - | - |
| Cup, 7 oz. | 20.00 | 25.00 | 70.00 |
| Deviled egg plate | 50.00 | - | - |
| Egg cup, 3-1/2 oz, ftd | 22.50 | 20.00 | 65.00 |
| Finger bowl, 5" d bowl, 7" d plate, piecrust edge. | 35.00 | 48.00 | 70.00 |
| Goblet, 8 oz, ftd. | 20.00 | 30.00 | 60.00 |
| Goblet, 8 oz, 7-1/2" h, low, ftd | 22.50 | 30.00 | 65.00 |
| Ice dish | 35.00 | - | - |
| Iced tea goblet, 11 oz. | 25.00 | 35.00 | 70.00 |
| Jelly, 5" d, ftd, scalloped edge. | 18.00 | 30.00 | 50.00 |
| Juice tumbler, 5 oz | 24.00 | 30.00 | 50.00 |
| Lamp, electric | 225.00 | 375.00 | 650.00 |
| Old fashioned tumbler, 5 oz. | 20.00 | 30.00 | 60.00 |
| Parfait, 3-1/2 oz, low, ftd | 27.50 | 40.00 | 75.00 |
| Pickle, 7" l. | 20.00 | 40.00 | 65.00 |
| Pitcher, covered, 9" h. | 175.00 | 350.00 | 675.00 |
| Pitcher, half gallon, 7-1/2" h | 100.00 | 165.00 | - |
| Pitcher, quart, scalloped edge. | 150.00 | 220.00 | - |
| Pitcher, tankard. | 190.00 | 650.00 | 900.00 |
| Plate, 6" d, bread and butter, scalloped edge | 6.50 | 9.50 | 20.00 |
| Plate, 7-1/2" d, piecrust edge | 8.00 | 12.00 | 22.00 |
| Plate, 7-1/2" d, scalloped edge | 8.00 | 12.00 | 22.00 |
| Plate, 8-1/2" d, piecrust edge | 9.00 | 12.00 | 30.00 |
| Plate, 8-1/2" d, scalloped edge | 9.00 | 12.00 | 30.00 |
| Plate, 9" d, scalloped edge | 18.50 | 24.00 | 55.00 |
| Plate, 10-1/2" d, center design, scalloped edge | 47.50 | 75.00 | 175.00 |
| Plate, 10-1/2" d, scalloped edge | 27.50 | 35.00 | 65.00 |
| Plate, 11-1/2" d, scalloped edge | 20.00 | 30.00 | 60.00 |
| Punch bowl and stand, 14" | 555.00 | - | - |
| Relish, 11-1/2" d, two parts | 35.00 | 50.00 | 75.00 |
| Relish, 12-1/2" d, five parts | 45.00 | - | - |
| Relish, 14" d, six parts | 45.00 | 65.00 | - |
| Roll tray, 13" d. | 35.00 | 60.00 | 125.00 |
| Salad bowl, 7" d, scalloped edge. | 25.00 | 40.00 | 65.00 |
| Salad bowl, 8" d, scalloped edge. | 32.00 | 42.00 | 67.50 |
| Salad bowl, 9" d, scalloped edge. | 35.00 | 50.00 | 85.00 |
| Salad bowl, 10-1/2" d, scalloped edge. | 25.00 | 50.00 | 90.00 |
| Salt and pepper shakers, pr | 80.00 | 135.00 | - |
| Salt dip | 35.00 | - | - |
| Sandwich server, center handle | 32.00 | 40.00 | 140.00 |
| Saucer. | 5.00 | 6.50 | 20.00 |
| Sherbet, 3-1/2 oz, ftd. | 15.00 | 20.00 | 25.00 |
| Spoon tray, 7" l. | 20.00 | 40.00 | 65.00 |
| Spooner. | 42.00 | - | - |
| Sugar, cov. | 50.00 | 65.00 | 155.00 |
| Sugar, 10 oz, open. | 18.00 | 20.00 | 45.00 |
| Sundae, 6 oz, low, ftd. | 12.00 | 15.00 | 35.00 |
| Syrup, lid. | 165.00 | - | - |
| Tray, 5-3/8" x 7-3/8", 7/8" h | 70.00 | - | - |

| Item | Crystal | Colors | Red |
|---|---|---|---|
| Tumbler, 9 oz, concave | 15.00 | 26.00 | 30.00 |
| Tumbler, 9 oz, straight | 15.00 | 26.00 | 30.00 |
| Tumbler, 12 oz, concave | 35.00 | 40.00 | 70.00 |
| Tumbler, 12 oz, straight | 35.00 | 40.00 | 70.00 |
| Vase, 11" h, ftd. | 75.00 | 95.00 | 170.00 |
| Vase, cornucopia | 70.00 | 95.00 | - |
| Whiskey, 2-1/2 oz | 25.00 | 35.00 | 65.00 |
| Wine, 2 oz | 22.50 | 30.00 | 50.00 |
| Wine, 3 oz | 22.50 | 30.00 | 55.00 |

*Rock Crystal, amber plate.*

# Romanesque

Manufactured by L.E. Smith Glass Company, Mt. Pleasant, Pa., in the early 1930s.

Made in amber, black, crystal, green, and yellow.

Romanesque, yellow luncheon plate.

| Item | Amber | Black | Crystal | Green | Yellow |
|---|---|---|---|---|---|
| Bowl, 10" d, ftd | 75.00 | 80.00 | 70.00 | 75.00 | 75.00 |
| Bowl, 10-1/2" d | 42.00 | 55.00 | 40.00 | 42.00 | 42.00 |
| Cake plate | 40.00 | 45.00 | 35.00 | 40.00 | 40.00 |
| Candlesticks, pr. | 27.50 | 35.00 | 25.00 | 27.50 | 27.50 |
| Plate, 5-1/2", octagonal | 6.50 | 10.00 | 6.00 | 6.50 | 6.50 |
| Plate, 7", octagonal | 8.50 | 14.00 | 8.50 | 8.50 | 8.50 |
| Plate, 8", octagonal | 10.00 | 18.00 | 9.00 | 10.00 | 10.00 |
| Plate, 8" d, round | 9.00 | 15.00 | 8.00 | 9.00 | 9.00 |
| Plate, 10", octagonal | 20.00 | 27.50 | 18.00 | 20.00 | 20.00 |
| Sherbet, plain | 8.50 | 14.00 | 7.50 | 8.50 | 8.50 |
| Sherbet, scalloped | 10.00 | 18.00 | 9.00 | 10.00 | 10.00 |
| Snack Tray | 15.00 | 20.00 | 14.00 | 15.00 | 15.00 |
| Vase, 7-1/2" h, fan | 50.00 | 60.00 | 45.00 | 50.00 | 50.00 |

# Rose Cameo

Manufactured by Belmont Tumbler Company, Bellaire, Ohio, in 1931. Made in green.

| Item | Green |
|------|-------|
| Berry bowl, 4-1/2" d | 15.00 |
| Cereal bowl, 5" d | 27.50 |
| Bowl, 6" d, straight sides | 30.00 |
| Plate, 7" d, salad | 16.00 |
| Sherbet | 16.00 |
| Tumbler, 5" h, ftd | 28.00 |
| Tumbler, 5" h, ftd, sterling silver trim | 30.00 |

*Rose Cameo, green tumbler.*

# Rosemary

Manufactured by Federal Glass Company, Columbus, Ohio, from 1935 to 1937. Made in amber, green, and pink.

| Item | Amber | Green | Pink |
|---|---|---|---|
| Berry bowl, 5" d . . . . . . . . . . 7.00 | | 17.50 | 17.50 |
| Cereal bowl, 6" d. . . . . . . . 30.00 | | 32.00 | 35.00 |
| Cream soup, 5" d. . . . . . . . 18.00 | | 25.00 | 30.00 |
| Creamer, ftd . . . . . . . . . . . 10.00 | | 16.00 | 20.00 |
| Cup. . . . . . . . . . . . . . . . . . . 9.00 | | 12.50 | 15.00 |
| Plate, 6-3/4" d, salad . . . . . . . 6.50 | | 12.00 | 12.50 |
| Plate, 9-1/2" d, dinner . . . . 10.00 | | 15.00 | 22.00 |
| Plate, 9-1/2" d, grill . . . . . . 12.00 | | 15.00 | 22.00 |
| Platter, 12" l, oval . . . . . . . 18.50 | | 24.00 | 35.00 |
| Saucer . . . . . . . . . . . . . . . . 5.00 | | 8.50 | 9.50 |
| Sugar, ftd . . . . . . . . . . . . . 10.00 | | 16.00 | 20.00 |
| Tumbler, 9 oz, 4-1/4" h . . . . 35.00 | | 38.00 | 50.00 |
| Vegetable bowl, 10" l, oval . . 18.00 | | 40.00 | 45.00 |

*Rosemary, amber vegetable bowl and berry bowl.*

*Rosemary, green platter.*

# Roulette

## Many Windows

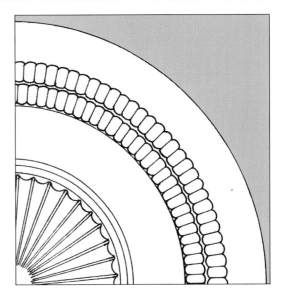

Manufactured by Hocking Glass Company, Lancaster, Ohio, from 1935 to 1939. Made in crystal, green, and pink.

| Item | Crystal | Green | Pink |
|---|---|---|---|
| Cup . . . . . . . . . . . . . . . . . . . . . . . . . . . . . . . . . . . . . . . . . . . . | 35.00 | 8.00 | 8.50 |
| Fruit bowl, 9" d. . . . . . . . . . . . . . . . . . . . . . . . . . . . . . . . . . . . | 12.00 | 25.00 | 25.00 |
| Iced tea tumbler, 12 oz, 5-1/8" h. . . . . . . . . . . . . . . . . . . . . . . | 24.00 | 40.00 | 35.00 |
| Juice tumbler, 5 oz, 3-1/4" h. . . . . . . . . . . . . . . . . . . . . . . . . . | 10.00 | 60.00 | 24.00 |
| Old fashioned tumbler, 7-1/2 oz, 3-1/4" h . . . . . . . . . . . . . . . | 24.00 | 40.00 | 40.00 |
| Pitcher, 65 oz, 8" h . . . . . . . . . . . . . . . . . . . . . . . . . . . . . . . . | 30.00 | 35.00 | 45.00 |
| Plate, 6" d, sherbet . . . . . . . . . . . . . . . . . . . . . . . . . . . . . . . . | 3.50 | 4.50 | 5.00 |
| Plate, 8-1/2" d, luncheon. . . . . . . . . . . . . . . . . . . . . . . . . . . . | 7.00 | 8.00 | 6.00 |
| Sandwich Plate, 12" d . . . . . . . . . . . . . . . . . . . . . . . . . . . . . . | 15.00 | 18.50 | 20.00 |
| Saucer . . . . . . . . . . . . . . . . . . . . . . . . . . . . . . . . . . . . . . . . . . | 2.50 | 4.00 | 3.00 |
| Sherbet . . . . . . . . . . . . . . . . . . . . . . . . . . . . . . . . . . . . . . . . . | 8.00 | 10.00 | 12.00 |
| Tumbler, 9 oz, 4-1/8" h . . . . . . . . . . . . . . . . . . . . . . . . . . . . . | 15.00 | 20.00 | 30.00 |
| Tumbler, 10 oz, 5-1/2" h, ftd . . . . . . . . . . . . . . . . . . . . . . . . . | 18.00 | 30.00 | 35.00 |
| Whiskey, 1-1/2 oz, 2-1/2" h . . . . . . . . . . . . . . . . . . . . . . . . . . | 10.00 | 18.00 | 18.00 |

*Roulette, green plate and sherbet.*

# Round Robin

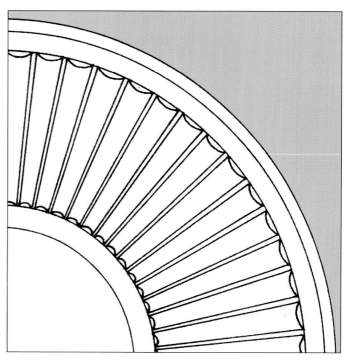

Unknown maker, early 1930s.
Made in crystal, iridescent, and green. Crystal, produced as the base for iridescent pieces, is found occasionally.

| Item | Iridescent | Green |
|---|---|---|
| Berry bowl, 4" d. | 12.00 | 10.00 |
| Creamer, ftd. | 7.50 | 12.00 |
| Cup | 7.50 | 8.00 |
| Domino tray | - | 120.00 |
| Plate, 6" d, sherbet | 4.00 | 5.00 |
| Plate, 8" d, luncheon | 9.00 | 12.00 |
| Sandwich plate, 12" d. | 15.00 | 17.50 |
| Saucer | 2.50 | 2.00 |
| Sherbet | 8.50 | 10.00 |
| Sugar | 7.50 | 12.00 |

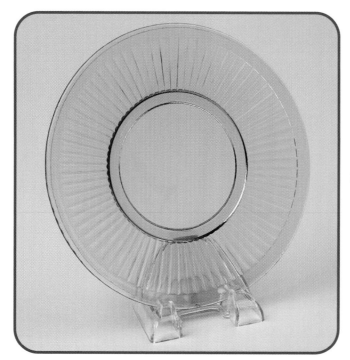

*Round Robin, green plate.*

# Roxana

Manufactured by Hazel Atlas Glass Company, Clarksburg, W.V., and Zanesville, Ohio, in 1932.

Made in crystal, golden topaz, and white. Production in white was limited to a 4-1/2" bowl, valued at $15.

| Item | Crystal | Gold Topaz |
|---|---|---|
| Berry bowl, 5" d . . . . . . . . . | 8.50 | 15.00 |
| Bowl, 4-1/2" x 2-3/8" . . . . . . | 8.00 | 15.00 |
| Cereal bowl, 6" d. . . . . . . . . | 9.00 | 18.00 |
| Plate, 5-1/2" d . . . . . . . . . . | 5.00 | 12.00 |
| Plate, 6" d, sherbet . . . . . . . | 5.00 | 10.00 |
| Sherbet, ftd. . . . . . . . . . . . | 8.00 | 15.00 |
| Tumbler, 9 oz, 4-1/4" h . . . . | 12.00 | 24.00 |

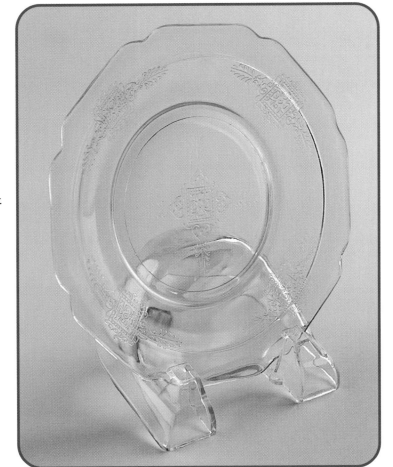

*Roxana, yellow saucer.*

# Royal Lace

Manufactured by Hazel Atlas Glass Company, Clarksburg, W.V., and Zanesville, Ohio, from 1934 to 1941.

Made in cobalt (Ritz) blue, crystal, green, pink, and some amethyst.

**Reproductions:** † Reproductions include a 5 oz, 3-1/2" h tumbler, found in a darker cobalt blue. A cookie jar has also been reproduced in cobalt blue.

| Item | Cobalt Blue | Crystal | Green | Pink |
|---|---|---|---|---|
| Berry bowl, 5" d | 50.00 | 18.00 | 38.00 | 35.00 |
| Berry bowl, 10" d | 100.00 | 20.00 | 35.00 | 45.00 |
| Bowl, 10" d, three legs, rolled edge | 650.00 | 225.00 | 125.00 | 100.00 |
| Bowl, 10" d, three legs, ruffled edge | 750.00 | 45.00 | 125.00 | 100.00 |
| Bowl, 10" d, three legs, straight edge | - | 24.00 | 75.00 | 65.00 |
| Butter dish, cov. | 865.00 | 90.00 | 275.00 | 200.00 |
| Candlesticks, pr, rolled edge | - | 45.00 | 85.00 | 60.00 |
| Candlesticks, pr, ruffled edge | - | 28.00 | 70.00 | 60.00 |
| Candlesticks, pr, straight edge | - | 35.00 | 75.00 | 55.00 |
| Cookie jar, cov † | 400.00 | 45.00 | 75.00 | 55.00 |
| Cream soup, 4-3/4" d | 55.00 | 18.00 | 35.00 | 30.00 |
| Creamer, ftd | 60.00 | 15.00 | 25.00 | 20.00 |
| Cup and saucer | 55.00 | 16.00 | 25.00 | 18.00 |
| Nut bowl | 1,500.00 | 275.00 | 425.00 | 425.00 |
| Pitcher, 48 oz, straight sides | 190.00 | 40.00 | 110.00 | 85.00 |
| Pitcher, 64 oz, 8" h | 295.00 | 45.00 | 120.00 | 120.00 |
| Pitcher, 68 oz, 8" h. ice lip | 320.00 | 60.00 | - | 115.00 |
| Pitcher, 86 oz, 8" h | - | 60.00 | 135.00 | 135.00 |
| Pitcher, 96 oz, 9-1/2" h, ice lip | 495.00 | 75.00 | 160.00 | 155.00 |
| Plate, 6" d, sherbet | 16.50 | 7.50 | 12.00 | 18.00 |
| Plate, 8-1/2" d, luncheon | 60.00 | 12.00 | 18.00 | 24.00 |
| Plate, 9-7/8" d, dinner | 55.00 | 24.00 | 30.00 | 27.50 |
| Plate, 9-7/8" d, grill | 40.00 | 20.00 | 25.00 | 22.50 |
| Platter, 13" l, oval | 60.00 | 42.00 | 45.00 | 48.00 |
| Salt and pepper shakers, pr. | 325.00 | 65.00 | 130.00 | 85.00 |
| Sherbet, ftd. | 50.00 | 20.00 | 25.00 | 18.00 |
| Sherbet, metal holder | 45.00 | 18.00 | - | - |

| Item | Cobalt Blue | Crystal | Green | Pink |
|---|---|---|---|---|
| Sugar, cov | 275.00 | 35.00 | 40.00 | 50.00 |
| Sugar, open | - | 12.50 | 25.00 | 22.00 |
| Toddy or cider set | 295.00 | - | - | - |
| Tumbler, 5 oz, 3-1/2" h † | 65.00 | 15.00 | 35.00 | 35.00 |
| Tumbler, 9 oz, 4-1/8" h † | 45.00 | 20.00 | 35.00 | 28.00 |
| Tumbler, 10 oz, 4-7/8" h | 245.00 | 25.00 | 60.00 | 60.00 |
| Tumbler, 12 oz, 5-3/8" h | 150.00 | 25.00 | 50.00 | 55.00 |
| Vegetable bowl, 11" l, oval | 60.00 | 25.00 | 35.00 | 35.00 |

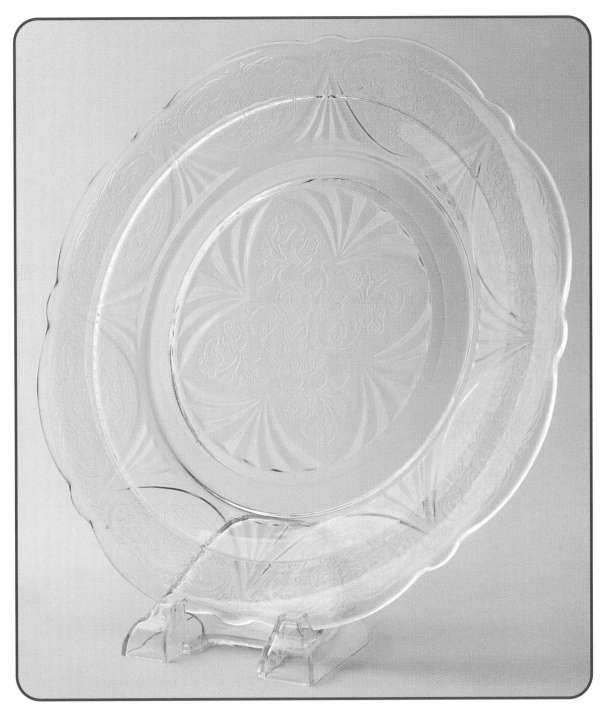

*Royal Lace, clear plate.*

# Royal Ruby

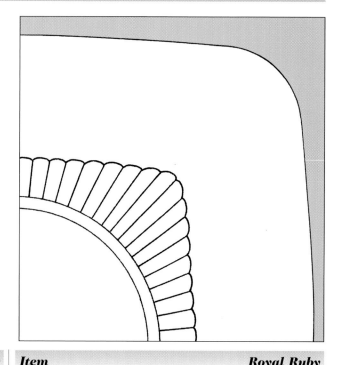

Manufactured by Anchor Hocking Glass Corporation, Lancaster, Pa., from 1938 to 1967.

Made only in Royal Ruby.

| Item | Royal Ruby |
|------|-----------:|
| Apothecary jar, 8-1/2" h. | 22.00 |
| Ashtray, 4-1/2", leaf | 5.00 |
| Ashtray, 5-7/8", sq | 9.00 |
| Ashtray, 7-3/4" | 32.00 |
| Beer bottle, 7 oz | 30.00 |
| Beer bottle, 12 oz | 32.00 |
| Beer bottle, 16 oz | 35.00 |
| Beer bottle, 32 oz | 40.00 |
| Berry, 4-5/8" d, small, square | 9.50 |
| Berry, 8-1/2" d, round | 25.00 |
| Bonbon, 6-1/2" d | 20.00 |
| Bowl, 7-3/8" w, sq | 18.50 |
| Bowl, 11" d, Rachael | 50.00 |
| Bowl, 12" l, oval, Rachael | 70.00 |
| Cereal bowl, 5-1/4" d | 12.00 |
| Cigarette box, card holder, 6-1/8" x 4" | 90.00 |
| Cocktail, 3-1/2 oz, Boopie | 8.50 |
| Cocktail, 3-1/2 oz, tumbler | 10.00 |
| Cordial, ftd | 15.00 |
| Creamer, flat | 10.00 |
| Creamer, ftd | 10.00 |
| Cup, round | 6.00 |
| Cup, square | 7.50 |
| Dessert bowl, 4-3/4" w, sq | 9.00 |
| Fruit bowl, 4-1/4" d | 6.50 |
| Goblet, 9 oz | 9.00 |
| Goblet, 9-1/2 oz | 14.00 |
| Goblet, ball stem | 12.00 |
| Ice bucket | 55.00 |
| Iced tea goblet, 14 oz, Boopie | 20.00 |
| Iced tea tumbler, 13 oz, 6" h, ftd | 10.00 |

| Item | Royal Ruby |
|------|-----------:|
| Ivy ball, 4" h, Wilson | 12.00 |
| Juice tumbler, 4 oz | 7.00 |
| Juice tumbler, 5-1/2 oz | 10.00 |
| Juice tumbler, 5 oz, flat or ftd | 12.00 |
| Juice pitcher | 39.00 |
| Lamp | 35.00 |
| Marmalade, ruby top, crystal base | 22.00 |
| Pitcher, 3 qt, tilted | 45.00 |
| Pitcher, 3 qt, upright | 38.00 |
| Pitcher, 42 oz, tilted | 35.00 |
| Pitcher, 42 oz, upright | 40.00 |
| Pitcher, 86 oz, 8-1/2" | 35.00 |
| Plate, 6-1/4" d, sherbet | 6.50 |
| Plate, 7" d, salad | 5.50 |
| Plate, 7-3/4" w, sq, salad | 7.50 |
| Plate, 8-3/8" w, sq, luncheon | 12.00 |
| Plate, 9-1/8" d, dinner | 14.00 |
| Plate, 13-3/4" d | 35.00 |
| Popcorn bowl, 5-1/4" d | 12.50 |
| Popcorn bowl, 10" d, deep | 40.00 |
| Puff box, ruby top, crystal base, orig label | 28.00 |
| Punch bowl and Stand | 75.00 |
| Punch set, 14 pieces | 200.00 |
| Punch cup | 3.50 |
| Relish, 3-3/4" x 8-3/4", tab handle | 16.00 |
| Salad bowl, 8-1/2" d | 19.00 |
| Salad bowl, 11-1/2" d | 40.00 |
| Saucer, 5-3/8" w, sq | 4.00 |
| Saucer, round | 4.00 |
| Set, 50 pcs, orig labels, orig box | 350.00 |
| Sherbet, 6-1/2 oz, stemmed | 12.00 |

| Item | Royal Ruby | Item | Royal Ruby |
|---|---|---|---|
| Sherbet, 6 oz, Boopie | 8.50 | Vase, 3-3/4" h, Roosevelt | 7.50 |
| Shot glass | 4.50 | Vase, 4" h, Wilson, fancy edge | 12.00 |
| Soup bowl, 7-1/2" d | 15.00 | Vase, 6-3/8" h, Harding | 15.00 |
| Sugar, flat | 8.00 | Vase, 6-5/8" h, Coolidge | 20.00 |
| Sugar, footed | 8.00 | Vase, 9" h, Hoover, plain | 20.00 |
| Sugar lid, notched | 11.00 | Vase, 9" h, Hoover, white birds on branch dec | 25.00 |
| Tray, center handle, ruffled | 16.50 | | |
| Tumbler, 5 oz, 3-1/2" h | 6.00 | Vase, 10" h, fluted, star base | 35.00 |
| Tumbler, 9 oz, Windsor | 8.50 | Vase, 10" h, ftd, Rachael | 50.00 |
| Tumbler, 10 oz, 5" h, ftd | 7.00 | Vegetable bowl, 8" l, oval | 45.00 |
| Tumbler, 14 oz, 5" h | 9.00 | Wine, 2-1/2 oz, ftd | 15.00 |
| Tumbler, 15 oz, long boy | 15.00 | | |

*Royal Ruby, punch set, punch bowl and six cups.*

*Royal Ruby, sugar, creamer, (on pedestal), cup and saucer.*

# S-Pattern

## Stippled Rose Band

Manufactured by Macbeth-Evans Glass Company, Charleroi, Pa., from 1930 to 1933.

Made in amber, crystal, crystal with amber, blue, green, pink or silver trims, fired-on red, green, light yellow and Monax.

| Item | Amber | Crystal | Crystal with Trims | Fired-On Colors | Yellow |
|------|-------|---------|--------------------|-----------------|--------|
| Berry bowl, 8-1/2" d | 8.50 | 12.00 | - | - | 8.50 |
| Cake plate, 11-3/4" d | 50.00 | 48.00 | 55.00 | - | 50.00 |
| Cake plate, 13" d | 80.00 | 65.00 | 75.00 | - | 75.00 |
| Cereal bowl, 5-1/2" d | 6.00 | 4.00 | 6.00 | 12.00 | 6.00 |
| Creamer, thick | 7.50 | 6.50 | 8.00 | 15.00 | 7.50 |
| Creamer, thin | 7.50 | 6.50 | 8.00 | 15.00 | 7.50 |
| Cup, thick | 5.00 | 4.00 | 5.50 | 10.00 | 5.00 |
| Cup, thin | 5.00 | 4.00 | 5.50 | 10.00 | 5.00 |
| Pitcher, 80 oz | - | 75.00 | - | - | - |
| Plate, 6" d, sherbet | 3.50 | 3.00 | 4.00 | - | 3.50 |
| Plate, 8-1/4" d, luncheon | 7.00 | 7.00 | 9.50 | - | 5.00 |
| Plate, 9-1/4" d, dinner | 9.50 | - | 12.50 | - | 9.50 |
| Plate, grill | 8.50 | 6.50 | 9.00 | - | 8.50 |
| Saucer | 4.00 | 3.00 | 4.00 | - | 4.00 |
| Sherbet, low, ftd | 8.00 | 5.50 | 8.50 | - | 8.00 |
| Sugar, thick | 7.50 | 6.50 | 8.00 | 15.00 | 7.50 |
| Sugar, thin | 7.50 | 6.50 | 8.00 | 15.00 | 7.50 |
| Tumbler, 5 oz, 3-1/2" h | 6.50 | 5.00 | 6.50 | - | 6.50 |
| Tumbler, 10 oz, 4-3/4" h | 8.50 | 9.00 | 7.50 | - | 8.50 |
| Tumbler, 12 oz, 5" h | 15.00 | 10.00 | 17.50 | - | 15.00 |

*S-Pattern, yellow tumbler.*

*S-Pattern, crystal yellow-satin plate.*

# Sandwich

Manufactured by Hocking Glass Company, and later Anchor Hocking Corporation, from 1939 to 1964.

Made in crystal, Desert Gold, 1961-64; Forest Green, 1956-1960s; pink, 1939-1940; Royal Ruby, 1938-1939; and white/ivory (opaque), 1957-1960s.

**Reproductions:** † The cookie jar has been reproduced in crystal.

* No cover is known for the cookie jar in Forest Green.

| Item | Crystal | Desert Gold | Forest Green | Pink | Royal Ruby | White |
|---|---|---|---|---|---|---|
| Bowl, 4-5/16" d, smooth | 5.00 | - | 4.00 | - | - | - |
| Bowl, 4-7/8" d, smooth | 5.00 | 6.00 | - | 7.00 | 17.50 | - |
| Bowl, 4-7/8" d, crimped | 20.00 | - | - | - | - | - |
| Bowl, 5-1/4" d, scalloped | 5.00 | 6.00 | - | - | 25.00 | - |
| Bowl, 5-1/4" d, smooth | - | - | - | 7.00 | 35.00 | - |
| Bowl, 6-1/2" d, scalloped | 7.50 | 9.00 | 60.00 | - | 35.00 | - |
| Bowl, 6-1/2" d, smooth | 7.50 | 9.00 | - | - | - | - |
| Bowl, 7-1/4" d, scalloped | 8.00 | - | - | - | - | - |
| Bowl, 8-1/4" d, oval | 10.00 | - | - | - | - | - |
| Bowl, 8-1/4" d, scalloped | 10.00 | - | 80.00 | 20.00 | 35.00 | - |
| Butter dish, cov | 45.00 | - | - | - | - | - |
| Cereal bowl, 6-3/4" d | 32.00 | 12.00 | - | - | - | - |
| Cookie jar, cov † * | 40.00 | 45.00 | 20.00 | - | - | - |
| Creamer | 6.50 | - | 30.00 | - | - | - |
| Cup, coffee | 2.00 | 12.00 | 24.00 | - | - | - |
| Cup, tea | 3.00 | 14.00 | 24.00 | - | - | - |
| Custard cup | 7.00 | - | 4.00 | - | - | - |
| Custard cup liner | 5.50 | - | 1.50 | - | - | - |
| Custard cup, crimped | 12.50 | - | - | - | - | - |
| Dessert bowl, 5" d, crimped | 18.50 | - | - | - | - | - |
| Juice pitcher, 6" h | 115.00 | - | 145.00 | - | - | - |
| Juice tumbler, 3 oz, 3-3/8" h | 12.00 | - | 6.00 | - | - | - |
| Juice tumbler, 5 oz, 3-9/16" h | 7.50 | - | 4.50 | - | - | - |
| Pitcher, half gallon, ice lip | 85.00 | - | 550.00 | - | - | - |
| Plate, 6" d | 5.00 | - | - | - | - | - |
| Plate, 7" d, dessert | 25.00 | - | - | - | - | - |
| Plate, 8" d, luncheon | 18.00 | - | - | - | - | - |

| Item | Crystal | Desert Gold | Forest Green | Pink | Royal Ruby | White |
|---|---|---|---|---|---|---|
| Plate, 9" d, dinner | 20.00 | 10.00 | 125.00 | 10.00 | - | - |
| Plate, 9" d, indent for punch cup | 12.00 | - | - | - | - | - |
| Punch bowl, 9-3/4" d | 18.00 | - | - | - | - | 15.00 |
| Punch bowl and stand | 32.00 | - | - | - | - | 30.00 |
| Punch bowl set, bowl, base, 12 cups | 60.00 | - | - | - | - | - |
| Punch cup | 3.00 | - | - | - | - | 2.00 |
| Salad bowl, 7" d | 8.00 | 25.00 | - | - | - | - |
| Salad bowl, 7-5/8" d | - | - | 60.00 | - | - | - |
| Salad bowl, 9" d | 24.00 | 20.00 | - | - | - | - |
| Sandwich plate, 12" d | 14.00 | 17.50 | - | - | - | - |
| Saucer | 3.50 | 5.00 | 15.00 | - | - | - |
| Sherbet, ftd | 8.00 | 8.00 | - | - | - | - |
| Snack set, plate and cup | 9.00 | - | - | - | - | - |
| Sugar, cov | 30.00 | - | - | - | - | - |
| Sugar, no cover | 6.00 | - | 30.00 | - | - | - |
| Tumbler, 9 oz, ftd | 32.50 | 125.00 | - | - | - | - |
| Tumbler, 9 oz, water | 9.00 | - | 7.00 | - | - | - |
| Vase | - | - | 27.50 | - | - | - |
| Vegetable, 8-1/2" l, oval | 10.00 | - | - | - | - | - |

Sandwich Hocking, crystal oval bowl.

Sandwich Hocking, amber round bowl.

# Sandwich

Manufactured by Indiana Glass Company, Dunkirk, Ind., 1920s to 1980s.

Made in crystal, late 1920s to 1990s; amber, late 1920s to 1980s; milk white, mid-1950s; teal blue, 1950s to 1960s; red, 1933 and early 1970s; smoky blue, 1976 to 1977; and green in the late 1960s and 1970s by Taira.

**Reproductions:** † Reproductions include a butter dish, decanter, and wine. Reproductions are found in dark amber, crystal, green, and pink.

| Item | Amber | Crystal | Teal Blue | Red |
|---|---|---|---|---|
| Ashtray, club | 3.25 | 4.00 | - | - |
| Ashtray, diamond | 3.25 | 4.00 | - | - |
| Ashtray, heart | 3.25 | 4.00 | 2.00 | - |
| Ashtray, spade | 3.25 | 4.00 | - | - |
| Basket, 10" h | 35.00 | 35.00 | - | - |
| Berry bowl, 4-1/4" d | 3.50 | 5.00 | - | - |
| Bowl, 6" w, hexagonal | 5.50 | 6.00 | 15.00 | - |
| Bowl, 8-1/2" d | 10.00 | 11.00 | - | - |
| Butter dish, cov † | 25.00 | 25.00 | 150.00 | - |
| Candlesticks, pr, 3-1/2" h | 18.00 | 20.00 | - | - |
| Candlesticks, pr, 7" h | 25.00 | 25.00 | - | - |
| Celery tray, 10-1/2" l | 17.50 | 14.00 | - | - |
| Cereal bowl, 6" d | 12.00 | 6.50 | - | - |
| Cocktail, 3 oz, ftd | 7.50 | 7.50 | - | - |
| Comport, low, ruffled | 15.00 | - | - | - |
| Console bowl, 9" d | 17.50 | 17.50 | - | - |
| Console bowl, 11-1/2" d | 20.00 | 20.00 | - | - |
| Creamer | 6.00 | 6.00 | - | 48.00 |
| Creamer and sugar, tray | 18.00 | 18.00 | 35.00 | - |
| Cruet, 6-1/2 oz, stopper | - | - | 145.00 | - |
| Cup | 4.00 | 4.00 | 8.50 | 30.00 |
| Decanter, stopper † | 25.00 | 25.00 | - | 90.00 |
| Fairy lamp | 15.00 | - | - | - |
| Goblet, 9 oz | 14.00 | 15.00 | - | 45.00 |
| Iced tea tumbler, 12 oz, ftd | 10.00 | 10.00 | - | - |
| Mayonnaise, ftd | 14.00 | 14.00 | - | - |
| Pitcher, 68 oz | 24.00 | 24.00 | - | 175.00 |

| Item | Amber | Crystal | Teal Blue | Red |
|---|---|---|---|---|
| Plate, 6" d, sherbet | 3.50 | 3.50 | 7.50 | - |
| Plate, 7" d, bread and butter | 4.00 | 4.00 | - | - |
| Plate, 8" d, oval, indent | - | 4.00 | 6.50 | 15.00 |
| Plate, 8-3/8" d, luncheon | 7.50 | 8.00 | - | 20.00 |
| Plate, 10-1/2" d, dinner | 9.00 | 8.50 | 20.00 | - |
| Puff box | 18.00 | 18.00 | - | - |
| Salt and pepper shakers, pr | 18.00 | 18.00 | - | - |
| Sandwich plate, 13" d | 14.50 | 14.50 | 25.00 | 35.00 |
| Sandwich server, center handle | 20.00 | 20.00 | - | 50.00 |
| Saucer | 3.50 | 2.50 | 7.00 | 7.50 |
| Sherbet, 3-1/4" h | 6.00 | 5.50 | 12.00 | - |
| Sugar, cov, large | 20.00 | 20.00 | - | 48.00 |
| Tumbler, 8 oz, ftd, water | 10.00 | 10.00 | - | - |
| Wine, 3" h, 4 oz † | 10.00 | 12.00 | - | 15.00 |

Sandwich, Indiana, crystal creamer, sugar, and tray.

# Sandwich

Manufactured by Duncan & Miller Glass Company, Washington, Pa., from 1924 to 1955.

Made in crystal with limited production in amber, cobalt blue, green, pink, and red. The molds were sold to Lancaster Colony which continues to produce some glass in this pattern, but in newer brighter colors, such as amberina, blue, and green.

| Item | Crystal |
|---|---|
| Almond bowl, 2-1/2" d. | 12.00 |
| Ashtray, 2-1/2" x 3-3/4" | 10.00 |
| Ashtray, 2-3/4" sq | 8.50 |
| Basket, 6-1/2", loop handle | 135.00 |
| Basket 10", loop handle, crimped | 185.00 |
| Basket, 10", loop handle, oval | 185.00 |
| Basket, 11-1/2", loop handle | 225.00 |
| Bonbon, 5" w, heart shape | 15.00 |
| Bonbon, 6" w, heart shape, ring handle | 20.00 |
| Bonbon, cov, 7-1/2" d, ftd, | 45.00 |
| Bowl, 5-1/2" d, handle | 15.00 |
| Butter, cov, quarter pound | 40.00 |
| Cake stand, 11-1/2" d, ftd | 95.00 |
| Cake stand, 12" d, ftd | 115.00 |
| Cake stand, 13" d, ftd | 125.00 |
| Candelabra, with bobeche and prisms, 10" h, three-lite | 200.00 |
| Candelabra, with bobeche and prisms, 10" h, one-lite | 95.00 |
| Candelabra, with bobeche and prisms, 16" h, three-lite | 225.00 |
| Candlesticks, pr, 4" h | 30.00 |

| Item | Crystal |
|---|---|
| Candlesticks, pr, 5" h, three-lite | 90.00 |
| Candy box, cov, 5" d, flat | 42.00 |
| Candy comport, 3-1/4" d, low, ftd or flared | 25.00 |
| Candy dish, 6" sq | 375.00 |
| Candy jar, cov, 8-1/2" d, flat | 60.00 |
| Celery tray, 10" l, oval | 30.00 |
| Champagne, 5 oz | 25.00 |
| Cheese comport, 13" d underplate | 60.00 |
| Cheese dish, cov | 125.00 |
| Cigarette box, cov, 3-1/2" | 24.00 |
| Cigarette holder, 3" d, ftd | 30.00 |
| Coaster, 5" d | 12.00 |
| Cocktail, 3 oz | 15.00 |
| Comport, 2-1/4" | 17.50 |
| Comport, 4-1/4" d, ftd | 22.00 |
| Comport, 5" d, low, ftd | 22.00 |
| Comport, 5-1/2" d, ftd, low, crimped | 25.00 |
| Comport, 6" d, low, flared | 25.00 |
| Condiment set, pr cruets, pr salt and pepper shakers, tray | 100.00 |
| Console bowl, 12" d | 45.00 |

| Item | Crystal |
|---|---|
| Cracker plate, 13" d | 32.00 |
| Creamer | 10.00 |
| Cup | 10.00 |
| Deviled egg plate, 12" d | 65.00 |
| Epergne, 9" h | 125.00 |
| Epergne, 12" h, three parts | 200.00 |
| Finger bowl, 4" h | 12.00 |
| Finger bowl underplate, 6-1/2" d | 8.00 |
| Flower bowl, 11-1/2" d, crimped | 60.00 |
| Fruit bowl, 5" d | 10.00 |
| Fruit bowl, 10" d | 65.00 |
| Fruit bowl, 11-1/2" d, crimped, ftd | 65.00 |
| Fruit bowl, 12", flared | 50.00 |
| Fruit cup, 6 oz | 12.00 |
| Fruit salad bowl, 6" d | 12.00 |
| Gardenia bowl, 11-1/2" d | 48.00 |
| Goblet, 9 oz, 6" h | 18.00 |
| Grapefruit bowl, 5-1/2" d or 6" d | 17.50 |
| Hostess plate, 16" d | 100.00 |
| Ice cream dish 5 oz | 12.00 |
| Ice cream plate, rolled edge, 12" d | 60.00 |
| Ice cream tray, rolled edge, 12" d | 45.00 |
| Iced tea tumbler, 12 or 13 oz, ftd | 20.00 |
| Ivy bowl, ftd, crimped | 35.00 |
| Jelly, 3" d | 8.00 |
| Juice tumbler, 5 oz | 12.00 |
| Lazy Susan, 16" d | 115.00 |
| Lily bowl, 10" d | 55.00 |
| Mayonnaise set, three pcs | 35.00 |
| Mint tray, 6" l or 7" l, rolled edge, ring handle | 18.00 |
| Nappy, 5" d, two parts | 15.00 |
| Nappy, 5" d, ring handle | 12.00 |
| Nappy, 6" d, ring handle | 15.00 |
| Nut bowl, 3-1/2" d | 10.00 |
| Nut bowl, 11" d, cupped | 55.00 |
| Oil bottle, orig stopper | 35.00 |
| Oil and vinegar tray, 8" l | 20.00 |
| Oyster cocktail, 5 oz | 18.00 |
| Parfait, 4 oz, ftd | 30.00 |
| Pickle tray, 7" l, oval | 15.00 |
| Pitcher, 13 oz, metal lip | 75.00 |
| Pitcher, 64 oz, ice lip | 125.00 |
| Plate, 3" d, jelly | 5.00 |
| Plate, 6" d, bread and butter | 6.00 |
| Plate, 7" d, dessert | 7.50 |
| Plate, 8" d, salad | 10.00 |
| Plate, 9-1/2" d, dinner | 35.00 |
| Relish, 5-1/2" d, two parts, ring handle | 15.00 |
| Relish, 6" d, two parts, ring handle | 18.00 |
| Relish, 7" d, two parts, oval | 20.00 |
| Relish, 10" d, three parts, rect | 27.50 |
| Relish, 10" d, four parts | 25.00 |
| Relish, 10-1/2" l, three parts, rect | 27.50 |

| Item | Crystal |
|---|---|
| Relish, 12" l, three parts | 25.00 |
| Salad bowl, 10" d, deep | 75.00 |
| Salad bowl, 12" d, shallow | 42.00 |
| Salt and pepper shakers, pr, 2-1/2" h, glass tops | 20.00 |
| Salt and pepper shakers, pr, 2-1/2" h, metal tops | 20.00 |
| Salts and pepper shakers, set, pr 3-3/4" h, metal tops, 6" tray | 35.00 |
| Service plate, 11-1/2" d, handle | 50.00 |
| Service plate, 13" d | 55.00 |
| Sugar shaker | 72.00 |
| Sugar bowl, 5 oz | 10.00 |
| Sugar bowl, 9 oz, 3-1/4" h, ftd | 12.00 |
| Sundae, 5 oz | 15.00 |
| Torte plate, 12" d | 48.00 |
| Tray, 8" l | 20.00 |
| Urn, cov, 12" h, ftd | 150.00 |
| Tumbler, 9 oz, 4-3/4", ftd | 15.00 |
| Vase, 3" h, crimped | 18.00 |
| Vase, 3" h, flared rim | 18.00 |
| Vase, 4" h, hat shape | 20.00 |
| Vase, 4-1/2" h, crimped | 25.00 |
| Vase, 5" h, fan | 40.00 |
| Vase, 5" h, flared or crimped | 25.00 |
| Vase, 10" h, ftd | 70.00 |
| Wine, 3 oz | 24.00 |

*Sandwich, 8" d crystal salad plate.*

# Seville

Manufactured by Fostoria Glass Company, Moundsville, Va., from 1926 to 1931.

Made in amber and green.

| Item | Amber | Green |
|---|---|---|
| After dinner cup and saucer | 32.00 | 40.00 |
| Ashtray, 4" d | 20.00 | 24.00 |
| Baker, 9" l, oval | 27.50 | 32.00 |
| Baker, 10-1/2" l, oval | 37.50 | 40.00 |
| Bouillon, flat or ftd | 15.00 | 17.50 |
| Bowl, 7" d, low foot | 15.50 | 17.50 |
| Bowl, 10" d, ftd | 35.00 | 40.00 |
| Bowl, 10-1/2" d, flared, ftd | 30.00 | 32.00 |
| Bowl, 12" d, deep, flared | 32.00 | 35.00 |
| Butter dish, cov, round | 195.00 | 250.00 |
| Canapé plate, 8-3/4" d | 37.50 | 42.00 |
| Candlesticks, pr, 2" h | 15.00 | 20.00 |
| Candlesticks, pr, 4" h | 15.00 | 22.00 |
| Candlesticks, pr, 9" h | 32.00 | 35.00 |
| Candy jar, cov, flat | 70.00 | 85.00 |
| Candy jar, cov, ftd | 90.00 | 125.00 |
| Celery, 11" | 17.50 | 20.00 |
| Cereal bowl, 6-1/2" d | 17.50 | 20.00 |
| Cheese and cracker | 42.00 | 48.00 |
| Chop plate, 12-3/4" d | 32.00 | 35.00 |
| Cocktail | 17.50 | 20.00 |
| Comport, 7-1/2" d | 22.00 | 30.00 |
| Comport, 8" | 30.00 | 37.50 |
| Console bowl, 11" d, rolled edge | 30.00 | 35.00 |
| Console bowl, 13" d, rolled edge | 35.00 | 40.00 |
| Console bowl, 13" l, oval | 40.00 | 45.00 |

| Item | Amber | Green |
|---|---|---|
| Cordial | 70.00 | 72.00 |
| Cream soup, ftd | 15.00 | 17.50 |
| Creamer, flat or ftd | 15.00 | 20.00 |
| Cup, flat or ftd | 12.00 | 15.00 |
| Egg cup | 30.00 | 35.00 |
| Finger bowl | 10.00 | 12.50 |
| Fruit bowl, 5-1/2" d | 10.00 | 12.50 |
| Goblet | 22.00 | 25.00 |
| Grapefruit, blown | 42.00 | 48.00 |
| Grapefruit, molded | 27.50 | 35.00 |
| Ice bucket | 60.00 | 65.00 |
| Nappy, 9" d | 30.00 | 35.00 |
| Oyster cocktail | 17.50 | 20.00 |
| Parfait | 35.00 | 37.50 |
| Pickle | 15.00 | 17.50 |
| Pitcher, ftd | 250.00 | 275.00 |
| Plate, 6" d, bread and butter | 4.00 | 6.00 |
| Plate, 7-1/2" d, salad | 6.00 | 7.50 |
| Plate, 8-1/2" d, luncheon | 7.50 | 12.50 |
| Plate, 9-1/2" d, dinner | 12.50 | 17.50 |
| Plate, 10-1/2" d, dinner | 30.00 | 35.00 |
| Platter, 10-1/2" l | 24.00 | 27.50 |
| Platter, 12" l | 35.00 | 40.00 |
| Platter, 15" l | 65.00 | 70.00 |
| Salad bowl, 10" d | 35.00 | 40.00 |
| Salt and pepper shakers, pr | 65.00 | 70.00 |
| Sauce boat and underplate | 75.00 | 95.00 |
| Saucer | 3.50 | 4.00 |

| Item | Amber | Green | Item | Amber | Green |
|---|---|---|---|---|---|
| Serving plate, 15" d | 37.50 | 42.00 | Tumbler, 5 oz, ftd | 15.00 | 17.50 |
| Sherbet, high | 15.00 | 17.50 | Tumbler, 9 oz, ftd | 17.50 | 20.00 |
| Sherbet, low | 12.00 | 15.00 | Tumbler, 12 oz, ftd | 20.00 | 24.00 |
| Soup bowl, 7-3/4" d | 24.00 | 30.00 | Urn | 72.00 | 95.00 |
| Sugar bowl lid | 75.00 | 100.00 | Vase, 8" h | 50.00 | 60.00 |
| Sugar bowl, ftd | 15.00 | 15.00 | Vegetable bowl | 24.00 | 30.00 |
| Tray, 11" d, center handle | 30.00 | 32.00 | Wine | 24.00 | 27.50 |
| Tumbler, 2 oz, ftd | 37.50 | 42.00 | | | |

*Seville, amber dinner plate.*

# Sharon

## Cabbage Rose

Manufactured by Federal Glass Company, Columbus, Ohio, from 1935 to 1939.

Made in amber, crystal, green, and pink.

**Reproductions:** † Reproductions include the butter dish, covered candy dish, creamer, covered sugar, and salt and pepper shakers. Reproduction colors include dark amber, blue, green, and pink.

| Item | Amber | Crystal | Green | Pink |
|------|------:|--------:|------:|-----:|
| Berry bowl, 5" d | 8.50 | 5.00 | 18.50 | 15.00 |
| Berry bowl, 8-1/2" d | 10.00 | 12.00 | 40.00 | 35.00 |
| Butter dish, cov † | 50.00 | 20.00 | 85.00 | 65.00 |
| Cake plate, 11-1/2" d, ftd | 30.00 | 10.00 | 65.00 | 50.00 |
| Candy dish, cov † | 45.00 | 15.00 | 100.00 | 65.00 |
| Cereal, 6" d | 24.00 | 12.00 | 32.00 | 35.00 |
| Champagne, 5" d bowl | - | - | - | 12.00 |
| Cheese dish, cov † | 225.00 | 1,500.00 | - | 950.00 |
| Cream soup, 5" d | 28.00 | 15.00 | 60.00 | 50.00 |
| Creamer, ftd † | 15.00 | 14.00 | 22.00 | 24.00 |
| Cup | 9.00 | 6.00 | 18.00 | 20.00 |
| Fruit bowl, 10-1/2" d | 24.00 | 18.00 | 40.00 | 55.00 |
| Iced tea tumbler, ftd | 125.00 | 15.00 | - | 65.00 |
| Jam dish, 7-1/2" d | 40.00 | - | 48.00 | 215.00 |
| Pitcher, 80 oz, ice lip | 145.00 | - | 150.00 | 165.00 |
| Pitcher, 80 oz, without ice lip | 140.00 | - | 150.00 | 150.00 |
| Plate, 6" d, bread and butter | 16.00 | 5.00 | 9.00 | 16.50 |
| Plate, 7-1/2" d, salad | 16.50 | 6.50 | 8.00 | 30.00 |
| Plate, 9-1/2" d, dinner | 17.00 | 9.50 | 27.50 | 24.50 |
| Platter, 12-1/2" l, oval | 24.00 | - | 35.00 | 40.00 |
| Salt and pepper shakers, pr † | 40.00 | - | 80.00 | 65.00 |
| Saucer | 6.50 | 4.00 | 36.00 | 15.00 |
| Sherbet, ftd | 14.00 | 8.00 | 35.00 | 19.50 |
| Soup, flat, 7-3/4" d, 1 7/8" deep | 60.00 | - | - | 65.00 |
| Sugar, cov † | 35.00 | 12.00 | 55.00 | 60.00 |
| Tumbler, 9 oz, 4-1/8" h, thick | 30.00 | - | 65.00 | 45.00 |

| Item | Amber | Crystal | Green | Pink |
|---|---|---|---|---|
| Tumbler, 9 oz, 4-1/8" h, thin . . . . . . . . . . . . . . . . . . . . . 38.00 | | - | 65.00 | 42.00 |
| Tumbler, 12 oz, 5-1/4" h, thick . . . . . . . . . . . . . . . . . . 55.00 | | - | 95.00 | 50.00 |
| Tumbler, 12 oz, 5-1/4" h, thin . . . . . . . . . . . . . . . . . . . 55.00 | | - | 95.00 | 52.50 |
| Tumbler, 15 oz, 6-1/2" h, thick . . . . . . . . . . . . . . . . . 125.00 | | 18.00 | - | 63.00 |
| Vegetable bowl, 9-1/2" l, oval. . . . . . . . . . . . . . . . . . . 25.00 | | - | 35.00 | 42.50 |

Sharon, pink sherbet, two bowls and creamer.

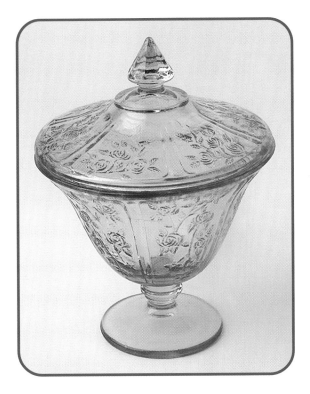

REPRODUCTION!
Sharon, pink covered
candy dish.

# Ships

## Sailboat, Sportsman Series

Manufactured by Hazel Atlas Glass Company, Clarksburg, W.V., and Zanesville, Ohio, late 1930s.

Made in cobalt blue with white, yellow, and red decoration. Pieces with yellow or red decoration are valued slightly higher than the traditional white decoration.

| Item | Cobalt Blue with White Decoration |
|---|---|
| Ashtray | 60.00 |
| Ashtray, metal sailboat | 120.00 |
| Box, cov, three parts | 250.00 |
| Cocktail mixer, stirrer | 45.00 |
| Cocktail shaker | 45.00 |
| Cup | 15.00 |
| Ice bowl | 45.00 |
| Iced tea tumbler, 10-1/2 oz, 4-7/8" h | 22.00 |
| Iced tea tumbler, 12 oz | 24.00 |
| Juice tumbler, 5 oz, 3-3/4" h | 12.50 |
| Old fashioned tumbler, 8 oz, 3-3/8" h | 22.00 |
| Pitcher, 82 oz, no ice lip | 85.00 |
| Pitcher, 86 oz, ice lip | 75.00 |
| Plate, 5-7/8" d, bread & butter | 24.00 |
| Plate, 8" d, salad | 27.50 |
| Plate, 9" d, dinner | 32.00 |
| Roly Poly, 6 oz | 10.00 |
| Saucer | 18.00 |
| Shot glass, 2 oz, 2-1/4" h | 250.00 |
| Tumbler, 4 oz, 3-1/4" h, heavy bottom | 27.50 |
| Tumbler, 4 oz, heavy bottom | 12.00 |
| Tumbler, 9 oz, 3-3/4" h | 18.00 |
| Tumbler, 9 oz, 4-5/8" h | 18.00 |
| Whiskey, 3-1/2" h | 45.00 |

*Ships, cobalt blue cocktail shaker.*

*Ships, cobalt blue luncheon plate.*

*Ships, cobalt blue dinner plate.*

# Sierra

## Pinwheel

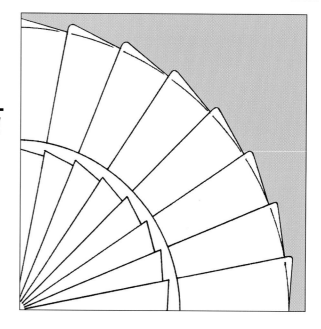

Manufactured by Jeannette Glass Company, Jeannette, Pa., from 1931 to 1933.

Made in green and pink. A few forms are known in Ultramarine.

| Item | Green | Pink |
|---|---|---|
| Berry, small | 25.00 | 25.00 |
| Berry bowl, 8-1/2" d | 40.00 | 40.00 |
| Butter dish, cov | 80.00 | 85.00 |
| Cereal bowl, 5-1/2" d | 25.00 | 20.00 |
| Creamer | 25.00 | 25.00 |
| Cup | 19.50 | 17.50 |
| Pitcher, 32 oz, 6-1/2" h | 160.00 | 135.00 |
| Plate, 9" d, dinner | 30.00 | 32.00 |

| Item | Green | Pink |
|---|---|---|
| Platter, 11" l, oval | 70.00 | 65.00 |
| Salt and pepper shakers, pr | 50.00 | 50.00 |
| Saucer | 10.00 | 10.00 |
| Serving tray, 10-1/4" l, two handles | 25.00 | 30.00 |
| Sugar, cov | 48.00 | 48.00 |
| Tumbler, 9 oz, 4-1/2" h, ftd | 90.00 | 80.00 |
| Vegetable bowl, 9-1/4" l, oval | 135.00 | 90.00 |

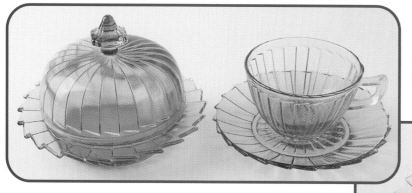

*Sierra Pinwheel, green butter dish and pink cup and saucer.*

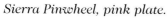

*Sierra Pinwheel, pink plate.*

# Spiral

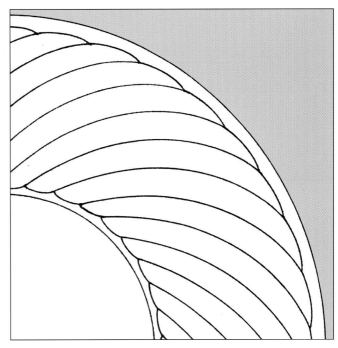

Manufactured by Hocking Glass Company, Lancaster, Ohio, from 1928 to 1930.

Made in crystal, green, and pink. Collector interest is strongest in green.

| Item | Green |
| --- | --- |
| Berry bowl, 4-3/4" d | 8.00 |
| Berry bowl, 8" d | 16.50 |
| Butter tub | 27.50 |
| Creamer, flat | 8.00 |
| Creamer, footed | 8.00 |
| Cup | 5.00 |
| Ice tub | 25.00 |
| Juice tumbler, 5 oz, 3" h | 5.00 |
| Mixing bowl, 7" d | 9.00 |
| Pitcher, 58 oz, 7-5/8" h | 35.00 |
| Plate, 6" d, sherbet | 5.00 |
| Plate, 8" d, luncheon | 6.50 |
| Platter, 12" l | 32.00 |
| Preserve, cov | 32.00 |
| Salt and pepper shakers, pr. | 37.50 |
| Sandwich server, center handle | 30.00 |
| Saucer | 4.00 |
| Sherbet | 5.00 |
| Sugar, flat | 8.00 |
| Sugar, footed | 8.00 |
| Tumbler, 5-7/8" h, ftd | 24.00 |
| Tumbler, 9 oz, 5" h | 12.00 |

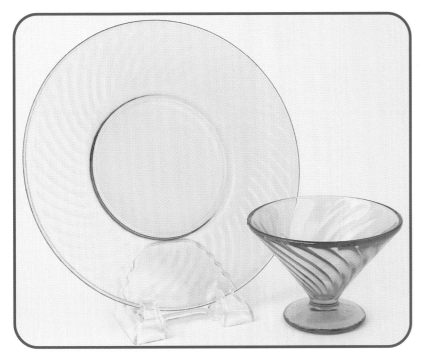

*Spiral, green plate and sherbet.*

# Star

Manufactured by Federal Glass Company, Columbus, Ohio, 1950s.

Made in amber, crystal and crystal with gold trim. Crystal pieces with gold trim would be valued the same as plain crystal.

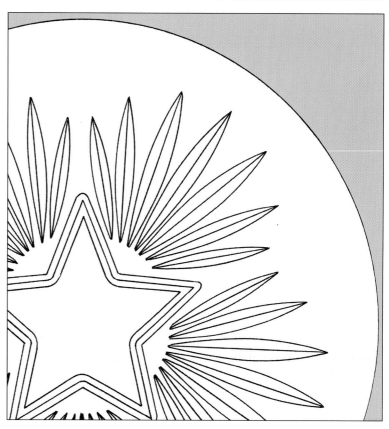

| Item | Amber | Crystal | Item | Amber | Crystal |
|------|-------|---------|------|-------|---------|
| Bowl, 5-5/8" d | - | 7.00 | Pitcher, 85 oz, 9-1/4" h, ice lip | 15.00 | 15.00 |
| Creamer | 7.00 | 9.00 | Plate, 6-3/16" d, salad | 5.00 | 6.00 |
| Cup | 10.00 | 10.00 | Plate, 9-3/8" d, dinner | 12.00 | 14.00 |
| Dessert bowl, 4-5/8" d | 4.00 | 5.00 | Saucer | 4.00 | 3.00 |
| Iced tea tumbler, 12 oz, 5-1/8" h | 8.00 | 9.00 | Sugar, cov | 15.00 | 15.00 |
| Juice pitcher, 36 oz, 5-3/4" h | 10.00 | 12.00 | Tumbler, 9 oz, 3-7/8" h, water | 15.00 | 7.50 |
| Juice tumbler, 4-1/2 oz, 3-3/8" h | 4.00 | 5.00 | Vegetable bowl, 8-3/8" d | 10.00 | 15.00 |
| Pitcher, 60 oz, 7" h | 12.00 | 14.00 | Whiskey, 1-1/2 oz, 2-1/4" h | 4.00 | 5.00 |

*Star, crystal bowl and two pitchers.*

# Starlight

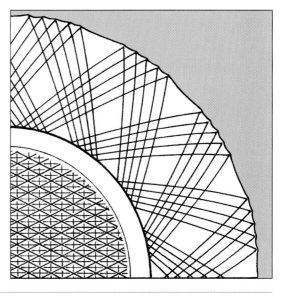

Manufactured by Hazel Atlas Glass Company, Clarksburg, W.V., and Zanesville, Ohio, from 1938 to 1940.

Made in cobalt blue, crystal, pink and white. Production in cobalt blue was limited to 8-1/2" d bowl, valued at $30.

| Item | Crystal | Pink | White |
|------|---------|------|-------|
| Berry bowl, 4" d | 9.50 | - | - |
| Bowl, 8-1/2" d, two handles | 18.00 | 20.00 | 18.00 |
| Bowl, 11-1/2" d, deep | 25.00 | - | 25.00 |
| Bowl, 12" d, 2-3/4" deep | 25.00 | - | 25.00 |
| Cereal bowl, 5-1/2" d, two handles | 7.00 | 12.00 | 7.00 |
| Creamer, oval | 10.00 | - | 5.00 |
| Cup | 6.00 | - | 4.00 |
| Plate, 6" d, sherbet | 4.50 | - | 4.00 |
| Plate, 7-1/2" d, salad | 5.00 | - | 4.50 |
| Plate, 8-1/2" d, luncheon | 5.00 | - | 5.00 |
| Plate, 9" d, dinner | 8.50 | - | 8.50 |
| Relish dish | 15.00 | - | 15.00 |
| Salad bowl, 11-1/2" d, deep | 27.50 | - | 27.50 |
| Salt and pepper shakers, pr | 30.00 | - | 30.00 |
| Sandwich plate, 13" d | 25.00 | 20.00 | |
| Saucer | 4.00 | - | 2.50 |
| Sherbet | 15.00 | - | 12.00 |
| Sugar, oval | 10.00 | - | 10.00 |

Starlight, crystal salt and pepper shakers.

Starlight, crystal plate.

# Strawberry

Manufactured by U.S. Glass Company, Pittsburgh, Pa., in the early 1930s.

Made in crystal, green, pink, and some iridescent.

*Strawberry, pink plate.*

| Item | Crystal | Green | Iridescent | Pink |
|---|---|---|---|---|
| Berry bowl, 4" d | 7.50 | 12.00 | 7.50 | 12.00 |
| Berry bowl, 7-1/2" d | 16.00 | 20.00 | 16.00 | 20.00 |
| Bowl, 6-1/4" d, 2" deep | 40.00 | 60.00 | 40.00 | 60.00 |
| Butter dish, cov | 125.00 | 185.00 | 135.00 | 195.00 |
| Comport, 5-3/4" d | 55.00 | 60.00 | 55.00 | 60.00 |
| Creamer, large, 4-5/8" h | 24.00 | 35.00 | 24.00 | 35.00 |
| Creamer, small | 12.00 | 18.50 | 12.00 | 18.50 |
| Olive dish, 5" l, one handle | 8.50 | 14.00 | 8.50 | 14.00 |
| Pickle dish, 8-1/4" l, oval | 8.00 | 14.00 | 8.00 | 14.00 |
| Pitcher, 7-3/4" h | 150.00 | 185.00 | 150.00 | 195.00 |
| Plate, 6" d, sherbet | 5.00 | 13.50 | 5.00 | 8.00 |
| Plate, 7-1/2" d, salad | 10.00 | 14.00 | 10.00 | 15.00 |
| Salad bowl, 6-1/2" d | 15.00 | 20.00 | 15.00 | 20.00 |
| Sherbet | 6.00 | 13.50 | 6.00 | 13.50 |
| Sugar, large, cov | 60.00 | 85.00 | 60.00 | 85.00 |
| Sugar, small, open | 12.00 | 32.00 | 12.00 | 32.00 |
| Tumbler, 8 oz, 3-5/8" h | 20.00 | 32.00 | 20.00 | 38.00 |

# *Sunburst*

## *Herringbone*

Manufactured by Jeannette Glass Company, Jeannette, Pa., late 1930s.
  Made in crystal.

| Item | Crystal |
|------|--------:|
| Berry bowl, 4-3/4" d | 7.00 |
| Berry bowl, 8-1/2" d. | 18.00 |
| Bowl, 10-1/2" d | 30.00 |
| Candlesticks, pr, double | 35.00 |
| Creamer, ftd | 16.00 |
| Cup. | 7.50 |
| Cup and saucer | 9.50 |
| Plate, 5-1/2" d | 12.00 |
| Plate, 9-1/4" d, dinner | 15.00 |
| Relish, two parts | 14.50 |
| Sandwich plate, 11-3/4" d | 15.00 |
| Saucer. | 3.00 |
| Sherbet. | 12.00 |
| Sugar. | 16.00 |
| Tumbler, 4" h, 9 oz, flat | 18.50 |

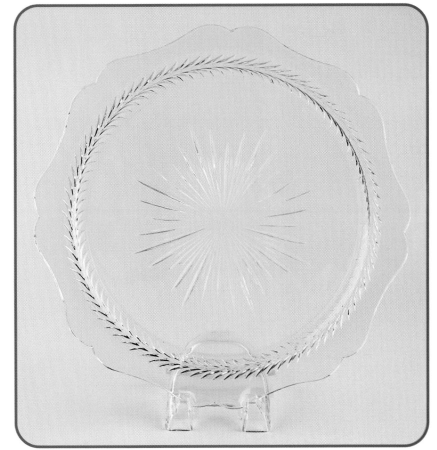

*Sunburst, clear sandwich plate.*

# Sunflower

Manufactured by Jeannette Glass Company, Jeannette, Pa., 1930s.

Made in Delphite, green, pink, and some opaque colors. Look for a creamer in Delphite, valued at $85.

*Sunflower, green cake plate.*

| Item | Delphite | Green | Pink | Opaque |
|---|---|---|---|---|
| Ashtray, 5" d . . . . . . . . . . . . . . . . . . . . . . . . . | - | 15.00 | 10.00 | - |
| Cake plate, 10" d, three legs . . . . . . . . . . . . . . . | - | 20.00 | 20.00 | - |
| Creamer. . . . . . . . . . . . . . . . . . . . . . . . . | 90.00 | 20.00 | 20.00 | 85.00 |
| Cup. . . . . . . . . . . . . . . . . . . . . . . . . . . . . | - | 15.00 | 15.00 | 75.00 |
| Plate, 9" d, dinner . . . . . . . . . . . . . . . . . . . . . | - | 22.00 | 20.00 | - |
| Saucer . . . . . . . . . . . . . . . . . . . . . . . . . . | - | 13.50 | 12.00 | 85.00 |
| Sugar . . . . . . . . . . . . . . . . . . . . . . . . . . . | - | 25.00 | 22.00 | - |
| Trivet, 7" d, three legs, turned up edge . . . . . . . . . | - | 325.00 | 315.00 | - |
| Tumbler, 8 oz, 4-3/8" h, ftd . . . . . . . . . . . . . . . . | - | 35.00 | 32.00 | - |

# Swanky Swigs

Swanky Swigs are small tumblers that originally contained a Kraft cheese spread product. Made from the 1930s until the 1950s, these colorful tumblers are popular with collectors. Lids are valued at $5 each when found in good condition. Certain advertisements can bring a higher price. Glasses with original labels will bring about 50 percent more.

| Item | Value |
|---|---|
| **Antelope and Star** | |
| Black and Red, 3-1/2" h | 4.00 |
| **Antiques Pattern** (3-3/4" h) | |
| Churn and Cradle, Orange | 5.00 |
| Coffee Grinder and Plate, Green | 5.00 |
| Spinning Wheel and Bellows, Red | 5.00 |
| Teapot and Lamp, Blue | 5.00 |
| **Band #2** | |
| Red and Black | 2.50 |
| **Band #3** (3-3/8" h) | 3.00 |
| **Bear and Pig** | |
| Light Blue, 3-3/4" h | 5.00 |
| **Bird and Elephant** | |
| Red, 3-3/4" h | 5.00 |
| **Bustlin' Betsy** (3-3/4" h) | |
| Brown | 6.00 |
| Orange | 2.75 |
| Red | 2.75 |
| Set, Red, Blue, Brown, Yellow and Green | 25.00 |
| **Carnival** (3-1/2" h) | |
| Blue | 4.25 |
| Green | 4.50 |
| Red | 3.00 |
| **Cars and Wagon** | |
| Black and White, 3-3/4" h | 4.00 |
| **Checkerboard** | |
| Red and White, 3-1/2" h | 16.00 |

| Item | Value |
|---|---|
| **Circle and Dot** | |
| Black | 4.25 |
| Blue | 4.25 |
| Red | 4.25 |
| **Cornflower** | |
| #1, Light Blue, 3-1/2" h | 9.00 |
| #1, Light Blue, 3-3/4" h | 15.00 |
| #1, Light Blue, 4-1/2" h | 18.00 |
| #2, Dark Blue, 3-1/4" h | 12.75 |
| #2, Light Blue, 3-1/4" h | 12.50 |
| #2, Yellow, 3-1/4" h | 12.00 |
| #2, Dark Blue, 3-1/2" h | 2.75 |
| #2, Light Blue, 3-1/2" h | 2.50 |
| #2, Red, 3-1/2" h | 2.50 |
| #2, Yellow, 3-1/2" h | 2.00 |
| **Daisy** | |
| Red and White, 3-1/4" h | 35.00 |
| Red, White and Green, 3-1/4" h | 15.00 |
| Red and White, 3-1/2" h | 25.00 |
| Red, White and Green, 3-3/4" h | 2.00 |
| Red, White and Green, 4-1/2" h | 17.50 |
| **Davy Crockett** | |
| 3-1/2" h | 8.50 |
| **Dog and Rooster** | |
| Orange, 3-3/4" h | 5.00 |
| **Dots** | |
| Red, 3-1/2" h | 3.00 |
| **Duck and Horse** | |
| Black, 3-3/4" h | 5.00 |

| Item | Value |
|---|---|

## Flying Geese
Red, Yellow and Blue, 3-1/2" h . . . . . . . . . . . 4.00

## Forget-Me-Not
Dark Blue, 3-1/4" h. . . . . . . . . . . . . . . . . . . 15.00
Light Blue, 3-1/4" h . . . . . . . . . . . . . . . . . . 12.75
Red, 3-1/4" h . . . . . . . . . . . . . . . . . . . . . . . 14.00
Yellow, 3-1/4" h . . . . . . . . . . . . . . . . . . . . . 13.00
Dark Blue, 3-1/2" h . . . . . . . . . . . . . . . . . . . 2.75
Light Blue, 3-1/2" h . . . . . . . . . . . . . . . . . . . 2.75
Red, 3-1/2" h . . . . . . . . . . . . . . . . . . . . . . . . 4.00
Yellow, 3-1/2" h . . . . . . . . . . . . . . . . . . . . . . 3.00

## Horizontal Lines
Black and Red, 3-1/4" h . . . . . . . . . . . . . . . . 3.00

## Kiddie Cups
Black, 3-1/4" h . . . . . . . . . . . . . . . . . . . . . . 13.50
Brown, 3-1/4" h . . . . . . . . . . . . . . . . . . . . . 12.75
Green, 3-1/4" h . . . . . . . . . . . . . . . . . . . . . . 12.75
Orange, 3-1/4" h. . . . . . . . . . . . . . . . . . . . . 12.75
Black, 3-3/4" h . . . . . . . . . . . . . . . . . . . . . . . 3.50
Brown, 3-3/4" h . . . . . . . . . . . . . . . . . . . . . . 2.75
Green, 3-3/4" h . . . . . . . . . . . . . . . . . . . . . . . 2.75
Orange, 3-3/4" h. . . . . . . . . . . . . . . . . . . . . . 2.75
Black, 4-1/2" h . . . . . . . . . . . . . . . . . . . . . . 20.00
Brown, 4-1/2" h . . . . . . . . . . . . . . . . . . . . . 18.00
Green, 4-1/2" h . . . . . . . . . . . . . . . . . . . . . . 18.00
Orange, 4-1/2" h. . . . . . . . . . . . . . . . . . . . . 18.00

## Posy
Jonquil, Yellow, 3-1/4" h . . . . . . . . . . . . . . . 18.00
Jonquil, Yellow, 3-1/2" h . . . . . . . . . . . . . . . . 6.00
Jonquil, Yellow, 4-1/2" h . . . . . . . . . . . . . . . 20.00
Tulip, Red, 3-1/4" h . . . . . . . . . . . . . . . . . . 15.00
Tulip, Red, 3-1/2" h . . . . . . . . . . . . . . . . . . . 4.00
Tulip, Red, 4-1/2" h . . . . . . . . . . . . . . . . . . 12.00

| Item | Value |
|---|---|

Violet, Purple, 3-1/4" h. . . . . . . . . . . . . . . . 18.00
Violet, Purple, 3-1/2" h. . . . . . . . . . . . . . . . . 5.00
Violet, Purple, 4-1/2" h. . . . . . . . . . . . . . . . 20.00

## Scotty
Red Dog, Blue Fence, 3-1/2" h . . . . . . . . . . . 6.00

## Spaceships
Blue, 3-1/2" d . . . . . . . . . . . . . . . . . . . . . . . 6.00

## Squirrel and Deer
Brown, 3-3/4" h . . . . . . . . . . . . . . . . . . . . . . 5.00

## Stars (3-1/2" h)
Black . . . . . . . . . . . . . . . . . . . . . . . . . . . . . 2.00
Green . . . . . . . . . . . . . . . . . . . . . . . . . . . . . 3.00
Red . . . . . . . . . . . . . . . . . . . . . . . . . . . . . . 4.00

## Tulip
#1, Green, 3-1/4" h. . . . . . . . . . . . . . . . . . . 14.00
#1, Black, 3-1/2" h . . . . . . . . . . . . . . . . . . . . 3.00
#1, Dark Blue, 3-1/2" h . . . . . . . . . . . . . . . . 2.75
#1, Green, 3-1/2" h . . . . . . . . . . . . . . . . . . . 2.75
#1, Red, 3-1/2" h . . . . . . . . . . . . . . . . . . . . . 3.50
#1, Blue, 4-1/2" h . . . . . . . . . . . . . . . . . . . . 15.00
#1, Green, 4-1/2" h. . . . . . . . . . . . . . . . . . . 14.00
#1, Red, 4-1/2" h . . . . . . . . . . . . . . . . . . . . 15.00
#2, Dark Blue, 3-1/4" h. . . . . . . . . . . . . . . . 15.00
#2, Dark Blue, 3-3/4" h. . . . . . . . . . . . . . . . . 4.00
#2, Dark Blue, 4-1/2" h. . . . . . . . . . . . . . . . 18.00
#3, Light Blue, 3-1/4" h . . . . . . . . . . . . . . . 14.00
#3, Yellow, 3-1/4" h . . . . . . . . . . . . . . . . . . 14.00
#3, Dark Blue, 3-3/4" h. . . . . . . . . . . . . . . . . 2.75
#3, Light Blue, 3-3/4" h . . . . . . . . . . . . . . . . 2.75
#3, Red, 3-3/4" h . . . . . . . . . . . . . . . . . . . . . 2.75
#3, Yellow, 3-3/4" h . . . . . . . . . . . . . . . . . . . 3.00
#3, Red, 4-1/2" h . . . . . . . . . . . . . . . . . . . . 15.00

*Swanky Swigs: six styles of Kiddie Cups.*

258

# Swirl

## Petal Swirl

Manufactured by Jeannette Glass Company, Jeannette, Pa., from 1937 to 1938.

Made in amber, Delphite, ice blue, pink and Ultramarine. Production was limited in amber and ice blue.

| Item | Delphite | Pink | Ultramarine |
|---|---|---|---|
| Berry bowl | 15.00 | - | 18.00 |
| Bowl, 10" d, ftd, closed handles | - | 25.00 | 35.00 |
| Butter dish, cov | - | 175.00 | 245.00 |
| Candleholders, pr, double branch | - | 40.00 | 60.00 |
| Candleholders, pr, single branch | 115.00 | - | - |
| Candy dish, cov | - | 130.00 | 150.00 |
| Candy dish, open, three legs | - | 20.00 | 29.50 |
| Cereal bowl, 5-1/4" d | 15.00 | 10.00 | 15.00 |
| Coaster, 1" x 3-1/4" | - | 15.00 | 14.00 |
| Console bowl, 10-1/2" d, ftd | - | 20.00 | 35.00 |
| Creamer | 12.00 | 9.50 | 18.00 |
| Cup and saucer | 17.50 | 14.00 | 22.50 |
| Plate, 6-1/2" d, sherbet | 6.50 | 5.00 | 8.00 |
| Plate, 7-1/4" d, luncheon | - | 6.50 | 12.00 |
| Plate, 8" d, salad | 9.00 | 8.50 | 18.00 |
| Plate, 9-1/4" d, dinner | 12.00 | 13.00 | 22.50 |
| Plate, 10-1/2" d, dinner | 18.00 | - | 30.00 |
| Platter, 12" l, oval | 35.00 | - | - |
| Salad bowl, 9" d | 30.00 | 18.00 | 35.00 |
| Salad bowl, 9" d, rimmed | - | 20.00 | 30.00 |
| Salt and pepper shakers, pr | - | - | 50.00 |
| Sandwich plate, 12-1/2" d | - | 20.00 | 27.50 |
| Sherbet, low, ftd | - | 13.00 | 23.00 |
| Soup, tab handles, lug | - | 25.00 | 35.00 |
| Sugar, ftd | - | 12.00 | 18.00 |

| Item | Delphite | Pink | Ultramarine |
|---|---|---|---|
| Tray, 10-1/2" l, two handles . . . . . . . . . . . . . . . . . . . . . . . . . . | 25.00 | - | - |
| Tumbler, 9 oz, 4" h . . . . . . . . . . . . . . . . . . . . . . . . . . . . . . . | - | 18.00 | 42.00 |
| Tumbler, 9 oz, 4-5/8" h . . . . . . . . . . . . . . . . . . . . . . . . . . . . | - | 18.00 | - |
| Tumbler, 13 oz, 5-1/8" h . . . . . . . . . . . . . . . . . . . . . . . . . . . | - | 45.00 | 90.00 |
| Vase, 6-1/2" h, ftd, ruffled . . . . . . . . . . . . . . . . . . . . . . . . . | - | 22.00 | - |
| Vase, 8-1/2" h, ftd . . . . . . . . . . . . . . . . . . . . . . . . . . . . . . . | - | - | 36.00 |

*Swirl, Ultramarine sugar and creamer.*

*Swirl, Ultramarine plate and bowl.*

# Tea Room

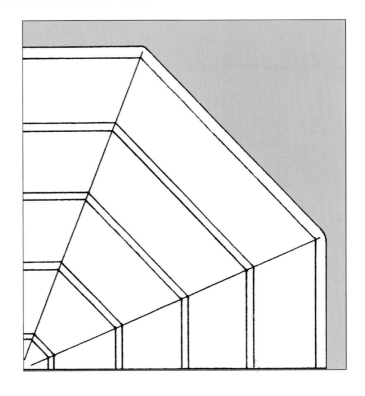

Manufactured by Indiana Glass Company, Dunkirk, Ind., from 1926 to 1931.

Made in amber, crystal, green and pink.

| Item | Amber | Crystal | Green | Pink |
|---|---|---|---|---|
| Banana split bowl, 7-1/2" l | - | 85.00 | 200.00 | 210.00 |
| Candlesticks, pr, low | - | - | 80.00 | 85.00 |
| Celery Bowl, 8-1/2"d | - | - | 35.00 | 27.50 |
| Creamer, 3-1/4" h | - | - | 30.00 | 28.00 |
| Creamer, 4-1/2" h, ftd | 80.00 | - | 20.00 | 18.00 |
| Creamer and sugar on tray | - | - | 95.00 | 85.00 |
| Cup | - | - | 65.00 | 60.00 |
| Finger bowl | - | 80.00 | 50.00 | 40.00 |
| Goblet, 9 oz. | - | - | 75.00 | 65.00 |
| Ice bucket | - | - | 85.00 | 80.00 |
| Lamp, electric | - | 140.00 | 175.00 | 145.00 |
| Mustard, cov | - | - | 160.00 | 140.00 |
| Parfait | - | - | 72.00 | 65.00 |
| Pitcher, 64 oz | 425.00 | 400.00 | 150.00 | 135.00 |
| Plate, 6-1/2" d, sherbet | - | - | 35.00 | 32.00 |
| Plate, 8-1/4" d, luncheon | - | - | 37.50 | 35.00 |
| Plates, 10-1/2" d, two handles | - | - | 50.00 | 45.00 |
| Relish, divided | - | - | 30.00 | 25.00 |
| Salad bowl, 8-3/4" d, deep | - | - | 150.00 | 135.00 |
| Salt and pepper shakers, pr, ftd | - | - | 60.00 | 55.00 |
| Saucer | - | - | 30.00 | 25.00 |
| Sherbet | - | - | 40.00 | 35.00 |

| Item | Amber | Crystal | Green | Pink |
|---|---|---|---|---|
| Sugar, 3" h, cov . . . . . . . . . . . . . . . . . . . . . . . . . . .- | | - | 115.00 | 100.00 |
| Sugar, 4-1/2" h, ftd . . . . . . . . . . . . . . . . . . .80.00 | | - | 20.00 | 18.00 |
| Sugar, cov, flat . . . . . . . . . . . . . . . . . . . . . . .- | | - | 200.00 | 170.00 |
| Sundae, ftd, ruffled . . . . . . . . . . . . . . . . . . .- | | - | 85.00 | 70.00 |
| Tumbler, 6 oz., ftd . . . . . . . . . . . . . . . . . . . . .- | | - | 35.00 | 32.00 |
| Tumbler, 8 oz, 5-1/4" h, ftd . . . . . . . . . . . . .75.00 | | - | 35.00 | 32.00 |
| Tumbler, 11 oz., ftd . . . . . . . . . . . . . . . . . . . .- | | - | 45.00 | 40.00 |
| Tumbler, 12 oz., ftd . . . . . . . . . . . . . . . . . . . .- | | - | 60.00 | 55.00 |
| Vase, 6-1/2" h, ruffled edge . . . . . . . . . . . . .- | | - | 145.00 | 125.00 |
| Vase, 9-1/2" h, ruffled . . . . . . . . . . . . . . . . . .- | | 50.00 | 175.00 | 100.00 |
| Vase, 9-1/2"h, straight . . . . . . . . . . . . . . . . . .- | | 175.00 | 95.00 | 225.00 |
| Vase, 11" h, ruffled edge . . . . . . . . . . . . . . . .- | | - | 350.00 | 395.00 |
| Vase, 11" h, straight . . . . . . . . . . . . . . . . . . .- | | - | 200.00 | 395.00 |
| Vegetable bowl, 9-1/2" l, oval . . . . . . . . . . . . . .- | | - | 75.00 | 65.00 |

*Tea Room, pink sugar and creamer.*

# *Teardrop*

## *Line #301*

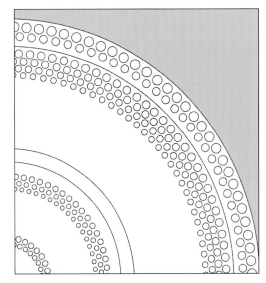

Manufactured by Duncan & Miller Glass Company, Washington, Pa., from 1936 until 1955.

Made only in crystal.

| Item | Crystal |
|---|---|
| Ale, 8 oz | 18.50 |
| Ashtray, 3" d | 6.50 |
| Ashtray, 5" d | 9.00 |
| Bonbon | 12.00 |
| Butter dish, cov, two handles | 25.00 |
| Cake salver, 13" d, ftd | 50.00 |
| Canapé set | 30.00 |
| Candlesticks, pr, 4" h | 20.00 |
| Candlesticks, pr, 7" h, two lite | 40.00 |
| Candlesticks, pr, 7" h, bobeches, prisms | 125.00 |
| Candy basket, 5-1/2" x 7-1/2" | 80.00 |
| Candy box, cov, 7", two parts | 60.00 |
| Candy box, cov, 8" d, three parts | 65.00 |
| Candy dish, 7-1/2" w, heart shape | 30.00 |
| Celery tray, 11" l, two handles | 18.00 |
| Celery tray, 11" l, two handles, two parts | 20.00 |
| Celery tray, 12" l, three parts | 24.00 |
| Champagne, 5 oz | 12.00 |
| Cheese and cracker | 48.00 |
| Claret, 4 oz | 20.00 |
| Coaster, 3" d | 6.50 |
| Cocktail, 3-1/2 oz | 17.50 |
| Comport, 4-3/4", ftd | 15.00 |
| Comport, 6" | 18.00 |
| Condiment set, salt and pepper shakers, two cruets, 9" tray | 120.00 |
| Cordial, 1 oz | 32.00 |
| Creamer and sugar tray, two handles, 8" or 10" | 10.00 |
| Creamer, 3 oz | 6.50 |
| Creamer, 5 oz | 9.00 |
| Creamer, 8 oz | 12.00 |
| Cruets tray | 12.50 |
| Cup | 8.50 |
| Demitasse cup and saucer | 12.00 |
| Dessert bowl, 6" d | 6.50 |
| Finger bowl, 4-1/4" d | 7.50 |

| Item | Crystal |
|---|---|
| Flower basket | 125.00 |
| Flower bowl, 12" d, ftd | 48.00 |
| Flower bowl, 8" x 12" | 48.00 |
| Fruit bowl, 6" d | 7.00 |
| Gardenia bowl, 13" d | 40.00 |
| Goblet, 5-3/4" h | 12.00 |
| Goblet, 7" | 15.00 |
| Hi-ball, 10 oz | 12.00 |
| Ice bucket | 70.00 |
| Iced tea tumbler, 12 oz or 14 oz | 20.00 |
| Juice tumbler, 3-1/2 oz, flat or footed | 7.50 |
| Juice tumbler, 4-1/2 oz, ftd | 10.00 |
| Lazy Susan, 18" d | 75.00 |
| Lemon plate, 7" d, 2 handles | 15.00 |
| Marmalade, cov | 37.50 |
| Mayonnaise, ladle, underplate | 35.00 |
| Milk pitcher, 5" | 20.00 |
| Mustard jar, cov | 30.00 |
| Nappy, 5" d | 6.50 |
| Nappy, 7" d | 12.00 |
| Nappy, 9", two handles | 25.00 |
| Nut dish, 6" | 12.00 |
| Oil bottle, 3 oz | 22.00 |
| Old fashioned, 7 oz | 7.50 |
| Olive dish | 15.00 |
| Oyster cocktail, 3-1/2 oz, ftd | 9.00 |
| Pickle dish | 15.00 |
| Pitcher, 64 oz, ice lip | 120.00 |
| Plate, 6" d, bread and butter | 6.00 |
| Plate, 7-1/2" d, salad | 6.50 |
| Plate, 8-1/2" d, luncheon | 9.00 |
| Plate, 10-1/2" d, dinner | 32.00 |
| Punch bowl, 15-1/2" | 115.00 |
| Punch bowl underplate, 18" d, rolled edge | 65.00 |
| Relish, 7" l, two parts, two handles | 12.50 |
| Relish, 7-1/2" d two parts, heart shape | 22.00 |

| Item | Crystal | Item | Crystal |
|---|---|---|---|
| Relish, 9" l, three parts, three handles | 32.00 | Sugar, 8 oz | 10.00 |
| Relish, 11" l, three parts, two handles | 32.00 | Sweetmeat, center handle, 6-1/2" | 36.00 |
| Relish, 12" d, five parts | 37.50 | Sweetmeat, star shape, two handles, 5-1/2" or 7" | 40.00 |
| Relish, 12" d, six parts | 37.50 | Torte plate, 13" d, rolled edge | 32.00 |
| Relish, 12" l, three parts | 35.00 | Torte plate, 14" d, rolled or plain edge | 37.50 |
| Salad bowl, 9" d | 30.00 | Torte plate, 16" d, rolled edge | 40.00 |
| Salt and pepper shakers, pr | 25.00 | Tumbler, 8 oz, ftd | 10.00 |
| Salt and pepper shakers tray | 12.00 | Tumbler, 9 oz, flat or footed | 10.00 |
| Saucer | 1.50 | Urn, cov, 9" h, ftd | 125.00 |
| Sherbet, 5 oz | 6.50 | Vase, 9" h, ftd, fan | 32.00 |
| Sherry, 1-3/4" oz | 32.00 | Vase, 9" h, ftd, round | 40.00 |
| Sugar, 3 oz | 6.00 | Whiskey, 2 oz, flat or footed | 15.00 |
| Sugar, 6 oz | 7.50 | Wine, 3 oz | 20.00 |

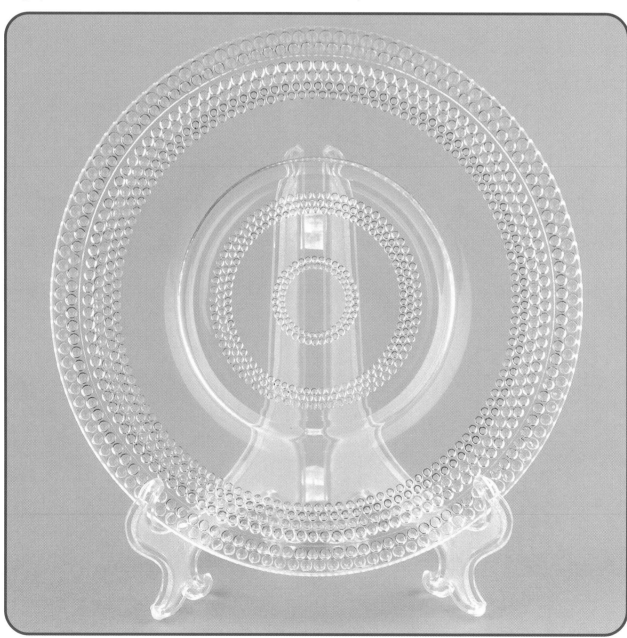

*Teardrop, crystal salad plate.*

# Thistle

Manufactured by Macbeth-Evans, Charleroi, Pa., about 1929 to 1930.

Made in crystal, green, pink, and yellow. Production was limited in crystal and yellow.

**Reproductions:** † Recent reproductions have been found in pink, a darker emerald green, and wisteria. Several of the reproductions have a scalloped edge. Reproductions include the cake plate, fruit bowl, pitcher, salt and pepper shakers, and a small tumbler.

| Item | Green | Pink |
|------|-------|------|
| Cake plate, 13" d, heavy † | 195.00 | 225.00 |
| Cereal bowl, 5-1/2" d | 50.00 | 60.00 |
| Cup, thin | 32.00 | 24.00 |
| Fruit bowl, 10-1/4" d † | 295.00 | 495.00 |
| Plate, 8" d, luncheon | 24.00 | 20.00 |
| Plate, 10-1/4" d, grill | 35.00 | 30.00 |
| Saucer | 12.00 | 12.00 |

*Thistle, green plate.*

# Thumbprint

Manufactured by Federal Glass Company, Columbus, Ohio, from 1927 to 1930.
Made in green.

| Item | Green |
|---|---|
| Berry bowl, 4-3/4" d | 10.00 |
| Berry bowl, 8" d | 25.00 |
| Cereal bowl, 5" d | 10.00 |
| Creamer, ftd | 12.00 |
| Cup | 8.00 |
| Fruit bowl, 5" d | 10.00 |
| Juice tumbler, 4" h | 6.00 |
| Plate, 6" d, sherbet | 4.50 |
| Plate, 8" d, luncheon | 7.00 |
| Plate, 9-1/4" d, dinner | 24.00 |
| Salt and pepper shakers, pr | 65.00 |
| Saucer | 4.00 |
| Sherbet | 9.00 |
| Sugar, ftd | 12.00 |
| Tumbler, 5" h | 8.00 |
| Tumbler, 5-1/2" h | 10.00 |
| Whiskey, 2-1/4" h | 6.50 |

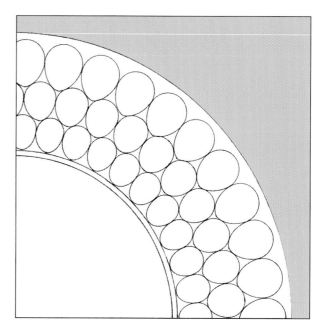

*Thumbprint, green plate.*

# Tulip

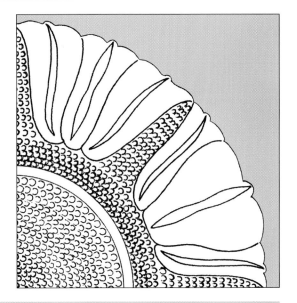

Manufactured by Dell Glass Company, Millville, New Jersey, early 1930s.
Made in amber, amethyst, blue, crystal, and green.

| Item | Amber | Amethyst | Blue | Crystal | Green |
|---|---|---|---|---|---|
| Bowl, 6" d. | 20.00 | 18.00 | 18.00 | 20.00 | 20.00 |
| Bowl, 13-1/4" l, oblong oval | 90.00 | 100.00 | 100.00 | 90.00 | 90.00 |
| Candleholders, pr, 3-3/4" h | 24.50 | 30.00 | 30.00 | 24.50 | 24.50 |
| Candy, cov | 175.00 | 195.00 | 195.00 | 150.00 | 165.00 |
| Creamer | 20.00 | 25.00 | 25.00 | 20.00 | 25.00 |
| Cup | 15.00 | 20.00 | 20.00 | 15.00 | 15.00 |
| Decanter, orig stopper | - | 500.00 | 500.00 | - | - |
| Ice tub, 4-7/8" wide, 3" deep | 70.00 | 95.00 | 95.00 | 65.00 | 75.00 |
| Juice tumbler | 15.00 | 40.00 | 40.00 | 15.00 | 15.00 |
| Plate, 6" d. | 10.00 | 12.00 | 22.00 | 9.50 | 10.00 |
| Plate, 7-1/4" d. | 12.00 | 24.00 | 24.00 | 13.50 | 24.00 |
| Plate, 10-1/4" d. | 35.00 | 40.00 | 35.00 | 20.00 | 35.00 |
| Saucer | 10.00 | 8.50 | 10.00 | 5.00 | 7.50 |
| Sherbet, 3-3/4" h, flat | 20.00 | 24.00 | 24.00 | 18.00 | 20.00 |
| Sugar | 20.00 | 25.00 | 25.00 | 20.00 | 25.00 |
| Whiskey | 22.00 | 35.00 | 35.00 | 20.00 | 25.00 |

Tulip, green creamer.

# Twiggy

Manufactured by Indiana Glass Company, Dunkirk, Ind., in the 1950s and early 1960s.

Made in crystal, some green and pink, and rarely in light blue with an opalescent edge. Collector interest is highest in the crystal.

| Item | Crystal |
| --- | --- |
| Jelly, 8" d | 12.00 |
| Nappy, 4-1/2" d | 5.00 |
| Nappy, 8" d | 8.00 |
| Plate, 8" d | 10.00 |
| Punch bowl | 45.00 |

| Item | Crystal |
| --- | --- |
| Punch cup | 12.00 |
| Relish, 10" d, divided | 15.00 |
| Relish, 8" d | 12.00 |
| Snack plate, 10" d | 10.00 |

*Twiggy, crystal nappy, 8" d.*

*Twiggy, crystal divided relish, 10" d.*

*Twiggy, crystal nappy, 4-1/2" d.*

# Twisted Optic

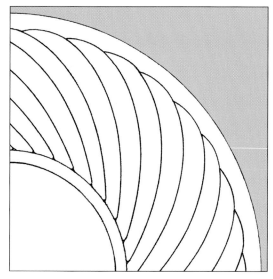

Manufactured by Imperial Glass Company, Bellaire, Ohio, from 1927 to 1930.

Made in amber, blue, canary, green, and pink.

| Item | Amber | Blue | Canary | Green | Pink |
|---|---|---|---|---|---|
| Basket, 10" h | 55.00 | 95.00 | 95.00 | 60.00 | 60.00 |
| Bowl, 7" d, ruffled | - | - | - | - | 18.00 |
| Bowl, 9" d | 18.50 | 28.50 | 28.50 | 18.50 | 18.50 |
| Bowl, 11-1/2" d, 4-1/4" h | 24.00 | 48.00 | 48.00 | 24.00 | 24.00 |
| Candlesticks, pr, 3" h | 22.00 | 40.00 | 40.00 | 35.00 | 22.00 |
| Candlesticks, pr, 8" h | 30.00 | 50.00 | 50.00 | 30.00 | 30.00 |
| Candy jar, cov, flat | 25.00 | 50.00 | 50.00 | 25.00 | 25.00 |
| Candy jar, cov, flat, flange edge | 50.00 | 90.00 | 90.00 | 55.00 | 55.00 |
| Candy jar, cov, ftd, flange edge | 50.00 | 90.00 | 90.00 | 55.00 | 55.00 |
| Candy jar, cov, ftd, short | 55.00 | 100.00 | 100.00 | 60.00 | 60.00 |
| Candy jar, cov, ftd, tall | 55.00 | 100.00 | 100.00 | 60.00 | 60.00 |
| Cereal bowl, 5"d | 8.50 | 15.00 | 15.00 | 10.00 | 10.00 |
| Cologne bottle, stopper | 60.00 | 85.00 | 85.00 | 60.00 | 60.00 |
| Console bowl, 10-1/2" d | 25.00 | 45.00 | 45.00 | 25.00 | 25.00 |
| Cream soup, 4-3/4" d | 12.00 | 25.00 | 25.00 | 15.00 | 15.00 |
| Creamer | 8.00 | 14.00 | 14.00 | 8.00 | 8.00 |
| Cup | 7.50 | 12.50 | 12.50 | 5.00 | 6.00 |
| Mayonnaise | 20.00 | 50.00 | 50.00 | 30.00 | 30.00 |
| Pitcher, 64 oz. | 45.00 | - | - | 40.00 | 45.00 |
| Plate, 6" d, sherbet | 3.00 | 6.50 | 6.50 | 3.00 | 3.00 |
| Plate, 7" d, salad | 4.00 | 8.00 | 8.00 | 4.00 | 4.00 |
| Plate, 7-1/2" x 9" l, oval | 6.00 | 12.00 | 12.00 | 6.00 | 6.00 |
| Plate, 8" d, luncheon | 6.00 | 9.00 | 10.00 | 6.00 | 5.00 |
| Powder jar, cov | 38.00 | 65.00 | 65.00 | 38.00 | 38.00 |
| Preserve jar | 30.00 | - | - | 30.00 | 30.00 |
| Salad bowl, 7"d | 12.00 | 25.00 | 25.00 | 15.00 | 15.00 |
| Sandwich plate, 10" d | 12.00 | 20.00 | 20.00 | 15.00 | 15.00 |
| Sandwich server, center handle | 22.00 | 35.00 | 35.00 | 22.00 | 22.00 |
| Sandwich server, two-handles, flat | 15.00 | 20.00 | 20.00 | 15.00 | 15.00 |
| Saucer | 2.50 | 4.50 | 4.50 | 2.50 | 2.50 |
| Sherbet | 7.50 | 12.00 | 12.50 | 7.00 | 7.50 |
| Sugar | 8.00 | 14.00 | 14.00 | 8.00 | 8.00 |
| Tumbler, 4-1/2" h, 9 oz | 6.50 | - | - | 6.50 | 7.00 |
| Tumbler, 5-1/4" h, 12 oz | 9.50 | - | - | 9.50 | 10.00 |
| Vase, 7-1/4" h, two handles, rolled edge | 35.00 | 65.00 | 65.00 | 40.00 | 40.00 |
| Vase, 8" h, two handles, fan | 45.00 | 95.00 | 95.00 | 50.00 | 50.00 |
| Vase, 8" h, two handles, straight edge | 45.00 | 95.00 | 95.00 | 50.00 | 50.00 |

# U.S. Swirl

Manufactured by U.S. Glass Company, late 1920s.

Made in crystal, green, iridescent, and pink. Production in crystal and iridescent was limited.

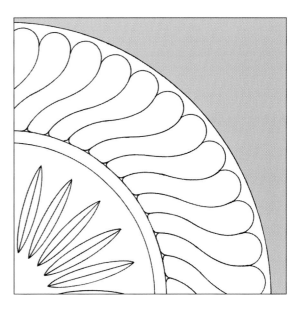

U.S. Swirl, green pitcher.

| Item | Green | Pink |
|---|---|---|
| Berry bowl, 4-3/8" d | 8.00 | 10.00 |
| Berry bowl, 7-7/8" d | 15.00 | 17.00 |
| Bowl, 5-1/2" d, handle | 10.00 | 12.00 |
| Bowl, 8-1/4" l, 2 3/4" h, oval | 40.00 | 40.00 |
| Bowl, 8-3/8" l, 1-3/4" h, oval | 50.00 | 50.00 |
| Butter dish, cov | 115.00 | 115.00 |
| Candy, cov, two handles | 30.00 | 32.00 |
| Creamer | 15.00 | 17.50 |
| Pitcher, 48 oz, 8" h | 55.00 | 50.00 |
| Plate, 6-1/8" d, sherbet | 3.00 | 2.50 |
| Plate, 7-7/8" d, salad | 6.00 | 6.50 |
| Salt and pepper shakers, pr | 48.00 | 45.00 |
| Sherbet, 3-1/4" h | 5.00 | 6.00 |
| Sugar, cov | 35.00 | 32.00 |
| Tumbler, 8 oz, 3-5/8" h | 12.00 | 12.00 |
| Tumbler, 12 oz, 4-3/4" h | 15.00 | 17.50 |
| Vase, 6-1/2" h | 25.00 | 25.00 |

# Vernon

## No. 616

Manufactured by Indiana Glass Company, Dunkirk, Ind., from 1930 to 1932.

Made in crystal, green, and yellow.

| Item | Crystal | Green | Yellow |
|---|---|---|---|
| Creamer, ftd . . . . . . . . . . . | 12.00 | 25.00 | 30.00 |
| Cup . . . . . . . . . . . . . . . . . | 10.00 | 15.00 | 18.00 |
| Plate, 8" d, luncheon . . . . . . . | 7.00 | 10.00 | 12.00 |
| Sandwich plate, 11-1/2" d . . | 14.00 | 25.00 | 30.00 |
| Saucer . . . . . . . . . . . . . . . . | 4.00 | 6.00 | 6.00 |
| Sugar, ftd . . . . . . . . . . . . . | 18.00 | 25.00 | 30.00 |
| Tumbler, 5" h, ftd . . . . . . . . | 16.00 | 40.00 | 45.00 |

*Vernon, yellow tumbler.*

# Victory

Manufactured by Diamond Glass-Ware Company, Indiana, Pa., from 1929 to 1932.

Made in amber, black, cobalt blue, green, and pink.

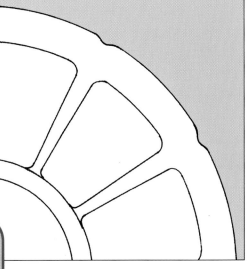

*Victory, pink creamer and sugar.*

| Item | Amber | Black | Cobalt Blue | Green | Pink |
|---|---|---|---|---|---|
| Bonbon, 7" d. | 15.00 | 20.00 | 20.00 | 15.00 | 15.00 |
| Bowl, 11" d, rolled edge | 30.00 | 50.00 | 50.00 | 30.00 | 30.00 |
| Bowl, 12-1/2" d, flat edge | 30.00 | 60.00 | 60.00 | 30.00 | 30.00 |
| Candlesticks, pr, 3" h | 35.00 | 100.00 | 100.00 | 35.00 | 35.00 |
| Cereal bowl, 6-1/2" d | 15.00 | 30.00 | 30.00 | 15.00 | 15.00 |
| Cheese and cracker set, 12" d indented plate and comport | 45.00 | - | - | 45.00 | 45.00 |
| Comport, 6" h, 6-1/4" d | 18.00 | - | - | 18.00 | 18.00 |
| Console bowl, 12" d | 35.00 | 65.00 | 65.00 | 35.00 | 35.00 |
| Creamer | 17.50 | 45.00 | 45.00 | 15.00 | 15.00 |
| Cup | 10.00 | 35.00 | 40.00 | 10.00 | 10.00 |
| Goblet, 7 oz, 5" h | 20.00 | - | - | 20.00 | 20.00 |
| Gravy boat, underplate | 185.00 | 325.00 | 325.00 | 185.00 | 185.00 |
| Mayonnaise set, 3-1/2" h, 5-1/2" d bowl, 8-1/2" d indented plate, ladle | 55.00 | 100.00 | 100.00 | 55.00 | 55.00 |
| Plate, 6" d, bread and butter | 6.50 | 17.50 | 17.50 | 6.50 | 6.50 |
| Plate, 7" d, salad | 7.50 | 20.00 | 20.00 | 8.00 | 7.00 |
| Plate, 8" d, luncheon | 10.00 | 32.00 | 30.00 | 8.00 | 8.00 |
| Plate, 9" d, dinner | 20.00 | 40.00 | 40.00 | 22.00 | 20.00 |
| Platter, 12" l, oval | 30.00 | 70.00 | 70.00 | 32.00 | 32.00 |
| Sandwich server, center handle | 30.00 | 65.00 | 65.00 | 32.00 | 30.00 |
| Saucer | 5.00 | 12.50 | 12.50 | 5.00 | 5.00 |
| Sherbet, ftd | 15.00 | 27.50 | 27.50 | 15.00 | 15.00 |
| Soup bowl, 8-1/2" d, flat | 20.00 | 45.00 | 45.00 | 20.00 | 20.00 |
| Sugar | 15.00 | 45.00 | 45.00 | 15.00 | 15.00 |
| Vegetable bowl, 9" l, oval | 35.00 | 85.00 | 85.00 | 35.00 | 35.00 |

# Vitrock

## Flower Rim

Manufactured by Hocking Glass Company, Lancaster, Ohio, from 1934 to 1937.

Made in white and white with fired-on colors.

| Item | Fired-On Colors | White |
|------|----------------|-------|
| Berry bowl, 4" d | 9.50 | 7.50 |
| Cereal bowl, 7-1/2" d | 12.00 | 8.50 |
| Cream soup, 5-1/2" d | 16.00 | 14.00 |
| Creamer, oval | 10.00 | 7.50 |
| Cup | 8.50 | 6.00 |
| Fruit bowl, 6" d | 10.00 | 8.00 |
| Plate, 7-1/4" d, salad | 7.50 | 4.50 |

| Item | Fired-On Colors | White |
|------|----------------|-------|
| Plate, 8-3/4" d, luncheon | 12.00 | 6.50 |
| Plate, 10" d, dinner | 15.00 | 10.00 |
| Platter, 11-1/2" l | 50.00 | 35.00 |
| Saucer | 7.50 | 4.50 |
| Soup bowl, flat | 48.00 | 35.00 |
| Sugar | 12.00 | 7.50 |
| Vegetable bowl, 9-1/2" d | 24.00 | 18.00 |

*Vitrock, white bowl and plate.*

# Waterford

Manufactured by Hocking Glass Company, Lancaster, Ohio, from 1938 to 1944.

Made in crystal, Forest Green (1950s), pink, white, and yellow. Forest Green production was limited; currently an ashtray is valued at $5. Yellow was also limited. Collector interest is low in white.

| Item | Crystal | Pink |
|---|---|---|
| Ashtray, 4" d | 7.50 | - |
| Berry bowl, 4-3/4" d | 8.50 | 18.00 |
| Berry bowl, 8-1/4" d | 12.00 | 30.00 |
| Bonbon, cov | 45.00 | - |
| Butter dish, cov | 30.00 | 250.00 |
| Cake plate, 10-1/4" d, handles | 15.00 | 20.00 |
| Cereal bowl, 5-1/2" d | 18.50 | 32.00 |
| Coaster, 4" d | 7.50 | - |
| Creamer, Miss America style | 35.00 | - |
| Creamer, oval | 6.00 | 15.00 |
| Cup | 7.50 | 18.00 |
| Cup, Miss America style | - | 45.00 |
| Goblet, 5-1/2" h, Miss America style | 35.00 | 85.00 |
| Goblet, 5-1/4" h | 18.00 | - |
| Goblet, 5-5/8" h | 20.00 | - |
| Juice pitcher, 42 oz, tilted | 30.00 | - |
| Juice tumbler, 5 oz, 3-1/2" h, Miss America style | - | 65.00 |
| Lamp, 4" spherical base | 45.00 | - |
| Pitcher, 80 oz, tilted, ice lip | 50.00 | 165.00 |
| Plate, 6" d, sherbet | 4.50 | 9.50 |
| Plate, 7-1/8" d, salad | 9.00 | 18.00 |
| Plate, 9-5/8" d, dinner | 12.50 | 24.00 |
| Platter, 14" l | 14.00 | - |
| Relish, 13-3/4" d, five parts | 16.00 | - |
| Salt and pepper shakers, pr | 12.00 | - |
| Sandwich plate, 13-3/4" d | 15.00 | 32.00 |
| Saucer | 3.00 | 5.00 |
| Sherbet, ftd | 5.00 | 15.00 |
| Sherbet, ftd, scalloped base | 8.00 | - |
| Sugar | 7.50 | 15.00 |
| Sugar, Miss America style | 35.00 | - |
| Sugar lid, oval | 5.00 | 25.00 |
| Tray, 10-1/4" l, handles | 10.00 | - |
| Tumbler, 10 oz, 4-7/8" h, ftd | 18.00 | 27.50 |

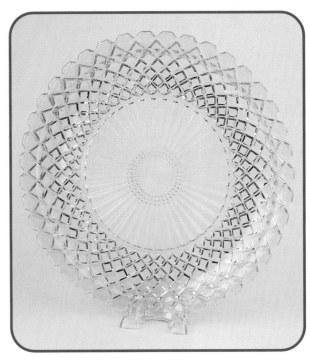

*Waterford, crystal plate.*

# Wexford

Manufactured by Anchor Hocking Glass Corp.
Made in crystal.

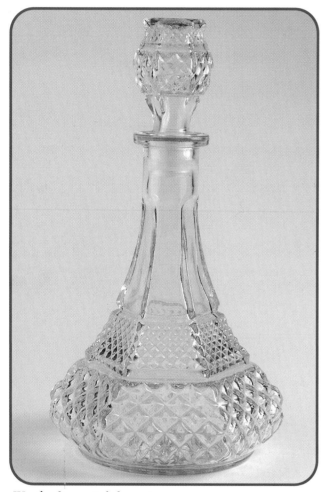

*Wexford, crystal decanter.*

| Item | Crystal |
|---|---|
| Bowl, 7-3/4" d, ftd | .30.00 |
| Bud vase | .12.00 |
| Butter dish, cov | .30.00 |
| Candlestick | .9.00 |
| Candy dish, cov, 7-3/4" d | .15.00 |
| Canister, cov, coffee, 5-3/8" h | .15.00 |
| Canister, cov, flour, 9-1/4" h | .22.00 |
| Canister, cov, sugar, 6-3/8" h | .18.00 |

| Item | Crystal |
|---|---|
| Centerpiece bowl | .18.00 |
| Champagne, 3-5/8" h | .8.00 |
| Chip and dip set | .20.00 |
| Claret, 5-3/8" h | .10.00 |
| Creamer, 4-1/4" h | .10.00 |
| Cruet, 7-1/2" h | .15.00 |
| Cup, ftd, 3" h | .6.00 |
| Decanter, 11-3/4" h | .30.00 |
| Decanter, 14-1/2" h | .35.00 |
| Dessert bowl, 5-1/2" d | .4.00 |
| Fruit bowl, 10" d, ftd | .30.00 |
| Goblet, 6-5/8" h | .12.00 |
| Iced tea tumbler, 5-1/2" h, 12 oz | .12.00 |
| Juice tumbler | .9.00 |
| Old fashioned tumbler, 3-3/4" h | .9.00 |
| Pitcher, 5-1/4" h, pint | .18.00 |
| Pitcher, 9-3/4" h, two quart | .35.00 |
| Plate, luncheon | .9.00 |
| Plate, salad | .6.00 |
| Punch bowl | .10.00 |
| Punch cup, 3" d | .3.00 |
| Relish | .20.00 |
| Relish, three parts, 8-5/8" l | .18.00 |
| Salad bowl, 9-3/4" d | .15.00 |
| Serving plate | .20.00 |
| Sherbet, low | .6.50 |
| Sugar, cov, 5-1/4" h, ftd | .15.00 |
| Toothpick holder | .12.00 |
| Torte plate, 14" d | .24.00 |
| Tumbler, 5-1/2" h, flat | .6.00 |
| Vase, ftd | .40.00 |
| Wine, 4-1/2" h | .10.00 |

*Wexford, crystal serving plate*

*Wexford, crystal goblet.*

# Wild Rose with Leaves & Berries

Manufactured by Indiana Glass Company, Dunkirk, Ind., from the early 1950s to the 1980s.

Made in crystal, iridescent, milk glass, multicolored blue, green, pink, and yellow, satinized crystal, satinized green, pink, and yellow, sprayed green lavender, and pink.

*Wildrose with Leaves & Berries, crystal bowl.*

| Item | Crystal, Satinized Crystal | Iridescent, Satinized colors, Sprayed colors | Multicolored |
|---|---|---|---|
| Bowl, large | 10.00 | 15.00 | 40.00 |
| Candleholder | 5.00 | 8.00 | 20.00 |
| Relish, handle | 6.50 | 10.00 | 25.00 |
| Relish, handle, divided | 7.50 | 12.00 | 25.00 |
| Sauce bowl, handle | 4.00 | 7.00 | 12.00 |
| Sherbet | 5.00 | 6.50 | 15.00 |
| Sherbet plate | 2.50 | 3.50 | 9.00 |
| Tray, two handles | 15.00 | 20.00 | 35.00 |

# Windsor
## Windsor Diamond

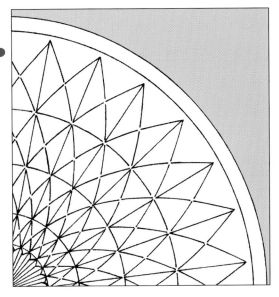

Manufactured by Jeannette Glass Company, Jeannette, Pa., from 1936 to 1946.

Made in crystal, green, and pink, with limited production in amberina red, Delphite, and ice blue.

| Item | Crystal | Green | Pink |
|---|---|---|---|
| Ashtray, 5-3/4" d | 15.00 | 45.00 | 45.00 |
| Berry bowl, 4-3/4" d | 5.00 | 12.00 | 12.00 |
| Berry bowl, 8-1/2" d | 7.50 | 18.50 | 30.00 |
| Bowl, 5" l, pointed edge | 10.00 | - | 25.00 |
| Bowl, 7" x 11-3/4", boat shape | 18.00 | 35.00 | 32.00 |
| Bowl, 7-1/2" d, three legs | 8.00 | - | 24.00 |
| Bowl, 8" d, two handles | 9.00 | 24.00 | 20.00 |
| Bowl, 8" l, pointed edge | 10.00 | - | 48.00 |
| Bowl, 10-1/2" l, pointed edge | 25.00 | - | 32.00 |
| Butter dish, cov | 30.00 | 95.00 | 60.00 |
| Cake plate, 10-3/4" d, ftd | 12.00 | 22.00 | 20.00 |
| Candlesticks, pr, 3" h | 22.00 | - | 85.00 |
| Candy jar, cov | 18.00 | - | - |
| Cereal bowl, 5-3/8" d | 10.00 | 32.50 | 25.00 |
| Chop plate, 13-5/8" d | 24.00 | 42.00 | 50.00 |
| Coaster, 3-1/4" d | 8.50 | 18.00 | 25.00 |
| Comport | 9.00 | - | - |
| Cream soup, 5" d | 6.00 | 30.00 | 25.00 |
| Creamer | 5.00 | 15.00 | 20.00 |
| Creamer, Holiday shape | 7.50 | - | - |
| Cup | 7.00 | 22.00 | 12.00 |
| Fruit console, 12-1/2" d | 45.00 | - | 115.00 |
| Pitcher, 16 oz, 4-1/2" h | 30.00 | - | 115.00 |
| Pitcher, 52 oz, 6-3/4" h | 20.00 | 55.00 | 35.00 |
| Plate, 6" d, sherbet | 3.75 | 8.00 | 6.00 |
| Plate, 7" d, salad | 4.50 | 20.00 | 18.00 |
| Plate, 9" d, dinner | 10.00 | 25.00 | 30.00 |
| Platter, 11-1/2" l, oval | 7.00 | 25.00 | 25.00 |
| Powder jar | 15.00 | - | 55.00 |
| Relish platter, 11-1/2" l, divided | 10.00 | - | 200.00 |
| Salad bowl, 10-1/2" d | 12.00 | - | - |
| Salt and pepper shakers, pr | 20.00 | 48.00 | 42.00 |
| Sandwich plate, 10" d, closed handles | 10.00 | - | 24.00 |
| Sandwich plate, 10" d, open handles | 12.50 | 18.00 | 20.00 |

| Item | Crystal | Green | Pink |
|---|---|---|---|
| Saucer | 2.50 | 5.00 | 4.50 |
| Sherbet, ftd | 3.50 | 15.00 | 13.00 |
| Sugar, cov | 10.00 | 40.00 | 30.00 |
| Sugar, cov, Holiday shape | 12.00 | - | 100.00 |
| Tray, 4" sq | 5.00 | 12.00 | 10.00 |
| Tray, 4" sq, handles | 6.00 | - | 40.00 |
| Tray, 4-1/8" x 9" | 5.00 | 16.00 | 10.00 |
| Tray, 4-1/8" x 9", handles | 9.00 | - | 50.00 |
| Tray, 8-1/2" x 9-3/4" | 7.00 | 35.00 | 25.00 |
| Tray, 8-1/2" x 9-3/4", handles | 14.00 | 45.00 | 85.00 |
| Tumbler, 4" h, ftd | 7.00 | - | - |
| Tumbler, 5 oz, 3-1/4" h | 9.00 | 42.00 | 25.00 |
| Tumbler, 7-1/4" h, ftd | 19.00 | - | - |
| Tumbler, 9 oz, 4" h | 7.50 | 38.00 | 22.00 |
| Tumbler, 11 oz, 4-5/8" h | 8.00 | - | - |
| Tumbler, 12 oz, 5" h | 11.00 | 55.00 | 32.50 |
| Tumbler, 11 oz, 5" h, ftd | 12.00 | - | - |
| Vegetable bowl, 9-1/2" l, oval | 7.50 | 30.00 | 25.00 |

*Windsor, crystal plate and pink pitcher.*

# Yorktown

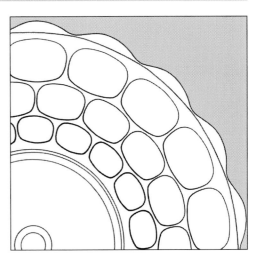

Manufactured by Federal Glass Company, in the mid-1950s.

Made in crystal, iridescent, smoke, white, and yellow. Values for all the colors are about the same.

*Yorktown, crystal fruit bowl.*

| Item | Crystal | Item | Crystal |
|---|---|---|---|
| Berry bowl, 5-1/2" d | 4.50 | Iced tea tumbler, 5-1/4" h, 13 oz | 7.50 |
| Berry bowl, 9-1/2" d | 10.00 | Juice tumbler, 3-7/8" h, 6 oz | 4.50 |
| Celery tray, 10" l | 10.00 | Mug | 15.00 |
| Creamer | 5.00 | Plate, 8-1/4" d | 4.50 |
| Cup | 3.50 | Plate, 11-1/2" d | 8.50 |
| Fruit bowl, 10" d, ftd | 18.00 | Punch bowl set | 40.00 |

| Item | Crystal | Item | Crystal |
|---|---|---|---|
| Punch cup | 2.50 | Snack cup | 2.50 |
| Relish | 3.00 | Snack plate with indent | 3.50 |
| Sandwich server | 4.50 | Sugar | 5.00 |
| Saucer | 1.00 | Tumbler, 4-3/4" h, 10 oz | 6.00 |
| Sherbet, 7 oz | 3.50 | Vase, 8" h | 15.00 |

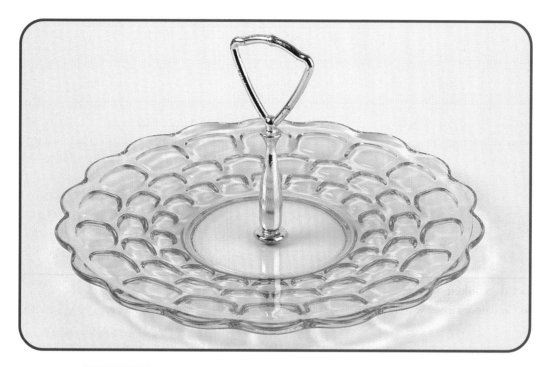

*Yorktown, yellow sandwich server with gold metal center handle.*

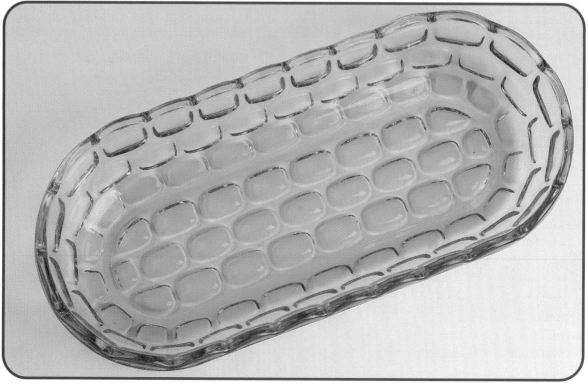

*Yorktown, yellow relish.*

282

# Index by Manufacturer

# Index by Pattern